Christopher, from England, arrived in Australia at 21-year-old as a '10 Pound Pom' in 1964. The effect of his torturous years growing up and at boarding school remain, as does his burden of dyslexia, but he compensated for the latter by recording his stories of his 'Drifter' days on his trusty reel-to-reel recorder. Some of his recordings and his stories were chosen to profile the *'10 Pound Pom'* Victorian Immigration Museum exhibition in 2017. He has always had a love of electronics, film and TV and in the switch from Drifter to mainstream, successfully developed his own business in this area. He is now retired, avidly listens to talking books, but his wandering spirit, and love of media remains to this day.

Dianne, an Australian, is a descendant of pioneers who arrived in the 1800s by way of convict (Port Arthur), free settlers, and through the Earl Grey Scheme (Ireland) during the potato famine. Her Great Grandfather was one of the 13 tried for treason in the Eureka Stockade, Ballarat. Dianne grew up on a farm, in Victoria, completed her nurse training in Melbourne in 1972 and then nursed in Alice Springs before relocating to Yuendumu, Northern Territory in 1973. She worked in academia at Federation University for many years, and is now Executive Dean at Lawson College Australia that has a focus on international students.

Christopher and Dianne met at Yuendumu, Northern Territory, Australia in 1973 and married this same year. Together, they have three adult children, and seven grandchildren. All are their pride and joy.

Christopher G Thompson and
Dianne L Thompson

THE BURDEN WITHIN

One man. Two countries.
Untold Stories

AUSTIN MACAULEY PUBLISHERS™
LONDON * CAMBRIDGE * NEW YORK * SHARJAH

Copyright © Christopher G Thompson and Dianne L Thompson 2022

The right of Christopher G Thompson and Dianne L Thompson to be identified as authors of this work has been asserted by them in accordance with section 77 and 78 of the Copyright, Designs and Patents Act 1988.

All rights reserved. No part of this publication may be reproduced, stored in a retrieval system, or transmitted in any form or by any means, electronic, mechanical, photocopying, recording, or otherwise, without the prior permission of the publishers.

Any person who commits any unauthorized act in relation to this publication may be liable to criminal prosecution and civil claims for damages.

All of the events in this memoir are true to the best of author's memory. The views expressed in this memoir are solely those of the author.

A CIP catalogue record for this title is available from the British Library.

ISBN 9781528932998 (Paperback)
ISBN 9781528986625 (ePub e-book)

www.austinmacauley.com

First Published 2022
Austin Macauley Publishers Ltd®
1 Canada Square
Canary Wharf
London
E14 5AA

Heartfelt thanks to my three children: Sophie, Benjamin and Matthew and to their partners: John, Jayne and Zara for their ongoing support and encouragement; and to my extended family who enjoyed the telling of my stories over the years and this inspired me to share them.

Prologue
One Man. Two Countries. Untold Stories

This is one man's story of his trials, tribulations, and triumph.

Born into a wealthy household in England in 1942, Christopher could've expected a privileged life. This was not to be. At six-year-old, Christopher entered boarding school. These school years were 'the lost years of his childhood and youth'. Undiagnosed and debilitating dyslexia led to an aversion to schoolwork, and violent sexual abuse by an older fellow boarding student was the impetus for refusing to return to school at age 14.

Extremely shy, inept socially and emotionally, and devoid of the most basic literacy and numeric skills, Christopher embarked on a life of hard manual labour in rural England. Returning to work on his parents' newly purchased farm at eighteen-year-old, continual frustrations led to an escalation of outbursts of anger culminating in a stint of involuntary commitment instigated by his parents. In 1964, at 21 years old, he left for Australia as a *'10 Pound Pom'*.

For the next 10 years, Christopher roamed Australia – its cities, country towns and outback. Searching, travelling, working, and living the Aussie way that many Australians have not experienced. His travels, adventures, and the people he met are tirelessly captured by black and white photos and audio tapes, recorded on his trusty reel-to-reel audio tape recorder that on many occasions was pawned to buy food.

But a rolling stone gathers no moss. Christopher, the adventurer, insidiously became a hardworking, hard-drinking, hard-playing *Drifter*.

'Warts and all' stories told are compelling: sometimes mundane, sometimes tumultuous; but always profoundly interesting, capturing the 'moments in real-time'. They provide a unique insight into the torturous journey of a lonely, insecure child and the young man in England; a unique view through the lens of a newly arrived immigrant who drifted around Australia three times between

1964 to 1973; and the rollercoaster ride of recreating himself from a *Drifter* to mainstream society.

Christopher's story of migration and 'Adventurer', is recorded in the 2017 Museums Victoria touring exhibition titled: British Migrants – Instant Australians?

There will always be one more tale to be told by this remarkable man until his final request is played out by his family: Wagner's Ride of the Valkyries, turned up very loudly, with the final announcement: 'Christopher has left the building'!

Part 1
The Burden
1942-1964

'If you can't get rid of the skeleton in your closet, you'd best teach it to dance'.
George Bernard Shaw

Chapter 1
The Beginning

There were some happy moments during my early childhood. Like the times my Father [Edward Marshall] bounced me on his knee and sang the nursery rhyme 'run rabbit, run rabbit run, run, run'. When the song got to the bit where the farmer shot his gun, Father would help me gently fall off this lap to the ground and then thrust me into the air. It was a lot of fun. Like the times my Mother [Gwendoline Annie] would play with me, hold me tightly, and laugh with me. And, like the times my big brother Tony, [Antony John] would try and teach me colours and numbers in his school holidays.

But always, I had to be in bed, out of sight by the time my Father returned from his factory in the evening. Mother was his, and he would not share her with anyone, including me. I was born ten years after Tony who was already at school, and then a boarder at Malvern College progressing towards a brilliant medical career. As such, I was like an only child – a lonely, only child. I did have an affectionate Mother who doted on me – when she was at home. Often, she disappeared – travelling overseas with my Father and I was left with my Nanny, whom I hated. She could never replace my Mother, plus she scrubbed my tongue routinely, for whatever reason she found.

My family lived the perfect social norm of the day for the level of society in which they found themselves, in the 1940s. This era is described in newspaper articles of the time as 'the-class-that's-too-snobbish-to-speak-its-name'. This name is not used contemporarily but did reflect the era of my parents, as it did my paternal grandparents.

Whilst my childhood was generally unhappy, I suspect my Father' was considerably worse, growing up in the early 1900s. Father was born and raised in a rigidly formal family and called his Father [Walter Percival]' *Sir'* and his Mother [Elizabeth] Mater – the German word for mother. They were a wealthy family that mimicked aristocratic life. Walter's [Percy] wealth came from his own endeavour and documents suggest how very generous he was to many family members throughout his life. When Percy married Elizabeth, she brought an element of aristocracy into the family via the 'Bartlam' line.

Father told me that Percy, his father was a complicated, interesting, but eccentric man. His passion for music meant he retreated to his library where he would play the gramophone at full blast and 'conduct' the concert being broadcast! He was known as a generous, but very restless and difficult man. He erected a permanent tent on the lawn and slept in it on a wood and canvas 'camp bed' when he felt like it. At a whim, he would leave the family home, to pick grapes in France – something that was 'not done' in the circle he and his wife belonged. And he boasted that he liked pepper on strawberries!

Percy had a wandering spirit that remained throughout his life. In his early twenties, he was a commercial traveller for Pathe Freres phonograph records and spent time living and working in Europe and Canada. In 1887 Percy and his brother William [Bill] a keen photojournalist, travelled to Alaska and took part in recording the Klondike gold rush in the Yukon region of Canada. They took many photos that were lost forever when the boat capsized in the Klondike River and Bill was swept downstream. They survived, but Percy's camera and all of his photographic plates were lost. Adventure or restlessness seemed to be part of the family at this stage. My father also wanted to migrate to Australia, early in his life but family and business pressures prevented this until later – much later.

Whilst I never knew my Grandpa Percy, I understand much about him. I think people who know me could say I am a little like him in some ways. I have a love of electronics, film and wild and passionate classical music, and spent much of my life in my 20's travelling and seeking adventure. And I remain restless to this day. Am I eccentric? I will leave this up to you!

Father told me that he came from an 'unloving family that lacked warmth', with the mantra that 'children should be seen and not heard'. He and his younger brother [Robert Arnold] had a full-time live-in Nanny and saw very little of their parents. Father went to boarding school at a very young age at St Cuthbert's College, now Worksop College, Sherwood Forest.

He confided that he was not a brilliant student and was beaten by the Master when he 'couldn't do his lessons'. However, he did excel at Officer's Training Corps, and was a highly respected pistol shooter; and became the honoured 'Silver Bugler' at the School he attended.

Father desperately wanted to join the Army when he left school at eighteen-year-old, but his parents refused. Instead, they wanted him to join the Anglican Church, as did his great Uncles after graduating from Cambridge University. Robert Edward Goddard became Cannon of Cambridge and later Sydney, Australia; and James Windett Goddard, a Priest who focussed on social welfare aspects of the times.

My Father resisted his parents' aim for him to become a clergyman. Instead, he pursued his passion of business and engineering and absorbed himself, in turning around his Father's ailing manufacturing business. Robert, his younger brother relented and gave up his ambition of working in electronics and became an accountant.

Despite Father's considerable business acumen and engineering skills, he had his challenges. Mother said he couldn't add up a row of figures correctly when they first married. Father loved reading very practical type books – particularly relating to engineering and invented a range of products and registered several patents during his lifetime. His success in business was due to his engineering and manufacturing abilities, and the very wise decision of surrounding himself with employees who were highly educated professionals and well-trained office staff.

Father did not get high grades at School, but he developed his business into a large and prosperous company over time. In later life, he joked that if he had become a clergyman, the diocese he held would've been very wealthy! But, whilst he did not preach, he was always very generous and provided the local Church at Elworth, with large donations. Father loved fishing, particularly fly fishing for trout in Scotland. He made his own 'flies' and was a great fisherman all his life. My oldest son seems to have inherited his grandfather's genes, as he too is a crack pistol shooter and talented fisherman.

Mother fared better with emotional development in childhood, despite the death of her father [Alfred Beaumont] when she was just three-year-old. Her Mother [Annie Davies] was very affectionate and had a great capacity to love and nurture. This she did with her own two children, and four other young children she raised when she remarried a widower. However, my mother and her brother, Horace, did not get on with their stepfather [Mr Clare] and refused to change their name to his, as a sign of respect for their dead father. This caused considerable friction, particularly as my mother and Horace grew older.

Horace attended boarding school but given the friction in the household with his stepfather, and two stepbrothers, he left at fifteen-year-old to become a jackeroo in New Zealand. It would be many, many years later before Horace would return to England to see his mother, who described him as 'very colonial'. My mother went to a local Grammar School, and excelled in her studies, including the French language which she had an affinity with, as her father's ancestors were French. She desperately wanted to leave home and be a 'children's nurse' and won a scholarship placement at King Edwards VI College. But her mother begged her not to leave her, so she obliged, and settled to work at Cadbury's as a head telephonist, taking overseas orders – a choice occupation of the time.

My father courted my mother for some years, and they had 'pet' names for each other. Mother was 'Silvo', and Father was 'Teddy'. Mother recalls that on one of their rides on 'Teddy's motorcycle, she was thrown over the handlebars! My father only enjoyed affection when he met and married my mother some 10 years after they met at school. She was his greatest asset. He held onto her dearly and resented the affection she directed towards her children, particularly me on whom she doted. I arrived later in their life together, at a time when Father was becoming extremely prosperous. I believe that he wanted to have all of Mother's affection and attention; and be free of the responsibility of a young child.

My father was a gentleman. He was a reserved and shy man, with a strong, distinguished presence. I loved him and always will be proud of him. But I spent my early life trying very hard not to be like him, or more precisely, escaping the class he represented and the money that went with it. I believe I have succeeded admirably with this!

It is only with time and wisdom, that I clearly see how my life could've been much easier and simpler, if I had embraced, rather than rejected what my family, and class, could've provided.

Chapter 2
My Early Years

It was the middle of World War II. I was born on 31st August 1942, via cesarean section at thirty-five weeks after which my mother found it difficult to recover. We returned to our home Westway's, a grand art-deco home in the grandly named Royal Town of Sutton Coldfield, then a part of Warwickshire – but today a suburb of Birmingham in the West Midlands of England.

The first few years after my birth, the 'war years' conjures up potent memories for those who lived through this period. Though I was too young to be involved, I understood what it was about. The aftermath of the war continued for years – food and petrol rationing bombed-out houses and cities and destroyed lives and livelihoods. Daily life in Britain during the second-world war was bleak.

As a family, we were relatively fortunate during the war years, compared to others. Father's business was classed as 'an essential business', which meant he did not see active duty in the forces, yet his brother Robert, an accountant did. Father was more valuable to the 'war effort' by manufacturing specific war parts at the direction of the government. However, he also did his duty diligently as an ARP-Air Raid Precautions – Warden. In his ARP uniform, he walked the streets of Sutton Coldfield after dark checking for road obstacles, bomb damage and making sure light was not escaping from any of the houses that might alert German bombers. He did this every night in addition to working long hours in his factory, making equipment for the forces.

While Father was doing his ARP Warden duty at night, Mother, Tony, and I slept in our 'safe room' – a cloakroom under the stairs that was covered in sandbags. Why in the cloakroom? Mother hated both heights and going underground 'like a mole', and therefore would not consider an underground 'Anderson Shelter', as other members of our extended family did. Mother felt safer in the cloakroom during Fathers' warden duties. She determined that if something was to happen – like a direct hit, then that would be it. We would 'go together'. Whist the sandbags dulled the sound of the buzz bomb carriers as well as the inevitable explosion; this 'safe room' would've done absolutely nothing should we have taken a direct hit, except maybe muffle the sounds of our dying screams!

Rosina, our live-in maid left our employ at the start of the war, and Jay, an American soldier who worked in intelligence was billeted with us. Jay was very well-liked, and Mother wrote to his mother regularly, who in return sent us food parcels at Christmas time that we appreciated. Communication continued between the two families long after the war ceased.

Despite Westway's being under the direct flight route of German bombers, we were very lucky. These planes flew very low, en-route to attempt to bomb the main electricity generating station [Ham's Hall]. The field opposite our house had anti-aircraft guns and searchlights – but luckily, we were not bombed as many others around us were.

During the war, our island nation was effectively cut off from the rest of the world thanks to the efficiency of the German U-boats sinking everything they could find. Food production was paramount at this time and for the next few years, there was severe rationing that I vividly recall. It was our duty to produce our own food – to become self-reliant. Prisoners were released from jail on day passes so they could help farmers tend their crops. Westways had a large garden, and my parents employed Oakey, a gardener, to maintain the produce for the family.

I recall this period as I spent time 'working' with Oakey in the garden at a very early age. Oakey had a severe speech impediment. The roof of his mouth was missing and the sounds he made to communicate were indistinguishable to most, except to me, as a small child. I became the only one in the family who could understand what he said! Oakey looked after the garden, the vegetable garden, and the chickens that he treated like children. He made sure they were caged at night to save them from foxes and collected their eggs for the household to eat. Produce was shared with Uncle Robert's family [wife Mary, daughters Judy and Rosemary] as he was serving in the army. Robert and Mary's third child, Andrew was born long after the war had ceased.

Rationing was part of our life for many years. I always looked forward to our free weekly bottle of orange juice dispensed from the government clinic. Orange juice was associated with sunshine and health, but the juice was a poor substitute for the ever-absent sun. Nevertheless, I looked forward to my sip of the sun and the sweets from the tobacconist, while my family lined up like everyone else for their pound of flesh from the butcher. Mind you, if you didn't have the correct ration coupons you were forced to go without.

Mother improvised and made sweets out of peppermint and dried milk. I loved them. They were a real treat. To this day, more than seventy years later, when I suck on a peppermint lolly it makes me feel happy remembering the sweets Mother made. Despite being a wealthy family, it was still a time of deprivation and the unavailability of certain food items meant no amount of money could buy what you wanted. The black market was not an option for us.

Father's factory – Thompson Alumine was in Scofield Street, Birmingham. The 'peacetime' output from the factory included pots, saucepans, kettles, teapots, and everything you could possibly need in a kitchen and canteen. These products were branded and marketed as the Chieftain brand. The factory was retained to manufacture aeroplane parts during the war.

Father did not seek to benefit financially during the war years – but benefits came to him. Demand for his peacetime products was much reduced, and the replacement of aluminium with steel and tin plate for the normal pots and pans, during the war impacted his quality product. At this time, the War Department chose him, and his factory to build specific parts for aeroplanes, quickly, secretly and at sometimes, odd times. Magnesium, a very light metal was often used for parts for aeroplanes and Tony who was twelve-year-old when the war ended recalls, that 'on one occasion he returned with some magnesium shavings from one of the parts made for an aeroplane, and when ignited, burned with a brilliant white light.'

Father, by now an expert toolmaker, worked weekends making amongst other things, parts for bombs, such as the 'Fin'. Tony again recalls: 'The man from the War Department would arrive at our house with plans for a certain part and sometimes would wait until Father could return with the completed orders'.

There was an increased demand for Thompson Alumine kitchen and canteen wares post-war, and Father ramped up production and built a new, bigger factory in Talke, Stoke on Trent. He incorporated a furnace to branch out into porcelain tops for tea caddies, which were the flasks and water bottles of their day. Every worker had one and carried them on their bicycles to work and back, for refreshment.

We moved from Sutton Coldfield to Sandbach, Cheshire to be closer to Fathers' factory. It was 1947 and I was five-year-old. I remember the emotions of excitement surrounding the move and shivering with the cold. I recall people talking about how the heavy snowfall was delaying the completion of the new factory, and Father was worried about the blow out of the cost, due to the continual delays. However, the trials of the factory were of little concern to me as we headed off to Dalton House our home for the next thirteen years.

Dalton House was a lovely, double storied house with beautiful gardens including an apple orchard set on an acre of land with a long, winding road with a gate before you reached the house. It had a kitchen, morning room, dining room, lounge, a study downstairs and four upstairs bedrooms and one bathroom. Beyond the French windows of the lounge, a sunken tennis court had been replaced with a lawn. Father built a pigeon loft to house the five, fantail pigeons that pranced around and put on a show. Tony made a fishpond when home from boarding school.

The combination of lawn edged with rhododendron bushes and assorted shrubbery that led up to the apple orchard at the side of the house along with the dancing pigeons made for something of an idyllic scene. The sense of secrecy was enhanced by a winding drive to the house that was set back from the road so that from the garden, you couldn't see the road. There was an air of isolation, yet just a few fields away stood the Foden family mansion. This family-owned Foden Works the company that popularised diesel trucks.

Our family were guests at the yearly garden parties hosted by the Foden family. It was a grand and social occasion and one looked forward to. There were even rides and activities for children. One year when I was six-year-old, I quickly spent all my pocket money given to me by my parents on rides. I wandered around the garden watching grownups and longing to hop aboard for another ride or three. I approached one of the guests, a man and asked if he could lend me some money for a ride and he said to my surprise: 'here you go 'lad', here is sixpence, go and have a good time'. I repeated this 'little boy lost' act and had a lovely day! I proudly told my Mother and Father on the way home that 'I just asked people for sixpence and they gave it to me'. My parents showed extreme displeasure and told me to never repeat this again.

At this period, my Father was everything I could have wanted. We walked together and played together and even my visits to the factory afforded me the joy of being fussed over by his workers. But still, Father was a figure of censure and Mother would call on his name to get me to go to bed before he got home so the house would be quiet, and he would have Mother to himself.

Mother and Father had a full social life, attending dinners, ballroom dancing and other social events in the district and had several friends – mainly professional people of the district. They hosted lavish Christmas parties every year. Father's shrewdness went beyond the factory and matters of business. Whilst very generous, when we hosted parties, his strategy was to offer his guests a first drink of stiff whisky with just a dash of soda from the soda fountain and every subsequent drink had less and less whiskey and increasingly soda. Father had determined that it was more economical to do it that way because after a good, strong, initial drink people were less aware of what they were being served and you could get away with more diluted drinks. Good advice, applicable today for both economy and safety!

Mother was a 'social butterfly'. She said that Teddy always told her: 'I don't mind whom you dance with at the ball or party, as long as you have the last dance with me.' Mother told me: 'once home, Teddy would call and pay for a taxi for my babysitter to go home. He would never be exposed to what could be considered a compromising situation'. Mother and Father were devoted to each other. Apart from her duties of hostess, Mother did a lot of charity work, particularly for the local hospital where she regularly distributed books to patients in the wards, from the library trolley. Father also had his activities outside work and home. He was a committed Freemason and rose to the position of Grand Master in Birmingham. His masonic memorabilia were left to the Melbourne Masonic Lodge on his death.

Being an essential business making war parts for the Government, contributed to our family's wealth. However, it was Father's expertise as a designer, engineer and toolmaker that made his camping gear famous.

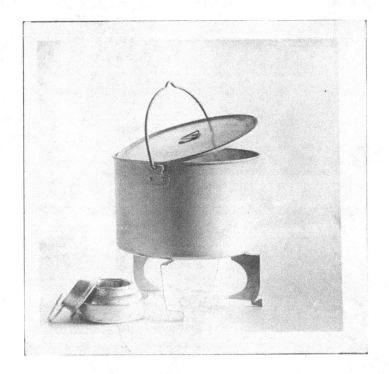

In the early 1950s my Father added the production of camping and picnic goods to his business. Edmund Hillary [later Sir Edward Hillary] his Sherpa, Tenzing Norgay and the rest of the party, carried camping equipment made at Father's factory on their conquest of Mt Everest. I do not know if the two main climbers took any of Father's wares to the summit on 29 May 1953; but I think that at least at a high base camp somewhere along the route, there is, frozen in time, Chieftain brand camping gear that worked its way from our Birmingham factory to the highs of Mt Everest. Interesting, the news of the successful ascent by Hillary only reached the 'outside world' the eve of the coronation of Queen Elizabeth on June 2, 1953.

TV was available in the UK in 1930 with limited programs five days a week. From around 1936-1939, television programs aired an average of 4 hours per day in the UK and the TV with around 12,000 to 15,000 receivers. Some sets in restaurants or bars might have 100 viewers for sports events. It is written that:

The Second World War caused the BBC service to be abruptly suspended on September 1, 1939, at 12.35 pm, after a Mickey Mouse cartoon and test signals were broadcast, so that transmissions could not be used as a beacon to guide enemy aircraft to London. It resumed, again from Alexandra Palace on June 7, 1946, after the end of the war, began with a live programme that opened with the line 'Good afternoon everybody. How are you? Do you remember me, Jasmine Blight?' The Mickey Mouse cartoon that was broadcast on the day before the war followed this introduction!

However, the above events are now termed 'popular mythology' as the BBC report indicates.

Father's business was going so well he was paying nineteen shillings in the pound tax at a time when the top tax rate was 19 shillings and six pence in the pound. In 1952, we bought our first TV, just before the boom in sales in 1953 – so people could watch the coronation of the young Elizabeth, Queen to be.

I love television and all things related to audio-visual media and the day Father brought home our first TV was a significant and memorable occasion. Prior to this, I occasionally watched TV at someone else's house. It was a 'Pye' TV – 'all in one' that had a radio, gramophone, and a small TV screen. Father and I watched TV together on that first night. We couldn't operate the volume control because we couldn't find it! We sat, watching silent TV. Neither of us thought about consulting the brochure for instructions!

The novelty for me was not what was shown on TV screen, but the TV itself. Most of the time there was the test pattern and we watched that and loved watching it! At this time, I loved the advertisements as much as I loved the television shows.

I watched everything on TV when I was home from school, even the 'Women's Hour' in the afternoon where cooking was the focus. The evening program was from 7-10 pm consisting of the daily news and other programs such as the police drama about a policeman on the beat in London and 'Z Cars' the first major detective drama along with some other variety shows. Children's hours went from five to six and the most memorable program I can recall was a toy horse – a puppet, bouncing on top of a grand piano! Thin on plot, I know, but I found it exciting viewing. The test pattern also excited us, so we were obviously not a very discerning audience, but there was not a lot of choice. Later, commercial television commenced with one station – ITV providing more choice of programs and a lot more ads. My love of audio-visual media continues to this day.

Father didn't like the radio that came with the TV unit, so he removed it and replaced it with a new tuner amplifier. I loved listening to the records piled eight high, enabling uninterrupted music. My parents had a portable wind-up record player that used to play 78 vinyl records. It literally was a big oak box with a record player in it. You wound up the handle at the side and two doors at the front were opened to let the sound out. I spent hours playing records such as 'We'll meet again' with Vera Lynn, 'Out in the Cold' with Gracie Fields and 'Teddy Bear's Picnic' and others of the time, such as the 'Sabre Dance' by Adam Khachaturian, [which drove Tony 'dotty'] and my all-time favourite, 'Ride of the Valkyries' by composer Richard Wagner.

But the gramophone needles of this portable record player were in short supply, so I picked a thorn from the hawthorn hedge and pushed it into where the stylus should be and the record played beautifully. If someone hadn't already come up with the cliché of necessity being the mother of invention, I might have invented it during those days of seeming deprivation but, for me, they were some of the happiest years of my life, because Father found time, even made time, to play with me. Rarely perhaps, but at least there were times I could cherish.

Father was an engineer, inventor and entrepreneur who always needed to be doing 'something'. Being idle was an anathema to him and one of his activities was repairing things for the antique shop in Sandbach, not for the money but because he loved 'tinkering'. He had all sorts of mechanical things and gadgets, such as a cylindrical gramophone and a concertina. One day he brought home a 1784 Grandfather Clock that he bought from Golding's Antique Shop in Sandbach Square, where the Christian Saxon Memorial Crosses still stand. These historical crosses were erected in the Ninth Century and are among the finest, surviving examples of Anglo-Saxon artistry. The grandfather clock my Father bought stood in my parents' home in England for years, then my own.

Dalton House was a busy, privileged household. Our four family members were joined by: the cook, gardener, chauffeur, and housecleaner. Nanny was ever-present, very strict, and would scrub my tongue with a toothbrush when any punishment was deemed necessary. I'm not sure why, because I really can't remember knowing any swear words at the time and I never took to the art of oaths.

Cook got the sack because she put salt in the cupcakes instead of sugar, the chauffeur got the sack for replacing the silver spoons with cheap ones when the cook took him a cup of tea; and Nanny's term ended when I went to school. Only Oakey, the gardener was a constant.

A sign of opulence as it is now, are cars of status filling a garage and lining a driveway. Mother's first car was a Triumph complete with running boards. In subsequent years she had a succession of Vauxhalls. Each year at Christmas time, she would get a new Vauxhall and her near-new car would be given to father's chief salesman, Mr Heath.

Mother did not like Mr Heath, because 'he was using the company car on the side to sell broom handles.' She urged Father to sack him, but he would not comply, telling her 'Mr Heath was a valued salesman, and making considerable money for the business…and if he wanted to make a bit of extra money on the side, then good luck to him.' So, Mr Heath continued to bring Mother a big bunch of flowers on Christmas Day, when mince pies and drinks were provided!

Father was far more reserved in his choice of cars and preferred Bentleys and Rolls Royce. When he migrated to Australia, Father brought his favourite grey Bentley with him. It had a grey leather interior and a lovely wooden dashboard and two mirrors in the back so that ladies could check their hair and make-up before they disembarked.

But Father was capable of perplexing decisions. Like the time he decided one of his Bentleys used too much petrol, so he removed the large mudguards and running boards to 'lighten' it and for good measure, painted it yellow! Mother told him 'it looked like an ice cream truck' as most cars were black in those days. A yellow Bentley was unheard of.

When Mother was about fifty-year-old, she stepped up to a grey Jaguar SK 120 sports car. Jaguar first released this classic car at the 1948 London Motor Show. It was only ever intended as a concept car but proved so popular it became a much sought-after model. If you're lucky enough to find the car she swanned around in, today, in 2017, you'll have to pay anything between $90,000 and $150,000 depending on condition! Not surprisingly, she turned many heads among the young men who would watch in envy as she sped past. Her regal bearing was with her forever.

When she aged and took up residence in a retirement home in Australia, the staff liked and respected her but soon dubbed her 'the Queen' for her regal, almost overbearing manner. She enjoyed this comparison. But I like to remember her as my Mother, the beautifully coiffured lady, resplendent in her ballroom gown and wrap-around fur, gliding into my bedroom to kiss me goodnight before she and Father spirited off to yet another evening and night of gaiety and dancing.

I arrived late in my parent's life, had a Nanny, and lived in idyllic, but isolated surroundings. Despite the impressive home, gardens, and cars we had, the war restricted movement, and rationing of petrol had impacted social contact with family and friends. Contact with our two cousins Judy [same age as Tony] and Rosemary [same age as me], was limited. I never knew my paternal grandparents as they died when I was a baby [Grandmother, 1942] and [Grandfather, 1944]. Occasionally I had contact with my maternal grandparents, Nana and Grandpa Clare, who lived in Bournemouth – a long way from Sandbach at the time. I was a lonely child.

As a young child, I liked to explore. I was forbidden to go through the gates that were halfway down the drive to Dalton House. But occasionally, I went through those gates and stood at the bottom of the drive to see the outside world.

I saw a steamroller flattening the tarmac on the newly surfaced road. The unforgettable image and the power it displayed remain with me. Steam, one of the main sources of power of the day, spurted out of all the steamroller openings! Around this time, I saw steam shovels and a steam roundabout in a fair ground. And, as a family, we occasionally went to Crewe to see the great trains and record the numbers of them in the 'train spotter book' provided by the railway. I was in awe of steam then, as I am today.

At the forbidden bottom of the drive, I saw a 'road sweeper' doing his job. I looked at him and he said: 'Hello lad, what are you doing?' I chatted happily with the friendly fellow for five to ten minutes before saying 'I'd better go as I am not supposed to come down here by myself.' I rushed back to Mother and proudly announced: 'I'm going to be a road sweeper when I grow up.' She was horrified and asked me why. With excitement, I replied: 'Because they are happy and talk to people all day.'

My response to this interaction with the road sweeper at such a young age shows insight into how my views were forming. That is, class distinction does not influence happiness.

I was a lonely child and yearned company. I was two-year-old when Tony went to boarding school around twelve years of age. But in 1947, school was on the horizon for me. This would solve all problems – I would not be lonely.

I was a described as a 'gregarious child' and now would have company with children of my own age for the first time in my life. It was expected that I would progress and make my parents proud, as my brother had done. Tony went to Malvern College and then studied medicine at St Bartholomew's Hospital Medical College in London, leading to a successful career in the UK, then Australia. Life for me would also be good, as it should be…. Wouldn't it?

The war was over, but my troubles had just started.

Chapter 3
Growing Up

Whatever choices are made, there are consequences. Perhaps because of the miscarriage Mother suffered between the birth of Tony and my arrival, and perhaps because of the War, she was fiercely protective of me. Commendable, but it did me no favours as I lacked resilience, and confidence in my abilities as a child. Combined with the burden of significant, but undiagnosed learning disabilities, my future was destined for a troubled, and torturous, path.

From my own childhood, I have learned how important it is to expose children to influences beyond that of parents. I know that parental influence has a major impact on a child's decision-making. Restricting children from the outside world means trouble for the child when the 'cord' is cut.

I grew up in a closeted and isolated environment, devoid of valuable experiences of playing and interacting with other children regularly as there were no 'suitable' children to play with. I may not have learned how to swear or steal silver spoons, but I learned something else far more debilitating during these early years. I developed a dependence on my Mother and felt great loneliness. To me, loneliness became a feeling of normality and one that I carried with me for most of my early life. The shy, lonely young boy grew into a shy and lonely young man.

Added to my deep feelings of loneliness was the infliction of ailments I suffered during my early years. The remedies to treat these ailments also shaped my childhood and teenage years. I had a reputation as a sickly, 'dorky' child, without the academic abilities that are often associated with this latter description. From four-year-old, I wore big round National Health Service glasses to cure or tame a very noticeable nervous squint. Or, more correctly, I wore glasses when I could because often, they were lost or damaged – one pair went under the lawnmower at school!

Unprovoked, and within a millisecond, my squinting eye would travel to the corner and startle and bemuse the person talking to me or looking at me. I wore an eye patch over my wayward eye – not all the time, but on alternate months to try and fix the problem. All this did was succeed in making me look like a dorky pirate! I suppose it was some sort of improvement, adding a devilish quality to me, but not sinister enough to strike anything other than unrestrained mirth in the minds of my school tormenters. My fellow school students called me: 'four eyes with the taxicab doors open'. 'Four eyes' related to me wearing glasses. The 'cab doors open' unkindly referred to my ears that stuck out each side of my head – the projection of the left ear almost at a 90-degree angle from my head!

I had been blessed with a squint, protruding ears, and large crooked teeth. I had too many teeth for my gums and some grew upwards into the distorted cavity of my upper palate a remnant of the consistent sucking of my two middle fingers as a child. At a glance, it was obvious that life was not going to be easy. Perhaps this was why Mother was so protective of me?

One day Tony and I were to have a professional photo taken together. I was four-year-old. We were told where to stand and sit. I sat on a bench, and Tony was to stand directly behind me. The photographer looked, and then told Mother he would pin my ears back with sticking plaster so that the photo wouldn't be ruined. I revolted when he tried to do this. I knew sticking plaster was painful when removed, especially when stuck to hair! The outcome? The photo was taken with my ear unimpeded. I had won a small, but important victory! But did I?

Years later I looked at that photo on the sideboard. I could not see my ears sticking out. My ears were not stuck back prior to the photo being taken, so how did the photographer manage to camouflage my protruding ears? I looked harder. I saw that the photographer had positioned me slightly off-centre ensuring Tony looked directly at the camera, and I slightly to the side. This resulted in the least protruding ear pressed into Tony's shirt collar and tie, and my most protruding ear totally hidden, apart from a very small outline of the tip – seen when you look hard, at the photo!

And the humiliation went on. My ears were syringed frequently to remove the accumulated wax due to twisted eardrums that made me prone to ear infections – at a time that antibiotics had not been sufficiently developed. Constant infection caused my ears to discharge profusely causing crusting and scabs on the outer ear and a very unpleasant smell. As a small child I found the scabs irresistible and would pick at them constantly. This resulted in the wounds being daubed with Mercurochrome – a 'cure all' red lotion and marked me as an object for further ridicule.

The local hall in Sandbach doubled as a casual medical centre. It was there I had my 'shots' for polio, visited the friendly optician and occasionally the dentist. Dentistry at this stage was akin to a registered form of torture, and I was rightly terrified. For a start, the Dentist who visited had an utter lack of social skills relating to children. I recall visiting him. I was roughly sat down in an alien space-chair and restrained by a nurse whilst the Dentist 'attacked' me. Some sort of a contraption was inserted into my mouth to keep it open, and a horrible smelling rubber gas mask placed over my mouth! It was a truly scary encounter and I genuinely thought he was going to kill me!

Self-preservation kicked in! I was fighting for my life! As the Dentist leant over me trying to put the gas mask on, I turned my head towards him and used the only weapon I had available – my teeth! I opened my mouth wide, lunged forward and bit him hard on his ear! Pandemonium broke out! The bleeding dentist roughly hauled me out of the chair and pushed me out the operating room door to my bewildered Mother waiting outside. He declared: 'He's an animal! He's bitten me! He's uncontrollable! Never bring him back again'.

I counted this as one of my earliest victories. Mother on the other hand, counted it as a humiliating experience. How could her cherub behave like that? After all, she, the 'lady' of the district had a social standing to uphold! From then on, my reputation as a sickly and 'dorky' child was extended too 'uncontrollable'. I never had to return to that dentist again, and Mother certainly refused to take me. But I did need to visit a dentist. What was the solution?

    I visited Father's factory on occasion prior to attending school and it was here that I met Laura, the nurse who worked in the packing area. I liked her – she had a good manner with children. Father asked Laura if she would take me to the dentist at Kidsgrove, the local shopping centre near the factory. She jumped at the opportunity. It was a morning off work, a ride on the bus with the boss' son, giving her increased recognition.

    I liked the dentist and his assistant and went there several times with Laura. The dentist gave me sweets to distract me from his intent. It worked. The dentist did whatever he needed to my teeth, and I on the other hand, was chuffed at earning sweets for visiting him on an outing with Laura!

    Laura and the packing staff became my friends at the factory. I played amongst the straw used for packing the product. One day Joe packed me in a wire crate and placed straw all around me. Just at this time, Father came looking for me. Excited, I jumped up out of the straw and said, 'here I am'! Father was furious with Joe for placing me in danger, but I enjoyed the fun.

    Shortly after the 'dentist' episode I had my tonsils and adenoids removed at a hospital in Crewe, Cheshire. The hospital was normal for the time – dreary, smelt of disinfectant and no discrete children's ward. I ended up in a room with two beds and in the bed opposite me was an old man surrounded by oxygen bottles and a mask attached to his face. He looked more dead than alive. I was terrified he would die and return to haunt me!

Medicine has always been a bit of a mystery to me. What I didn't understand then, and still don't is: why they gave me, a six-year-old, an enema before wheeling me in for a tonsillectomy? Chloroform was used as the anaesthetic and anyone who has been 'put under' with this gas knows how horrible it is. I tried desperately to push the mask away to get away from the vile smelling gas. I literally felt like I was being suffocated. But I was held down firmly and could not escape! My tonsils were removed.

The only good thing about my hospital stay was the ice cream and jelly I was given after the operation. Other than that – it was a dreadful experience. I was discharged two days after the operation – earlier than normal, as I was not a compliant patient. Mother told the staff that she could look after me at home just as well, so I was sent home to heal. The staff seemed very relieved to see me go!

In 1948 at six-year-old, I contracted a severe dose of whooping cough and became delirious due to a temperature of 104-degree F. It was a frightening, and life threatening, ordeal. Mother, a great knitter, taught me the art to keep me amused and sedate indoors during the long recovery period. I knitted a string vest, which I proudly wore after softening by washing and drying!

One day, I went for a check-up with the local doctor. He asked me to pull up my vest, so he could listen to my chest. I had been knitting a long time, and didn't know how to caste off, so the vest went down to my knees! I started pulling the vest up, and up, and up – a bit like Rapunzel let down your hair, but in reverse! The Doctor said to me with a smile: 'I can see you have been very busy'!

From this time on, bronchitis would become a yearly ailment that I battled with all my school years. I spent many days recovering from these debilitating episodes at home, licking brown sugar and butter to relieve my throat and cough, and knitting. I even graduated from knitting string vests to string underpants! Unbelievably, they were warm and tailored and I wore them in the winter, at home.

I had one school holiday friend – Alistair – the vet's son who lived nearby. Alistair was one of five children of which he was the only boy. We looked forward to the company of each other. We played in the garden and around the pool that Tony and his friend David built. We listened to records and sometimes went to tea at each other's houses.

Alistair was an 'alter' boy at the local Catholic Church. On a Sunday, he rushed off from our play to perform his duties. He returned about an hour later and we resumed our play. We had great discussions about his church and my church – we were inquisitive about the two religions. Later, at an older age, Alistair told me that he thought I was the one who invented stereo sound. He thought this as I put two speakers either side of the room and ask him to stand in the middle and tell me which speaker the sound was coming from. Our school holiday friendship ended when school did. Alistair joined the Navy on leaving school and I hope he had a good life. He was a very good friend and made the school holidays enjoyable.

From an early age my interests were in all things practical, particularly those relating to electronics, electricity, and film. I recorded radio plays, placed a speaker in my parents' bedroom and 'broadcast' the plays I had recorded. I rigged the door of my room to buzz if anyone opened it. My electric train set was well used. I attached power plugs to pieces of electrical wire to create extension cords, making Father very nervous, and once he brought in an electrician to check on my work. My work was correct. How I did this without any guidance or reading was a mystery to others. To me it was not. I understood the principles – it was simple. It just made perfect sense to me. Circumstances in the future did prove that I had above average intelligence, but at this time, it was not recognised. The focus was my lack of abilities that dominated.

My proficiency in things mechanical grew when Father allowed me to manage our home projector by hiring ten-minute movies such as 'Popeye' in the days before television. But, for me, the excitement wasn't in watching the black and white films, but rather, in splicing the film and running it through the 11.5mm projector so that everything worked perfectly. Many years later I obtained a 16mm projector license. I always wanted to get a 35 mm license and work as a projectionist in movie theatres, but never did. One of many unfulfilled dreams, like we all have.

Surely, with the aptitude and abilities I demonstrated at an early age in the intricacies of complicated technical and mechanical procedures, I would excel at school? However, this was not to be. I started my crucial years of schooling at a time when schools in England had just started recovering from the severe and widespread interruptions brought by the war. Teachers did their best, but were not always qualified. This environment, coupled with my learning disabilities, had long lasting effects on me.

The cat sat on the mat. It made no sense to me, no sense at all, no matter how hard I tried. It just didn't make any sense. My inability to make sense of the written word led to me being described by my family as 'not as talented as Tony'. This was the nicest description I heard.

The description my teachers used was different. They gave up on me early because they determined I couldn't be taught. They believed I was stupid and acted on that 'truth'. I didn't like being treated as if I was stupid and withdrew from participating in their charade. As a child, I didn't have the armoury with which to fight this battle, so, I challenged their authority in the only way I knew how – by withdrawing my participation and becoming the class clown. It was at this point, the sickly, dorky, uncontrollable child now had 'stupid and disruptive' added to the description.

I hated school – apart from the daily half a pint of milk at the mid-morning break in which we blew bubbles through the straw. Other than this, school was a totally, negative experience. I believed the teachers didn't want to teach me, so I didn't want to learn. Well, it wasn't so much that I didn't want to learn but because every effort I made to learn I didn't succeed. I lost heart and was quickly dismissed as someone who either didn't care or was somehow unable to care. I was someone not worth the effort. I'm not saying that everything that went wrong at school was entirely the school's fault, because I did contribute to my own academic demise. Well, not so much demise as a 'failure to launch'!

Elworth Primary School was my very first school – a local day school I started at the age of five-year-old. Up until this time, my life had been reclusive and protected. Suddenly, unprepared for the event, Mother dragged me to school. I screamed, cried, and dug my heels in the whole way – every day!

Mother was persistent and disciplined – I was going to school – it was the law she told me. Her mantra was, always: *'If I say something, I mean it!'* And she did mean it. Mother did try to cheer me up on the dreadful journey to school by getting me to sing along with her. She sang, and I cried and together we made quite a spectacle of ourselves. We conducted this daily drama amid the 'waves' of cyclists peddling their way to Foden Work Factory, at Elworth!

To me it was a daily walk to the gallows, and I wasn't cheered in the least by mother's exhortations to, 'Come on dear, let's sing'. And she would trill: 'Oh what a beautiful morning, oh what a beautiful day, I got a beautiful feeling, everything's going my way…' it might have worked on stage for Oklahoma, but for this reluctant pupil it was a dirge, a proclamation of dire consequences.

I often wonder if I was the youngest child ever expelled from Elworth Primary School? I was asked to leave after a few short months, having been labelled 'a disruptive child, not conforming and trying to attract attention by being the class clown'. During my time at Elworth, I spent some time in the corner of the classroom wearing the cone shaped hat with the 'D' on it. This 'dunces' hat' was reserved for children who could not learn or got things wrong or were disruptive.

The Headmaster of Elworth suggested to my parents that I should be 'assessed' for a 'special needs' school to receive 'professional care'. To this day I am not sure what type of professional care he was suggesting, or indeed if I had it. All I know is that I was quickly shipped to Bereton Hall, another day school via an old, rickety bus. This form of transportation morning and afternoon was so much more exciting than being dragged to school by Mother!

Brereton Hall school was a much more palatable school than Elworth. At Brereton, I made mats out of bottle tops, had a sleep on a camp bed in the afternoon, and then boarded the bus to go home. A nice school indeed! But I still didn't learn much, except to not confuse what I imagined, with reality.

One day after school I described in detail to Mother about the foxhunt I had witnessed at school, complete with smartly dressed riders and baying hounds. Mother mentioned this to the teachers at school who assured her there was no foxhunt to witness! I had either started to create in my mind the experiences I couldn't achieve through conventional learning; or I was transporting my mind to more exciting activities, than the learning I could not fathom.

I liked Brereton Hall but was there only for a term before Mother and Father decided to send me to 'boarding' school. I was just six-year-old. Boarding school was common… 'boys from upper-middle-class families had to go to boarding-schools, it was what always happened to them, poor things, and there was nothing anyone could do about it.' Boarding School may have been common, but wise for a six-year-old?

Staple Hill was an exclusive boarding school for around thirty boys. There were two dormitories and as boarding schools go for a six-year-old, this was pleasant as it was small and homely.

Mrs Bustard, the owner had long golden hair and was like a surrogate mother to me. When I was lonely and upset, which I was, often, she would kindly say to me: *'come on dear'* and take me into her room and console me. I would sit on the soft cream coloured sheepskin on the sofa, and she would talk to me. This frequent interaction made my stay bearable.

Staple Hill had a large garden where we played games such as 'oranges and lemons' and 'ring a ring of roses'. We would sneak through the gap in the hedge of the boundary of the School and walk through the woods and out onto the open meadow where an old house stood in the middle and statues dotted in the overgrown garden. It was like entering a magic realm, a hidden garden.

We played a lot of games and went a lot of walks. School-work was at a minimum and this is probably why I liked it. I was not challenged with the written word – it was more about creating and adventure.

There were some memorable classmates at this 'exclusive' school – one, I recall. If he was touched, even slightly, he 'crumpled' and fell to the floor, as if he had been pushed. As you could imagine, with a group of small boys, this occurred frequently. Others had epileptic fits, which was frightening when I saw this for the first time. The teacher quickly told me, 'don't worry, they will get over it'. And they did.

I've never been quite sure about the type of school Staple Hill was, but the school did provide some entertainment. It was here that I was introduced to the world of movies, albeit by stealth. Boys, those more than ten-year-old, went to watch movies once a week at the picture theatre in Warwick. One night, I snuck into the old army truck they used to transport them to the theatre. I crawled under the seats and hid until I felt the truck stop at the destination. Only then I crawled out. The teacher was not pleased with me at all but reluctantly resolved: 'We can't send you home now as we will miss the movie – we'll have to sort it out tomorrow.' So, I stayed and watched some spooky movie with the older boys. I felt so proud – the only youngster ever to join the older boys, and see, a film!

It was the very first film I had seen on a big screen at a picture theatre, and, as a six-year-old, the atmosphere was something I have never forgotten. Even to this day, I love watching movies. Every time the cinema darkens, and the screen lights up with the picture, I am transported back to my adventure and the initial exposure to this wonderful, make believe world. My impertinent behaviour so early in my school life was worth every bit of displeasure directed at me by the Teacher!

My time at Staple Hill ended abruptly when the school relocated back to its pre-war premises. My parents needed to find another school for me. But where could they find a suitable one? I was not a gifted student, or even a passable student. They did try to get me into Malvern College as a boarder, which was where my brother Tony was schooled from twelve-year-old, but being 'special', I failed the entrance exams miserably. Mother suggested I have private tutoring at home to improve my studies to a level that was acceptable to the schools they aspired me to attend; but Father flatly refused. I was to go to a boarding school, and that was that!

There are some things in life that define you, and over which you have little or no control. Family circumstance and influence dictated the early part of my life, but an even greater influence was the 'gift' of undiagnosed dyslexia, which was not well known in the 1940s. It was only many, many years later – in 1975 that my wife Dianne and I were listening to 'breakfast' radio and heard the guests – experts and an actor, discuss a significant learning disability called dyslexia. The actor who had dyslexia explained to the experts how she learnt her lines to enable her to act. Her friend read and recorded the script lines on audiotape; and then she replayed the tape repeatedly, until she memorised the words.

I was stunned. I immediately recognised the symptoms the experts and the actor were talking about. I knew, and lived this affliction dyslexia, and its cousin, dyscalculia every day of my life.

This radio session was enlightening, as at one stage I dreamed about becoming an actor or working in television as a movie presenter or newsreader. But I determined that I could only do this if I could read, learn my lines, *and* had the confidence to do so. But now in an instant I recognised what had constrained me for years. Finally, 'it', had a name – dyslexia. And there was a valid reason for the pain and humiliation I had consistently endured over the years.

I can identify with the following articulated by the well-known architect Richard Rogers regarding his own struggle with dyslexia in the 1940s – a period of childhood we shared.

In my youth, in the 1940s, I was called stupid. Not only could I not read but also, I couldn't memorize my schoolwork. I was always at the bottom of the class. I became very depressed. When I was young, 7 or 8, I remember standing on the windowsill and saying, 'should I jump, or shouldn't I jump?' At that time, dyslexia, was not recognised. In fact, it wasn't until I had my first child that I realised I was dyslexic....

I was gregarious. People who are excluded from society tend to express themselves in ways not acceptable to society.... I believe it important to have someone who believes in you and is supportive which in turn builds your confidence whether it is your parent, teacher, or a friend. I also went to a special school for a year, which saved my life because they understood my difficulties and I realized that there were other students who also had great difficulties.'

Unlike Richard, I did not have this support from anyone who understood my difficulties when growing up – not even qualified teachers. I couldn't learn like others did and couldn't pass exams. I was the class dunce and treated as such. My self-esteem was non-existence. I felt useless and despaired.

However, I did think that one day I would be able read and write and do sums – it would come naturally, when I am older. To some extent it did – in much later life, but never to the extent I would like.

My older brother Tony was a gifted academic who worked jolly hard – and I saw just how hard he worked – to achieve his qualification that allowed him to be a respected medical professional. But that type of pathway was closed to me.

Dyslexia prevented me from reading and writing sufficiently and thwarted any possibility of me developing a nurturing and loving relationship with the written word. And without that relationship, the chances of me ever developing an interest in academia, never mind conquering any chosen field, evaporated.

Even now, with the telling of my story, I am relying on the help of Dianne who did develop a relationship with the written word. My contribution to this story is mostly through the spoken word diaries I developed in my 20s and 30s. I have improved my literacy since this time using computers. Where once I shied away from being challenged by the written word, or sums, as I knew from repeated experiences, I would 'fail'; the use of a computer lets me fail until I succeed, without judging me.

I am now comfortable with my abilities. I can expose myself to criticism whilst having the confidence of not being crushed, as I was in my school years and beyond.

I still lament how my undiagnosed dyslexia stunted my abilities, and confidence, and prevented me from reaching my true potential.

Dyslexia, has remained, my greatest burden. It has impacted, and shaped, every aspect of my life.

The need to find another school when Staple Hill closed was about the time my parents were jetting off on regular overseas jaunts. With Tony independent at Medical College, I was the only impediment to their sense of freedom. The solution was boarding school. But, after being rejected by a credible one, the next best option found was Cloverley Hall, a school that did not require an entrance exam. It was perfect for me – a boy who couldn't read or write or pass exams.

I would spend seven torturous years at this school – an understaffed and badly run large boarding school for boys; and it was here I suffered the other defining and devastating experience of my life, the first being coping with undiagnosed dyslexia.

Chapter 4
Potent Memories

I was not meant for boarding school. Who is, at just seven-year-old?

I have potent memories of my time at Cloverley Hall Boarding School for Boys in the 1940s and early 1950s. The despair I endured during a boarder at this school from seven, to fourteen-year-old, makes it hard to speak of my experiences to this day. I prefer not to reflect on or speak about the painful and emotional aspects of my time at this school, but my story must be told. Undoubtedly boarding school had a significant impact on my life.

Many articulate and well-qualified people have spoken, and written, about the long-lasting effects of boarding school, particularly when starting from an early age. I concur that boarding school does not 'build one's character' or 'make the man'. Instead it steals a young child's innocence, breaks the confidence, and replaces what's lost, with a coat of armour, plated with fear and filled with loneliness and alienation.

The pain experienced each term from being wrenched from my parents and incarcerated in an alien and often hostile environment is still etched in my brain and psyche.... I am sure that other boarding survivors of the era I attended boarding school, must feel the same. I suspect my learning disabilities added to, and compounded, the relentless trauma I experienced. Surely, boarding school in this day has improved? I hope so.

George Perkins, a fellow boarder of the same period I attended boarding school sums up his feelings of how this experience of leaving his mother for boarding school impacted on his life. He describes this leaving and going to boarding school as 'the most potent memory of my life'. His feelings reflect that of my own. He writes that he directly:

...Links the 'distraught state' of his twenties and the 'wreckage' of his emotional life with the ploy he used when watching his mother recede in a cloud of steam as the school train left. It was at such moments that I learned early on, not only how to suppress all feeling and emotion, but also not to feel anything at all.

I was in a state of trauma for most of my years at school. For days before returning to school for another term, I pleaded to Mother: 'please, please don't send me back' and cried enough tears to fill a bucket. The cleaner refused to come to Dalton House for the three days prior to my return to school, as it upset her to see and hear my distress. But my parents told me 'this will make a man of you...you will thank us in years to come.' I never did. I was time, and time again, betrayed. Taken from home and sent back to school, – an environment where I was ignored, ridiculed, and humiliated.

I couldn't wait to leave school, but my parents told me that 'I needed to learn how to read and write and do sums, as even if you work on a farm as a labourer, you will need these skills so that you give the right type and amount of feed to animals.' Besides they said, 'the law of the land dictated that children must attend school until the age of fifteen.'

I'd watch Father's Bentley drive into the distance and out of sight, hoping that once, just once, my parents would realise their mistake and turn back to collect me. They never did. Time, and time again, I felt abandoned and devastated. Another long term commenced. I immediately started to countdown the forty-two days before I would return home for a reprieve of five days after which time, the same heart-breaking rift from my home and family would be repeated.

I was nearly seven-year-old when I entered Cloverley Hall – a boarding school for boys who couldn't pass entrance exams. It would be a long and torturous seven years before I would finally leave, abruptly, at fourteen-year-old.

Cloverley Hall Boarding School was owned and managed by the Church of England and run by the Headmaster, Reverend Duncan. Prior to being converted into a private boarding school, it was a large, and stately home. The building was impressive when viewed from the outside. There were tracks and narrow paths and walkways that weaved beautifully within the grounds. Squirrels ran up and down the trees and rhododendron bushes. Different sorts of flowers and trees were planted across the estate in that specific British way – carefully placed and impeccably managed. Inside was a different story.

There were two downstairs junior dormitories, separated by an archway, and housed about sixteen boarders in each area. I resided in these bitterly cold dormitories for five years. There was no heating at all, and the doors couldn't be closed properly. There was a gap of half an inch where the wind blew in a draft that cut through the only warmth allowed-one sheet and a red blanket on the thin mattress, and a travelling rug from home.

As we returned for another term, our case from home was stored as were our clean clothes that were distributed weekly. Our 'tuck box' was locked away in the passage. It was a Spartan existence – a bed, chair, rug, and a Bible. The junior dormitories were previously used as stables and the only noticeable difference was that the stable now housed young boys, and not horses! There was a bullring over my bed where cattle had been tethered. That bullring is still there – I have a photo of it as evidence to where my bed stood all those years ago. Unfortunately, my time at Cloverley Hall was not just a long, recurring nightmare!

The upstairs loft that housed older boys from the age of twelve, was slightly better. The loft was divided into three dormitories with a big archway between each of them and exposed beams that rose high up to the roof. In each dormitory there were twelve steel beds set along the wall in a familiar pattern of bed, chair, Bible. In this upstairs area it was warmer, and sanitary arrangements were slightly better as there was a toilet at the far end – a proper toilet with a proper door that you could shut. There were no such luxuries in the junior dormitories.

We made our beds, folded the rug, and placed it on the back of our chair, at the side of our bed. Sharing the chair with the rug was one of our two Bibles – the other was used in the classroom. Every week we had a change of bed sheets, underclothes, shirt, and trousers. It was a very orderly approach. Staff left the clean, folded clothes on the bottom of our bed one day, and we left our folded dirty clothes on the bottom of the bed the following day. If your school blazer got dirty, too bad, it had to last until half term to be taken home and cleaned.

In the junior dormitories, boys shared a bucket to pee in late evening and night. At times the boys played jokes on other boys, as you could imagine. A thin piece of string was tied around the bucket and when an unsuspecting boy approached and was about to pee, the trickster would pull the string that moved the bucket, leaving the poor boy peeing over the floor!

Sometimes the 'jokes' played in the dormitories were not so innocent. Once, while sleeping, a couple of boys came over and peed on my bed. I remained quiet and did not make a fuss when they did this and slept in the wet bed, on the side. Why did they do this? Why did I not retaliate?

I don't know and can't explain, but I know I was considered different and was 'an easy target', for what would now be called bullying – a word not mentioned at this time. I was a gawky, weak, and small boy who had led a sheltered life. In fact, I was a 'poor little privileged rich boy'. Most other boys were from farming families from the local district, and well known to each other. I was insignificant to both teachers and fellow students. I was ignored for the most part of my schooling, apart from when I was disruptive – the class clown, or bullied, the latter I thought was normal for me at this time. Boarding school was never going to be an environment in which I thrived, and undiagnosed dyslexia assured this.

The Headmaster a Reverend was previously a missionary in Canada and had developed a love for all things frozen. I think he thought he was preparing us for a life in the frozen wastelands he so loved, hence the need to live, and exercise, in perpetually cold surroundings.

Six days a week, we had a cold shower in the morning. We had one hot bath a week, with juniors two to a tub and seniors by themselves. At night, we had to wash our hands and face and the teacher would pull our ears to check they were clean. The justification for a cold shower was that we needed it to wake us up, but of course, the truth was far more mundane – cold showers were a lot cheaper than hot ones. Needless-to-say, cold showers were never good, not even in summer. It was the UK after all! To add to this, every year I struggled with bronchitis and at the time, there weren't any antibiotics available.

Mother used to get very upset and told the Headmaster:

What is the use of giving out cough mixture to Christopher if you make him have a cold shower in the morning in a room with no heating, then go outside and do breathing exercises in the bitterly cold air? You should pour the cough mixture down the drain for all the good it does!'

I don't remember the Headmaster's response, but I think he was not at all comfortable dealing with spirited adults. He was more used to compliant or cowering children.

There were 12 showers in a semicircle that the boarder's walked under to shower. Many just put their heads forward under the cold stream, pretending that they had a full body shower before leaving and towelling off. But, some Masters, stood on a raised platform so they could see who was not having a full shower. Yes, I've often reflected on the strange arrangement of grown men spying on young boys under the pretext of checking if they were properly cleaning themselves. At the time I simply accepted that this was common practice for boarding schools.

Opposite the showers where the bathtubs stood, were hooks. And by each hook there was a number – mine was 60. After our shower, we dried ourselves, put the towel back on the correct hook, and then, completely naked, ran up, or down the stairs wherever our dormitory was, got dressed, made our bed, and knelt beside it and said our prayers.

Then, there was inspection of the beds by the master. Any beds not made to his satisfaction were stripped, and the offender, ordered to remake them. It was like the army. After inspection, we went to the quadrangle to do breathing exercises. In three rows, with the Headmaster in front, we vigorously threw our 'hands up and out, breathe in, breathe out, breathe in, breathe out', for fifteen minutes.

After the exercise ritual came breakfast. How we looked forward to this! Food was plentiful in the early stages of my boarding school life. Breakfast was a feast of porridge, bacon and eggs and thick slices of bread and butter. Lunch was a stew; and for tea, we were treated to brains or liver, or something resembling this; and on occasion for supper, a drink of orange cordial in the summer and warm milo in the winter, with a biscuit, that was placed on a table outside the kitchen for self-service. And, we had our own tuck box that had been filled with anything we liked from our home before returning to school after the holidays. However, whilst you could fill the tuck box with anything you like, the quantity was limited by the size of the tuck box allowed. And it was a small size allowed. I packed my tuck box with sweets, eggs, a fruitcake, and a jar of jam to spread on the bread and butter that was provided. We boiled our own eggs when we were hungry and wanting a treat. We wrote our name in pencil on the shell, before lowering the whole egg into the boiling water so we knew which one belonged to us.

After a time, there was a change. Food became sparse. There was a great speech from the Headmaster to the Boarder's. School fees would have to go up unless we economised. So, 'to spare our parents the cruelty of having to pay more fees, we all had to make do with less'.

From this point forward, we were always hungry. Breakfast became porridge and thick slices of bread and butter. Lunch was still something like a stew, but tea became bread and butter only. There was no supper. Our tuck box was now not for treats, but rather, accessed for survival.

The emotion surrounding the tuck box was palpable and visible, but access was not guaranteed. If a student had done anything wrong, they were denied access to their tuck box as punishment. However, if the offence was shared, or had widespread implications, all students would be denied access to their tuck box – for a day, week or even longer. Once, our tuck boxes were banned for a whole term!

Deprivation of your tuck box was severe punishment indeed – it was the ultimate weapon for boarders. It meant your precious comfort foods brought from home – eggs, sweets, or cake were denied. Given the circumstances of our lives at his time, this deprivation was as close to as cruel punishment as you could imagine.

There was good reason for our obsession with food – there was never enough of it. We were growing, we exerted a tremendous amount of energy and our need for fuel in the cold environment was great, but one that was never fully satisfied. If you look at photos of me taken at the time you will see a blonde haired, blue eyed, skinny kid with a gaunt face and hungry, desolate eyes.

There was only one qualified teacher who focused on the 6th form, the last year of senior school, trying to prepare them for the School Leaving Certificate.

The rest of the staff were trainee teachers. The war had interrupted education and I suspect that well qualified available teachers, were employed by prestigious schools. I expect Cloverley Hall had no choice than to employ, inexperienced trainee teachers.

What can I say about lessons? I attended reading, writing, arithmetic, sport, woodwork, and religious education. What do I recall of the '3Rs' apart from waiting for the bell to ring for recess and end of the day and waiting for the torture of the lesson to end? I daydreamed. I thought of spaceships and anything else that would take me away from the present. However, for some reason I could relate to how to structure sentences with nouns, pronouns, adjectives, and verbs. I spent a lot of time copying directly from the blackboard on how to construct a sentence, which kept me amused for hours.

Thank goodness for Norris! He and I alternated in being bottom of the class. Lee was just above us, but he had a 'saving grace'. He was very good at sport, and where he failed in academia, he more than compensated with his prowess in sports. I did not excel in either area.

My years as a student, was plagued with learning disabilities, and assistance was non-existent. However, I do give Cloverley Hall and my parents credit, for their focus on grammar, and insisting on speaking the 'Queen's English'. This one attribute has held me in good stead over the years. That is, apart from when my 'plummy' accent caste me as a 'misfit' in the type of jobs I was destined to be employed in the future.

Cloverley Hall was very keen on sport and physical fitness. In addition to breathing exercises prior to breakfast, we had physical education after our two lessons in the morning. We changed into our white gym shorts, and a white singlet, and exercised for 30 minutes. Press ups, handstands, hands above your head, all that sort of thing. In the afternoon, after lessons finished, you donned your black shorts and a long-sleeved black singlet before going for a run or participating in whatever sport was on offer. I mainly did running, boxing and rugby – the latter not very well as 'too many legs and feet got in the way of the ball'! I did one term of tennis on the court that was built by Father's donations. I recall being told that I should try a different sport as I had very poor eye – hand coordination.

Boxing, however, was different. I didn't like it, but was good at it. It brought out my developing sense of self-preservation. The Headmaster sat in the boxing ring on training day and kept punching at my face. I had to retaliate. And I did.

I was selected for the Cloverley Hall boxing inter-school sports day team. I fought a boy of similar age and weight from a competitor school in three, three-minute rounds. A mouth guard was provided, but no headgear. The equation was simple. You either punched, or, got punched. I knocked him out in the second round! Overall, I liked these inter-school challenges, particularly when we went to another school and stayed for a meal. It was a feast compared to the normal Cloverley Hall fare.

On Tuesday afternoons, we went 'grounding' looking after the extensive, grounds, garden, and woodland. I enjoyed this outside physical work as I did as a young child at *Dalton House*. The Boarders kept Cloverley Hall garden very tidy, indeed – it was our responsibility to do so. We chopped trees, mowed lawns, and tidied the grounds and woodland. My glasses suffered during this activity, and every term I needed to have them straightened. Once when 'grounding', I lost my glasses completely and the lawn mower ran over them! When I returned to Cloverley Hall many years later, the grounds were not as well kept as when the students were 'grounding'. My love of physical work, and gardening, remains.

In the evenings, we roamed the corridors in the school after finishing our homework of thirty minutes, five nights a week. Comics were not allowed. The only books allowed was the Bible and the small library – really a corridor more than a library, which contained books that were above my capacity to read. Other evenings, after homework there were places you could build model ships or play with plasticine. Most of the time, however, I paced the corridors aimlessly. Juniors used to go to bed about half-past 7, and the seniors an hour later.

A commendation and conduct point system were intrinsic to Cloverley Hall. A Commendation – was received for good work or good behaviour. Not surprisingly I rarely received any commendation points for the gold team to which I belonged. In fact, I received only one in my time at Cloverley Hall. It was for good woodwork and I received it in 1957 just before leaving school.

Conduct points were the opposite of commendation points. I received many conduct points, mostly for talking in the dormitory after lights out. My loud, clear penetrating voice – an asset now – got me into a lot of trouble at school. 'Thompson – you are talking – who else?' the teacher would ask. No one ever owned up. I was on my own! When teachers became frustrated with our behaviour in class, they would throw chalk at us. One teacher, completely 'lost it' and kicked the panel out of the classroom door! We all went very quiet. The Headmaster announced at one lunchtime after this event, that this same teacher had left unexpectedly.

When conduct points were issued, you were handed one card while a duplicate was given to the Headmaster. The points you 'earned' for unbecoming conduct were deducted from the commendation points your team had won, but that wasn't the end of the humiliation. Once you received a Conduct Card you had three days to front up to the Headmaster and hand your card to him to receive your punishment.

The three days in which to present your Conduct Card was not a period of grace. It was a time of torment as the prospect of presenting yourself for a ritualized caning meant every day delayed was a day of dread. When delay and procrastination ceased to be an option, I would go to the Headmaster's office to receive my punishment. Once inside, the Headmaster pressed a button, and a red light would go on outside his door indicating he did not want to be disturbed.

The Headmaster glared at me over his desk reinforcing the message that I was wrong for whatever I had done. He would order me to go over to the green chair, take down my trousers and underpants, and put my hands, on top of the chair and lean over, presenting my naked backside for my punishment. He would then pick up an old gym shoe and deliver 3 great whacks – one on each buttock, and one down the middle, depending on the severity of the crime. All boys who received a Conduct Card had the same punishment. That night, in the dormitory, we would show the marks of the whacking to the other boys, as a way of displaying your hard-earned badge of honour.

I never worked out why spanking naked boys was something that needed to happen behind closed doors or if the red light was an automatic locking device or simply a warning that terrible things were going on behind that locked door. My suspicions and other boarders were even more aroused when we noticed the red light outside the Headmaster's door used to go on in the evening when Miss Skewers, deputy head was spending the evening with the Headmaster. Was she being beaten too, we wondered?

The Headmaster 'dished' out punishment that was normal for the time. But he also read to the young boarders before lights out at night. Although the stories were normally something from the Reader's Digest, we really looked forward this act of normality.

Sunday was the day I hated most of all. The Sabbath. But I did not hate it for the reasons you may think. Sunday started off with getting up as usual, even though I might have wanted to spend the day in bed. There were no exercises in the morning on this day. We had breakfast, and then we trooped off to church. Originally, we went to the local church at Carvahall, which was quite nice. We used to walk down there in crocodile formation and, at some time during the service, we would put money that had been allocated to us from our account, in the collection plate.

The Headmaster, a Reverend was a lay preacher. When he preached at local churches in the area, he asked if any of the 'boarder's' would like to accompany him – to boost the congregation. There was no shortage of volunteers as it was a pleasant drive in the country, and he went to some nice churches. We joined in the service, and then returned. On the odd occasion the whole school would travel by buses to sing at a large cathedral, which was appreciated.

The agony of watching sixty students put in a shilling, two shillings, or whatever, into a collection plate that was going into someone else's coffers and not directly benefiting Cloverley Hall was too much for either the Headmaster of the School Board, to bear. It was decided that church would be held at the School, and the collection plate money retained, for the charities the Headmaster supported. So, the boarder's donated to the School Church, and continued to donate to charity causes periodically.

The Headmaster was obsessed with raising funds for missionary work in his former frozen domain in Canada and the students were constantly being asked to donate for a 'noble cause'. Of course, we did donate because it was very hard not to. We were children. How could we say no to such an authority figure? By giving to the collection plate in church and charity donations, we were left with precious little discretionary money in an environment where we received precious little.

Donations to charity went down like this. We queued up in the morning, and the Reverend Headmaster would say, *'How much?'* The responses came from each of the boarders ... normally sixpence. But when it got to my turn, I gave double the amount of donations but not for the right reason! I had developed a stutter, particularly with 'C' and 'S' and it remains to this day, surfacing when I am under some sort of duress. Therefore, my name was hard to say [Christopher] and I couldn't say sixpence, so I always said 'shilling'! I gave a shilling each week to the Sunday collection plate, and a shilling to the charity collection!

My two shilling and six pence weekly pocket money soon went with donations, and my account also had deductions for newspapers for the library. My Father was not pleased and said: It's a joke, Christopher donating to a newspaper. He can't even read! He was right. I never did read a newspaper at school but did donate for them. Occasionally I had enough money left to buy an ice cream from the ice cream van that came twice a week in the summer months.

When you think about it, it was a clever way of taking money from children. Initially, when we went to a church outside the school if we didn't want to put anything in the collection plate, we would simply rattle our fingers among the coins and pass on the plate and no one was any the wiser! But, when the biggest authority figure in your life is standing there, towering over you, and asking, 'how much can I deduct from your account?' it's virtually impossible to say: 'nothing, thanks'!

After Church we went for long walks, followed by lunch. Then, we had 'Crusaders', a scripture-type reading. After this, we sang hymns, followed by another long walk. Then we had tea, which consisted of our tuck box wares, bread and butter and a jug of tea. After tea there was letter writing to home, with a nib pen, as we weren't allowed to bring biros into the School.

I struggled with letter writing and only ever managed half a page of scrawl or illegible writing which conveyed to my parents that I was still alive, but that's about all. I amused myself the rest of the time drawing spaceships and imagining living in one. My spaceship that I drew was tall, thin, and multi-storied with fins on the side. Inside it had bedrooms, control room and a kitchen. I loved spaceships.

After 'letter writing' we gathered around for scripture or Bible reading. The younger children went to Miss Skewer's sitting room for Bible reading, the older boys into the Headmaster's study. In the hot weather, we would sit on the terrace or under the Monkey Puzzle tree in the grounds, while the Headmaster read Bible stories to us.

No, Sunday was never a very good day. Yet, somehow, I have retained my faith. Not necessarily a belief in the institutions that promote adherence to any faith, but something approaching an acknowledgement of a higher power.

Even though I hated school and every day of schoolwork, I enjoyed the excursions. We went to Wedgewood Potteries and Cadbury's Chocolate Factory that delighted us. We were handed free samples of chocolate, so we could taste just how good freshly made chocolate tasted! Another particularly interesting outing was to Birkenhead where a boat was launched.

Sometimes, on a Saturday, two to three times per term, we watched films in the coach house – the assembly area of the School. Each boy carried a chair out of the dining room into the coach house to sit on and watch the film. The 'seniors' set up the 16 ml projector that the Headmaster operated. They were quite good quality G rated films, such as Tom Brown's Schooldays. Sometimes, if we were terribly, terribly good and there was a special program broadcast such as the Trooping of the Guards and the Edinburgh Tattoo we were invited to watch television in the Headmaster's study. There we sat cross-legged on the floor in our pyjamas and dressing gown and felt genuinely privileged to be afforded such a treat.

I occasionally 'escaped' from schoolwork to have dental treatment. I had sucked two fingers as a small child, which distorted my palate, resulting in considerable 'crowding' of teeth. As a result, a lot of my teeth needed to be removed and I wore braces for many years. Father said my teeth literally cost him a fortune!

Mother would pick me up from school to go to the dental specialist in Liverpool. We would drive through the Mersey tunnel under the Mersey River.

Mother did not like driving through the tunnel, because it scared her. I think she was afraid the tunnel would collapse, and we would drown. Other times we went by train, boarding at Crewe Station, a major terminal for the steam trains. The station was full of grit and grime that belched from the chimneys of the locomotives, majestic machines that seemed to come to life as the steam spewed out of all the pistons, building the power to pull the carriages. The train windows were closed to prevent the soot from coming in and the train would stop occasionally to fill up with water to keep the supply of steam constant. Mother and I would go to the buffet car, where tables were laid with white tablecloths and we enjoyed steward service. I loved these trips on the train, but not visiting the dentist.

Every three weeks of the twelve-week term, Mother would visit on a Saturday and take me out on a Sunday afternoon to Market Drayton to have lunch, returning by the mandated half past six. One day Father came with her and we were late returning to Cloverley Hall. The boarders were watching a movie in the Coach House when we arrived back from our outing. Father had the high beam lights on in the car and these bright lights apparently flashed through the window onto the projection screen. This was not deliberate, and Father was not even aware of the incident. However, what followed highlights the animosity that the school directed at my parents and me.

At school assembly the next morning, the headmaster said: 'I have to apologize for last night and the headlights on the screen. Thompson's father drove into the yard with his Bentley and his headlights went all over the screen.' This unnecessary declaration made the boys hate me even more and this seemed to be acceptable to the Headmaster. The boys all looked around and glared at me, making me feel even smaller than I already felt. I was devastated. It is one thing for students to bully and ridicule you but this humiliation by the Headmaster gave permission for fellow students to dislike me further, adding to my woes.

From this moment, I blamed the wealth and the almost aristocratic mannerisms of my parents that, in my mind, brought so much misery upon me, and influenced my life decisions for many years. But it would be many more years before I eventually came to see the reaction to the incident for what it was: A vindictive and immature response from an adult picking on a defenceless child.

Mother had a few run-ins with the Headmaster over the years, but at the end of one term, on sports day, he asked her if she could give out the prizes as the dignitary originally asked, was unable to attend. Mother, looking a million dollars in her fur coat, was very happy to oblige, and carried the role out perfectly. Unfortunately, her son did not win a prize this year, or any year.

There are incidents in one's life that are so significant that they leave unhealed wounds that are carried for life. 'Mountain', a big senior schoolboy, committed a violent sexual assault on me in 1957. I don't know if Mountain was his given name or a nickname he had earned because of his size, but I only ever knew him as Mountain. He was about 18, an overly large African and I was a small, skinny, 14-year-old. This incident abruptly caused the end of my schooling and impacted my life's journey. I must tell you what happened, even though I am not comfortable in doing so.

It was a normal evening, much like any other. I was in the arts and crafts room, just above the bell tower, working with balsa wood and doing some painting. Mountain came up to me and grabbed my arm. He snarled, 'Hey you, you've got to come with me.' I said, 'let go!' *'No,'* he snapped, 'I've got something for you.' Still holding my arm tightly, he pulled me out of the room, downstairs and across the quadrangle to a place where there were two classrooms with stairs up to the second classroom. There was a large toilet between the two stairs. He shoved me in the toilet and pulled my hand behind my back and upward. It hurt.

He pulled out a penknife and opened the blade. He said, 'Now you're going to do what I tell you, else I'm going to hurt you with this.' He was aggressive, and substantially larger than me. I was frightened and intimidated by him – not only because of his size but also because he was a rarity at school, a black African in a land of mostly white faces.

With his penknife at my throat he told me to take down my trousers and lean over the toilet. I refused. He pressed the penknife into my neck further. I did as he said. He penetrated me with his penis. It felt very bad. He was hurting me, and I shouted at him: 'Stop…I don't like it!' He continued, then suddenly stopped, and told me not to move until I heard the door close behind him. I did as he said. I was petrified. Afterwards, I sat on the toilet seat and sobbed for some time before I left. I did not tell anyone about this incident.

You might ask why I didn't shout from the rooftop about this incident. I have asked myself this question, many, many times over the years. I now know why. I literally did not have the words or understanding. I genuinely didn't know what Mountain had done to me. I didn't even know what rape was at that time. It just shows how naïve I was. I knew nothing about the world or about how the human body worked or anything. I was oblivious to everything. How could this be? I know that my ignorance about these matters reflected the times of my youth. I am angry at Cloverley Hall and my parents for not preparing me for life. This is a sad indictment of my parents, but at the same time I know my ignorance about these matters reflected the times I lived.

To my horror, Mountain repeated the same attack on me, just before the end of half term. He literally frightened the life out of me because of pressing the knife to my throat and his threat: 'If you turn around, I'll use this knife.' I kept protesting to him: 'I don't like it, why are you weeing in me?' That protest was a fair indication of my very limited understanding of all things sexual. This shames me to this day, but one cannot judge another unless having walked in the same shoes. What I did do after this attack, and what I am proud of to this day, I got the courage to immediately go to the 'sick bay' and report what had happened to me, to Matron. Distressed, she called a senior teacher, a kind man whom I trusted. I told him, 'Mountain comes up to me with a knife and threatens me. He makes me bend over and 'wees' in me. I don't like it'.

I was in a state of trauma and bewildered at this time and afterwards. It is a blur to me as to what happened after I 'blew the whistle'. What I do know is that it came out that some other senior students were also raping other junior students. It became the 'talk' – in whispers, of the school. A fellow student of the same age told me that the same sort of thing was happening to him when he was in the woodland pick up kindling wood for the furnace – a chore we all had to do as well as maintenance to the grounds. He was grateful to me for reporting what had happened to me as it was benefiting all others, who did not have the courage to talk to someone.

I never knew what happened to Mountain, or indeed if anything did. His violent assaults on me should've been reported to the police. But were they? Nothing further was said to me, and as normal in those days, no counselling was given – in fact nothing was mentioned again. I don't know if Mountain was charged but I think not. He may have been expelled because I did not see him during the few days after reporting the incident and the end of half term. I didn't care – I just wanted to forget about the assaults and how they made me feel.

A few days after I had 'blown the whistle' Mother collected me for the half term break. She never mentioned anything to me about the assault, so I am not sure if the school had contacted her. I don't think they did, otherwise why didn't she collect me immediately, and not wait until end of term? It was me who told her about the assault in the car on the way home and said: 'I am never going back'. Mother who was well known to never speak, read or view anything that was considered 'nasty' or un-tasteful in her whole life simply said something to the effect of: 'All right dear, don't speak of it again. We will just put all this behind us.' She lived to ninety-seven-year-old, and true to her word, never ever spoke again of the brief conversation we had in the car the day I left school for good.

I don't know if Mother told Father about the reason for my leaving school abruptly, but I don't think he ever knew because he never ever mentioned it to me. Although, I suspect even if he did know, he still would never have spoken to me about it. His response on my return to Dalton House was: 'if you're not going back to school, then you need to work and pay your wa*y'*. If he did know, this was a callous response, but probably one to expect – 'British stiff upper lip'. Plus, he himself went to boarding school at a very early age. I told myself he did not know what had happened to me. It was easier that way.

Without any type of discussion or counselling to heal the pain, I tried to bury what had happened deep inside me, convincing myself that what had happened was a 'childish interaction' and the 'incident that dare not speak its name.' But I never succeeded. The assaults were much, much, more than that.

I know the school changed my life and after these acts of violence and humiliation, I felt empty. My self-esteem, already almost non-existent, had totally evaporated. I am not alone in having experienced and survived child abuse, and I believe many of my responses and feelings would be shared. It would be forty years after the assault before I spoke of it again with my wife, and almost sixty years before I could put into words.

I was woefully unprepared for boarding school when I entered at seven-year-old. I was hopelessly unprepared for life outside Cloverley Hall when I left at fourteen-year-old. The rocky road of life was never going to be easy for me.

Chapter 5
Hard Toil

It was March 1957. I was fourteen-year-old, small, and skinny and just left school after enduring, and reporting gross humiliations by a fellow boarder. Thoughts of my future were not important to me – I was just relieved to be safe at home, and, most importantly with the knowledge that this time, finally, after seven and a half years, I would never have to return to Cloverley Hall, or any other school.

I had to earn my keep. The very day I returned home from leaving School Father reminded me of this. He did not offer me a job in his factory. I never asked why he didn't suggest this, and never understood why he did not see any value in training me, his son to be part of his business – at any level.

I was not suited to office work of any description, but I did understand the manufacturing side of his business, and liked it, having spent time there in the holidays. My aptitude for electricity and electronics was also apparent, and this could've been utilized in the business. 'Why didn't he ask me?' is the question I have asked myself over the years. I do not like to think that he was embarrassed or ashamed of me, his son that could never meet his expectations.

So, what to do? I had to think of something that suited my practical skills and literary abilities. In retrospect, this was a time I should've followed my interest and abilities that had been evident for many years. I should've seized the opportunity to work in any capacity in the developing area of electronics – such as audio radio, TV, or film. With guidance and encouragement, I might have. However, in all honesty, I don't think I would have. To do this, I would've needed an enormous injection of confidence in myself and self-esteem to choose this path. This, I sadly lacked. So, without any real thought, I chose farming. Why? I liked animals and being outdoors and resolved that farming would be an easy option. Important in my decision-making was the false perception that as a farm labourer, I would never, ever, be challenged with reading, writing, and doing sums again.

After deciding on farming, Father arranged for me to work for no wages on Holland's farm at Bradwall, near Sandbach, seven miles away. Why no wages? Perhaps it was a trial, he was testing me to see if I would like the work, and stick it, or return to school. The latter was never going to happen! Perhaps it was because I was not yet fifteen-year-old – the legal age to leave school and therefore, could not be paid a wage? Most likely it was a mutually beneficial arrangement. It was hard to find me a job, and the farmer would never refuse free labour.

This, my first job as a farm labourer, was challenging in many ways. I cycled seven miles to and from the small farm every day in the dark to reach the farm in time for milking. It was a very cold and unpleasant trip. The mixed farm was small – mainly cows and a few pigs. My job was to milk the cows, feed the pigs, clean the farm areas, and manage the muck.

I love cows, and the milk they produce to this day. Like most dairy farms the herd were a mixture of Friesians, Ayrshires, and Jersey cows. The Jerseys and Ayrshire milk had more butterfat than the Friesians. At this time, no one worried about eating or drinking butterfat; nor was milk pasteurised, homogenized, or anything else. It was just plain milk!

Milking in the 1950s was not automated – it was very labour intensive, even for a small farm. There was no power in the milking shed so a Lister engine delivered compressed air to operate the milking units. Before dawn, I lit the Tilley lamps in the cowshed. When heated, the paraffin would evaporate up the Tilley lamp mantle, and glow very brightly as compared to the ordinary lamp with a paraffin wick and gave out a small amount of light.

There were three milking units at this farm. Units were covered buckets that held about a gallon of milk, with a 'pulsator' attached to the lid. Once everything was in place, a compressed air tap was pushed to turn the unit on to start the milking. This pulsator caused the teat cups, attached to the cow's udder, to pulsate, and squeeze out the milk. When the bucket was full, the milk was tipped into the milk churn, and milking continued.

The milk churn held 12 gallons. On top of the churn there was a sieve with a cloth filter. The milk worked its way through the sieve and into the milk churn. Once filled, I carried the milk churn to the farm dairy where there was a cooling device made up of three pipes with cold water running through them. On the top was a rotating mechanism that you put a water hose in to make it rotate. As it rotated, the cold water went through the three prongs and cooled the milk. When the milk was cool, it was placed in an area for the milk lorry to collect the following morning. I would help load the milk onto the lorry and the driver would then take it to the commercial dairy for processing and distribution in milk bottles. I milked the cows every morning and night resulting in 4 churns of milk per day – about 48 gallons of milk.

For three months during the harsh winter, the cows were chained up in the stalls of the shed all day and night. There was a concrete partition between every two cows, and they stood on a raised platform to enable the dung to be collected in the depressed gully. I kept putting straw under the cows to make them comfortable and cleaned out the dung area and wheeled the full barrow to the 'muckheap'.

There was an art to managing the 'muckheap'. I couldn't simply tip a barrow load in front of the previous one because if I did, I'd have the whole yard full of it! When the muckheap got to a certain level, I placed a wooden plank on the muck and tipped the barrow of muck over the end, until it became a giant heap. Then, and only then, I used the muck spreader, hooked to the tractor. It was a real masterpiece – equipment that sprayed the muck all over the field via revolving spindles. This muck was great fertilizer for the next year.

At this farm, I learned about hard work, good work ethics no matter what the job, and the responsibility of working with animals. I was now just fifteen-year-old and ready to find a paid job. This I did by myself.

I worked forty-seven hours per week at a large mixed farm at Wheelock, three miles from Dalton House from December 1957 until May 1958. I enjoyed cycling to and from this farm, particularly beside the canals, watching the lochs and long boats of which I am fascinated even today. My wage was 3 pounds 9 shillings for 47 hours work per week. I paid Father 3 pounds for board and lodging and kept the 9 shillings. Years later Father said it was his way of teaching me the value of money. I don't think I really understood the lesson at the time, and learned instead, that no matter how hard you worked there was always someone ready to take it off you…if not your Father, then the taxman!

This farm was large, and had a lot of cows, calves, sheep, and pigs, as well as chickens. I worked with Howard – a large, burly, and over-confident chap. I disliked him immediately and was wary of him when we first met, and this feeling proved correct. As the youngest farm worker, Howard gave me all the worst jobs. I looked after all the farm animals – I mucked out the cowshed, fed the pigs and cleaned the pigsties. Ammon, the owner's father looked after the chickens. I remember asking Howard, what was the name of the old man who keeps going into the chicken pen? In a thick broad accent, he replied 'Ammon'. I thought he said, 'Old Man'. So, every time I saw Ammon, I said: 'good morning Old Man, how are you'? Politely, he always used to say good morning back – he never corrected me!

There are no real holiday periods on a farm. It was very, very, cold working outside over Christmas in England. Sometimes, to compensate, the boss brought us out a coffee with a nip of rum in it. This was very well received as it warmed us up. And on Christmas Day, he brought out mince pies for us! A merry Christmas, indeed – rum *and* mince pies!

There was a lot of hard, heavy manual handling in this job. For example, the calves were 20 to 50 yards from where the hay was stacked. I carried numerous hays bale up to the pens, threw them over and stacked the hay into the mangers – v-shaped racks, from which calves could eat the hay. After this, I swept the yard.

Wheelock's was unique in the district as this farm mixed its own feed. Every week a truck came with sacks of different sorts of grain that we unloaded by placing the great big sacks on our back and carted them to the sheds where they were lifted into the loft. There was a big 'mixing hopper', where we placed three bags of this, two bags of that, one bag of the other in to mix up the food for the cows.

Winter was a busy time for farmers in England and a time when I appreciated being busy. The cows were tied up in the cowshed during winter. Before putting the milking units on the cow's teats, I would wheel the barrow of feed down the corridor and scoop some into the cows feeding manger. Either one, two or three scoops depending on how much milk they gave. If a cow gave a lot of milk, she got a lot of feed. But if she didn't give much milk, she got very little feed. Sounds cruel, but that's how it went. After evening milking, I pushed a slab of hay into the feeding manger, so they could chew on it during the night.

At this farm I learnt how to drive a tractor and how to back a trailer. Every day we took the hay out to the 'dry' cows in the paddock. Howard or I would either drive the tractor or throw out the bales of hay. There were two tractors used. One was a small Ferguson that was a nice smart, zippy little tractor. The other a Ford tractor, was old but very popular. The Ford started on petrol and then was switched over to kerosene. It was quite a complicated matter managing this very big, cumbersome but powerful tractor.

Silage making is a seasonal activity. Grass was cut green and brought into the barn with a 'buck rake' that fitted onto the hydraulic arms of the Ferguson tractor. The grass was piled high – about 6 feet into a section of the barn that had concrete walls. We kept piling, rolling, and compressing it, enabling fermentation. The secret of silage is to keep rolling and compressing, because if you don't the air that is trapped within the rolled silage will heat to the point of combustion. And nobody wants all their hard work to go up in flames! The silage mixed with molasses was fed to the cows in the winter. Not surprisingly, the cows loved silage, because of the 'buzz' the fermentation delivered!

At a time before the combine harvester, the thrashing machine came once a year to process the sheaves of wheat or barley. The arrival of this thrashing machine was considered a big event in the district.

A binder cut the wheat or barley crop when ready to be harvested. The long stems of straw and the heads of the grain facing upwards were then manually made into sheaves and placed in small stacks resembling small pyramids. These stacks of sheaves were left dotted around the fields ready for workers with two-pronged pitchforks to load them onto the trailer behind the tractor. When the trailer was full, the sheaves were taken and stacked in the barn ready for processing by the thrashing machine.

The day the thrashing machine arrived was a great event for the whole district. The neighbours came and helped the owner of the farm at this time. The machines were a novelty because of their rarity. With only two servicing the whole district, you had to book them well ahead.

A tractor drove the thrashing machine. When the tractor was started, the main pulley connected to the thrashing machine gave a great whirring noise signalling the machine was coming to life. The sieves in the middle of the machine started clattering, and the drum that fed the wheat or barley into the containers began whirring. And if all that clatter wasn't enough, fans sprang to life to push the grain and the chaff along. It was a hell of a noise once the thrashing machine really got going and the whole thing took on a life of its own. Looking back, it was quite dangerous. There were no guards on any of the pulleys, and the main belt went from the thrashing machine to the drive wheel on the tractor. But it was exciting!

It took quite a lot of people to man this 'monster', the thrashing machine. There were one or two people on the stack who fed the grain into the top of the thrashing machine that made its way then into the 'guts' and sieved. On one end of the machine – usually where the owner worked, there was a chute where the grain came out and filled up the sacks. That was the most important end, at least as far as the owner was concerned. But at the other end, a lot of action took place. A baler was connected to that end and as the straw came out it was tied with two pieces of baling twine and made into a bale. Depending on the farmer's direction, there could be very compact bales that made them heavier, or not so heavy bales that made them easier to manage. Some farmers used the good barley straw as feed.

A big worker, one like Howard, took the bales of straw and stacked them – in art form. He stacked a layer right across the bottom of the barn, then, when he put the other layer on, he left the first row of straw, so he could use it as a step. There were probably 10 or 12 layers of straw bales going up, and up, high into the barn. At the same time straw was being turned into bales, chaff was being bagged from a chute at the side of the thrashing machine. But the chaff wasn't much good for anything.

Working on the principle of giving the least important job to the least important worker, I was positioned bagging chaff. It was dusty and dirty. As the large sacks filled with chaff, I quickly unhooked the full one and replaced it with a new one. When the number of sacks had reached the limit, the excess of chaff was tipped on the ground and was later either burned on a dry day, or, collected by someone to be used for bedding.

As well as the people involved in 'manning' the thrashing machine, there were a few auxiliary staff that helped stack away the grain and tip out the chaff. Plus, the women of the district made tea, coffee, scones, and sandwiches for all the workers to drink and eat during the breaks. The thrashing machine event was pleasurable and memorable for the precision of the machine, its enormous productivity, and its ability to bring the surrounding community together. There were other jobs on this farm that were also memorable, but do not evoke positive memories.

Winter was a time for farm maintenance. In the days before electric fencing or barbed wire, 'laying' a hedge to ensure that it presented an effective stock-proof barrier was part of the regular winter maintenance work in the countryside. Hedges – hawthorn hedges mostly, grow alongside most English roads and need regular maintenance. In autumn I cut the hedges – miles of them! It was very monotonous and hard work. I used a hand 'slasher' which is a very cumbersome tool and to make things worse, some roadside hedges were grown on a steep bank, adding to the hardship. The hedge cutting went on for several weeks. It was not my favourite job!

Perhaps a tenth of a farm's hedges might be slashed each year and re-laid on a 10-year cycle. Hedge laying and slashing, is a craft, and requires a good deal of skill. Hedge laying competitions were often included in agricultural shows in the early days. A properly laid hedge is a highly distinctive, but comparatively rare sight, nowadays.

To cope with the excessively wet English winter, all the fields had underground earth-ware drainage pipes to manage the floods. If the drains got blocked great puddles in the field resulted. A hole was dug to find out where the blockage was, and rods placed in the pipes to clear them. It was just another winter job that needed to be done. Sometimes, if there was a lot of frost around, you had to light the blowtorch to thaw out the water pipes that serviced the dairy and house.

I did not like Howard from the beginning and this feeling did not change when working with him. He was a big, burly, bully. He was a grown man, but always wanted to wrestle with me to demonstrate his strength and power. I had been there a few months when one day when we were throwing down hay from the loft, Howard tackled me to the floor, grabbed me around the neck and pinned me down in the hay and then pulled out my penis! I struggled to get free and shouted at him to stop. He said he would stop when I 'came'. I did not know what he meant when he said this – until it happened.

He laughed at me when he saw my reaction, and confusion. Humiliated, I jumped up and scrambled to get out of the barn as quickly as I could. Ashamed, I did not tell anyone what had happened. Who would I tell? What would I say? I reasoned, in comparison to the violent sexual assault I experienced at school, this incident was minor. How *could* I reason like this?

To some my non-action would be unfathomable, to some unreasonable, and to some distasteful. Certainly, in today's environment I would agree with all those responses. However, remember the times. It was 1958 and I was a young and naïve fifteen-year-old with a severe lack of confidence and self-esteem and knowledge of life. Further, I had been clearly told not to speak out and keep quiet about such things. I justified my reasoning for ignoring what had happened at this time. But I was soon to learn that not speaking out, or taking any action exposes you to further abuse, and humiliation. A few weeks later the same thing happened, again in the hayloft. I demonstrated my considerable anger and vowed not to work with him again. I found another job a long, long way from this farm.

I became a weekly boarder at Manor Farm, Cheshire from June 1958 until October 1959. This farm had 'battery' chickens, and this was the first time I saw an automated food and watering system for animals. The owner, his wife and small child lived in one half of the double storey house and the retired parents in the other half. I had a big comfortable room by myself upstairs. I boarded Monday to Friday and went home to Dalton House, about ten miles away at the weekend. Mother collected me from Manor House and took me back on Sunday night for tea. I was paid 5 pounds for 58 hours of work a week. I paid Father almost 75% of my pay for weekend board and lodgings.

Mother bought me a small, red portable transistor radio to keep me company in my room at night. It made me so happy! It was my first radio, and it was portable, which was novel in those days. There were only three channels from which to choose. The Light Programme was my favourite. It had popular music, variety shows, comedy and drama. I listened to this channel often and recall Hancock's Half Hour, Life with the Lions, Raise a Laugh, and the great music of the 50s. The other channel I listened to was Home Service that provided the news. The Third Programme, only on at night, was a bit highbrow for me.

What do I recall about Manor Farm apart from lots of battery chickens to look after? I recall a very kind and generous Methodist family, and the Sunday trifle – laced with oodles of sherry, and the best I have ever had! And, I recall my red portable transistor and listening to The London Palladium, with Bruce Forsythe, the compere.

I was safe and happy at this farm, but I wanted to make my own way in the world and get further away from the influence of my parents. I applied for, and attained, a full-time live-in position on a big old farm in Somerset. This time, I would not be returning to my parents' home at weekends. I was seventeen-year-old and now for the first time, I would be independent of my parents.

I worked at Ashbrittle Farm at Wilverliscombe, Taunton, from January 1960 until May 1960, earning 2 pounds a week plus board and lodging. The old farmhouse had a huge fireplace and a TV. Sometimes we watched television on a Sunday night, which was good, more for the sense of family it gave me rather than the quality of the programs broadcast.

The owner was an 'old school farmer', a mean but fair old bloke who taught me a lot about farming and life in general. He had a mixed farm of cows, pigs, and sheep. I looked after all the animals – feeding and mucking out and milked the cows.

Milking was not an easy process at this hilly farm. The cows were milked at the bottom of the hill and, the dairy was on top of the hill. This meant that *everything* had to be carried down, and up. I milked the cows at the bottom of the hill and then carried all the milk to the top of the hill.

There was no power on this farm, other than the Lister engine that powered the generator for electricity for the dairy and house. I had worked with this method of generating electricity for milking before, but not for the house. The old farmer monitored this arrangement fiercely, particularly in his house, which I was living. The first person to turn on a light switch automatically started the Lister engine. That meant if you got up at night and turned on the light, the engine would start. And God help you if you did that! The old man got very annoyed. So, you never turned on a light at night. His 'waste not, want not' philosophy extended to all aspects of the farm and living, in general.

The old farmer was going away for the day. He said to me: 'the butcher's coming today to kill the pig. I want you to help him when he comes.' 'No worries, I'll do that,' I replied with all the good cheer I could muster. Although I'm not sure I would have said 'no worries' because that's really an Australian saying, isn't it? The butcher came and said: 'Have you got the pig?' It was a nice, big sow, that was chosen. 'Alright' he said, – We'll have to shoot her first then do the rest. Now just hang onto her tail, and I'll put a bullet in her head.' So, I hung onto her tail, and closed my eyes to avoid the inevitable brutality. The next thing I knew he had cut the pig's head off and handed it to me saying: 'Go and wash that under the tap now.' I don't remember hearing the bullet being fired but I guess it must have been.

Washing the pig's head, was 'bloody awful'. I had looked after her for some time, and now I was washing her severed head! But worse was yet to come. For the next few months I ate her!

It's true what the old man said: 'you can eat everything but the squeak of a pig'. There were no fridges of any substance in this house, and everything was salted. We had bacon, liver, chops, sweetbread – everything. And that's what kept us going: 'The pig that saw us through winter.' Believe me, it was certainly a memorable experience and not one I was keen to repeat!

A sheep died in the paddock and the old farmer said to me: 'I want you to go and pluck the wool off that sheep, put it in a bag and bury her.' I had to wait three days to make the wool easy to pull off the decaying sheep. I placed the wool in a bag for selling, dug a hole and buried her. The smell of the decaying flesh was revolting. I can pinpoint this time as when I started smoking!

The brutality of the beheading of the pig and the decaying flesh of the sheep were the two things I vividly recall about my time at Ashbrittle Farm. That is, apart from the pleasurable memories of my introduction to Somerset Cider!

On a Sunday after milking, I would visit the farmer's newly married son and his wife who lived on a small farm close by. I would take my red transistor radio and listen to the compiled episodes of The Archer's – a story about everyday country folk as I walked through the valley, down an incline, over the bridge of a little stream, and up the other side to his farm. I used to help him clean out the pigpens and any other odd jobs around the farm. In return, he and his wife would ask me to stay for Sunday lunch – bread and dripping which was always very 'tasty' and ate sitting by the fire. It must have been pork dripping I suppose seeing how we had to eat the pig. Not very healthy, but it was nice. It was also good to have the company of younger people.

On the way home, I listened to Movie Roundup, a BBC radio show that discussed new movies and had the signatory tune of the musical Carousel. As I was milking in the evening my mind drifted as to how I could make a movie. I pictured myself leaning against a large old fireplace with a raging log fire burning, and the camera slowly zooming in on the log fire and fading as the movie commenced. Maybe it was a movie of my life that I was introducing? Well, I've now got the book; maybe the movie will come?

Somerset was the first place I got drunk. It would not be my last. Somerset cider is a really, really, good drop. I remember the day. The old farmer's son said: 'we're going to see some friends up on the hill. Would you like to come?' 'Yes please' I responded. It was a beautiful summer evening and we sat outside on the wide veranda of the old house talking. The friend asked me: 'Would you like some cider?' I'd never really tasted cider, but I soon found it to my liking and had another glass, then another, and another. It was good – and I got *really, really* drunk.

At the end of the session, late at night, I had to get back to the old man's farm. While my memory of that journey is fuzzy to this day, I *think* I was all right walking down to the son's place. But after leaving the son and his wife at their home, I had to walk further down the valley, over the stream, up the other side of the bank, and back to the old man's farm. It was a precarious and challenging journey at any time, but particularly so for one in such a condition, and so late at night.

There were obstacles and distractions along the way. There was a haystack in the middle of the field. I remember climbing up the haystack and then, walking right off it! It's a wonder I didn't kill myself, but I must have been limp and fell like a rag doll. Then, I could have fallen and drowned in the stream I crossed. But luckily, I didn't, I got back safely, but not in a good condition.

The old man met me and was *very* annoyed. 'What are you doing going out and getting drunk… we all thought you were going to kill yourself'! He knew of my drunken state before I got to the farm, as his son had telephoned after I had left to tell the old farmer that I was on the way home, and I was 'rather worse for wear.'

Perhaps emboldened by the effects of the cider or perhaps knowing the likely outcome of my challenge, I responded cheekily to the old man saying: 'What, are you going to do? Sack me?' 'Sack you!' came the angry response. 'No, I'm not going to sack you. You're going to have to milk those cows in the morning, with your hangover. That'll be enough punishment for you!' And he was right – it **was** the worst punishment! Having to get up and down, all the time, putting the milking units on – it was very, very hard. Torture. I remember that well.

There were many other encounters with Somerset Cider during my stay at this farm. My Sunday visits to the old farmer's son and his wife continued. His son would say: 'We'll go and see so-and-so today. He's got a nice cider.' It seemed that all the farmers in the district made cider. The farmers had big vats underneath their houses and took pride in sharing the toils of their labour; and for most – it was a labour of love. 'Oh, come down here lad and have a taste of the cider. See what you think of it.' And at almost every farm I visited the quality of the cider was top notch.

I've never tasted cider as good as I did then. The commercial cider wasn't like that made on the farms. The farmers used cider presses, and the methodology of making the cider was ancient and not to be tampered with. First, you put cider apples on the press, then straw, then another layer of cider apple, some more straw, then, wind down the press. The juice of the apples filtered through the straw and left to ferment, resulting in the cider. I used to visit two or three farms regularly and got very friendly with the families that ran them, but never again got as drunk as the first time I drank Somerset Cider!

Not surprisingly, I had quite a happy time in Somerset and even today my pleasant memories are revived when I get the opportunity to drink a glass of Somerset Cider. *Cheers!*

But I left this Somerset farm after working five months. Father had purchased Firs Farm, at Stone, and asked me to return to help him run it. At this time, I had 3 years' experience as a farm labourer and was seventeen-year-old.

I remember the old farmer's parting words to me: 'you'll never do any good lad. You're not ready for managing a farm yet.' I replied: 'Well, Father's bought this farm at Stone and I've got to go back to manage it.' The farmer replied: 'oh, well, good luck to you, but I don't think you'll do any good. You're not a bad lad, but you're not ready to manage a farm, that's for sure.'

Time would tell that the wise old farmer's words were indeed correct. I wasn't ready to manage my parent's newly purchased farm at Stone; and as it turned out, I didn't.

Why would Father buy a farm? He had retired from his business once plastics came in replacing aluminium, the foundation his business was built on. He didn't want to convert the business to plastics, so he sold the factory. As I was showing an interest in farming, he thought that by buying a farm, he could manage it with my help. I expect he genuinely was thinking of my future.

However, this venture was doomed to fail for various reasons. I was still young and inexperienced; and at the same time, finally demonstrating the confidence and courage to assert my independence. I was also becoming less inhibited by my past. Father on the other hand was inexperienced in farming, but *always* used to being right, and in charge!

Now was not the time for me to return to the family 'fold'. That is, to return to the past. But the scene was set. I foolishly returned to living with my parents and working with them.

Chapter 6
Folly and Tension

It was 1960 – the beginning of the decade of the 'swinging sixties' – a time of great social change and challenging of traditions. I was seventeen-year-old. Within the next three years the birth control pill was approved (1960), the Berlin Wall built (1961), and the music group the Beatles recorded their first single in 1962. In 1963, the first episode of 'Dr Who' aired and the first James Bond Movie hit the screen; and in this same year, JFK, the President of the United States, was assassinated.

It was in this environment of change that I left Somerset to return to Dalton House in preparation for taking over Firs Farm, Coton on July 1, 1960. I was headed for torrid times and a path of no return.

The move to Firs Farm was in two stages. I helped the removalists, Ray and Bill, load up for each stage. Firstly, the outside wood, goods and chattel were taken to the farm and sorted by me. As the house was not yet furnished, I stayed locally, with the Hines family and worked at the farm during the day. Mother and Father remained at Dalton House until all renovations were completed at Firs Farm and the surroundings tidied. Renovations included an additional bedroom in the loft for Tony that required a staircase up to the new bedroom and insertion of two windows in the solid building.

Once Mother and Father were ready to move, Ray and Bill returned, and I again helped them. It took two full days to move, and seven large truckloads! The hard work and heavy lifting didn't bother me – I enjoyed working with people around my age again. Ray and Bill told me that they had delivered coal to Dalton House on some occasions. Small world, but then, it was a small corner of a small country. Much later, I would see just how small it was when I met up with Ray and Bill again, under much different circumstances.

Firs Farm was impressive by any standards. It was a huge gentleman's country residence with 60 acres of land and a nice garden. The house had 4 bedrooms, a lounge, and a very beautiful bathroom. It had a nice big kitchen with a big Aga cooker that was an extremely efficient contraption, relying on wood for its fuel and warmed the house in winter. Lawns and rhododendrons and other shrubs framed the building, and a small greenhouse at the side of the house completed the ambience. A long drive to the residence swept around a central garden where the Statuette of Mercury stood. Only time would tell if this statuette – the god of financial gain, commerce, messages, or communication, amongst others, would provide guidance in these areas.

The farm – yard and the sheds were very well situated, having a separate drive-in entrance plus direct access from the back of the house. The three outhouses housed milking cows over winter, and behind these buildings there was a large cowshed, dairy and cooling complex, and beside these a Dutch barn for storing hay. The cowshed, dairy and cooling complex were a masterpiece. Coated from top to bottom in cream-coloured tiles, and big enough to milk 50 cows at once. I'd never ever seen anything like it on any of the farms I had worked or visited.

All-in all, Firs Farm was fitting for a wealthy, recently retired, successful businessman, and his wife. But the question remained: could it be a hobby farm for the owner and a working farm for his son? And importantly, could the venture succeed?

The first thing I did after taking over the farm, was to go to Uttoxeter Market, about 10 to 15 miles away, a large rural town with a well-known stock market. I bought 14 Friesian cows and housed them in the cowshed at Firs Farm. From then on, I went to Uttoxeter Market on a regular basis, and it doubled as my outing.

I ended up with a mixed herd of Friesians, Jerseys and Ayshires. I knew what a good cow looked like including a thin face and tail and firm udder. In the end, we had about 100 milking cows, along with the calves that were born on the farm. All the cows were given names, which I wrote on a chalkboard in each of the milking stalls. I treated them as children, and, talked to them when I put the chain around their neck to tether them.

My cows were very intelligent animals. They each had their own personality – for example, some were more greedy or opportunistic – dashing to take a mouthful of another cow's feed before moving into their own stall to eat. They filed into the milking shed in the same order and went to the same milking stall every day. Grace and Duchess were my favourite cows. Grace was exceptional. She was a feisty, determined and thoroughly naughty cow that pushed the boundaries. If there was any trouble at all, Grace was the ringleader. Duchess was a big cow, and 'mothered' all others.

I bought a kelpie dog – a 'Border Collie cross', called Flash. She was a very loyal dog and helped me round up the cows for milking. Tessa our other dog was allowed into the kitchen. I had a hand fed pet lamb that when older, accompanied the two dogs and I believed the lamb thought she was a dog. Flash, Tessa, and the lamb, slept together in the barn.

Father was very trusting of me. He gave me a signed cheque to go to the market. I could have fiddled and diddled him for millions, but never ever did. I was honest and always did the right thing by him.

I learnt a funny custom attending the market, which may or may not be practiced today. When a cow was bought, the new owner had to seek out and approach the previous owner, who in turn would give a couple of pounds back to the new owner as 'luck money'.

I went to the Hereford bull sales and bought a Hereford bull – a very placid one that needed some guidance on his role, but was a quick learner. It was good to cross a Friesian with a Hereford because the offspring was a sought after, beef calf – black calf with a white face that sold for quite a lot at market. We castrated all the bull calves by putting a ring around their testes and sold them as steers at Uttoxeter Market.

The herd increased, as did the workload. Dennis, a young person a couple of farms lower down the hill came to help me milk to free me up to do other things around the farm. But he didn't stay long as he headed off to New Zealand as a '10-pound Pom'.

I became friendly with our neighbours. I could speak their 'language' and understood the work and farmer's ways. In short, I had a rapport with them. But Father never got along well with anybody in the small village, and they with him. Basically, he was a businessman and used to a different lifestyle and acquaintances. It was like 'mixing oil and water'. To the locals he was a 'hobby farmer', that is, not the real thing. As such he was never accepted in the district.

Farming life went on. We made our own hay. Contractors cut the grass into swathes in the field, and turned it until it was dry, and then it was made into hay bales. I drove our Ferguson tractor and trailer to pick up the bales and put them in the barn. I harvested and chopped up turnips to feed to the cows. I purchased brewers' grain from the brewery in Stone, and mixed it with molasses, bought in forty-four-gallon drums, to feed the cows.

I never kept the cows locked up all day during winter. I thought it a cruel practice, and I saw the damage that it did to the cows' knees and other parts of their body when I worked on other farms. Instead, in winter, I let them out for two hours in the home paddock. This kept them healthy, and gave me time to clean out the shed, put more feed in and clean straw for bedding. It was not hard to get them back into the shed. Rather, they would run back in because they knew they would have a shovel full of brewers' grain flavoured with molasses waiting for them!

A contractor – our neighbour came to plough the fields and plant kale for the winter and strip grazed it using a battery-operated electric fence. Every day I moved the fence 2-3 feet enabling the cows to eat a certain amount of fresh kale every day. The cows loved it. On a Sunday, I fed them hay thrown from the back of the tractor-trailer. The 100 Suffolk black faced sheep grazed in the 13 acres that had been specifically netted off to fatten them up for market. In England sheep to the acre was considered; in contrast to Australia where how many acres to the sheep is calculated.

Not long after we moved, and the farm was 'ticking' over nicely, Father decided that Tony and I should go on a skiing trip to Italy, financed by him. I resisted strenuously, as I loved my animals, and the trip coincided with 'lambing' and I felt obligated to stay and tend them. However, with pressure, I reluctantly conceded and went for two weeks all kitted out. Mother took me to Hanly, one of the towns of Stoke-on-Trent, collectively known as 'The Potteries' to buy skiing clothes – a bright multi-coloured jumper, ski trousers, boots and gloves.

It was my first aeroplane trip and very exciting. We left for Italy, from Manchester airport and first flew to Geneva. Here, we visited the United Nations building built next door to Lake Geneva and saw the fountain that is so well known. We took an interesting tour with a guide from the United Nations Geneva building. We saw great conference rooms with headphones and speakers and rooms where languages were converted in readiness for functions. I was fascinated by the electronics behind the scenes.

We then went for a walk and bought croissants for lunch. As we walked out the door, the shopkeeper gave us a chocolate in the shape of a mouse to eat. We passed a cuckoo clock shop, and we both decided to buy one. These same clocks would hang proudly from our respective homes in the future.

We caught a train – a strong, solid train built for the climate and steep climbs, then a bus to Sauze d'Oulx, Italy, on the border of France. We stayed in a small chalet, and in the evening drank heated red wine, and ate bread sticks before enjoying a different cuisine. It was all very glamorous for the time.

The first few days we skied on the nursery slopes and then Tony, more adventurous than I, determined to go higher. We stood on a ski anchor, one on each side, and halfway up, I fell off and lost one ski. Given the anchor was unbalanced Tony also fell off but retained his skies and then located mine.

Dusk was approaching quickly, and the professional skiers were combing the slopes for stragglers and came across us. They spoke fast in a language we couldn't understand and pointed furiously towards the bottom of the slope then suddenly pushed us hard in our backs!

We took off at a rapid speed, trying to remember all that we had learnt in the past 3 days. Snow plough! Snow plough, stuck in my mind to slow the descent. But we didn't act on this. The light had gone, and we couldn't see any light or shade to prepare us for bumps. We managed to get to the nursery slopes and fell over – out of fatigue and fright. We were both extremely lucky. That night we had an extra glass of warm red wine as we relived our adventure!

The next day, we tobogganed to a small town. Again, the speed of tobogganing was surprising. We 'flew' down the slope and through a small space between two donkeys being led down to the village! Again, someone was looking after us – or the donkeys!

We both bought a brass cowbell in the village, as a souvenir. Cowbells were placed around the neck of the cow so that the ringing bells alerted the farmer as to their location when grazing on the grassy plains below the mount. I still have this cowbell – it reminds me of my time in Italy as a young man, and was useful later in my life, in another country.

We went to a local dance on the Saturday night. It wasn't Tony's 'scene', and we left. But, all-in-all, it was a good holiday, and I should've enjoyed it. And I did to some extent, but my mind was on lambing, at home. I kept referring to this, which annoyed Tony immensely. He told me 'to get over it', or words to that effect.

Fond memories of this trip remain to this day. I was lucky to have a good brother to share the experience. My Father was right – the trip would be good for both of us.

Father loved pigs. He converted the two long sheds at the back of the farmyard previously used for free range chickens, into a piggery. He had six brick pigpens built with a half-acre run for them to root around and an electric fence kept them from straying. The pigs only needed to touch the electric fence once before they learned the wire marked the beginning of their 'no-go' area. The pigsties had bars at one corner, so the piglets could squeeze through to stop them being leaned on by their mother, and infrared lamps to keep them warm. The pigs were Father's pride and joy.

Pigs need to be monitored very well as they roll recklessly when farrowing, and the newly born piglets need protecting. Normally I milked the cows and tended to them, but not the pigs, as that was Father's job. However, I often sat up all night with a farrowing sow, busily moving the piglets out of harm's way. As the pigs were born, I picked them up, made sure they were all right, and put them in a box, until the last one – the runt, was born. Then, the bars were put up at the side of the pigsty to provide a barrier between the sow and her litter, so she couldn't roll on them. At ten weeks old, it was time to take them to market to make some money.

Bibby's was the firm from which we bought all the food for the farm, and the salesman convinced Father he should go into intensive chicken farming because 'that's where all the money is.' I did not agree with him. But Father built a huge foundation for the planned massive broiler shed at enormous cost because it was built on a slope. However, the shed was never built – circumstances prevented it.

My cows liked music, as I did. Most dairies had a radio playing when the cows were being milked. I determined to take the access to music further. Father had a lot of loudspeakers in storage at *First Farm*, left over from his redundant factory. I wired these speakers up in the cowsheds.

On a Sunday night I took my reel-to-reel recorder out of my bedroom and plugged it into the radio downstairs and recorded the top twenty music of the week. Songs like 'It's now or never' by Elvis Presley, 'Only the Lonely', by Roy Orbison and 'She loves you yeah, yeah, yeah' by the Beatles, and many others of the time.

I set up a system to integrate the music with my daily work. I rigged up a bell on a piece of wood that dangled on the end of a cable outside my bedroom window. When the farm labourer who helped me do the milking in the morning rang the bell to let me know he had arrived for work, I would start off the recorder that piped the music into the cowshed and head off to do the milking. We all listened to the music while we milked, and throughout the morning – workers and cows alike!

Later, when, I realised Tony had left his amplifier behind when he went to Australia, I integrated it into my music system. I connected the speakers to the microphone socket, resulting in the speakers becoming a microphone. Then, if I turned the amplifier up full blast at night, I could hear the chains rattling and the cows snorting in the cowshed as I went to sleep. It pleased me no end and I had a great sense of achievement in working out how to rig up the equipment to hear sounds in the distance. However, I learned more than this when the amplifier overheated due to excess workload and blew up. Tony was hoping this amplifier would eventually join him in Australia. Even now, more than 50 years later, he still mentions how I blew up his amplifier!

My experiments continued. There were no lights outside and darkness descended early in the winter. I used the electricity cable left over from the closed factory and wired up the barn. I plugged the lights into the mains and turned the switch on. The lights lit up the area brilliantly! The barn didn't burn down! The lights allowed me to tend to the cows before they settled down at night.

I was very confident of my ability in this area – to me, it was simple. Little did I know at this time that the knowledge and skills I had gained as a young child with my electric train set and wiring up speakers and lights in the dairy at this time, together with my sustained interest in music, radio and films would provide the impetus for a different life. But that was not now, but long into the future.

I returned to Firs Farm and the district more than 40 years later after wiring up the dairy. There had been many changes, as you would expect. Our next-door neighbours owned all of Firs Farmland, the dairy complex, and the Dutch barn at the back of the farmyard and a small field to the side of the house. The gentleman's residence was a private residence and the outhouses had been converted into small flats. The farm was not a farm anymore. Time had moved on. But, incredibly, my light holders – those installed all those years ago in the barn, remained.

The Wheatsheaf Hotel and farm owned by George and Isabelle was right next to Firs Farm. Along with their family, they lived in the run-down hotel and were the publicans, plus farmed the surrounding acreage. George ran the hotel and had a 'bad toe' and always limped, possibly from gout. The beer at the Wheatsheaf was always cold as it was kept in a cellar, in contrast to most English beer that was warm. Whilst my regular 'local' hotel was around 3 miles away from Firs Farm, I did spend some time in the Wheatsheaf in the evening drinking Worthington E and Stone Brewery beer and chatting around the roaring fire in winter. Despite the Wheatsheaf only being 100 yards away from the farm, after an evening of excess, I was sometimes 'dropped' off at the gate of Firs Farm.

Isabelle was responsible for the farm with her nephew Len. Isabelle's daughter [also named Isabelle], and her son Ben, went to school, but did a lot of work on their family farm such as tending the 'poddy' calves. Ben was also a big help to me with the milking when he came to Firs Farm each day after school.

Len was very obliging and the one who did all the milking and most of the farming at Wheatsheaf Farm. Isabelle called him Lenny. She'd say, 'Lenny can do that for you.' Lenny was Isabelle's sister's son. The sister lived about three miles away and had asked Isabelle to look after Lenny when he was little as she 'had too many children'. So, it was sort of an informal adoption and everybody was happy. Lenny knew where his birth mother was and saw her often, but he called Isabelle 'mother'. There was no animosity at all. Apparently, that sort of thing went on quite a lot in England.

Isabelle was a good farmer, a strong woman and an authoritarian who ruled her farm with an iron hand. She wore strange attire, namely a sack as an apron, tied around her middle with binder twine. However, her children respected her and did exactly what they were told, as did others. I enjoyed talking with Isabelle and saw her as a mentor. She advised me on a lot of things related to farming. But this advice was at odds with my Father's view and subsequently caused great friction between us as time went on. I would like to believe that Isabelle was giving advice to assist the management of the farm, and maybe in her way, she was. However, with reflections over time, I wonder as George and Isabelle eventually purchased our farm.

Mother and Father travelled widely. They often went for two months or more – a favourite was the Canary Islands, to escape the cold in England and relax. At these times, I successfully ran the farm on my own – and at the same time, also had some fun with my mates and enjoyed the freedom.

While my parents were away, I had 'a kind of' holiday away from them. I brought my bed and TV into the large kitchen and took advantage of the warmth exuding from the Aga stove, and Tessa, the dog, slept on the end of my bed. I invited the neighbours – Ben's whole family around to watch TV, as they didn't have one at their home. They brought the beer and chips and we watched TV together. I loved the company, and we all had a good time.

My parents never knew of the 're-arranged' house and the next-door neighbour visits whilst they were away. Nor did they know about me having to replace the exhaust on the tractor before they returned home as I had accidentally pulled it off when driving intoxicated, after drinking with my mates. My parents would never have approved of any aspect of my life whilst they were away.

The Royal Dairy Show was held once a year in London, at the same time as the Motor Show. Ben and I decided to go to both the Dairy Show in the morning to see all the techniques in milking and then onto the motor show. It was about this time the new M1 motorway had just been opened in 1959 – with no speed limit, just slow and fast lanes. A journey that used to take 3 hours, now took 1 hour! Another novelty on this fast road to London; was the new idea of cafes and roadhouses along the way, where you could just pull in and get something to eat and drink before resuming your journey! It was a brave new world, and I was eager to be a part of it!

I was not going to let a small thing like the lack of a driver's license, stop me from driving. Somehow Ben and I managed to convince ourselves that it didn't matter that I didn't have a driver's license because 'they' would never catch us. And, anyhow, I was having driving lessons in Stone but had not yet gone for my test. Besides, we had a cunning plan. I would drive to the outskirts of London, and park the car, and from there we would go by train avoiding the traffic. So off we went down the freeway – not a care in the world.

The journey was a real experience! We were used to winding country lanes where you almost had to drive off the road to allow a car to pass in the other direction. But here we were, speeding along on a four-lane highway – with that number of lanes in each direction! There were fast cars in the fast lane and trucks in the slow lane. I drove in the middle lane, as fast as I could, in my Land Rover that I had bought a few months earlier. This type of trip was new to us. I was familiar with going to Llandudno once a year for our summer holidays and taking the whole day to travel the 50 or 60 miles to our destination. But now, zoom. On the freeway you just raced along!

When I exited the freeway, there were traffic lights. I was not only an unlicensed driver but also a very inexperienced one. I was distracted by the 'bright lights' of the city and suddenly, I bumped into the car in front of me. Ben, who was as bad at making sensible decisions as I was, suggested we could make a run for it in the car, and in my panic, I thought that was a good idea! I headed for the back streets where I thought I would stand a fairly good chance of losing the driver of the car I had bumped into. I rationalized by saying, 'maybe he hadn't noticed that I had hit him'. 'Good idea', said Ben and off we sped. I whizzed around back streets, left, right, straight, left again and so on… and got terribly lost! Eventually I asked Ben, 'anybody behind?' He reassured me there wasn't. 'Great,' I thought, 'I've got away with it…I've lost him'. I pulled up shaking and breathing heavily, but relieved.

About five minutes later, a middle-aged man tapped on my window. I looked up, and slowly wound the car window down. The man said, 'you're the one that hit my car in the back aren't you. Don't deny it, I can see you are the same person. What do you think you're doing trying to lose me…you're not that smart, are you?' I was forced to agree with him. He went on: 'Have you got a license?' I muttered something without much conviction, allowing him to interpret it as he would. He responded 'you haven't, have you? You haven't got a license! That's why you tried to lose me. I'll have to report you.'

This comment shook me into trying to defend the situation – very, very politely. 'Look', I said, 'I am very sorry, but I didn't do any damage to your car – I just nudged it and there's no damage – you don't have to report me do you?' He hesitated, then replied: 'No, no, but still. It was careless driving. I don't know. I'll have to think about it. I'm not going to say yes, and I'm not going to say no, but I might because it wasn't the right thing to do to hit my car and then take off. It wasn't right. You know that don't you?'

I had learned over time that the best thing to do when faced with undeniable confirmation of your 'crime' was to confess. 'Yes. I'm very, very, sorry for doing that. I just got frightened.' 'Well, I'll see,' he said, softening in the face of my obvious contrition. He then left us and drove off.

Ben and I drove to the train station and parked the Land Rover. We went to London, visited the dairy show and the motor show; returned on the train to my car and drove home. I waited, and waited, but never heard any more about the accident. The man obviously never reported it, but for some time I had the same feeling as when I received a conduct card at school. The waiting for punishment that may, or may not, come *was* punishment in itself. Perhaps he knew this, or perhaps he had children himself?

The piglets were ready for market. Normally, Father arranged a lorry to take them to market. This time was different – my parents were away, and I was 'resourceful'. Father had two Bentley cars. 'The Grey' had mahogany inside and beautiful smelling grey leather seats. This was the Bentley that he drove to visit me at Cloverley Hall, my old school. 'Katie' was the one he 'mauled' by removing the running board and mudguards and replacing them with two half-moon guards over the front wheels. To top it off, he painted Katie yellow, much to mother's disgust. In short, he managed to turn an elegant car into an ugly hybrid, devoid of all the glamour you normally associate with a Bentley.

Father's butchery of Katie encouraged me to do a bit more manipulation. Or perhaps an 'apple doesn't fall far from the tree'? Anyhow, I removed the back seat, placed cardboard on the floor to protect the carpet, then a layer of straw and then placed two panels from the wire crates previously used to pack and freight the pots and pans at Father's old factory, at the side behind the front seat. Then, I placed the five, ten-week-old piglets that were to be sold within the panels and headed off to market. No problems!

I never told Mother and Father about this incident. I know they would not have been pleased. Nor did I tell them about other escapades whilst they were away enjoying themselves. When I returned to Firs Farm and district, more than 40 years later, I met up with some of the friends I used to 'hang' around with. They were still talking about the day Chris took the pigs to market in a Bentley!

When Mother and Father were due to return from holiday I went to the florist and bought a dozen bunches of flowers and placed them around the house, to welcome them home. Not that I missed them, but it was the right thing to do. After their arrival home, Ben and his family never visited again. The Bentley was clean, and Father never found out I used his beloved 'Katie' his Bentley to transport the pigs to market, and that made everything right in my world. Small victories. Mother and Father felt relaxed after their holiday, as was I because I had enjoyed my freedom.

I liked rowing which I had learned on a holiday at Rhyll, a seaside resort in Wales. My mates and I decided to go rowing down the River Trent, Stone. Given my 'prowess' in rowing, I was to be the sole rower. Halfway down the river, my 'crew' argued and wanted to change their positions. As they moved to different sides, the boat capsized and we all fell into the river and our Wellington boots filled with water quickly, dragging us down. I could swim, but none of the others could so they all jumped on top of me and clung tightly to me. I almost drowned. Luckily, we were able to reach the shore, only a few feet away. Again, 40 years later, when I met up with some of the lads, they were still talking 'Remember when we went rowing down the river?' It was good fun, they recalled. And it was despite my near-death experience. Activity, even dangerous activity, undertaken in the company of friends becomes memorable.

At nearby Coton there was a small Anglican Church. I heard via the grapevine that an elderly person was unwell and wanted someone else to ring the local church bells. I went to meet him and said I could do it, not all the time but every so often. 'Come along next Sunday and I will show you how itits works' he said. Along I went. Standing at the bottom of the bell tower I saw 3 ropes hanging from the Belfry, at the top of the tower. Two of the ropes were at normal hand height and had padding to place your hands, and the third rope was a bit longer with a loop at the end to place your foot. The old bellringer said, 'This is how you do it'. He put his foot in the loop and his hands on the padded ropes and showed me how to work the bells.

I enjoyed the challenge and learning the skill of bell ringing and practiced some days during the week. I had great satisfaction when I got the peal of the three bells right, plus waking everyone up on a Sunday morning! The Minister asked me to attend church after ringing the bells, but I told him I had to get home. He persisted, and I ended up not only ringing the bells, but also singing in the choir – for a while!

I spent three years at Firs Farms and during this time, there were periods of civility between Father and myself. There were also many arguments between us – mainly related to the management of feeding the cows, and my lack of opportunity to be involved in the business side of the farm.

Father said you had to feed the cows only so much if you wanted to be a good farm manager. You were supposed to weigh how much milk each cow gave, and then allocate the share of feed accordingly. Grain needed to be a part of the equation. Hay and grass weren't that expensive, but the grain you allocated the milking cows was an expense. So, a good milking cow got more feed than a cow that only gave a little milk, which made economic sense and mirrored what I had learned on earlier farms, even though I didn't like not feeding the cows as much as they wanted.

Isabelle 'egged' me on in this battle with Father. Her view was that 'you have to feed the cows well. Give them plenty of food. You don't want any skinny cows. You've got to have them well covered.' But Father and I had these arguments all the time about how much to feed the cows. Ben, who came and helped me milk was of the same opinion as his mother. Arguments continued between my Father and myself.

But now, I know my Father was right. He was a businessman and was implementing current and future practices. I was a pawn – and easily persuaded by Isabelle who at that time I believed was the expert. I never knew whether Firs Farm made a profit or loss. Father would not share this information or help me understand the accounting side of the business. He did not seem to want me to be fully involved, but rather, remain a farm labourer. But, learning to me was now relevant and I was interested in doing so – something I was never ready to consider or do at school. I desperately wanted to understand all parts of the farm business. But all I knew was that of a labourer – milking the cows, cleaning out the cowshed, giving them hay, and other manual farm jobs. And this was set to continue if things didn't change between Father and myself.

From afar, Tony was annoyed and frustrated at my treatment and the pound I was paid a week. Both our relationships with our Father soured. Tony could not tolerate the increasing family conflict anymore and planned to get as far away as possible. He determined to migrate to Australia when he could.

Over time I became an angry and frustrated young man. Father and I argued endlessly resulting in me often exiting the house and slamming the door behind me at such strength that the glass would shatter. The small wage I received was used to pay for replacement glass on each occasion. My inability to deal with the pent-up emotions, soon become obvious to everyone around me.

Tony came home one day from where he lived and worked at the Stafford Hospital. I do not know, but I expect Mother was at loss to know what to do regarding the friction and tension between Father and I and may have asked Tony to intervene in the family farm situation before he left for Australia.

Whilst Tony was always sympathetic to my situation and relationship with Father, on this occasion we argued. I suspect he was speaking to me as a much older and wiser brother would. But as I always saw him as a father figure, I mistook his comments as that of repeating Father's stance. Uncharacteristically, I lashed out in an expression of frustration – not at Tony, but at the nearest thing I could, which unfortunately was a window! Blood gushed from the deep cuts on my wrist. The tension between us was certainly broken. Mother and Tony wrapped the wound tightly and rushed me to hospital. I still bear those scars as a reminder.

A few weeks later, at the Wheatsheaf Hotel, I got into a 'heated' argument with another man around my age – about something I do not recall. It's easy to do. Frustration, pent up emotions, and alcohol do not mix well. Again, I lashed out at the man I was arguing with, hitting him square on the jaw. He crumpled. Shocked by the seething anger I felt, I quickly left the hotel for home.

The next day a policeman came to the farmhouse door and asked to see Christopher Thompson. 'I am here,' I responded with some trepidation. The policeman said: 'Do you realise you assaulted a special constable in the hotel last night?' 'What?' I said horrified. 'He didn't look like one to me… he was not in uniform…how was I to know?' The policeman said: 'Well, I'm here to give you an official warning. If anything happens like this again, you will be prosecuted.'

My over-reactions were escalating and becoming more frequent and unpredictable. The relationship with my parents was rapidly deteriorating. How would this ongoing issue that was splitting the whole family, be resolved – or could it ever be resolved?

Like an extra drop of water that makes a cup overflow, one night, some three years after I had started in the family farming business, the same issue of running the farm arose. Father and I had a long and 'heated' argument. This time the unthinkable happened. I lashed out and struck him in the stomach. He looked at me stunned, slowly turned, and walked away. As a father now, I can only imagine how he felt at this time. A range of emotions swept over me including intense shame.

My relationship with my parents was at 'an all-time' low after this incident. Father and I avoided each other after this time as much as we could: he in his beloved piggery and me in the cowshed, fields, and Wheatsheaf Hotel in the evening. Mother, as always, remained loyal to her husband.

A few days after this incident, when tensions began to rise again between us, I decided I'd had enough and could not live this way. I said: 'I'm leaving'. I slammed the back door behind me. I heard the familiar sound of glass breaking in the door.

I did not look back and quickly left the farm, on foot. I was twenty-year-old.

Chapter 7
Break Out and Break Free

I left Firs Farm abruptly after a terrible argument with my Father. I walked out with the clothes I had on and my wallet. I had no distinct plans. I just needed to leave, there and then. My Land rover was in the garage being repaired as it had a bent tail shaft. I walked, faking a limp to try and get a lift from passing cars. It never worked, and there were very few cars in the surrounding country lanes, especially at night.

I walked and walked, until I reached the roadhouse frequented by lorry drivers. I had something to eat and as it was getting late, I asked for a room to stay the night. I thought I would get a lift with a driver early in the morning when they set off on the road. But, when I saw the dormitory style bedroom available, I decided against staying. I didn't want to sleep in the same room with other people. I was shy of people – crowds of people, and still am. It reminded me too much of school. I made a quick apology to the owner and made my exit. I kept walking, arriving at the Stone railway station very late at night.

It was too late to get a train, anywhere. Everything was closed. I found an opening in the railway station fence and walked around the goods yard looking for a place to sleep. I tested the doors of the goods trucks parked on a siding of the main track. Luckily, one door was open! That night I slept on straw in an empty railway goods truck. The straw appeared to have been cushioning for electronic insulators being transported, given the discarded labels in the goods truck. I settled down. The enormity of my current situation weighed heavily on my mind, but there was no going back to farming with Father. I took a while to go to sleep but sleep I did. This was my first experience at sleeping rough and being homeless – it would not be my last – but that is in the future.

Sometime during the night, I heard voices approaching and thought it was probably the railway police. I kept very quiet. I knew I would be hard to spot because it was very dark inside the goods truck and I was curled up in a corner, right at the back. Luckily the 'voices' with their powerful torches did not check inside the goods truck I was in. But they did tightly close the door of it then continued. I did not move to check if the door had been latched. I remained still. I would know soon enough if it had been locked.

In the morning I opened the unlatched door, and it was a bright day. I jumped out and walked down the siding wondering what to do. I needed time to think. I kept walking. In the distance I saw two men loading coal from the heap on the siding, onto their truck to deliver to households. I recognized them. It was the coal merchants, Ray and Bill who had moved us from Dalton House to the farm and I had helped them at that time. I was so pleased to see them! I told them I had left home and had nowhere to stay and no job. They said, 'help us load up these sacks of coal and we'll decide what to do with you.' At the end of the day, they said 'you'd better come home with us to meet mum and dad if you have nowhere else to go. You look as though you could do with a good meal.' That night I tucked into the meal provided and felt a lot better afterwards.

For the next 2 days I helped them and stayed in the guest room at their parents' house. I enjoyed the days, and the idle banter between us was good, as it took my mind off my problems. The third day I helped again and at lunch time Bill said he'd drive me to the bus station as I had decided what I was going to do.

I went to Auntie Valerie, my godmother, who was also my cousin once removed. I thought I would tap into her wisdom and see what she suggested about how to resolve the predicament between my parents and me. Valerie was an optometrist and worked in Birmingham and lived outside the city. She was exceptionally good company, the life of the party and drove a red sports car. She certainly livened up a dull place. Valerie was single and having an affair with a married man she'd known for years. Eventually she married her lover, and they lived happily thereafter. But that was still well into the future.

I told Valerie what was happening at home. She listened but not having any exposure to the responsibilities or commitments relating to children or young adults, I sensed she was 'put out' at me arriving unannounced and confronting her with my problems. I also sensed that she had absolutely no idea what to say or do in response to my outburst of family problems! So, she took the only response she could – one of action, and not words. She said she had arranged to have a round of golf that afternoon and decided I should go with her, which I did. This was the first game of golf I'd ever had so I duly followed her around the golf course. At the end, we went back to her house, had tea together and I stayed the night.

After tea, she told me her solution to my dilemma. The solution? She said she didn't have a clue what I could, or should do, but whatever I was going to do was up to me, because I had to face up to my problems! In all the ensuing years, I was never sure if she was incredibly wise or singularly uncaring! Anyhow, I took her advice.

With my Auntie Valerie's words in my mind, I determined to face up to my problems with my parents. I telephoned to see if my Land Rover was fixed, and then Firs Farm, and spoke with Mother. I said calmly and without any animosity as I felt none, 'Enough is enough, I am coming home and we're going to have this out, once – and for all'. Valerie drove me to the bus station in her sports car. I then collected my Land Rover and drove home. My welcome home was unimaginable, and still to this day, unforgettable.

I opened the front door of the house at Firs Farm and went in, expecting Father and Mother to greet me. But instead, two police officers were inside waiting for me. I was immediately concerned, not for myself, but for my parents. I said in a panic: 'what's wrong? Has something happened to my parents?' 'No' they said, 'your father has taken out a restraining order against you and committed you for two weeks to a mental asylum'.

I was devastated to hear what my parents had done. Why are they doing this? I told the police, 'I just wanted to talk with my Father, and I did not threaten him'. The police didn't want to hear any of it and escorted me to the police car parked outside the back door, which is why I didn't see it when I arrived home. As I got into the police car, Mother came to the door and said, 'Sorry dear, it's for the best,' and closed the door. It was very upsetting. I was on my own. I felt betrayed and abandoned. The same sort of feelings I had throughout my boarding school years came flooding back. But I wasn't a child now. With that act, the relationship between my Father and I changed.

'Why did my Father do this?' was the question I repeatedly asked myself at the time. I never asked him directly then, or ever, as we never talked about anything that was remotely 'deep' or reflective in a stereotypical English way.

As time passed, I thought that perhaps he misinterpreted my telephone conversation with Mother as a threat. When I said, 'enough is enough, I am coming home and we're going to have this out once and for all', I meant: should

I leave the farm for good and go my own way or could we work in a different way, in a more open relationship with me being taught all aspects of running a small, family farm? After all, that had been the original brief when I left Devon to return home, rather than the poorly paid labourer I had become. Perhaps Mother and Father sought advice on my statement, and was advised to take this action? I don't know.

What I do know is that what I meant at the time of the conversation with Mother was not the message received, and because of that I was now in a police car being escorted to a lunatic asylum, about 10 miles from Firs Farm! On the way, I tried to understand and speak with the police in the car. The response from one was: 'we don't like doing this 'lad'. We don't like it at all.' I said, 'I don't know why you're doing it!' A policeman said: 'We've got to. Your father signed an order and we have to take you there. I'm sorry. It's not up to us.'

The police were very nice to me and I responded in a similar manner as there was nothing I could do about it. This has been my philosophy throughout life. 'You just have to roll with the punches. Time is a marvellous thing because it keeps on moving. So, if you're going through a bad patch, eventually you should come out the other side. It's like wading through mud.' Here I was, in a police car. I couldn't jump out as it was moving. I just had to accept my predicament and go along with it and hopefully everything would turn out all right.

It was dark when the police car drew up at the front of St George's Lunatic Asylum, Stafford, an historical building, and facility, joined to the Stafford Gaol via a covered corridor. Two male nurses about twenty-five-year-old and dressed in white coat and trousers came out and escorted me inside saying, 'come with us. I was taken to a room and given some pills to swallow. Then I was told to strip off – everything. As I stood there naked, thinking of what had just happened, I felt the depth of despair wash over me. I put on the smock handed to me and they gathered up my clothes and left. I did not resist. I was in shock, exhausted and crushed. I'd been through a horrific experience and wasn't feeling up to arguing, or in fact doing anything. What had happened was reeling in my mind going over what I have done. 'Why did I...? Why did they do it? I only wanted to talk to him.' I climbed into the bed, feeling very 'fuzzy'. I looked around and my last thoughts were: 'this is a nice little room...but unusual...has grey quilted walls...this must be the padded room....'

When I gained consciousness the next morning, the impact of the previous day hit me. I lay there for quite some time, wondering just what had happened over those 24 hours. After a time, a nurse opened the door and gave me back my clothes to put on. He said: 'How are you, Christopher?' I replied: 'All right' He continued: 'Well, it's time to get up. I'll show you where the common room is, and you can have some breakfast. There will be time to talk afterwards.' 'All right' I said. I couldn't say much else – I was feeling exhausted, confused, and hung over from the drugs I had been given the night before.

Many seriously messed up people were in the mental asylum. I was not one of them, but lived the life associated for a short time. What did I learn during my stay at the asylum? I learned how to use the floor polisher that would come in very handy, in the future. I learned to keep my mouth shut as anything said could be misinterpreted and you would be recommended to stay longer. I learned that danger lurked behind closed doors. I learned not to trust those in authority who are meant to be looking after you. And I learned to escape.

There were two main areas of the asylum that inpatients frequented – the dormitory and common room. Each of these rooms, along with a few other offices, consulting rooms, x-ray rooms and dark rooms were situated to one side of a very long corridor, and the other side had windows that wouldn't open, of course. At the very end of the corridor, there was a door, and behind the door, stairs connected this building, to the gaol next door.

The dormitory was a lot like a boarding school and housed about 25 people. The large common room was used for most things. It had a big table about twice the size of a standard billiard table in the centre of the room where the patients sat to eat. All around the outside of the room, there were easy chairs, but they weren't that 'easy' as they were the sort you get in waiting rooms – hard, with sides on them.

I walked into the common room with some trepidation. There were about 20 people just sitting around. The nurse introduced me: 'this is Christopher. He's going to be with us for a while'. The other patients looked at me disinterested, with no real expressions. There was a very, very, long pause. Then, one inpatient said: 'yes, well, the end of world is coming soon. You've got to be prepared. God is coming down. The end of the world is coming'. 'Oh yes' I said politely. The nurse directed me to a chair saying: 'just sit here. Soon we'll be serving breakfast.' With this, all the patients got up out of the easy chairs around the wall in a very orderly way and sat up at the table with me. There was no conversation. Breakfast arrived, and we ate. I can't remember what I ate, or indeed much else at this time.

There was a routine during the day. After breakfast, if you weren't assigned for any treatment or other sessions, you worked as per the cleaning roster. On this first day, I was to be assessed. I was escorted to a small room and asked to do puzzles, recite numbers backwards and other tests…. I think I passed them. A few days later, I was told: 'You're going to Birmingham in an ambulance to have some tests. 'That's all right', I said. I was very compliant.

I had a brain scan whereby they stick leads all over your head – almost like a lady's perm, and look at your brain activity. It was an interesting experience. A few days later I had a lumbar puncture at the asylum. This was not so interesting – it was rather frightening. I was told: 'You're going to have a lumbar puncture. Now this is very dangerous. You've got to lie down here on your side, and you have to keep perfectly still because if we move the needle the wrong way, you could become paralysed.' No need to tell me twice! I remained perfectly still. So, they took out some fluid from the bottom of my spine. My results were normal.

I was lucky as these were the only two tests I had. Other patients were not so lucky. The most unfortunate ones had electric shock treatment carried out at the asylum. This treatment seemed to be 'all the rage' at that time. After this shock treatment, patients had short-term memory loss. This was particularly noticeable in those who smoked, as after the treatment, they didn't know what had happened to their cigarettes. So, before their treatment, they would give me their cigarettes and say: 'when I come out, give me my smokes won't you, because I'll forget. 'Yes, no worries, I'll do that for you.' I didn't smoke so they trusted me, and I did not betray their trust.

It was Saturday morning. After breakfast the orderlies came in and said: 'we've got a treat for you today. We're going to the main gaol to see a movie this afternoon. There's been two rows of seats allocated to us in the picture theatre.' There was great excitement! Then the rules: 'there'll be prisoners in there and you're not to make a noise. You must behave because these are real prisoners locked up for various offences. Do you understand?' 'Yes, yes, we do'.

We were led down the long corridor of our abode, to the very end, where there was a door unbeknown to us. Behind the door, there were steps up into the main gaol. We entered the theatre room in the gaol and saw the two rows of seats allocated to us. The prisoners – 'hard core' criminals, murderers, thieves, and other thugs, all in prison uniform were already seated, and looked at us with suspicion. We, from the mental asylum, didn't make a noise and sat down ready to watch the selected movie.

The movie was Perry Mason, a crime courthouse detective series – one of my all-time favourites. Perry – Perry Mason, defended the accused, and always got them off. Interesting choice of movie by the gaol authorities you may think, given we were sitting in a gaol amongst prisoners! But the program was interesting. It always depicted that justice wins over crime, which, on the outside world no-one queries – it is expected and applauded. But here, in this room in the prison, it was the reverse… the prisoners loudly cheered on the baddies – those who Perry was pursuing for murder, robbery and the like! We, the mental patients, joined the prisoners in their cheering for the baddies and jeering of authority. This was a wise move given the circumstances. When the movie finished with Perry again succeeding in exposing the real criminal, we stood up quietly and walked back through 'the' door and into the building from whence we came. To this day, I recall the movie and the response to it with humour.

This brief visit to the adjoining gaol was my first and only experience of being inside a *real* gaol for convicted offenders. Later, in another country, and in another life, far removed from that in England, I would mix with a range of people from all walks and backgrounds during my travels and work, including some ex-prisoners and those evading the law. I would also be interrogated by police for a false accusation and briefly spend time in police lockups for various misdemeanours. But this is yet to come. Thank fully, never again would I see the inside of a real gaol.

I had one visitor wishing to see me while at the asylum – my Mother. I refused to see her, responding: 'No … I'm not going to see anybody. They put me in here. They can get me out.' I knew this refusal would be upsetting for her, but my emotions were still too raw for me to even consider the feelings of my mother.

Like all institutions a routine started to appear. With no further assessments required, I just needed to be compliant and serve out my 'time'. The results of my assessments revealed that I'm well above average intelligence, and there was absolutely no reason to keep me committed. Whilst this was good news to celebrate, it seemed at odds to where I was at the time, and my current predicament. Despite all signs being good for my pending release, I could not be confident that this would occur. In the circumstances I was currently in, nothing is assured, thus a highly anxious state is inevitable.

The routine continued. In the mornings, we would clean. In the afternoon, we used to laze around. It would not be long before I would be discharged, and my incarceration would become a distant memory. I hoped.

One morning, just before I was due to be discharged, I was 'buffing' and 'stripping' the floors along the long corridor. I went into the dark room to do the same. An orderly followed me in. I took no notice of him, as there were always orderlies and nurses present, observing the patients. Then the orderly, a big, oversized bloke spoke to me: 'Hello, Chris… would you like to have a bit of a play?' Not understanding this strange comment, I said: 'What are you talking about?' His voice altered as he replied: 'You know, what I'm talking about!'

With that response, it hit me, like a blow! I suddenly knew *exactly* what he was talking about! I panicked and roughly pushed passed him to get to the door saying with all the conviction I could muster, to once-and-for all, reject his proposition: 'No way, I'm not going to do that!' His reply to my rejection of him burned into my ears as I bolted past him into the safety of the corridor: 'Remember Chris, I'm an orderly and you are the mental patient. What I say will be true. They won't believe you… whatever you say.' Frightened, I blurted: 'I'm not going to say anything. Just leave me alone!'

His words rang in my ears, continually, and triggered painful memories. His words were true – nobody would believe me – I'm a 'mental patient', he is not – he is in a position of power and authority. I thought: 'This is a dangerous place and a terrible situation to be in because I am the mental patient and they are the law and what they say goes and they can do, or say, whatever they like, and no one would believe me!'

I felt like a caged lion. There were barred windows down one side of the corridor that I could see cars driving past, and doors leading off to rooms on the other side, where treatment was given. Whilst I could see freedom, I did not have it. I reasoned that this was not a place for me – no control over the situation and determined to get out. Not once did I think about the repercussions of escaping from the asylum – that is, breaking the law. All I could think of was the threat, and the reality of the threat I had just received from the orderly. I desperately needed to get out of this place.

I walked up and down the corridor thinking there must be a way out. I 'cased' the toilet thinking this would be a good place to escape as no one was around all the time. There was a small sash window in one of the toilets that could be opened about 4 inches but no further due to a piece of wood having been screwed to the side of the sash. I decided if I stood on the toilet seat and then the cistern, I might be able to get out – if I could make the window open further. I devised a plan to escape. I decided I could easily prise off the wood preventing the window from opening, *if* I had a knife. Knives were not accessible in the asylum for obvious reasons, so I waited for an opportunity.

The next day when I was having lunch with the other unfortunate men in various stages of sanity, I slipped a metal dining room knife up my sleeve. I waited until late afternoon when all the patients were sitting around the table in the common room and most of the staff on their tea break, to make my move. I casually left the room and went to the toilet and closed the door. I stood on the toilet seat, then onto the cistern and prised the wood on the small sash window off with the knife. I was elated! It wasn't as hard as I thought it would be! The hard part was climbing through the window, as I had to go headfirst. But then, the unthinkable happened. I got stuck – half in and half out. My head seemed to be a long way from the ground. I wriggled, and wriggled, propelling myself forward, hard. There was no going back! I roughly fell to the ground and looked around to see if anyone had seen me. They hadn't, and I thought: 'I'm out! How clever I am!'

I was exhilarated! I had an overwhelming sense of achievement almost as if this was the greatest thing I had done up to that point in my life. I didn't contemplate that this might be the single greatest achievement of my life, but that really was the euphoria I was experiencing. I had felt this once before, as a six-year-old, when I escaped from school and saw my first movie!

I decided not to rush so as not to draw attention to myself. I stepped onto the pavement and casually walked the opposite way to the asylum and gaol. I should've crossed the road but didn't. Bad move! Walking toward me were two men I recognized. They were off-duty orderlies from the asylum I had just escaped! They also recognized me and called out: 'Stop!' 'Stop!' I ran. They chased. I pictured in my mind what was happening as I ran. It was laughable – 'Cops' and robbers? Hardly. It was more like Keystone Cops and an episode of 'Z' cars!

I have never been a very good runner. At the school sports, I saw the finishing post in front of me, ran through, and stopped excited as I had won! Then, I was told, you have another lap to go – you are last and at the back of the rest of the runners! Disheartened, I plodded on.

I kept running, but, in the end, I was totally puffed, and stopped, placing my hands on the fence, and looked around. The 'off duty' staff were gaining so I waited and then said: 'All right, all right you win – but before you take me back, let's have a drink at the pub – it's very hard to break out of these types of places.' The Keystone Cops theme continued. I somehow managed to persuade them to go to the pub with me. How I don't know. Together we downed a couple of pints each. I told them: 'I can't be in the mental asylum anymore. I should not have been there in the first place.' I did not mention the threat from their colleague that was the impetus for my breakout. I concluded that there was no point in doing this, as the accusation may have made things worse for me on my return. They responded as expected – they had to take me back, and they did.

On return to the mental asylum the staff showed their extreme displeasure of what I had done as it reflected badly on them. I had breached security, broken the law and damaged property – the wood on the window. I was immediately slammed into the padded cell again and injected with something that knocked me out. What a spectacular great escape that was!

When I came to, I found out that the authorities were going to charge me for breaking the law. They were curious as to why I had broken out so close to my discharge date. I never disclosed the reason. Fortunately for me, Tony worked at Stafford North Hospital as a doctor and knew the psychiatric director of the asylum. Between them, they managed to persuade the authorities not to charge me.

At the end of my two weeks stay at the asylum, Mother collected me, and I went home to Firs Farm. Nor my Mother, Father or Tony ever spoke of these dark days and my involuntary commitment again, even in later years. It was a time that everyone tried hard to forget. I am sharing it here, many, many years after it occurred; and now know that the St George's Lunatic Asylum was closed in the 1990s.

My involuntary commitment was the talk of the local neighbourhood for some time and the collective opinion of my Father plummeted. Locking up your son in an asylum was not done in the circle in which we moved, or indeed in the farming area we lived. Despite this, I did return home to recover. I worked on the farm for a month, cutting hedges with Ben who was 'agog' with what had recently happened. But nothing was the same anymore. I just couldn't force myself to work on the farm, or for my Father who I told I was leaving farming for good but would remain at Firs Farm until I found another job. Shortly after this incident Tony left for Australia. He could not bear the family situation and rift any longer.

I found a job in the Stone Town Council fixing up Council Houses with the tradesmen and emptying dustbins. I was happy working finally, with no family pressure. I would not use the Land Rover to get to work as it belonged to the farm. Instead I rode to work on my bicycle – hard to pedal up the hills, but fun riding down. With money I saved, I bought a Triumph Tiger Cub motorbike and drove this to work. It was a 'slap in the face' to Father, who was against his sons owning a motorbike and had refused Tony to do so. I just went out and bought one myself. To be honest, at this time after all that had happened, I couldn't care less about my Father's opinion. I wanted to take a stand and make the point that I was my own man, and I would do exactly as I wanted – he had no say in it anymore!

My 21st birthday arrived. There were no plans for a party at home with my parents who gave me a long-playing record and wished me happy birthday on the day. There was no other celebration with them, but I did celebrate with some friends. There was a good hotel about three miles away that I frequented to play darts. I liked this hotel. I judged it as a good hotel as the proprietor put nibbles on the bar. I had made a lot of acquaintances there since moving to Firs Farm and established some friendships with five lads in particular – Ben and Len my neighbours and three others that went on the rowing escapade with me. I held my party in the 'Snug', a small room off the bar, and the table was laid nicely. I paid for the meals and opened a tab for the drink, and the hotel put up a bunch of balloons. It was a happy day, and a good night was had by all present. I remember it fondly.

Tony was sending audiotapes back to us about his life in Australia. Mother suggested that perhaps I would like to go to Australia and join Tony for two years and he would sponsor me. As things were so bad at home, I thought for 10 pounds I could go to Australia for two years. If I didn't like it, I could always come back. It struck me as a plan with no downside.

What did I know about Australia, apart from Tony living there? I must admit, very little. I could draw the map of Australia at school quite well and I interpreted that as a sign that this was meant to be!

I was lucky to be considered eligible to migrate to Australia as a '10-pound Pom'. I say this for two reasons. Firstly, there was a lot of detailed information required on the application form. Mother helped me fill in the never-ending paperwork. If she hadn't, I would still be in England today. I would never have been able to apply because of my aversion to filling out forms, due to dyslexia. Secondly, if a conviction had been made on me after escaping from the mental asylum in Stafford, I may not have met the legal or good character requirements.

I was accepted to migrate and told that I would be travelling by ship to Australia, the same way as Tony. But then I received a letter asking if I was prepared to fly out with 48 hours, notice. I responded yes, but deep down I really did not want to go. But I was caught up in the 'flow' and it was too late to opt out. A few weeks later, I received the phone call from Australia House giving me the date and flight details and stating, 'we want you to be at Qantas at the London Airport where we'll give you the appropriate papers, and you will head off to Australia for at least two years.' It was now an immediate reality. I was going to Australia.

It was time to say my goodbyes. I went to the Wheatsheaf Hotel to give Flash, my farm dog to Ben and say a final goodbye to all the regulars. They all said: 'you're going to Australia? Let us know what happens. Don't forget us.' They gave me a rousing send off to remember. Drunk, I moved onto the Hotel where I had my 21st birthday and said goodbye to my friends and those I played darts with.

But I walked home with a tear in my eye. I wasn't just leaving my mother, but 'Mother England' and all that I knew. I've still got a soft spot for my country of birth. I like the countryside. To leave all that you know and the way of life and go to the other side of the world is a big thing to do. Communications were better now, than when the convicts were shipped to Australia, but there was still no satellite telecommunication. I would be relying on audio-tapes sent to and from my parents, and the occasional letter from Mother, written in green ink.

I was very apprehensive about what my future would be. I was heading into the unknown. But as there was precious little for me in England and in the back of my mind I thought: 'I only have to go for two years and could come back'. So, it wouldn't be that bad…would it?

Chapter 8
Into the Unknown

I was 21 when I left England for Australia as a '10-pound Pom' on February 15, 1964. I left England with what was allowed by the authorities. The 'princely' sum of 52 pounds in cash and one suitcase packed with life's essentials. I said an unemotional goodbye to my father, at the farm. Mother drove me to the airport office based in London and, after a short, teary goodbye, she left.

It was a great day to leave England because it was a grey, very cold day and the rain and sleet was coming down in 'sheets'. This weather depicted how I was feeling inside and at the same time helped me focus on what might be a sunny future. I boarded the bus for the quick ride from the airport office to the terminal. I sat down with a great big sigh, wondering what I'd done, and stared at the wipers as they fought to clear the sleet from the windows. The weather gave me the confidence to think I might be making the right decision even though my heart was beating faster than could have been good for me.

At the departure gate I showed the papers that the Australian Embassy had sent me because that was all I had. No identifying passport and no identifying driver's license were required. Nothing, in fact to prove I was the person mentioned in the papers that bore my name! Travel was not complicated at this time.

We were ushered onto the plane where light music played as we were seated. I was upset after saying goodbye to Mother and apprehensive about the future. It reminded me of the times I would weep uncontrollably when I was being packed off to boarding school. It struck me at this time, sitting on the plane that the only reason that I cried so bitterly at that time of returning to boarding school was because I didn't want to leave Mother. I suddenly realized that I was something of a mummy's boy! Now, waiting for the aeroplane to take me further away from my mother than I had ever been, panic began to set in.

I was abruptly roused from my bout of self-pity by the sound of an elderly man calling out in a broad English accent for *'someone to turn off this racket'*, meaning the music that had been having a very soothing effect on me. Disappointingly, someone did his bidding and I remember thinking how great it would have been if I could have swapped that grumpy old bastard for my lovely mother as the aeroplane climbed into the sky and the country of my birth disappeared beneath a thick band of clouds. I felt a surge of excitement – we were off, off into the unknown.

The four-propeller new Electra plane that took me away from one home and delivered me to another was very noisy and made four or five stops before landing in Perth. At the third stop, the voice of the pilot came over the intercom saying: 'We're very sorry but due to industrial trouble… all our flights will be terminated in Singapore. We don't know for how long. Please fill in the departure forms that will be handed out around the cabin, and we'll be landing in about half an hour.'

I felt a tremendous surge of panic. Not because I would be stranded in a foreign country, but because I had to fill in a form! All my insecurities about writing and the dreaded forms flooded back and I was overwhelmed with gripping panic. But at the same time, I was immensely excited thinking: 'Wow, what an adventure…what's going to happen now? I struggled, but eventually managed to fill in the form and was ushered off the plane to the terminal where I waited with all other passengers.

Eventually we boarded a bus that took us to the very smart Goodwood Hotel, Singapore. The Doorman at the Hotel had strict instructions not to let any of us out, and we had designated areas that we were able to go in the Hotel. As this was a very plush 5-star hotel, there were no complaints. Single people were billeted in double rooms. I shared a room with a young Australian, from Fitzroy, Melbourne and we got on well together. The room had double glass doors that opened out to the inviting pool. The routine was: wake up, swim, dress in shorts and shirt, have the free breakfast provided, then laze poolside. Overall, it was turning out to be the best value '10-pound junket' I had ever bought! Mind you, alcohol wasn't included so I just stayed sober.

One evening, the young Australian saw me put on my cravat; one of several I had brought with me. Interested in the look, he asked me about it. I told him a cravat can replace a tie and is worn with an open neck shirt in hot weather, usually when going out in the evening. 'Can I buy one of those? They look great.' 'Yes', I said, and promptly sold him one!

Periodically Qantas officials would come by and ask: 'do you want to continue your journey? We have a charter plane for people who urgently need to continue their journey.' I would reply before diving under the water again: 'No, no, no. I am sure there are more deserving people – I'm in no hurry'.

I was enjoying all that the Hotel provided. In fact, if I'd had my way, I would have stayed there for two years rather than go to Australia! For those who volunteered to stay longer, a half-day bus trip around Singapore was arranged. We were not allowed to get off the bus, as we weren't officially in the country, but it was good to see something of Singapore. It did not look like a prosperous country, and there appeared to be poverty in some areas. A total contrast to the Hotel, where cocktails with mini umbrellas were prevalent. After four days of luxury in Singapore, Qantas resolved its industrial problem and we boarded the plane and headed off to Jakarta, Indonesia for refuelling.

Indonesia at this time was in a sort of 'defacto' battle with Britain and other countries, due to Malaysia being granted independence in 1957. Indonesia believed Britain was still trying to control the region by being a behind-the-scenes ruler of Malaysia. The tensions resulted in a brief war between Indonesia and Malaysia, and we had arrived just at the start of it.

The aeroplane landed and was greeted by heavily armed soldiers. The pilot informed us before leaving the plane that we were in a hostile environment and that we were to do exactly what we were told by the soldiers escorting us to the room we were to wait until refuelling had been completed. Being mostly British travellers, we were the enemy. The soldiers lined up either side of us and we walked the gauntlet in 'crocodile' form into a bare room with rows of cups of tea on trestle tables. The extractor fans roared overhead as we sipped our tea while the plane was refuelled which took about an hour. We were careful not to give the soldiers any reason to use their weapons as we returned to the plane the same way that we had left.

It suddenly hit me when I was sipping tea, how small the world was. Only a few days ago, I had been in England – peaceful and serene England, and now here I was, in a war zone with guns being pointed at me. Further, it dawned on me that Britain and British people were not highly regarded in Indonesia. Prior to this experience I was oblivious to the history, politics, and perception of the British, in other countries.

With this short experience in Jakarta, I started to open my eyes, albeit briefly, to the extent of the tentacles of the British Empire, and the resulting outcomes. And further, how this interference was viewed outside of Britain. I had begun to view my country and myself differently. But then, almost immediately, we boarded the plane, and normality resumed. The purr of the engines lulled me into a sense of security. The stewardess came along and asked if I'd like something to eat or drink, and everything was right with my world again.

The pilot said: 'the next stop is Perth'. There was restless excitement, as our journey was soon ending. I thought: 'I'll soon be in Australia and see Tony'. Little did I know that it would take another full flight day after landing, to reach my destination – Brisbane via Sydney, then onto Toowoomba, Queensland!

We landed at Perth, Western Australia – the gateway to Australia at the time, on February 20, 1964. My first glimpse of Australia from the plane revealed red soil everywhere. It was a beautiful, sunny day and the vivid colour of the land really hit me between the eyes. My first glimpse of Australia on the ground was just as memorable. Lots of young, beautiful girls with tanned skin, and big, swaggering men with large trilby hats. I thought: 'wow, what a place!'

We disembarked. The officials – custom officers seated at a table on the runway, beckoned us and asked to see our travel documents. They scrutinized them and nodded as if in approval, and then stamped them in the appropriate place. And, with that, we were officially accepted into Australia and declared to be Australians! No standing on ceremony in this big, beautiful land. In fact, no ceremony at all, just a nod and a barely audible grunt.

We were escorted a bit further into the large terminal. The waiting room had large glass windows in the front to give us a grand view of our new home and I remember being very taken with the rich, red soil of Western Australia. We stayed there for about an hour before we were ushered back onto the plane and headed for Sydney.

I was positively lightheaded with excitement. I thought, well I have arrived in Australia. I'm here! In a couple of hours, I will be in Toowoomba, saying hello to Tony. Everything was going to be fine. Perfect, in fact. The only thing was, we flew for another five hours! Five hours! I mean in five hours; you could go all around Europe by plane and that's how long it took us to fly from one side of the country to the other!

I disembarked in Sydney, a bustling major air terminal. Incredibly I didn't have to show passports or papers or anything because I was now an Australian, that is, for at least 2 years! I waited for about an hour before catching a plane to Brisbane – a two hour journey. So, seven hours after Perth, I'm still in the air!

Finally, we touched down in Brisbane. My jaw dropped in amazement, because there was this little wooden hut on the side of the runway where the waiting room housed only about 50 people. It was very similar to airports at some country towns, in Australia now. And guess who was standing there waiting to greet me? Tony, with a sort of happy, but at the same time, unhappy look on his face. *'Where have you been'*, he demanded to know. He was upset because I was four days late in arriving, and he was worried about what might have happened to me on the way. I told him that I had been at the Goodwood Hotel in Singapore and had the time of my life. 'The Goodwood' he spluttered, 'That's one of the smartest hotels in Singapore!' However, he did know where I was as he had the foresight to phone Qantas and been told about the problem. Still, he wasn't too happy because he had to drive down from Toowoomba, which was a couple of hours away by car to get me. I suspect that he also suddenly felt the burden of a younger brother, and the associated sponsorship responsibilities.

After the hugs, and 'lovely to see you', we got into his car and had a nice, long drive to Toowoomba – plenty of time for a catch-up, and exchange of pleasantries. Except it wasn't as pleasant as I would have liked. He wasn't too happy to learn what happened to his amplifier. 'You brought my amplifier?' he queried.... I responded: 'what do you mean your amplifier? 'Well I specifically asked you to bring my amplifier.' I then had to tell him why I hadn't brought it – the amplifier had been blown up. *'How did you manage to do that?'* I told him it was very interesting. I wired up the speakers that came out of the factory, around the farm and played music through them. One day I plugged a speaker jack into the microphone jack as speakers can be turned into microphones. I turned the amplifier volume up quite loud, and I could hear the chains rattling and the odd moo, in the cowshed, which was fascinating. I thought it was ingenious... but the amplifier got overheated and blew up. So, that was that. 'Very sorry Tony, I didn't mean to do it.'

It was a sore point with Tony for quite some time. He was obsessed with having decided anything electrical was far too expensive, and amplifiers were an expensive item in Australia at that time. My inventiveness that resulted in the blowing up of his amplifier did flash pounds and shillings in his mind. But I did bring his thick duffle coat, carried it over my arm, all the way from England, which I reckoned he should've been thanking me for, instead of criticizing. Why he wanted a thick duffle coat in one of the hottest states in Queensland, God knows! Anyhow, the brotherly 'banter' was good after such a long time.

In time we reached the edge of the Toowoomba Ranges that served as a barrier between the high and the low land. Along the way, Tony explained that when the first white settlers came to Australia, they couldn't find a passage to get up over the Ranges, so they settled on one side. Now there was a narrow road that wound up the Ranges from Gympie to Toowoomba – the latter being the largest city on that great plateau and second largest in Queensland. We eventually arrived in Toowoomba, around mid-afternoon. By this time, Tony had settled down a bit and forgotten about his amplifier. Tony lived in a top flat, too small to be described as a penthouse, and owned by the Sherman's who lived on the ground floor.

When Tony first arrived in Australia, he was met by a welcoming committee and interviewed on the radio. Such was the status of an English doctor, in

Australia, at the time. He was readily accepted into the 'right' circles. Into this mix, Tony's younger brother had just arrived, looking like an older Little Lord Fauntleroy. Would my arrival add to the sense of mystery and interest that surrounded Tony, or merely bring him down a peg or two in the eyes of the locals? I hoped it would not be the latter.

It was 1964 in Australia – the land down under. History would record the following in the year I arrived:

...Robert Menzies was still the Prime Minister, and would refuse to ratify equal pay for women, but announced the re-introduction of National Service, by implementing a conscription lottery. The first edition of 'The Australian' newspaper was published. The Olympic swimmer Dawn Fraser would be named Australian of the Year, but later be banned from amateur swimming due to 'misbehaviour'. In this year, both Latrobe University and Macquarie University would be founded, and 'Beatle mania' would grip Australia, with the tour of the Beatles in June 1964.

... The sixties revolution continued and in 1965, the miniskirt would burst onto the scene. Two feminists, Merle Thorton and Rosalie Bogner would chain their ankles to the front bar of a Hotel in Brisbane in protest about liquor laws that banned women from pubs. The Rolling Stones would tour Australia and the iconic Australian group, The Seekers single 'I'll Never Find Another You', would reach number 1 in the UK charts. Charles Perkins would lead the Freedom Ride – protesting about racial discrimination against Aboriginal people and Australian combat forces would be sent to South Vietnam.

Could I, a newly arrived '10-pound Pom' that had left England for a new start in life look forward, and not back, in the Australian environment of the 1960s? Would I embrace the times of change and opportunities that a new country and the sixties revolution offered? Or would I find it difficult to adjust culturally and shake off the baggage of the past? Would the cursed dyslexia continue to inhibit and crush me as it had done in my life to date? Would I stay in Australia after the 2 years was up or would I return to the home of my birth?

Only time would tell. But in my turmoil of thoughts I was confident of one thing. Whatever was to happen here in Australia I was sure it was going to be the adventure of a lifetime!

Part 2
The Drifter
1964 – 1973

'A life spent making mistakes is not only more honorable but more useful than a life spent doing nothing'.
  George Bernard Shaw

Chapter 9
Square Peg in A Round Hole

It was February 1964, and I was twenty-one-year-old. I was finally in Australia as a '10 Pound Pom.' I spent my first night in Toowoomba, Queensland, with friends of my brother Tony who emigrated the year before me.

I awoke and dressed for breakfast, which Tony and I had together, at a small table in his flat. We had toast and marmalade and there was much discussion about missing England, our parents, and how Tony had decided to remain in Australia. We then went to the Sherman's, for morning tea with a few other people I was to meet, who were also friends with Tony. The Sherman's owned the block of flats and lived on the ground floor.

Resplendent in my shorts and long white socks, polished brown shoes, nicely combed fair hair, and sparkling blue eyes, everyone seemed very pleased to see me, particularly, the women. However, I was never as popular as Tony with the ladies. He was viewed as a very, very eligible bachelor, a medical doctor, with a promising future. I on the other hand was much younger, less worldly, and did not have, nor would ever have the prospects or the status that Tony did.

I sipped on a cup of tea. It was all very refined, polite, and formal. I was asked what I intended to do in Australia. I explained I was experienced in farming, and without giving much thought, I said I'd like to go be a Jackeroo. No one found this response as unusual as Pommy Jackeroo's were common in Australia at the time.

However, in hindsight, looking for my first job in Australia in a remote and isolated area would not be the best choice as far as adjusting to an alien land, people, and culture. What I needed, as many other migrants need, is a resemblance of familiarity, and company to prevent loneliness and homesickness. Outback Australia was a total contrast to what I was used to. But the dye was cast.

Not long after commenting I was experienced in farming, Mark – a friend of the Sherman's, and a land agent, appeared. He told me he intended to travel inland to the towns of Chinchilla and Roma in a couple of days and asked: 'Would you like to come with me…? I'd be happy to show you around.' I replied to the effect: 'that would be very nice, thank you very much. I would very much like to go and look at the countryside.' At the same time, I thought: 'this is very kind of this chap, taking the time to show me around and we have only just met.'

So, just three days after I arrived in Australia, I was on my way to look at the countryside in outback Queensland. There was no familiarity with what I was used to in the countryside or the towns that I saw. I literally felt like a 'fish out of water'. I had left England in mid-winter. I arrived in Australia in mid-summer. It was hot, very hot. There was a heat shimmer, rising from the bitumen road.

In England, I was used to brick bungalows both semi-detached, and two-story houses; whilst almost every house I saw as we drove, was weatherboard, and perched precariously on tall stilts! Mark explained that the stilts let the cool air flow underneath to keep the houses reasonably cool, and they let the floodwaters flow freely under the house. Very sensible, I thought, but the feeling that I had been dropped into an alien land remained.

In England, I was used to rolling hills of green grass and manicured hedges, with farmhouses and animals dotted around the gentle landscape. Here, I was being driven through miles and miles of acres and acres of harsh, brown dusty land that was being savagely cleared. Two very large bulldozers joined together with chains with a huge steel ball suspended in the middle ripped unmercifully through the brigalo and bush scrub to claim the land for farming. Another bulldozer trailed behind pushing all the upturned bushes into piles waiting to be burnt. This was a common scene as we drove towards Chinchilla and Roma. I have never forgotten this day and what I saw. It was extremely interesting, and history in the making.

I was very familiar with pubs in England. They were small, homely, and friendly, with oak beams, low ceilings, and brass hooks on the wall, and a dartboard. Mark announced that we would have lunch along the way at a pub. I started to feel 'upbeat' as lunch in a pub would provide some familiarity. It didn't.

We stopped at a brick building with a wide veranda – the pub, on the side of the road and walked through swinging half doors, which gave the pub, a 'real' western feel, and reminded me of a Wyatt Earp movie! Whilst this felt strange, inside was truly amazing. The walls were covered in gleaming cream tiles from top to bottom – everywhere – making it look like to me, a toilet block! Mark explained the simple reason for the tiles on the wall – to keep the pubs cool. I understood this, given the heat, but I suspect it also made the walls easy to clean, just as the tiles did in the cowshed at Firs Farm in England!

Then, just as my mouth was still gaping in surprise at the inside of the pub, I was asked to 'put my money on the counter', by Mark. This was a very strange request, so I politely asked him why? The custom of 'putting money' on the counter was quickly learned and stayed with me all my Drifter days. It went like this:

'What will you have to drink? '

'I'll have a schooner or a half-pint or a half of whatever.'

... Then you put your money on the counter, and the fellow next to you at the bar, puts his money on the counter. And you just chat away and as the beer is drained, the barman takes the money out of the appropriate pile on the counter and furnishes you with another full glass. It was a novel system but one I quickly became used to. It was very important that you had your shout.'

...I found out later in life that it's best to shout first, because it may only be you and your mate at first, and then 'Charlie' comes along, that makes three that he's got to shout, and the next person who arrives shouts for four, and the next for five, and so on. And at the end of the shout, you might have had 10 beers. And if it's your shout again, you've got to drink another 10 beers, before your level again! So really, you don't want to get into a big shout because it's just suicide, and you end up getting very drunk. You say, 'no worries mate I'll have a beer with you, but I'm just drinking by myself. I'm just having a couple. That's the way to do it. Don't get in a big shout because otherwise you're going to lose a lot of money or get very drunk. It took me some years to learn this.'

Anyhow, the conversation with Mark at lunch revolved around land, farming and opportunities and potential in Queensland. Mark was a very good guide and went to a lot of trouble explaining about the districts and the potential and opportunities that abounded for those that 'got in early'. He asked: Would I like to meet some farmers, that 'had got in early'? 'Yes, thank you' I replied.

After lunch, we drove to a couple of small farms and met young farmers and their wives who had cleared a few acres and were planting edible crops, and 'making a go of it'. They all exuded enthusiasm about what they had done, were doing, and expected to do in the future.

Back in the car Mark said to me: 'just look at the potential. You can buy 1000 acres here for so little money, and here's another 2000 acres up the road you could buy. This is a good investment. It's a new country and we're clearing the land, and we want settlers to settle the land, people with real pioneering spirit.' How much money have you got to spend?

I had enjoyed the day seeing the countryside but was not looking to 'buy in early', So, I responded honestly: 'Well I've actually got about 500 – 1000 pounds – maybe'. My confession of my limited funds really 'killed' the conversation. 'Oh. Well, we'd better go back now, it's getting late,' Mark the agent replied.

His attitude changed completely. If I'd said I had 30,000 or 40,000 pounds and was thinking about investing, he would have continued to be very attentive and interested. But as soon as he knew I wasn't in the running for buying land, he quickly turned the car around and started driving back to Toowoomba.

With hindsight I realise the Sherman's must have thought that with my background, and their knowledge of Tony, I was wealthy, and would be looking to purchase a property. But I was not thinking of buying land – I had only been in Australia for 3 days! Even if I did have the inclination and funds to purchase land at this time, I would not have. The environment I had seen on this day was so unfamiliar to me that I felt I was truly in an alien land. I would never had been happy or made a 'go of it'. There would be considerable time pass before I would take the plunge and purchase land in Australia.

The mood in the car as we travelled was strained, and the conversation between us ceased for some time. Then, Mark said, 'I've got a very exciting invention here. It's an electric kettle, and all that I do, is plug it into the cigarette lighter and I can boil the billy. We can stop and have a cup of tea on the way back to Toowoomba.' Pleased that he had finally spoken, I replied in my very clipped BBC news accent: 'that would be lovely'. With that, he stopped the car on the side of the road and said to me: 'You go and sit over there by that tree in the shade, and I'll boil the billy.'

I did as he told me and sat down, under the tree. Unbeknown to me, but something he was probably aware of, was that there was a nest of bull ants at the base of the tree. I was not sure what sort of ants they were and said: 'Oh look at all these little ants. Mark didn't reply, he just smiled, watching the kettle boil away. I said: 'Oh look, they're climbing up my leg.' I had worn shorts for the day and the ants climbed right up my trouser leg to places that I didn't want to talk about, and they started to bite and hurt. I said: 'We don't have ants in England that bite'! Mark finally said: 'you must have sat near a bull ant's nest.' He found the whole incident highly amusing, and I suspect had his revenge after wasting the day with this Pommy Jackeroo! This was my very first introduction to Australian humour, but not my last.

During the long drive back to Toowoomba, I started thinking about finding a job. But when I got back, I found out that a job had been arranged for me.

Tony had been speaking with the Sherman's who had in turn, spoken with a friend, Barry Reynolds who owned a Hereford stud farm at Oakey, about 20 miles outside Toowoomba. Barry was very well respected in the cattle industry and, in fact, was one of the main judges at the Royal Sydney Show. They asked him if he'd like to employ a fresh faced, new Pommy Jackeroo. 'Hmm, I could do. I could do with a lad, especially if he's a Pommy. Is he strong?'

I understand the need to be strong, but never found out what the appeal of a Pommy Jackeroo was over an Australian one, but maybe it had something to do with the novelty of watching a singularly white man being burnt to a cinder by the Australian sun; or perhaps, being eligible for the butt of many jokes; or perhaps it was the novelty factor during the Royal Sydney Show? Barry went on: 'Well we've got sales coming up here, so there's a bit of work, and we're thinking of moving the other fellow employed into a house by himself, so it will be comfortable for the Pommy as well. Yep. Yep. We could do with him. When do you think he could start – in a couple of days? Sounds great. Bring him down.' And that was what passed for an employment contract in those pioneer days!

Tony said to me, 'It's a live-in position, in the country and you'll be happy there'. The next day he drove me to Oakey, a rural town, named for the river oaks that dominate the banks of the Oakey Creek. This same town would become 'famous' many years into the future due to the Australian 'soap opera' Neighbours, with main characters both originating from Oakey.

I had been in the country for two weeks. It was scorching hot weather, and from now on I would be living and working in outback Australia. It was like a 'baptism by fire'!

Barry, the owner of the stud farm, was married and his son Ken and daughter Carol worked for him as well as Ray, another Jackeroo, who was about twenty-three-year-old. Carol lived in the main house with her parents. Ken and Ray lived in a very comfortable flat and I was to join them. The flat was an extension to the main homestead accessed inside the home by stepping down a couple of steps and opening the entrance door to the flat. The flat had 3 single beds, its own toilet and shower but no cooking facilities, and was just like a little motel unit. I joined the family in the homestead every night for a meal.

A common practice at outback stations and farms at the time was to have a relatively formal evening meal. It was no different at the Reynolds. Everyone came to dinner in nice, clean clothes and I followed suit. We sat at a beautiful table with a white linen tablecloth laid with bone knives and forks, white bone china and drank out of cut-glass vessels. It was silver service and decidedly posh. The meals prepared by the cook fitted the grand surroundings. After our meal, we adjourned to the lounge with a glass of wine in hand and watched *The Fugitive* on the black and white TV, as that was Barry Reynolds' favourite show.

It was hard to get my head around. Australia was such a contrast. Here I was living in a unique homestead with a very distinct presence enjoying refined living, in a huge vast land that could be considered the outback. This is not at all what I, and others from England, would've expected. Just a few days ago, I was travelling inland in a harsh environment where brigalo salt bush and scrubland dominated, and now I am in a very civilised and formal dinner environment. I was reminded of the formal grand homes in England, and it was comforting. But, at the same time, it reminded me of a scene from Bonanza and probably a bit better than Bonanza – the popular TV show of the time that depicted the lifestyle on a cattle ranch, in America. It was all very pleasant and cosy, but things were about to change.

I had lived in luxury for a couple of weeks when Ray and I were moved into the little colonial cottage on small stilts, on the side of a road about half a mile from the main homestead. At this time, things took a sharp downward turn, at least as far as the cooking and accommodation was concerned. We had to cook and look after ourselves. However, there was compensation.

There was a vegetable garden at the back of the cottage, and watermelons were abundant. This was my first encounter with watermelons, and they tasted *so* delicious! They were very sweet, incredibly juicy, and tremendously thirst quenching. I learnt the rules of eating watermelon by Ray: don't swallow the pips as they would give me appendicitis, spit them out in the vegetable garden bed and they would reward you by growing into the next crop of ripe watermelons. Good advice I followed often. Watermelon is still one of my favourite fruits and when I see or eat watermelon, it prompts memories of outback Queensland and this time of my life.

The yearling sales were imminent. There was a lot of work to be done to get ready for this sale. A lot of individual pens had to be built inside the shed to house the bulls, and for the public to walk amongst them in safety. The pens were about 12ft x 9ft with wooden rails, and a small door about 4ft to get in and out. Ray and Ken did most of the carpentry, and my job was to do the painting – all glossy white and it really looked quite impressive when the job was finished.

All the work was carried out in the sun, and as I didn't have a hat to start with, it was inevitable that I got sunstroke. At the time I didn't realize or have the respect for the sun – nor did many others of this era. It was normal to work in the full sun, without your shirt. Sunscreen was a product and term not known, and hats were not always used. All the very things that the anti-cancer campaign of 'Slip on a Shirt, Slop on some Sunscreen and Slap on a Hat' some years later warned against. My brush with sunstroke early on in my working life in Australia was a lesson well worth learning.

One of my jobs was to clean out the bullpens and replace the straw. Another job was leading the valuable bulls around. I put a halter on their head and took them for a walk around the yard to familiarise them with the process required for the sale. After this, I groomed them to make sure their deep, red hide shone. Luckily, Hereford bulls pampered like this are placid animals and there was not much effort to get them to move and perform.

Water is a scarce resource in the outback. I went to fill up a canvas water bag that is then strapped to the front of the car and when driven, the wind on the canvas helps keep the water cool. As I filled the water bag from the outside tank, I saw little insects, larvae and tadpoles going into the water bag. 'Oh look,' I said, 'there are things alive in this water. I can't drink this'. Barry turned around to me and said, 'Look mate. If they can live in it, I'm bloody sure you can drink it!' I suddenly realised that this is true, because there was stagnant water around the property, and nothing lived in it. So, if the larvae lived in it, it meant you could drink it! That was another very good lesson to learn.

There were three resident carpet snakes at the farm to help keep the number of mice and rats down. Now, to me, a snake is a snake and in the first month I worked there I saw more deadly snakes than I have in all the years I've been in Australia since and that is more than 50 odd years. When we walked around the paddocks, the skins that once housed big, brown snakes were lying on the ground. Probably because I wasn't used to or didn't understand snakes, I just didn't like them, and let this be known.

My aversion to snakes played into the unique Australian humour. One of the fellows I was working with said 'Pommy', go and get that shovel that's leaning against the shed over there.' Dutifully, I did this or rather I just got my hand on the long handle of the shovel and he shouted, 'Look up!' I did as he said, and my immediate reaction of fright to what I saw almost caused me to jump out of *my* skin! One of the resident carpet snakes, all nice and warm from lying on top of the sliding rail, had 'flopped' it's head down and was looking directly at me. I was – definitely, not impressed, but my fellow workers thought it was a big joke!

I have not overcome my fear of snakes to this day. I have a photograph taken of me with a koala and carpet snake when at Lone Pine, a wildlife sanctuary near Brisbane. The wildlife handler gave me the carpet snake to hold and told me to look terrified. And I did look terrified, but it wasn't an act! I sent that picture along with one holding a koala – a cuddly little creature, home to my parents.

Life progressed day after day – mundane, with no real surprises or excitement. One night, Ray said, 'would you like to go down to the pub and have a drink? Do you ever drink?' I said, 'Yeah, I don't mind.' We drove the 'ute' to the pub, but we could not see a soul around. 'Don't worry about that,' Ray said. 'We'll go around the back, knock on the door, and it'll open up.'

The pub was closed, looking as though everything was right, the way it should after six o'clock that was closing time in Queensland. We walked around the side of the pub and through the unlocked back door, and saw about 20 or 30 people drinking, after hours! Here, the publicans pretended the pub was closed, but the patrons entered via the back door and continued drinking! Now this was in the outback, but I suspect in the cities, it probably would have been a lot harder to be so sociable, after closing time. It's amazing how people have always found way around laws that try to get them to behave in an 'approved' manner, much like the drug laws of today, I guess. Somebody once said, 'you can't legislate to make man moral' and I guess they were right.

I was working by myself a lot – driving a tractor, pulling a 'Scarifier' around a huge paddock that took me half a day to go around the perimeter! In comparison, Firs Farm biggest field was 13 acres! I sat on the tractor, going around and around the paddocks, day after day. There was much time for thought and all the time I fought back the tears in my eyes, feeling more, and more home sick – not for my parents but homesick for England. The landscape, environment and people here were so different from what I knew. I was in a foreign land. I could understand the language – mostly, but even then, the culture was different and there were so many differences and difficulties to overcome. I liked England. I liked the countryside, and I liked the cows in the fields. I was becoming very unsettled.

It was time to have a weekend off and Tony came to pick me up in his car and we went to the annual Toowoomba Show. This event was recorded on a tape sent by Tony to my parents in England:

'It's the 9th of April 1964. I'm speaking from Toowoomba, the Garden City, and the Gateway to the Darling Downs. The Royal Toowoomba Show. The show was opened yesterday but unofficially. And yesterday being Wednesday and my half-day, Christopher and Glynne and I went along to see the show. Yesterday, as today, was a glorious, sunny day.'

I wonder, was the summing up of the weather by Tony on that perfect day all those years ago and captured on tape, the inspiration for the slogan many years later: 'Queensland – beautiful one day, perfect the next!'

I had a great day at the Show, and particularly enjoyed looking at the massive machinery on display. It seemed to be three times as big as that I was used to in England! Then, all too soon, it was time to return to the stud farm, the tractor, and the huge never ending, paddocks. I tried very hard to settle down again after spending the weekend in Toowoomba, amongst people and all the action. I tried but was not successful.

Not long after returning, Tony phoned me to see how I was – a general 'chit chat'. I confided in him that I wasn't happy and said something that was critical of Barry – just a throwaway line. Next minute we heard: 'how dare you talk about my father like that. Don't you talk about my father like that'! Carol, Barry's daughter was listening in on the phone extension line! Well, with that comment, we realised that *nothing* was private. Tony slammed the receiver down as if it was on fire! I never mentioned the phone call. But Tony was incensed and wrote an eloquent but critical letter to Barry and sent a copy to me that basically said: 'how dare they listen in on phone conversations! He was coming to get me – I was leaving. I shouldn't be out in the middle of nowhere looking after myself and everything else!

Tony arrived, and we left together, but only after I went to say goodbye and thank Barry who said: 'you'd be a good 'lad' if only your brother would stop interfering in your life.' Many years later, Tony told me that Barry told him when I wasn't present that he was very sorry I was leaving. He said he had plans for me in the future, 'bright young man like me'. But Tony had made up his mind. I was leaving. So that was the end of that.

Why did I just do what Tony told me? I'd let Tony make up my mind, but it took me a while to realise this. There were two things at play. Firstly, I was used to my family telling me what I should do and shouldn't do, and right at this time, I was extremely lonely and homesick for England. Perhaps I was just pleased that Tony had taken control of the situation, as he had always done before. Secondly, Tony had sponsored me and therefore felt obliged for my welfare, both as a sponsor, and a brother.

In hindsight, I should've stuck it out and not taken the easy option. I could've learned a lot from Barry, and about myself. It wasn't a bad job after all. Sure, it was lonely, but there are worse things than being lonely. Barry was a clever man, a good boss and had treated me well. If I had stayed, the next few years of my life may have been less disjointed and traumatic. But this was not to be. I was at the world-renowned Australian Hereford Stud Farm only about two months before ending up back in Toowoomba. The time would come that I would finally stand on my own two feet, but not yet.

On return, I stayed with Tony until I got myself sorted. During this time, a friend of Tony's, Owen, a highflier, recently separated from his wife, offered to drive Tony and I to Surfer's Paradise in his car. Owen decided to make a day of it and stop at all the pubs on the way to have a drink. I thought this was a natural thing to do on a day out and enjoyed the drive and the sights – particularly after being on the tractor, going around and around, on the stud farm. But Tony was hesitant. I expect he had seen the outcome of many accidents from people drinking to excess. But, drinking and driving was normal at the time. It would be many, many years later before Australia's 'drink and drive – bloody idiot' campaign would alter the perception of what was normal.

Despite Owen having much to drink, we did arrive home safely, eventually. An extract of a tape sent to my parents in England recounts my impressions of the day:...

Well we got as far as Sea World, which was so exciting for me seeing all the dolphins and all the tricks that they use to perform. I was really impressed. I only had ever seen scenes like that on television and on movies like South Pacific, but this was real life! Australian wildlife!

Tony and I visited a sawmill just outside of Toowoomba. Alan, the owner was a friendly bloke, and occasionally we had a drink and a meal at his place. One day I was at the sawmill and Alan said to me, 'Have you got a driving license? 'No, not yet' I said. He quickly replied: 'Oh well, I will have to get you one. Come with me'. 'Okay Alan sounds good', I said.

Owen drove me to the small local police station. We opened the door and saw a Sergeant standing at the counter with a big smile on his face. 'Hello Alan, what can I do for you today? 'Alan replied, 'How are you, Bert? I've got a little job I'd like you to do for me. This 'fellow' has just come out from England and I've got to get a driving license for him. Do you think you can give him one?' 'Ah', the policeman said to me, 'Have you driven before?' 'Yes', I said. 'I've got an English driving licence – here it is'.

He was happy with what he saw. 'Alright then, what sort of licence do you want', he asked. Alan said straight away, 'He wants a full license. He wants to be able to drive semitrailers and everything'. Bert said to me, 'Have you read the highway code here yet?' 'Not yet, but I will shortly' I said. 'Alright then, I'll give him one,' said Bert. So, with that brief interaction I was given a full Queensland driving license, which entitled me to drive anything including semitrailers! Bert called out to me as we were going out the door of the police station: 'You won't forget you've got to read the highway-code, will you?' 'Yes, no worries Bert I'll do that', I replied. I immediately felt a surge of acceptance and felt with this interaction I had just experienced the true Australia! Friendly, relaxed, obliging, informal and actions with minimal red tape!

Outback Queensland has many long dirt roads. Cattle trains – huge trucks with long trailers towed behind, transported cattle around the country. One day, Alan suggested to me in Tony's presence: 'it would be a good job for you to drive one of those cattle trucks. You could make a lot of money and you would see a bit of the country. Would you like to do that?' Interested, I said: 'I'll think about it'. But with that Tony piped in and said, 'No way. I don't think you'd be able to do that, no way. No, he doesn't want to drive semis. 'It's very dangerous you know on these roads you have a huge responsibility driving these cattle trucks.

Based on this response, and my lack of confidence in my ability to manage this 'huge responsibility' at such an early stage in a country I did not know, I declined the offer. However, again with hindsight, I should've given it a go – it was an opportunity lost. I knew cattle, could drive, enjoy roving from one place to another, and only had to learn the truck side of the business. As a consolation, I bought a Holden Ute, and put the license to good use.

A friend of Tony's patient was looking for someone to work on his dairy farm in the Darling Downs and enquiries were made. Mr Lawrence said, 'Yes, he'd love to have Christopher.' Tony said to me, 'you'll love it there. They'll treat you as one of the family. You'll be one of them. You'll have a glass of wine with your meal in the evening. They will treat you as one of their sons. So, I went out to work on the dairy farm.

I lived in a detached room – the 'worker hut'. It was a shed that was just four walls and a bed and a wardrobe. That's all it was. I was about 100 yards or so from the house. After we finished milking in the evening, I'd go inside the farmhouse and have a meal. There was no wine served at the meal, but that didn't matter. The meal and the company at mealtimes, was appreciated. Straight after the meal I was sent off, back to my little hut of four walls, for the evening – a long evening, without the company of a TV.

After about a week, I awoke with terrible asthma that reoccurred over the next few days. One night it got so bad, I could hardly breathe. It was frightening. I didn't know what to do. It was about 2am, so I got in my 'ute' and drove all the way into Toowoomba, about 25 miles, to Tony's flat. I arrived about 3am and woke him. He was less than pleased. 'What do you want Christopher? Why are you waking me up at this hour of the morning?' I spluttered: I can hardly breathe! I'm getting asthma! He replied: 'you're just upset. Sit down for a minute. I'll give you something for it.' He gave me some tablets and a puffer and made a cup of tea. And he said, 'Are you all right now? I've got to back to bed. I've got to go to work tomorrow.' 'I'll be all right now', I replied, and drove back to the farm.

But the same extreme breathlessness happened again a couple of nights later. This time, I used the puffer that Tony had given me. I told Mr Lawrence in the morning that I couldn't work for him any longer – I'm getting terrible asthma. I packed, left the farm, and returned to Toowoomba. The asthma disappeared. It was 'nervous asthma'.

A married couple – Murray and Glynne, friends of Tony offered board and lodgings to me on my return. They charged me a steep fee, but I stayed with them for several months. Glynne was a socialite, and there was prestige in having a doctor's brother staying with them, and Glynne liked Tony's company. He regularly came for meals, and sometimes we all went out together.

My Auntie Trix [Louise] and her husband George, the Head of BOAC in Japan, were coming to Australia and Trix wanted to visit Tony, her godson. I just happened to be there at the time. I was not her favourite nephew – she considered me immature – which I was. Anyhow, when Glynne got wind of their impending visit, she enthusiastically arranged for drinks and a meal for them, at her house and gave them 'red carpet' treatment – like royalty. It was an extremely prestigious event in Glynne's calendar; and Trix and George enjoyed the visit, and more than adequately met Glynne's expectations.

My work in Toowoomba over the next few months revolved around factories – meat, malt, and yeast. Murray, an accountant, worked at KR Darling Downs, a large meat processing company and said, 'I'll see what I can do to get you a job at KR Darling Downs – they need causals for a short time – they have a big order coming in.' And before I knew where I was, I was working there. My job was to follow the order through, and I worked in all areas: packing the meat, getting it into the blast freezer, then into the waiting large, refrigerated trucks. The process was that the meat came along the conveyor, slid onto the table we worked at to be wrapped, then packed in a box and labelled then sent down the chute next to the table, to the blast freezer – a huge fridge the size of a room.

Extremely cold air is blasted into the blast freezer, and the meat is 'snap frozen'. We had to rug up as if going to the South Pole when working in the blast freezer and were only allowed to stay in there half an hour to an hour, before coming out for a break, warm up, and go back in again. The frozen boxes of meat were then manually transferred to the refrigerated containers on the back of big semi-trailer trucks and then the meat was distributed to the shops. Sometimes it was my job to carry a clipboard and tick off the various boxes that had been loaded onto the semi. This part of the process was good – I was out in the fresh air.

KR Darling Downs had a full range of meat products, and a lot of it was sausage meat-salamis and all the other type of meats with spices in them. At the end of the day, the excess meat was processed in a 'digester', where preservatives, and various flavours were added. This is probably a normal process – I wouldn't know. I just know that I have always been very wary of processed meat since I worked there. I left this job when casuals were no longer wanted as the large order was filled.

I needed another job. I did the rounds, knocking on doors. I eventually found one at the Malt Works in September 1964. This was a milestone in my life in Australia. I had found my own job, at last.

The Malt Works – a big old building with large wheat silos at the side of it had chutes opening onto four red concrete floors each the size of a tennis court. This is where we spread the wheat and kept it moist to enable germination. It was a perpetual operation. When one floor was in the germination stage, we were busy preparing the wheat coming down the chutes to another floor. To do this, we used large wooden paddles to spread the wheat evenly over the floor and every four hours turn the wheat, so it didn't get soggy and spoil. By the time we'd done that on one floor, we had to go to the other floor and repeat the action. When the wheat started sprouting, we shovelled it onto the conveyor to the big kilns where it was roasted, shovelled out, bagged, and shipped out to make malt-based products such as beer and bread. I liked the shovelling where the smell of roasted malt was intense. I enjoyed my stay at the Malt Works and in fact, stayed there quite a long time.

During my time of working at the Malt Works, I met Noel and Ismay a young married couple and friends of Murray and Glynne. Noel and Ismay owned a small farm – a house on the corner of a street with about five acres of land next door on the outskirts of Toowoomba. They had not long moved into the house and Noel had been in an accident and couldn't walk very well.

I went to their farm at the weekend to chat with Noel and give them both a hand. They grew sweet corn on one acre and when it became ripe, I helped them pick it. I also helped them put linoleum down on the floor in the kitchen. We first put down newspapers and then the linoleum on top. I stayed and watched TV with them on a Sunday night. They were young, and I enjoyed their company. In the end, they sold their property, and bought a Neptune Service Station. I didn't see much of them after that, as I didn't have much affinity with service stations.

Glynne, my married landlady, got annoyed that I kept going out to see Noel and Ismay on the farm. She clearly wanted me to stay and keep her company. I felt much more comfortable out on the farm helping Ismay and Noel. To me, Glynne seemed to be a frustrated 'housewife' – a very manipulative and seductive woman who had a big impact on those she favoured. I started to feel compromised and trapped by my living arrangements.

I sensed Glynne was 'making eyes' at me telling me more than once that she only ever made love with her husband once a week, on a Sunday. And that obviously wasn't enough for her. I wasn't sure if she was expecting me to 'step-up' to fill the gap, but it was never going to happen. Not only was I still incredibly ignorant in matters sexual, but I would also never have entertained the thought of doing anything 'dodgy' with a married woman. On reflection many years later, this situation has some broad similarities with the film 'The Graduate' written in 1963 and hit the screen in 1967.

Things were already tense with Glynne when I queried to steep rent I was paying her in the presence of Tony and this led to a disagreement. Tony said, 'Well, if you leave, don't think you're coming back to stay with me. You're very ungrateful after they took you in.' Well that comment from Tony was the last straw and I was incensed! I was paying incredibly high rent and could've stayed anywhere! I thought Tony should've stuck up for me. He didn't. I thought, 'he is my brother and friends are the outsiders'. Soon after this, I left Murray and Glynne's and distanced myself from Tony and his circle of friends.

This incident severely damaged my relationship with Tony for some time. However, I am eternally grateful for this argument and resulting rift, because I finally shook off the emotional shackles that had for so long restrained me and became independent from that time on. I believe Tony also would've been relieved that I finally broke out on my own, as he would be no longer be responsible for me.

I moved into a boarding house in Hume Street, Toowoomba. Ron, the owner was about forty-five-year-old, unmarried, but very friendly with a woman who lived there. This woman had a son who kept locking himself in his room because he was recording records onto tape. We all had to be quiet because he was using a microphone placed near the playing record to record onto the tape.

There were about twelve people in the boarding house most of the time, all different sorts of people. We had a common area where we all ate. Ron cut a packed lunch for boarders to take to work every day. The weekends were free.

Starting on Friday night, Ron and I would go on a pub-crawl. Several times I was asked if I was over 21 years of age – the legal age to drink in Australia at this time. On our pub-crawl, we went down one side of Toowoomba and up the other, and had a couple of drinks at each pub. By the time we got to the top one, we were both very 'happy'. And then, it was the time to have fish and chips out of rolled up paper or a hamburger. Ron was a strict Catholic so fish was a must for his meal each Friday. I wasn't too keen on fish, so I sometimes opted for a hamburger. Every Friday night walking home, the following conversation occurred. Ron would say: 'You should have fish on a Friday.' And I would reply, 'But I'm not a Catholic.'

He was good company and I got on well with all the people in the boarding house. I learnt to iron there, but burned a few pair of synthetic trousers, as the iron was too hot! We were a happy 'family', and my life was taking a turn for the better. I wasn't being told what to do, or being treated, as if I couldn't make-a-decision for myself. I was, in charge of my own life – at long last; and being treated as an equal.

I was living in the boarding house when I received a letter from my Nana Clare, written just before she died from bone cancer in Bournemouth, England. It was sad. She knew she was going to die, and she wrote wishing me all the best in my life. Nana was always very strict with me, and I only saw her about once per year, so we never developed a strong bond. She did get on well with Mother, and my Father both liked and respected her. He made it his duty to replace the normal curtains in our spare room with heavy velvet curtains when she visited so that she would not be woken early, with the morning light.

I was also living at this boarding house when my parents arrived in Sydney, Australia by ship on July 22, 1964. They had auctioned their farm and brought two container loads of household goods and Father's grey Bentley. Unfortunately, some antiques and valuables such as the mint records of my grandfather from Pathe Freres were left behind, but electrical goods were brought, from irons to washing machines and fridges! Soon after they arrived, I went to see them. They were living in a rented house right on the estuary, at Mooloolaba, on the Sunshine Coast beach and seemed very happy. I stayed for the weekend and returned to Toowoomba. I repeated that eight-hour trip periodically.

You might wonder as I did, why my parents migrated to Australia, after all the family trouble endured in England, just a few months earlier?

Both their children were in Australia. That is one reason. However, the real reason was that my Father always wanted to come to Australia as a young man, to live in the warmth and now there was a perfect opportunity to do so. My mother always wanted to stay in England with her mother and friends and the countryside she loved. She regretted coming to Australia until the day she died. However, at the time, the fact that both Tony and I were in Australia was a convincing factor to migrate.

Life went on. My last job I had at Toowoomba was working at the yeast factory separating yeast from water. Here, there were two concertina presses in operation. Firstly, liquid yeast was pumped into the presses under pressure at one end. At the opposite end, we manually turned the large wheel with spokes – one like that on a pilot boat, that when turned, squeezed the water out, through the cloth filters. Once I got my chin too close to the rapidly spinning wheel as the press was opening. The wheel whacked me hard on the chin and broke the skin. I felt a fool – getting my chin in the way! So, I simply shook my head, to clear it, stuck a plaster on the wound and went back to work. I've still got the scar at the bottom of my chin where one of the spokes caught me. I was very, very lucky as it could've been much worse.

One day, the foreman came onto the factory floor grim faced and said, 'I'm sorry to say that one of the members of this team has been caught 'flashing' in the park and you may have seen it reported in the local newspaper. Not a very savoury thing to do. We've told him he could come back to work, but if anybody has any reason that they feel that they can't work with this particular person, they have to tell us.' I hadn't read the newspaper of course, reading was an aversion of mine, and I was not about to turn into a judge, jury and executioner of some, poor misguided individual so I didn't raise any objection. But I think we should have suggested the poor guy receive treatment so that his behaviour did not progress into anything more antisocial. But, in those days that sort of problem was best not talked about.

It was 1964 and the first year I became aware of the Melbourne Cup. Just before the big race, the yeast factory came to a halt. Everybody downed tools. I was a bit confused and said, 'what's happening'? The person I was working with said, 'The Melbourne Cup is on the TV in the canteen shortly.' I said, 'But it's not smoko time.' He set me right saying, 'it doesn't matter, we always watch the Melbourne Cup – even the bosses.' It was the first time I'd seen the horse race that stopped a nation and Polo Prince stormed over the line. Little did I know at that time that horse racing would become a big part of my life and that I would be actively involved in the Melbourne Cup race day in the future. But that's well into the future.

Christmas time was looming. I decided that it was time to leave Toowoomba. My parents had bought their home 'Noogee' at Alexandra Headlands, Queensland in September 1964, and 'Blue Horizons', a block of four flats on the sea front of Mooloolaba in October 1964. They were settling into retirement in Australia.

I stayed with my parents for a year, working locally and helping them with renovations of their home. You might wonder how I could live with my parents again, or they with me, even for a short time after what had happened in England? The old saying blood is thicker than water is true. I loved my parents. I loved my Father, and I still do. He was a bit misguided I suppose at times, but then aren't we all at some stage?

I enjoyed this time of living with my parents. My Father treated me as an equal and we had a good time. He gave me a glass of whiskey each night before dinner and sometimes afterwards. There were no in-depth discussions – only topics that we were both comfortable with. We listened to old records – Frank Sinatra, Dean Martin, and Perry Como, and one of Father's favourites, Shirley Bassey. We watched TV programs, such as The Avengers, The Mavis Brampton Show and other live variety programs. It was a time of healing and our relationship strengthened.

1964 was a very significant year for me, and the rest of my family. A new era had started. The '10-pound Pom' had determined to stay – there was no going back to England. If my parents had remained in England, I probably would've returned at the end of my two-year stint. Whether I would then have come back to Australia, is unknown. I am glad that I did not have to make the decision at that time. I know I have had a better life in Australia than I could possibly imagine in England.

However, there was a rocky road ahead for me. It would be nearly 10 years of 'wilderness' before I would finally find my true destiny.

Chapter 10
The Life of a Drifter

I had reconciled with my parents and was living with them on the Sunshine Coast, Queensland. Mooloolaba was a very scenic, quiet, and laid-back part of Australia.

I was energetic and enthusiastic and put my landscaping and gardening skills to use for a wealthy man who had just relocated from Victoria. I jumped at the chance to work outside when the job was offered, as I liked gardening and creating beautiful spaces. I wheeled a lot of soil, moved a lot of rocks, and made an impressive, landscaped garden for him.

He was very pleased with the garden and arranged a job for me as a groundsman, at the Mooloolaba Bowling Club where he was a member. There, I mowed the lawns – first one way, and then the other. The club had two greens. I 'top dressed' one with soil and rolled it, making sure it was level by using a long piece of straight edged wood, while the other green, was used by the bowlers.

At the end of the bowling season, I got a job at the Alexandra Headland Golf Club mowing the fairways and greens. I liked this job as there were kangaroos hopping around everywhere at this time. Life was easy. But despite the job, the environment I was living and working, something was missing. I became restless and unsettled with my life – something that would become a pattern and stay with me for many years to come.

One night I watched a program on TV about sheep shearing in Tasmania, Australia. I couldn't get it out of my head. I thought 'I could go to Tasmania for a while'. A few days after this I was talking to Bob White the real estate agent my parents knew and told him I was thinking of going shearing in Tasmania. He said, 'Why don't you go and see my friends who live in Melbourne on the way'. I said, 'That's a good idea.' He replied, 'I'll arrange it, just go down for a weekend and see them.'

When I left the Sunshine Coast as a wide-eyed young man in a new country, I had no idea that this was the first of many times that I would leave, and subsequently return at a point of time in the future, only to 'take off' again for extended periods. It was a cycle that I would repeat, time-and-time again, over the next nine years. Does anyone plan or choose to become a Drifter, or does this just happen? It was never my intention to become a Drifter, but insidiously, very insidiously, a Drifter I became. But for now, I was simply just going to 'Tassie' via Melbourne.

In January 1965, almost one year after I arrived in Australia, I packed my brown suitcase with work clothes and boots. I said goodbye to my parents and boarded the train for Melbourne carrying my newly purchased audio reel-to-reel tape recorder. At this time, I did not give a thought as to how important this audio recorder and tapes would be to me for many, many years to come.

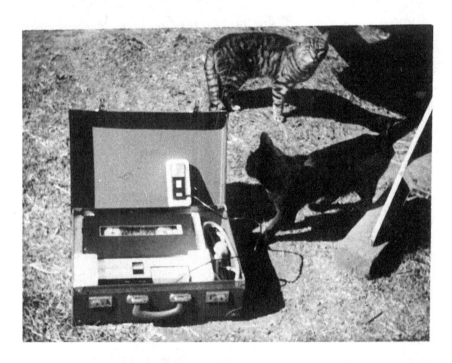

My audio reel-to-reel tape recorder would be my constant companion. It would be a source of music and entertainment and a communication system with my parents' as I would not write letters and public telephones were not always accessible. Significantly, my tape recorder would help me to survive when drifting around Australia over the years. It would become my 'bank' when pawned in hard times to buy the food and shelter I desperately needed in the many inhospitable and 'unsavoury' environments I found myself. But sometimes, the amount of cash received for the pawned recorder would run out before I got on my feet again, leaving me the only option available – homelessness.

I recorded numerous audiotapes over the next 9 years in all states of Australia, situations, and environments. I sent these tapes home to my parents, telling them where I was, and what I was doing. They would view their large map of Australia, positioned on the wall, and locate where I was when the tape was made. They often commented on their return tape to me: 'What a lovely lot of experiences you are having – you are very lucky. Even those born in Australia would not have seen as much of the country as you have or had the experiences.

I tried hard to sound 'upbeat' on the tapes sent to them, despite circumstances and situations I found myself in. But some tapes were made at very challenging times, and some at my very lowest points. When I was obviously melancholy or down, Mother would send a tape back to me with words of encouragement that boosted my morale. Father was shy, and very hesitant in speaking on the tape.

On occasion, at my darkest times when I was wandering aimlessly, thoughts did cross my mind that perhaps I should make my way back to the familiarity of the Sunshine Coast, but I never did at these low times. I would not allow myself to do this, I only returned when I was on a 'high'.

I learned to survive and fit into any circumstance, be resilient and take charge of my own life – the latter after a long 'apprenticeship'. Besides, there was no encouragement from my parents for me to either return or stay for any length of time. In retrospect, I appreciate this, and think they were wise not to interfere and try and disrupt my life's journey.

I now relate to and appreciate the wisdom of the respected Irish author and playwright, George Bernard Shaw:

'A life spent making mistakes is not only more honourable, but more useful than a life spent doing nothing.' And 'Life isn't about finding yourself. Life is about creating yourself.'

I am enormously grateful to my long-deceased parents for keeping the audio reel-to-reel tapes I sent to them during my years of roaming Australia.

Transcribed many, many, years later, the tapes provided the impetus for sharing my stories in: *The Burden Within*.

I arrived in Melbourne, Victoria after changing trains at Mildura. This change was necessary due to the different gauges of the train tracks throughout Australia. Little did I know at this time that on the next leg of my journey to Melbourne, I would travel through the countryside near where my future wife lived – at the time a schoolgirl, just entering her teens. It would be many years before we would meet on a remote Aboriginal settlement in the Northern Territory. By this time, I had travelled many, many miles – 3 times around Australia. Over this time, I had numerous jobs and many, many experiences: some good, some, not so good. But I'll start at the beginning.

Bob, the real estate agent's friend had a lovely house in Hawthorn, a suburb of Melbourne and made me very welcome. It was Saturday night, and Nigel their son, about my age said, 'I'll take you out and show you the sights of Melbourne.' We ended up at Luna Park, St. Kilda. Nigel bought a whole handful of tickets that enabled us to ride on any ride we liked. He said, 'I like the Big Dipper. Let's go on it.' Well, I've never been too keen on these sorts of things, where you feel as if your life is on the line. But, not wanting to sound frightened or ungrateful, I said: 'if you want to, I'll give it a go'.

We boarded the Big Dipper. The ride took us up, up, up, and then zoomed down to the bottom. When the ride finally stopped, I gave a huge sigh of relief, and thought, 'Thank God it's finished!' But immediately, Nigel said, 'That was terrific, wasn't it? We're going again… here we are' and he handed me the ticket. Three times we went on that Big Dipper! Finally, I said, 'I'm not going anymore, that's it.' Nigel relented, but then we went on the 'Mad Mouse' and it was worse than the 'Big Dipper'! The Mad Mouse was a zigzag ride at very high speed. You 'zoomed' right to the end, and then came a hairpin zigzag. By this time, your body is going forward, but at the same time you're going backwards! This Lunar Park experience is ingrained in my memories – probably because of the fear of heights and falling, I have had, all my life.

On Monday morning after a memorable weekend, Nigel very kindly drove me to the Melbourne airport where I bought a one-way ticket to Tasmania. After buying the plane ticket I had 7 pounds left in my pocket – all the money I had in the world. It might seem to be risky and highly irresponsible to 'flit' off to Tasmania with only seven pounds in my pocket, and it was, but those were different days. It was 1965 and seven pounds went a lot further than the equivalent would now. Even so, it was not a large amount. I reasoned: even if I don't have a lot of money, I will only need to get a job as soon as I get there. I'm a young person – I've got thousands and thousands of dollars stored in my body that I can cash through my hard work. I figured, once I got to Tasmania, I'd have a nice meal, buy a night's accommodation, before looking for a job the next day. So, with this positive plan, I confidently boarded the plane.

I arrived in Launceston, Tasmania and booked for one night at the first pub I came across, had a good meal and a deep sleep in a comfortable bed. I woke refreshed, had breakfast, and checked out of the hotel. It was a beautiful summer morning. With a spring in my step, I walked to the outskirts of the town, and stuck my thumb out in the universal sign of a young man looking for a free ride.

Very shortly, a cattle truck drove up and the driver said, 'Where are you going mate? I said, 'I'm looking for a job really. I'll go anywhere. Do you know anyone around here who has any work?' The reply from the driver: 'I'm going to Quoiba and then on to Scottsdale where there are market gardens. They're always looking for people to hoe up all the weeds and whatever and I know they've got a lot of cabbages, at-the-moment. I'll drop you off when we get there, and you can try your luck.' 'That sounds terrific, thanks very much for that.' I replied.

The truck driver dropped me off on the side of the highway opposite a pub. I looked down the valley and saw a few people working in the fields. I hesitated, but as the driver drove off, he called out, 'Go and have a chat with them and see what they say.' So, I walked down and said to the farmer, 'I'm looking for a job. I heard that you were putting on people'. The farmer replied, 'Yeah, no worries, we can give you a couple of weeks' work. When do you want to start?' I said, 'As soon as possible.' 'OK,' he said, 'First thing tomorrow morning at 7:00. See you then.' I was relieved and said, 'Thanks a lot – I really appreciate that.' I walked back up the hill to the hotel.

Now in those days, people trusted you. I had no money to pay for the hotel but said to the lady in charge, 'Can I book in for bed and breakfast please? I will pay you at the end of the week. Will that be all right?' The lady replied, 'No worries, that's fine'. So that was that. Once again, I felt at home in this country, and honoured my debt to the hotel once my weekly wage was paid to me.

I enjoyed working with the other itinerants who were mainly women – some local and some foreign. But I didn't enjoy doing the hoeing around carrots and lettuces and other small produce. It was very 'fiddly' work. I am not meant for 'fiddly' type work. But I stayed for two weeks until the work finished.

I needed another job straight away. I heard in the same pub I was staying that Kraft Foods Limited, a big factory at Scottsdale just up the hill from where I was living, was hiring people to work in the pea vines. I also heard that it was very hard work, but you got good money. I decided to give it a go. Early the next morning I walked up the hill and found out that the talk in the pub was correct. The personnel officer said, 'Go and see the foreman and you can start working tomorrow.'

I worked with the pea vines. A four-tonne tip truck would pull up in the courtyard, to unload the big slabs of twisted pea vines with the peas still in the pods that had been harvested. The slab was about the size of the tip truck. Two of us worked on each slab of twisted pea vines. We stood on the top of the slab and with our pitchforks we pulled the twisted vines out of the very tangled mess and forked them onto the small conveyor. From there the pea vines were delivered to a cylindrical drum with small holes in the side and a few lead balls inside. As the drum turned the lead balls belted the vines and the peas in the pods fell out through the small holes onto a conveyor that transported them into a processing shed. The waste pods and vines were discarded.

It was very hard, hot, and sweaty work during the twelve-hour shift. The workers were not provided gloves to protect our hands and we ended up with terrible, terrible blisters. Once, I was working with a fellow, who was a Disc Jockey on one of the local radio stations. He was working casually for Kraft Foods, as he wanted some extra cash. As we continued to pull and tug the pea vines the whole shift, he turned to me and said quietly: 'This is hard isn't it mate?' I wholeheartedly agreed with him.

At the end of the shift, your body had taken a real punishing. It was very, very sore, and I was exhausted. I would return to the pub I was staying, have a hot bath, something to eat, set the alarm and go to bed, only to do the same thing the next day. I managed to do this job for a fortnight and thought this is just too much. Even though I was living in a most beautiful area in Tasmania, I thought, 'I have to move on'. In hindsight I should've stayed longer and just 'sucked it up' because I didn't have that much money saved to enable me to survive.

I left Kraft and went to close by Devonport. The only place I could afford to stay was a very sleazy boarding house down near the docks that housed a few men. Three people shared one room. I looked around the shared bedroom and wondered how clean the single bed was that I would be sleeping in? The wallpaper was peeling off the walls and money had to be put in a slot in the meter to watch the TV. The only attraction for me to stay at this boarding house was that I had just enough money for about a fortnight's board. I thought I could look around for a job while I was there and move out when I did. But I only had a few days to find a job. The pressure was on.

One day one of the blokes I was sharing a room with asked me to lend him my good white shirt because he was going out on a date. I lent it to him, but he came back with grass stains all over it. I naively said: 'What have you been doing – rolling in it'? I wasn't very worldly in those days – more's the pity. Strange to think about it now, but sex education was not taught at school in the UK in the 1940s. In the 1950s basic things were taught in science classes as the biology of how plants and non-human animals reproduce. This meant that 1950s teens had a lot to figure out for themselves. Girls were more likely to have lessons as biology wasn't seen as a subject for boys – at least where I went to school. I didn't study science or biology and there was no discussion with my parents about this topic. It's no wonder that I had a lot to learn in this area!

I was acutely aware that I was not living in a good environment and was constantly exposed to the lifestyle of my roommates and others at the boarding house. But, here, I learned how different types of people live, and a few survival skills that would equip me well for the future. One night, both of my roommates came back early in the morning, and menacingly waved a bottle of beer in my face saying, 'Hey, Pommy, wake up and have a drink with us'. I roused and replied to the very happy pair, 'Why do I want a beer at 3am in the morning?' 'Oh, come on mate, have a drink with us' they said. They weren't thugs, just young blokes who were drunk. I decided to sit up and have a drink with them, as I knew they wouldn't leave me alone until I did.

I desperately needed work, but it wasn't easy. My money was running out – quickly. I learned that Edgell's at Quoiba [now Simplot Australia Pty Ltd] was putting on people for work. As the Edgell's factory wasn't very far from where I was boarding, I went to ask if there was any work but was told, 'No, not today, come back in a few days.' I returned in a few days, and the response was, 'No, there's still no work.' A week had passed, and I thought, 'I've only got another week to go, and then I'm out on my ear, all my money gone.' So, I decided I've got nothing better to do so I might as well just go to Edgell's and wait.

For three days in a row I quietly sat on the steps, outside the Edgell's personnel office. Nothing happened. I sat there, waiting. I literally had no money to travel anywhere to look for work. Luckily, on the fourth day, a lady came out and said to me: 'You can't just sit there all your life, you'd better get inside, and we'll give you a job'. So, that's how I got a job at Edgell's! Today, if this approach was taken, I suspect they would have simply called the police or security to move me on, but those were kinder days.

I had a job! I immediately moved out of the boarding house into the hotel at Quoiba, about 4 miles from the Edgell's factory. I enjoyed staying in the pub – there were others working at Edgell's that also stayed there. The pub supplied food for our breakfast that was stored in the small fridge. Cereal, bacon and eggs, the latter we cooked ourselves before heading off to work, travelling in the bus provided. The only trouble was if you worked the late shift – until 11pm, there was no transport back to the hotel and you had to walk on your own. The large trees on either side of the isolated country road, 'whooshed' in the wind; and this coupled with a very dark sky, the unfamiliar night sounds, and no one else around, was scary. But I didn't really think I would be mugged, because Tasmania seemed a fairly safe place to live. One weekend, I walked down the street to go to the pictures. The outside of the picture theatre looked quite normal, until I walked inside. The auditorium was open air, and full of very comfortable deck chairs. I enjoyed watching the Beatles movie, 'Help'.

I worked on the factory floor, in the processing area. It was a very noisy job because it was all to do with tins, more precisely, putting vegetables in tins. Earmuffs were not provided or thought about. I put cotton wool in my ears to try and reduce the noise.

I worked at both ends of the production line. Jobs involved placing empty tin cans from the pallet on the conveyor belt, and after filling and processing, placing them back on a pallet. To do this, I used what could be described as a large fork. There were about 12 spokes on the fork, spaced the width of a can. These spokes were hooked under the layers of cans on the pallet and placed onto the circular conveyor. The conveyor was positioned under a round processing table with openings that matched with the position of the cans underneath. Lots of ladies with rubber gloves sat around the table and pushed the freshly blanched peas or beans that had been dropped from an overhead chute, into the cans below. Further up the processing line, lids were fixed on the cans of vegetables and from there they went into a pressure cooker, before coming out the other end where I would again place the fully processed cans on a pallet to be labelled then marketed.

Frozen vegetables were also processed here, but I was not privy to the exact details of this. What I saw was frozen vegetables in plastic bags exiting a large glass tunnel where they had been snap frozen. These bags of frozen vegetables were manually placed by me on a pallet and then whisked away when full. What I did learn from my time at Edgell's was at the end of the process, vegetables were branded differently – Bird's Eye, Eskimo Peas, or whatever. But the vegetables were all the same and underwent the same process – they were just put into different tins, bags, or frozen packs, or just labelled differently. I know this, as the shift was half a day on this, half a day on that, and the vegetables used were all the same. Peas were round and green; and beans were beans!

The peas season finished, and I had to leave Edgell's. Luckily, a lady named Mrs. Jones who lived in Quoiba and worked at the hotel I was staying, knew a few people and she managed to get us both a job picking apples in one of the orchards, in the area. One day she said to me: 'A nice boy like you shouldn't be living in a hotel.' I think she thought I was lonely, and I guess I was. She and her husband offered private board to me, and I accepted. They were a nice family with two children, a girl, Abby about 18-year-old and a boy, Louis, about 16-year-old. I stayed in this family environment a few weeks. When not working, I would join them going to the beach, at Burnie.

I made my first tape to send to my parents while I was living with the Jones'. I had not made one before, as I did not want to tell them my woes when I was trying to survive. My first tape is descriptive:

...Around here you can say picturesque, and it really applies to any part of Tasmania. I find it very refreshing to see the green trees, the green vegetation, and the fields are divided up into small acreages like they are back in England. The people over here have been most friendly and most hospitable to me. Especially Mr and Mrs Jones and their family I am staying with.

...Most of the orchards are well into the midst of picking now. At the-moment they're picking for size and colour, for export to the British Isles and other countries less fortunate than us to have such an abundance of apples. The key varieties of apples are Jonathan, Stomas, Delicious, and Crocktons. Crocktons are a late apple, and they're usually the last ones picked and are the most

delicate of apples. The most common was the Delicious, but not the most popular.

...Probably in about a fortnight's time, we will be stripping the trees, and then most of those apples will go for local use, but there will still be quite a large quantity earmarked for export. There have been one or two boats, which have been turned away this year due to the shortage of apples. I hope this won't mean that the price of apples will go up. But I've got the pick of the crop because I can eat what I want, and more-often than not, get a tummy ache in the process.

...It's a very pleasant way of earning a living, and I hope before the end of the season I shall be quite good at picking. We have a bag over our head, strapped over our head and around our shoulders. The bag hangs about waist high and holds about a case of apples, and we drop the apples into the bag. By the time you've been doing that for about a day, it gets quite heavy. The average weight for a case of apples is about 43 pounds.

...I was out in the orchards for a couple of weeks picking with Mrs Jones and others, and we used ladders and picked for size and colour. The tractor came along periodically with all the empty boxes in. We got off our ladders to empty our bags into the boxes that were transported to the packing shed. It was an enjoyable working experience. Then the boss came to me and said we've got a vacancy in the packing shed where we want you to pick up the boxes and put them on the conveyor for the girls to sort the apples. Would you be interested? Is it more money? Yes. Well, of course I would be.

...So, I ended up in the packing shed, which was good fun. All the boxes I had packed in the orchards ended up in the packing shed. My new job was to help unload them off the trailer when they came into the packing shed, and then stack them on top of each other. When the trailer had gone, I tipped the contents onto conveyor belts which was how they we delivered to about five or six young ladies who selected them for size and colour and packed them in their appropriate cardboard box for export to various parts of the world.

We had a lot of fun and a lot of laughs in that shed. It wasn't hard work for me being a young man. And when I left, they were so pleased with me, that they gave me a gold propelling pencil and a tiepin, which was very nice of them.

My audio recorder strengthened my interest in this medium and I turned my hand to 'reporting' and 'interviewing', imitating the TV reporters.

... I'm, going to tell you a little bit of the history of Tasmania, especially about the northwest coast where Latrobe, Devonport, Sorel, and the other forts are. Devonport is situated on the river Mersey and up the river about seven miles is Latrobe, where I'm staying. At one time, Devonport wasn't what it was now, and Latrobe was a shopping centre. Latrobe has quite a thriving shopping centre, and the boats used to come up the river and disembark at Latrobe, but now none of that exists anymore, and as you can see in the photographs, I sent you, it is more a very nice trout stream.

... I have with me, Louis who is a pupil at St. Brendan's College, Devonport. He might be able to tell us a little bit more about Tasmania than me, as he is a native of Tasmania and has lived in Port Sorell for several years before coming to Latrobe.

CT: Now, Louis, what can you tell us about the northwest coast in general?

LS: The northwest coast is known generally for its farming produce and apples, and around Devonport it is a thriving industrial area.

CT: Now could you tell me what industry there is around Devonport, for instance?

LS: The main export is Ovaltine and Edgell's, where you have worked. And then, there's a Scottish carpet industry situated in Devonport. The new dairy factory at Devonport produces butter and cheese. Also, we have the berry factory that is near the Ovaltine factory, and the storage sheds for Edgell's and Ovaltine. Then we have the other storage facilities...

CT: So, as you can see, Devonport has quite a lot of industries supporting it in that area. Now let's look at Burnie. How far would you say Burnie is away from Devonport – Just roughly?

LS: I should think it's about 36 miles. I believe the Empress goes from Burnie, as well as Hobart. It's only been in operation for about three months. Goes to Sydney, doesn't it?

CT: Yes, it does. The Devonport will not stand up to such a big ship. So, you could really say Burnie was bigger than Devonport as far as the port goes.

LS: Oh yes, pretty big, it's deeper but not in size. But now the big, 25-million-pound scheme is going up to make a breakwater.

CT: I'd like to thank Louis for giving us a bit of insight into Tasmania. I expect if we want to know any more, we can always consult the history books.

It would be here that I would learn a little more about females in general, and the birds and the bees. I was twenty-two-year-old. Mrs Jones a mother figure to me often dried some 'rubber things' by the fire. One day I pointed to the bits of rubber and said to her quite seriously, 'what are these – pincushions? She laughed and laughed and said, 'No, they're my falsies.' That was, quite an 'eyeopener' for me.

Soon after moving in with the family, Abby and I became friendly and when we could, sneaked a kiss and a cuddle. I suspect it was obvious to Mr and Mrs Jones that the relationship was becoming closer and would be concerned that I was living with them. I know I would be, if it were my daughter! It was time to leave this family environment, before the harmless friendship between Abby and myself could escalate. I left the Jones' on good terms and did not seek to see Abby or the family again. I thought it best not too.

I moved to Quoiba, which was closer to the city and got rooms at a house with a nice elderly lady. I liked living there. We never really had much to do with each other, other than exchange polite conversation. This was fine with me as it was time to have a bit of solitude and not get too entrenched in somebody else's family, or life. In the evening after work, and having a meal at the pub, I would enter through the back door straight into my room, at the back of the house.

I stayed working at the apple sheds until the season finished and kept myself busy on the weekends by getting paid work at Quoiba picking up stones in the paddocks and placing them in small heaps for loading onto the truck by the farmer. It was then time to return home to prepare for my brother's impending wedding. Tony had asked me to be best man, who I was very happy to be.

I'd earned quite a lot of money in Tasmania and I was 'flush' again. But I only had old work clothes because that's all I'd been wearing in Tasmania. I decided that I must dress to impress for my return home. I went to a large shop in Devonport and chose a good charcoal suit, nice shirt and matching tie, black shoes, and some other impressive outfits. I bought an aeroplane ticket to Queensland and when I stepped off the plane at the Brisbane Airport, I looked a million dollars! All I had to do then was catch a coach to Maroochydore and I was home again, all ready for the wedding.

This process of 'dressing to impress' for my return home would occur time and time again, over the next eight years. No matter how tough things had been for me on the road, no matter what conditions I had been living and working in, I would *only* return home when I had money in my pocket and could exude confidence. The reasoning was simple – pride, and first impressions count. My Grandmother had always said: 'to be poor and look poor is the devil itself'.

Tony and Helen married on May 15th, 1965, in a nice little Church in Nambour where Helen, her brother and parents lived. Helen's parents owned a pineapple farm, and her father was also the local bank manager. They were a well-established Australian family that lived in a large colonial house situated on a hill, overlooking Nambour. Tony and Helen have two children, twins – Timothy and Anne. I am very fond of them, and when they were small, I bought them their first bikes.

After the wedding, I stayed at home for a while – I helped my parents with the garden, digging out the soil under the house, making a laundry and a darkroom for photography for my Father. I turned the excess soil into a garden with native plants. I bought a lawn mower and mowed lawns as a living.

This was a time of stability, enjoyable outside work in a very pleasant environment. I decided to stay on the Sunshine Coast and attempt to 'put down some roots'. It worked for a while.

Chapter 11
The Sugar Shack

I spent a very pleasant winter at Maroochydore on the headlands, and Mooloolaba. In Spring I gave my lawn-mover to Tony as a belated wedding present when I got a job with Les Carhart the owner of a local building company, 'Carhart's'.

I helped build a lot of houses in the area, including one extremely large house on the headlands and one right on the Esplanade at Maroochydore. This latter house was right next to a small surfing shop that made and sold surfboards and owned by Hayden Kenny. Little did I know that this name Kenny would become synonymous with elite surfing, a generation on. I never took to a surfboard but did do a lot of body surfing.

Amongst other building jobs, including the extension of the Buderim Ginger Factory – the largest ginger factory in the Southern Hemisphere, I spent days on the jackhammer. This jackhammer was run by compressed air delivered by a one-inch pipe running from the jackhammer to a standalone compression unit with a petrol engine situated a few yards away. The jackhammer broke the large stones enabling a trench for a large wall perimeter wall. Operating this jackhammer made my teeth 'rattle'. At the end of the day my teeth still 'rattled'.

There was no ready-made concrete delivered for foundations for houses and driveways. I literally spent days shovelling sand, stone and gravel into the small concrete mixer driven by a 2-stroke petrol engine. The mixed cement was then tipped into a wheelbarrow that I then pushed to various places on the building site. It was hard work.

The highlight of the build was when the roof was finished, making the house waterproof. At this stage, we 'wet the roof' with a keg of beer supplied by the builder. Les, the owner of the business provided a bar-b-que, with drinks and food and everyone had a good time. He did the same at Christmas time. He was a very fair boss and good to work for. I got to know the carpenters and the apprentices working on the build, so I was never lonely. The skills I learned from this job and building my own house would later hold me in good stead when I worked as a builder on Aboriginal settlements in the Northern Territory.

During this time of working for Carhart's, I joined the amateur dramatics in Nambour and worked behind the scenes and enjoyed it. I met a girl named Dorothy. We went out for a while and had a few meals at a restaurant at Alexandra Headlands and attended dramatic functions. It didn't last – she didn't kindle a flame in me.

I got talking to Bob White, the real estate agent who lived on the same street as my parents and had previously sold mother and father their home and investment flats. I was 'flush' after saving a nest egg in Tasmania and regular builder work at Mooloolaba. It was time to buy some land and put down some roots. I became a landowner. In October 1965, I bought 21 acres of uncleared land at the bottom of Buderim Hill – an area that became very exclusive, some years later. At $1200 for the 21 acres, it was good buy and a sound investment for the future.

I stayed working as a builder and threw myself into improving my land. I cleared some and planted 600 banana plants over two acres and a few broad beans. The rest of the land remained woodland. I decided to build a house on my land. A carpenter friend helped me build a 'shack' – a shed like structure built of wood and fibrous sheeting with an outside 'dunny'. It could be described as a shed on stumps – the stumps to keep out the snakes and 'crawlies' that existed in the area.

My shack had a tank to supply drinking water and I used the sea front and public showers. I connected the shack to electricity – cost of one pole to bring from the road. Inside, the house the layout was simple, but practical. There was a bedroom at one end and a kitchen at the other, with a lounge/dining area with a coconut mat on the floor, in the middle, and a TV. It was very liveable, for one person. Today it would be called a studio apartment on stilts.

Father and I decided one day to blow up the large tree stump beside my house. We bought some gelignite, dug a big hole under the stump and placed the gelignite in and packed rocks tightly over it – as we were told to do. We sheltered under some trees and lit the fuse. Yes, you guessed it. The tree stump split but remained secure in the ground. However, the twelve-inch rocks we had placed over the gelignite were blown high up into the sky, and then pelted down to earth. Father and I watched in amazement and then decided we needed more lessons in blowing up trees! Luckily the hole we packed the gelignite in wasn't facing the house, so the rocks flew out away from the house.

It was 1966. I lived in my home on my land. I bought an Alsatian dog I called Billy to keep me company in this very isolated area.

I've always been a very shy person and still am in some respects. When I walked into the bar of a hotel, I would think that everybody was looking at me. So, I would go and sit in the furthest corner of the bar and get 'half-charged'. Then, and only then, I would start talking and ended up 'the life of the party', which probably means I was a clown, and made a fool of myself! I was not a good drunk but did not realise this for many years.

I met some lifesavers at the Maroochydore pub, and they encouraged me to join the Cotton Tree Life Savers Club that was next door to the Caravan Park. I became an honorary member of the Life Saver's Club. It was wintertime when I joined, so luckily, I didn't have to swim for my bronze medallion!

One of the things we did on a Saturday was to have a 'chook' raffle at the local pub with the funds going to the Life Savers. A lot of people bought tickets in the raffle as it was for a good cause. I had great fun being part of arranging and overseeing the 'chook' raffle. Sounds mundane now, but the 'chook' raffle was a very social activity at the time.

I drank with the Life Savers and their friends at the pub – on Friday and Saturday night. I would drive in, and home. Billy, my dog would run after the car, and eventually find me in a pub. I was warned to change my ways when driving when the local policeman told me: 'If I follow you home one more time after you've had a night out, I am going to have to book you!'

After this warning, I decided to stay in town with a lot of Life Savers that came from Brisbane for the weekend. We all stayed in the dormitory above the Life Saving Club. One morning when I was in a deep sleep after a night of drinking, one of the lifesavers, tipped me out of the top bunk, mucking around. I jumped up from the floor completely disorientated and punched him all the way to the end of the building! I only stopped when I was pulled off him by other lifesavers that said: 'Thomo, that's not like you.' My response: 'I don't like being woken up this way!'

Sometimes we would take a five-gallon keg of beer down to the beach and sit around a fire we had lit and talk and sing the night away. One night when I was a bit 'worse for wear' and unsteady on my feet, I stood up, and promptly fell backwards into the fire. Only the lifesaver telling a joke at the time saw me fall into the fire and weaved into his joke: 'Thomo has fallen into the fire.' Other lifesavers scrambled to pull me out as I heard the joke teller saying: 'Aren't you going to hear my joke first?' Luckily, I had done no real harm, but grog, water and fire are not a good mix.

Often, the partying continued at my place once the pub closed. A group of us – male and female, used to go to my house on a Friday and Saturday night to 'finish off' the five-gallon wooden keg that was perched on the table. I nailed two pieces of wood either side of the keg, so it wouldn't roll around. These pieces of wood became permanent features.

The lifesavers named my house the Sugar Shack – I think inspired by the popular song in 1962 by Jimmy Gilmore and the Fireballs with words: 'There was a crazy little shack beyond the track, and everybody called it the Sugar Shack.' The only difference between the song and my shack was that beer was served and not coffee!

I always had a tape recorder blaring with music, giving everyone the incentive to dance at the Sugar Shack. God knows what else they did – it was the 1960s after all – the age of drugs and free love! Food in the Sugar Shack was limited at these all-night parties – 'grog' and music were the focus – there were no drugs that I knew of at least. As no food was supplied inside, the broad beans growing outside my house on my block of land, were routinely raided and half my crop eaten by my drinking 'buddies'!

But some good did come out of the Sugar Shack hosting this very friendly and harmless mob. There were no proper steps leading up to the front door of the Sugar Shack. Instead, four logs served as makeshift steps. It was a very dangerous exercise getting into and out of the shack, particularly after you'd had a few beers. So, the Life Savers donated a set of steps and put them up, so they wouldn't break their necks. The partying continued.

There was a slump in housing and Carhart's downsized. I had to look for alternative employment. I now had a mortgage and no income. I got the only job I could find in the area. A job with the Maroochydore Council emptying 'night carts', which was well paid, about 30 pounds, a week. I mentally struggled with having to take such a job, thinking 'I don't know if I can do this, but I'll have to give it a go'. And I did.

I started on the 'night cart' at 5am and finished early leaving plenty of daylight to do what I wanted on my land. In those days, most houses didn't have inside toilets, and instead were serviced by an outhouse – a 'dunny' out the back. In the dunny there were squares of torn up newspaper secured on a hook and pulled off when needed. The new-fangled thing called 'toilet paper' was not common. The use of the squares of newspaper was twofold. They could be used for reading the local news while doing your business, and afterwards for cleaning before getting off the toilet. Wood chips were then sprinkled into the can to contain the odour.

I went into the backyard of each house to the dunny. I refilled the wood chip container and opened the door at the base of the seat, pulled out the used can, and replaced it with a fresh one. A lid was placed on the used can and if too full, the fluid was strained off at the back of the outhouse before being lifted onto my shoulder and carried to the red 'night cart'. Little wonder why the grass always grew well around these little out houses!

The night cart had two shelves one on the bottom and one on the top either side to put the cans on. The used cans were on the bottom and new ones, half filled with wood chips, on the top. At the end of the shift, the night cart returned to the depot where the cans were processed. What this meant was that we dug a hole with a spade the size of a grave on the plot of land that was allocated. It was sandy soil, so it was easy digging. We tipped the contents out of the used cans into the hole and placed a scattering of soil on top. In the nearby shed, we sprayed the inside of the cans to clean them. The cans were then dipped in tar, in the vat nearby and placed on a rack to dry. The cans processed the previous day were loaded onto the night cart after placing a couple of scoops of wood chips in, ready to repeat the procedure the next day. Then it was home time where I showered and put on clean clothes. To me, the smell of the chemicals we used to clean the cans was more offensive than the smell of human waste.

I remember one day I woke from an afternoon nap at about 5pm and it looked very similar to 5am. It was dusk, and I thought it was dawn. I rushed and got dressed, sped to the depot to go to work and thought at the time, there was a lot of activity so early in the morning. I wondered why and then discovered it was 5pm!

I was on the night cart for about three months before scoring a job 'on the dustbins' which was better. With both jobs I had to lift the bucket or the bins on to my shoulder before emptying the container of its contents so between this job and other hard work I've done over my life, it's no wonder I ended up with crook shoulders, knees, and widespread arthritis. Sometimes when lifting a dustbin with a rusted bottom you felt your hand going through the bottom into the rotting rubbish, but you couldn't stop until it was emptied.

During my time working for the Council a significant change in Australia occurred. On February 14, 1966 Australia's currency changed from pounds and shillings to dollars and cents; weights from pounds and ounces to grams and kilograms; and miles to kilometres. There was a lot to learn and get used to. This change in currency and weight was integral to my next job.

In November 1966 I bought the Golden Bread, a bread-run that came with a Holden 'ute' with a wooden canopy and three shelves inside and doors that closed at the back. The previous owner showed me around the bread run at Maroochydore for a week and then I was on my own. I was in business!

I was up at 4am to drive to the Golden Bread Bakery at Caloundra to collect the bread and started the deliveries at 5am and finished at 10am. I couldn't be late and had to work quickly. Most of the deliveries had to be completed before 7 or 8am because households wanted fresh bread to make sandwiches to take to work or for the kid's school lunches.

The first day I had my torch on and had a list of all the houses. People were trusting and left bread bins outside the door with their notes stating what they wanted based on the pricelist: Vienna loaf, half a white, or a tank roll, or two whites and three coffee scrolls; and the correct money. I delivered the goods, collected the money, and placed it in my moneybag.

On my bread run, I passed the milkman, and we would swap goods – iced buns for a pint of milk. I drank a lot of milk, straight from the bottle. The beauty of travelling early in the morning was you didn't have to obey the road rules, so I could zigzag from one side of the road to the other.

This was an interesting period. Before my bread run, I had watched the Mooloolaba estuary being dredged so that the pilot boats could get in and out to navigate the shipping into the Brisbane docks. With excess tons, and tons, and tons of soil available, the land was reclaimed, and a road built that enabled driving straight from Mooloolaba to Caloundra. It was only about six or seven miles, but before this, it was a very long and indirect route. As the land had newly been claimed, there were no housing estates, just land. Today, 50 years later, this road is absolutely 'chocker block' with houses and entertainment. Anyhow, after a short time, I had a good offer, so I sold the bread run with the Holden Ute. It was February 1967. Now, what to do?

The local BP station had a gas pie warmer for sale. I asked the owner, 'What do you do with that?' He said, 'You just put the pies in it, warm it up, and then you can sell them.' He said: 'Why don't you buy it and get a little van, and you'll be able to sell pies – you'd 'make-a-killing' selling pies along the beaches – Mooloolaba, Cotton Tree and Maroochydore over the holiday season.' I thought that's not a bad idea.

After a couple of days thinking about it, I bought the two-door, two-shelf pie warmer, a silver Austin van and had a rack made to fit the pie warmer. I bought a gas bottle, mounted a gas ring on top of the pie warmer, had the car sign written, and bought the uniform – white shorts, tee shirt and hat. Guy's Pies – Hot and Tasty was in business! Guy is my second name and the rhyming of Guy's with pies pleased me no end.

I made a special deal with the bakery at Caloundra. I wanted to buy from them, prime meat pies – not the normal meat pie in gravy; plus, pasties, sausage rolls and apple pies. The bakery obliged with the quality. I went to the bakery early in the morning and watched them make them. They were good pies. Over time, I would place an increasing order each day for pies and other pastries as the business 'took off'.

I enlisted the numerous kids running around the local caravan park to increase sales. I had a cowbell I'd bought in Italy when skiing and I would say to kids: 'Would you like a free pie?' 'Yes', they all replied. 'Well, just stand on the side there and ring this bell and yell out, Guy's Pies Hot and Tasty!' I made a 'killing' over Easter, in particular! Well, it would've been a killing if I did not give a lot of pies away. In the end, it was not a very profitable business, but it was fun for a time.

At night, from about 7 to 10pm I parked outside the pub at Cotton Tree where I sold chook raffle tickets for the Life Savers Club and outside the Life Savers Club at Mooloolaba. There was good trade in these areas, but the trouble was, most of the patrons knew me. 'Hey, Thomo,… give us a pie?' How could I resist? I knew most of these people and had drunk with many of them. A lot of pies went as 'freebies' – but this was okay as the lifesavers and their mates had been good to me.

The police working the 'beat' would pull up beside me in their car. 'How are you going today Guy?' My reply? 'All right officers – would you like a pie?' I never charged the police for a pie – for a good reason. The rule was there was supposed to be 100 yards between a shop selling pies, to where you're vending pies. The position of my van and the caravan-park and the shopkeeper, was borderline. The shopkeeper made a complaint to the police saying, 'he's illegally trading.' But the police said, 'No, I don't think so.' There were no further complaints.

The business developed! I thought I might add the option of peas and potatoes with the pies. Gourmet Guy's Pies started! The pies sold for 9 cents, pie and potatoes were 15 cents and with the lot, pies, peas and potato, the grand total of 20 cents. Very popular and a great success – I just lifted off the lid of the pie, put a scoop of potatoes and peas into the pie, and sold them for 20 cents! I thought this is good. I'm making a great profit now. However, when comparing with selling cappuccino coffee today, the amount of ingredients and the intensive labour required to get the 'gourmet pies' ready for sale, it was not very profitable. Never mind, it felt like it at the time.

The gourmet deal added extra work, and this was undertaken with my parents' help and in their house. I bought a hundredweight of dried potatoes and dried peas in sacks and soaked them, with the peas soaked in bicarbonate of soda to make them a lush green. Like it or not, we – my parents and I were forced to feast on left over pies, peas and potatoes and the apple pies.

There were some disasters. Once, I'd loaded up several trays of pies on the van 'tail-board' as the rest of the van was full. I thought they would be safe, but one tray dislodged, and fell off, scattering about a dozen pies over the road. Fortunately, this order was frozen. Oh my God, I thought, I can't throw them all away. So, I gathered them all up, brushed them down and put them back on the tray and continued. During the day, somebody said, I think there's a bit of grit in this pie. I responded, 'Madam, please, don't be ridiculous! You're just imagining it.' But I replaced the pie immediately.

I gave the pie with grit to a dog hanging around the van – he didn't complain. The health authority wasn't as vigorous then as it is now or maybe people were just hardier in those days! This is the only time I had a slight lapse in standards, and I always had clean hands and a nice clean white apron. The holidaymakers left at the end of the season and Guy's Pies suddenly became unprofitable.

I'd been living at the Sugar Shack with Billy my dog on the 21 acres of land for several months and had many friends in the Life Savers. I had a nice coconut mat, sink, bed, and everything I needed. Life had been sweet. But again, I needed a job – I knew I needed to explore further afield to find one.

At the time of thinking what I was going to do to survive, I met a young couple Peter and Rose, with a small baby from Sydney in the pub. They were short of money and had nowhere to stay. After a few beers, I said: You can stay with me a couple of days if you like and look around. This they did, and within the two days, Peter, a second-generation 'wharfie' talked me into going with them to Sydney, as there were jobs available. So, within a few days I left the Sugar Shack and followed them in my car to Sydney.

I very quickly got a job at Australia Containers – a company that made containers of all types including 44-gallon drums. After the drums were made, they were dipped in a vat of black paint and went through a drying tunnel. I was at the other end of the tunnel with a stencil of the Celtics Red Star, and I placed it over the top of the drum and sprayed the can with red paint. It wasn't the healthiest environment with all that paint and a lot of chemical smells around. The compensation was a free pint of milk every day! I did other things around the factory apart from spray red stars on the drums – but I must admit that I had a sense of great achievement after seeing my beautifully produced red stars on top of the forty-four-gallon drums. They may still be around today?

I normally parked my car at the back of Peter and Rose's house, out of sight, out of mind. One night I heard a noise in the back yard. I went out to check the car and saw a wheel lying on the ground and somebody in the process of taking another off! I said, 'What the hell are you doing!' The would-be robber jumped up and threw a punch at me and ran off. I put the wheel back on and never parked the car in the back garden again that's for sure. I parked it a little way down the road under a streetlight. I thought it was safer there, than in the backyard of the house I was living. This incident set the scene for my stay in Sydney.

Sydney had a lot of leagues clubs – very plush places. I went to them every weekend with Peter and Rose and Peter's father. The attraction for them was the poker machines – how the clubs made their money. As if to compensate the punters for doing their dough, the club would offer really good food very cheaply as well as entertainment. The pokies were old style, so you did get some exercise by pulling the lever down and apples and oranges whizzed up.

We sat around the table, pooled our money and in turns, played a poker machine. The belief was that eventually we would win the jackpot from this poker machine. There was a flap at the top of the poker machine that you could flip over to indicate it was reserved, when you left the machine. Before I was familiar with the 'rules' and practice of the place, I went to a 'vacant' poker machine and started playing it. A fellow came up to me and said gruffly: 'what do you think you are doing. This machine has a reserved sign!' He pointed to a small sign right at the top of the machine that I hadn't taken any notice of. I quickly said, 'I'm sorry', and left.

We played the pokies every week and I got sick of it. We just seemed to drink, put our $20 on the table to play pokies and never seemed to win very much. One day I said, 'I'm not coming with you'. My 'friends' weren't happy, but I resisted.

Peter was in a foul mood when he came back drunk. I was asleep. He started banging on my door shouting: 'You Pommy bastard. You're a mean Pommy bastard. I'm going to kill you. I don't like you Poms coming to Australia. I'm going to shoot you.' I heard him get his rifle out as he continued to rant and rave. I thought the best thing to do was retreat as he pounded almost breaking the door down. He was really going berserk. So, I quickly slipped out of the bedroom window, slid under the house, and hid for a little while – petrified.

After a while Peter seemed to have calmed down and there was silence in the house. I crawled from under the house and quietly walked down to my car where I dozed in the front seat for the rest of the night. Very early the next morning I got out of the car and went back to the house to retrieve my case and belongings. I quietly opened the front door of the house and had a look around. There was no one up, or sound anywhere. They were all in a drunken sleep. I crept down the hallway to my bedroom. I packed my case and got out quickly. I did not return.

To this day, I thank God I didn't bump into Peter's father. He was a brute of a man – stereotypical of those days – a 'wharfie' with a huge stomach. Most of the evenings that I saw him, he was leaning on the kitchen bench drinking beer. His enormous belly simply hung over the kitchen bench – it looked like the undercarriage of a plane! I often wondered if he didn't lean on the bench to support himself, would the weight of his belly force him to fall face forward?

After this incident, I decided Sydney wasn't the place for me, so I got in my little Austin van and drove back to Maroochydore. I sold it to the wreckers as it was clapped-out and had blown smoke the whole way back from Sydney.

I decided to leave the Sugar Shack and the district and return to country work and country living where I felt most at home – but where?

Chapter 12
Driving Mrs Jorgie

1967 was another year of change in Australia and again, one to be remembered. History records the following...

...There were extreme drought, bushfires, and cyclones. A referendum to enable Aboriginal people to be counted in the census and the Commonwealth to legislate on Aboriginal affairs was overwhelmingly passed. The word 'British' was dropped from the cover of Australian passports; the last man to be legally executed – Ronald Ryan was hanged. 'Open line' radio began, STD calls were possible, and the ABC launched the TV news program, 'This Day Tonight'. Fashions, language, and behaviour were changing; and the film industry remained undeveloped. Normie Rowe won the inaugural King of pop award and Johnny Farnham released 'Sadie, the Cleaning Lady'. There were claims that the contraceptive pill was eroding living standards and the government immigration policy aimed to maintain homogeneity to 'retain our characteristic Australian identity'. The Vietnamese war was raging, as was the opposition to it with protests escalating and becoming more violent, with dissident University students planning to send money to the enemy! Further, to cap it off, the Prime Minister, Harold Holt, disappeared without trace into the surf at Portsea surf mid-December leaving speculation as to what really happened to him.

In this environment of change, unrest, and tradition, I headed to Victoria on August 1, 1967. My recent disturbing experience in Sydney had hardened my resolve to return to country living where I felt most at home. There was no purpose for choosing Victoria, just as there had been for choosing other places I had been, or things I had done previously, or would do in the future.

I left by Pioneer Coach from Maroochydore to Brisbane and then by train and changed at Mildura to head down to Melbourne – the same trip I had done before going to Tasmania. I stayed overnight at a hotel opposite the Spencer Street train station. After local advice in the pub the night before I purchased a ticket to Gippsland, the dairy farm belt of Victoria. Travelling through the lush countryside was very pleasant and I was reminded of England – cows dotted around, grazing peacefully on the green grass. The train passed through the towns of Morwell and Traralgon – I was not compelled to get off. As the train pulled into Maffra, I made a quick decision to get off and look around – it seemed to be a quiet rural town.

I walked into Dalgety's a large pastoral company with offices all over Australia and met Jim the cattle manager for Maffra. I asked him if there was any work around. 'Yes', he replied immediately – 'my mother is living by herself on the dairy farm, as my father died a few months ago. I go out to the farm every day with my daughter, to milk the cows. Maybe you'd like a job staying out there and looking after the cows, putting out the hay and just general farm work? There's a caravan in the home paddock that you could stay in, and my mother is only about 25 yards away in the house. So, if you're in trouble or want anything, you can always go and see her. Are you interested?' I replied quickly, 'That sounds a good idea and yes, I would like the job'. He said 'I've got to go out there at lunchtime to see my mother, so I'll take you with me and introduce you to her. If you get on with her, you've got the job.'

Jim drove me out to the farm, a few miles out of town. I met his mother who approved of me, and the arrangement we made included the use of her old Holden car to do my shopping in Maffra, each Saturday. I did not have access to any other transport and the farm was isolated. So luckily, I got the job, and stayed there for a few months.

I lived in the small caravan, parked in the home paddock. This paddock was also home to Roany, a horse that was blind as it had 'pink eye', and Peter, the farm dog. The 50 cows I milked night and morning were in the next large paddock and were rotated to other paddocks that were routinely irrigated from channels drawing water from the local Glenmaggie Weir.

I was woken each day with what seemed like an earthquake! Early in the morning, the small caravan was shaken vigorously with me in it, as Roany used it as a personal scratching post! It was time to get up and start the day.

It was quite easy to get the cows in for milking as I called them as loudly as I could. The strong clear voice that got me into so much trouble at school was now an asset. I would lean on the fence post and shout at the top of my voice. Some people in the local district said they could hear me five miles away when I was calling up the cows!

But there was always one cow that would not come when called – just like there's always one person who's late to get on the bus. There was one cow that used to just stand her ground and wait – wait for me to walk down and follow her to the milking shed. Sometimes I sent Peter, the dog instead, if he was in a co-operative mood, as occasionally he was like me in the morning – not too bright. On these 'off' days, Peter would just sit, and look at me. The expression on his face, said it all.

Apart from breakfast, I cooked all my meals in the caravan. Breakfast for me was easy. After getting the cows in and putting the milking units on, I simply walked to the adjoining dairy, put my bowl of cornflakes under the milk cooler to collect the milk for my cornflakes and finished eating them before removing the first units! Other meals I cooked in the caravan. There was a radio in the milking shed and I listened to all the 50s and 60s music, which I loved, and Jason and The Argonauts on the ABC every night.

The milking shed was a very ordinary one with five stalls and five milking machines. After the cow was milked, a lever was pulled which in turn opened the rail in front of the cow. The milked cow walked out, down a little alley into another holding paddock. Then, the next cow walked into the stall that had just been vacated and the process was repeated. Cows are very intelligent animals – they know which stall to walk into and in which order, which made the job much easier. After the last cow was milked, water and chlorine were drawn through the hoses and pipes to rinse them. The yards were cleaned with a high-pressure hose ready for the next milking.

Every morning the milk tanker came to the farm and collected the milk. The driver attached pipes to the bottom of the stainless-steel vat that held the milk, and it was transferred to the tanker. After this, I thoroughly cleaned out the stainless-steel tank plus the milking units. Night and morning, I sucked water and chlorine through the milk pipes to make sure they were clean. After finishing milking the cows, I showered in the bathroom attached to the milking shed.

I had never ridden a horse. One day I asked Jim if I could ride Roany, the horse with pink eye. He replied, 'you can have a go. He's a quiet horse, but remember when you go through any shades, like that of a shady tree, he's liable to buck a bit because he can't tell the difference between light and shade, so you have to be a bit careful.' Roany and I got on well, and together, we rounded up the cows every so often. This skill of riding a horse would come in handy later when I was working in the outback of Australia.

After a few weeks, I got to know Mrs Jorgie quite well – her initial indifference towards me had subsided. She was a nice old lady. She would say, 'Come up tonight and watch a bit of telly with me if you like.' That's very nice of you,' I replied. So, I would wander up to her home at night after getting something to eat in my caravan. I usually arrived about 7pm and we watched television together and she would make cup of tea around about 9pm. Sometimes she made me a sandwich or offered me cake or biscuits. It was very nice and homely. We spent the evening together for quite some time and then one day she said, 'I think you'd better come up on Sunday, and I'll cook dinner. I'll cook you a roast.' So, from then, every Sunday I had a roast with Mrs Jorgie. Once, I went to Jim's place in Maffra and had a meal with his family.

What transpired during my time on this dairy farm was a bit like something out of the future movie Driving Miss Daisy.

Mrs Jorgie couldn't drive, but she had an old Holden car that I drove to Maffra on a Saturday to do my shopping. One day, Jim said to me: 'my mother wants you to drive her to Morwell. She's got some friends there. But she doesn't like going fast. You've got to be very careful with her. Would you be able to do that for us?' 'No worries', I said, having by now mastered the popular Australian phrase. So off we went.

I drove no more than 50 kilometres per hour the whole way to Morwell, which was around 80 kilometres away. After I drove her successfully the first time, every few weeks she would ask: 'Chris, do you think you could drive me again? I want to go and see my sister.' I always replied, 'No worries Mrs Jorgensen, I'll be happy to drive you.' She would 'shout' me lunch, or I would have tea with her as a token of appreciation. It was a good arrangement and we got on well.

Life continued at the farm and the following excerpts from a tape I sent to my parents when I was living in Maffra outline the ordinary and mundane existence and from my perspective the intriguing situation of the family that was unfolding.

...It is Wednesday, and I just finished the cows. It's about quarter past 7, and I've tied up Peter and shut up the horses, and now I'm going to have something to eat. I'm going up to see Mrs. Jorgie. I go up most nights and look at the television till about nine when the 'Graham Kennedy Show' ends. We both like that program and I have a cup of tea and sometimes a piece-of-cake before heading back to the caravan and bed. I'll get up about half-past four and start all over again. Today it's been quite a nice day. It's a bit overcast but hasn't been too bad at all really...John's on holiday.

Yes, John was a sore point with me. John appeared 'out-of-the blue' one day. Jim explained that John had come to help me as the number of cows to be milked had almost doubled in the time I had been there. The first question I asked was, 'Where's he going to sleep?' Jim's reply was not what I wanted to hear – 'In the caravan with you of course!' I was not happy. The caravan was very small, with two single beds either side of a sink with a grill underneath on which you could cook. It was very cramped for two grown men and I didn't like the decidedly uncomfortable living arrangements as evidenced by my recorded tape.

...Jim has three brothers who live in Maffra – Fred and Bill and another one. Jim's the only one we ever see here. Jim said he doesn't get anything out of the

farm, but he runs quite a bit of stock of his own here, and he gets the profit from his stock, I suppose. I reckon Mrs. Jorgie gets 50 pounds a month, that's about 11 pounds a week, to live on, and she's always saying that she's not making enough, not getting anything out of the farm. She told me she has told her children that she isn't going to leave the house because it's her house, and she can live there as long as she wants. She is not going to move for anybody. It is her house, but the farm is not hers – she has a life interest.

...The reason the farm, I suppose, is in financial difficulty is because it's got to pay off all the death duties, for her late husband. All the profit they are making is being used to buy dairy cattle because it wasn't a dairy farm up until last year. So, all the cows they've bought are new. So, John and I live in this caravan – there is no money for another house. Mrs. Jorgie says if there's enough money to build us a house, there's enough money to give her some money so she can go on holiday again. So, this makes a stalemate.

...I frankly refused to live in the caravan with John because of his dirty habits. He never showers, he doesn't have clean clothes, and leaves them lying around. I am not going to live like this. I don't think he likes living in the small caravan with me either. We tolerate each other. So, now, we're all in a topsy-turvy way, in a stalemate sort of thing. Jim says he doesn't want to get rid of either of us given the work to be done. I say I am not going to live in a caravan with someone else. So the only solution is to create alternative accommodation for one of us. But Mrs. Jorgie is still living up there at the house. She has two spare bedrooms, which she will not rent to us. I think it is very stubborn of her really. Even so, Mrs. Jorgie is the only person who really bothers about our welfare at all, and if we didn't have her, it would be very dull here because I think twice Jim has asked me to his place. He doesn't really care much about John or me for that matter, as long as we do our work.

...John went on holiday after working a month or two. Now I am back to normal again – a caravan to myself.

... There were a lot of people in Maffra this morning when I went in. I go in on a Saturday. That's when I do my shopping. On Sunday I do my washing. Mrs. Jorgie always pays great attention to my washing, especially how I hang things out on the line. She's always telling me 'no, you hang these this way, or you hang those that way'. When I brought the car back on Saturday, Mrs. Jorgie asked me for dinner which consisted of ham and a couple of rounds of bread and butter. I suppose she's taking pity on me at Christmas time because I sometimes tell her that I'm a bit discontented, and I think the farm is being run in a cockeyed manner, which it is, I think. They should have a share farmer and Jim should just leave it to the share farmer.

...The time is 5:12 Christmas evening. I got up at five this morning, about half-past four I suppose. The cows are up about five, and I started the milking. I wasn't expecting Jim to come out to help me, but I suppose the Christmas spirit runs through all people, and Jim came out this morning and helped me with the milking. Then I went up to Mrs. Jorgie's and had a piece of toast and a cup of tea. About half-past 10, we went into Maffra where Kenny and Joanne, Jim's two smallest children were. Kenny is 5 and Joanne is about 3. They were playing with all their new toys and showed them to me. I gave Joanne a doll and Kenny a couple of bulldozer things. We had dinner about 12. Nice dinner – a joint of lamb and some ham. A lovely Christmas pudding afterwards, and we had quite a pleasant day. After dinner, we went for a ride to Glenmaggie Weir where the water reservoir is, to follow the channels. It was a very pleasant run up. The water level is down more than half. It's a great big weir there, I suppose it's about three miles square. After that, we came back and did the milking. We didn't start the milking until about four. But Jim helped me again tonight, and after we finished the milking, I went back in for tea where we had cold ham and salad and looked at the television. I have just come back now, and the time is 5 to 12.

...We had a successful Christmas. I went to bed, and the next morning, we started all over again, without Jim this time. And that was Christmas 1967.

...It is January 8, 1968, today and I thought I must talk to you. Such a lot of interesting events have taken place over the last weekend. Saturday I usually go to Maffra to do my shopping. I had to go into Maffra to buy a new pair of boots because my old ones had sprung a leak. There I met Ellen, who is a typist at Dalgety's and serves on the counter. I've seen her several times when I've gone there. She's a very pleasant girl, a strict church-going girl who goes to church every Sunday. She teaches at Sunday school as well, and doesn't have a terribly glamorous figure really, but she's got a nice smiling face, and she's always smiling and always been very pleasant to me. Several times she's asked me if I'd like to come to the church socials. I say I can't, I'm working, and I haven't any transport. This time she said would you like to come to our place for tea. We have nothing much, but it'll be nice for you to come out for a change. I couldn't resist. She's about 23 and doesn't stand for any 'funny business'. And you would appreciate nice girls these days are far and few between. So, I decided I would accept the invitation. And, I still hadn't any means of transport. Once before when she asked me, I asked Mrs. Jorgie if I could borrow the car, but something came up and I couldn't have it. Tony suggested in several of his letters I should get a second-hand bike, so I can go into Maffra when I want, and I've decided I will.

...The shop had no second-hand bicycles, so I had to buy a new one, which was $53 or 27 pounds. It sounds a lot of money, I know, but considering the one I bought about 15 years ago cost 20 pounds, it's not too bad really. And I can always give the bike to Tim and Anne when I get older. Besides it's a lot cheaper than running the car. I've ridden around on it a bit. At least I can get out now. I can pop into Maffra if I want to because it's only about three miles away, and I might hear of another job if I go around and meet people. I shan't be so isolated. So, I bought it, and that's why I haven't paid you the money this week for my land. But at least I shall have a nice outing on Tuesday. As you said yourself, I can't be stuck away in the never – never and not meet anybody. I'm 25. If I never meet anybody, I should just stay a lonely old bachelor the rest of my life.

... John was due to come back on Saturday, the 7th, by train. He arrived in Maffra at two. He was supposed to arrive at one, but the train he was coming on hit a lorry and they were delayed for an hour. In any case, he got in at two to Jim's place in Maffra where he was entertained until nine. Jim didn't bring him out here until nine. I was up with Mrs. Jorgie looking at television. I didn't say much to him. I was pleasant to him, and he put down the table and put out his hard mattress. Next morning, we got up and did the milking. Halfway through milking he said, 'I asked Jim what he thinks about building a house for us to live in?' I said to John, that's like waiting for the cows to come home! Excuse the expression. In any case, to cut a long story short, yesterday afternoon at two, John picked up his bundle and went. I saw Jim a bit later, and said Jim, John's gone. Everybody seemed surprised and shocked that he had just 'shot through'. I was not surprised. After our discussion the previous night where I told John I did not think that anything would change, I was not surprised. Anyhow, I was quite happy that he had left.

...Yesterday was quite a big day because Jim and I had to get all the cattle up and spray them along their back for Tsetse fly.

...Pink eye is quite severe here in Gippsland, and if the cows get it like Roany the horse has, their eyes will glaze over, and they won't be able to see. So, we treated them for pink eye as well.

...*Here we're still suffering with the drought. It hasn't been too severe for us, but now we're not allowed any more water rights, and Glenmaggie Weir is going down. And if we don't get some rain soon, it will be quite a serious problem here in Gippsland. There isn't any rain forecast for the immediate future, but we're still milking 97 cows, and John's gone now, and Jim says he's not going to get anybody else. I say well are you going to come out and help me in the morning? Jim says if I have to come out and help you in the morning, I might as well do it myself and save John's wage and my wage, which I suppose together would come to about 35 pounds a week he would save. So, then that's another stalemate. But I'm going to tell him I can do the milking in the morning and evening, but I'm not going to do any work in between. It's a very ticklish situation. A few weeks later when we were talking about it, I said to Jim, I think you anticipated John leaving as no one in their right mind would stay living in these conditions. I'll see what happens.*

...*A man named James was here before I arrived and unbeknown to me, he was on shares, and would have been getting about 50 pounds a week I suppose when the milk price was high. That was an interesting piece of information that Mrs. Jorgie shared with me one night. I never realized there was a share farmer here before I took up the position. I don't know if Jim ended the share farming with him, but I think he made life awkward for him as Jim wanted to put more of his livestock on the farm, and share farming was hampering him.*

...*Wednesday, and I had a lovely evening last night when I went to see Ellen. I finished milking about seven and got on the bike after changing into nice long trousers I bought. I got to Ellen's at 20 past 7, and they were all seated round a big table in the kitchen ready to tuck into a nice casserole she'd made. I sat down. But, after cycling about three miles, my face started to pour with sweat. I was so embarrassed, really. After dinner, Ellen had to take her brother, who I guessed to be about 13 and a very nice boy, up to a farm to do a few days milking for them until the weekend. So, we got in the car, and drove him there. It must have been about nine when we got back. Ellen and I had a couple of games of drafts, and she made me a nice cup of tea, and I didn't get back here until about eleven. I had quite a busy evening.*

...*The date today is the 19th of January, and I'm recapping from Wednesday the 10th, when Bruce came out. Now you know the Lamberts who I have talked about who Mrs. Jorgie went to spend Christmas Day with; well their son Bruce, who is about 15, knows a lot more than John ever did about farming. Mrs. Jorgie* very tactfully asked him to stay with her for a week. He's been here 10 days now because he came on Wednesday. So, he has been giving me a hand with the milking at night. And he wanders around and is a bit of company and knows about farming.

...On Saturday, the 13th, Ellen and I went to the drive-in. I arrived at Ellen's place about quarter past seven, and we went with friends of hers, a married couple, to the drive-in to see Thoroughly Modern Millie, starring Julie Andrews. It was a very good movie. On Sunday the 14th, Jim had to bring a lot of black cattle up to Brandon, and Bruce said he'd like to go the movies. So, Jim gave Bruce and me a pound and I drove us to the drive-in again on Sunday in Mrs. Jorgie's car to see Sampson and Delilah, one of those old-fashioned pictures.

...Every day this week, Mrs. Jorgie has asked me up for dinner, and I've had really all my meals up at the house. I haven't got any groceries. In the morning, Jim comes out and helps me milk. He comes out about half-past five, and when we finish milking, we both go up to the house, and I have a couple of pieces of toast and a cup of tea. Then I potter around. At about 12 I appear again, and have something else to eat, and then I usually have something to eat again at tea. This has gone on all week. I'm going to offer her some money tomorrow, that'll be the 20th, for the last week, to be fair. You never know, things might go on like this for a while.

...Bruce might be going to the pictures tomorrow night to see African Texas Style, and I'm wondering if I might be able to go. I haven't seen Ellen again. I should probably go and see her sometime during the week.

...The date is Tuesday, the 23rd of January. Last Sunday, the 20th, I told you I might be going to the pictures to see African Texas Style. I did. I went in a nice white Hillman car, very comfortable, with one of Bruce's friends – which turned out to be the milk tanker driver that collected the milk from the farm. His name was Darryl, and about my age. Quite a nice person, easy-going like me, and he came and picked Bruce and I up about half-past seven, and we went to the pictures. It was nice to meet somebody my own age, and through him, I'll probably meet more people, or I might start up a social life to a certain extent. We have since been for a couple of day trips, to Sale which has a big air-force base, and Lakes Entrance a nice sea-side place which is holiday orientated.

... I haven't been out with Ellen again. For one thing, it was causing a lot of controversy because Jim kept teasing her when she went to the office, and she didn't like that. Then she kept writing me letters and phoning me up and leaving *messages with Mrs. Jorgie, saying Jim shouldn't tease her. So, I decided I should probably distance myself from her because it was causing a lot of complications, and I don't really want to settle down in Maffra and get married, and that's what Ellen wants. In any case, I don't mind if we don't see each other again, I just want to go out somewhere and have a bit of a life. Maybe I'd get into less trouble if I just go to the drive-in and buy a couple of cans of beer and drink there and come home than if I start going steady with a girl. But I would like to settle down eventually. In the meantime, if I can meet a few friends, they might ask me out to somebody's place or somebody's house where I might meet another girl, just for a bit of female company – no strings attached at this stage.*

... As I said, Bruce has been out here, and he's still out here. He's been out here almost a fortnight now. He's gone with Jim today into Sale where there's a beef markets because he likes going around there. He likes beef farming. He doesn't like dairying much, but he's been very helpful, and he's helped me around and about the farm. I have been nice to him because I think they thought that I sent John away because I wasn't very nice to him. Well I wasn't, really. My intentions were to get rid of John, and it worked out well. But never mind. Everything comes out in the wash. Things seem to be sorting themselves out well, and I'm still getting good money, 20 pounds a week.

... The date today is 31st of January, and I'm recapping from Saturday the 27th. We did go to the drive-in. Bruce, Darryl and me. This time we saw a funny film. It was an English comedy. I've forgotten the name, but it was very funny, and we enjoyed it a lot. Saturday afternoon before going to the drive-in, we had to go and do Harry's cattle against lice and we had to go and spray them with Jim. We managed to get finished in plenty of time to get changed to go to the drive-in because it doesn't start until about half-past 8. I think we got there about 8.

... Sunday and Monday were big days for us, as we had to milk the dairy cows plus brand and tattoo with earmarks 230 Hereford cattle belonging to Jim. I had to go out on the horse with Bruce and Jim to round up the cattle to bring them in to the yards. I felt as if I was on Bonanza or some such! It was good fun. The horn span on some of their heads must have been at least 3 feet, and they were very wild. It took us all day Sunday and Monday to do them, and we had a lot of fun doing it.

... We still have the kookaburras in the tree over the bull paddock. I haven't heard them today actually. The three bulls are grazing there peaceably, and the

sheep, they're going down slowly because Jim kills about two a week, and we all get a little bit each. Not lamb, I'm afraid, it's mutton. But it's still quite nice and tender. The weeping willow trees are still budding around the paddock. They are on the side of the channel base, so I expect they get quite a lot of water. The grass is very dry all around because of the lack of water. It doesn't seem right, does it?

... I went to Maffra, and they told me I couldn't vote there, I'd have to have an absentee vote. I have to go to Sale. So, I went into Sale and a funny little man came behind the desk and said, 'Sorry mate. You can't vote here. You've been in Maffra more than a month, and you haven't put yourself on the electoral roll. I said well then, give me a form and I'll post an absentee ballot. 'Oh no,' he said, 'you can't have an absentee vote. You've been away from your other electorate more than a month!' Which was obvious I suppose? I said what if I say I don't care one way or the other, but if I get fined, I shall blame you. He said, 'Oh, that's all right. Just tell them you notified us.' And that's exactly what I did. I wrote on the 14th, well I posted it on the 14th of January – no, that was a Sunday. I must have posted it on the Monday. So, I think all that is cleared up, thank goodness. I would hate to be fined all that money. I've had quite a busy month really. John left on the seventh, didn't know he'd left until the eighth. Bruce came on the seventeenth and left on thirtieth. I've been going up to Mrs. Jorgie's for dinner since the seventeenth, but now Bruce has gone she says I've got to cook my own meals again because she only cooks for herself. It's February now. Twenty-nine days in February. Must be a leap year.

...It's about the middle of March – winter is coming towards us quickly. I feed the cows with hay every night and morning. They're like a lot of naughty children, all 97 of them. I put the hay on the truck, and as I go down the paddock, they pull at the bale, and they pull them off. They can't wait until I get there, and I slap them and some of them are very cheeky. Just like getting the first bite of ice cream before their brother does. So, they're all right. The horses, Roany, Brumby, Creamy and the little Shetland, they're all very well. The cat had kittens – four of them. Peter still sleeps under the caravan and tugs at the wheel that I put his chain around every so often, but he hasn't managed to shift the caravan yet. We all seem to be trucking on I suppose. And we all talk to each other each day and ask how we are, so we don't really get lonely.

This tape sent to my parents, with my mundane day-to-day life and activities ended with a rendition of Talk to the Animals from Dr Doolittle! I think when you start talking to the animals, it's time to reassess your life, and move on. So, I left the farm and Maffra, as really, I was going nowhere fast. The family had their problems to sort out and there was no possibility of becoming more than a farm hand, and at that, one that was destined to live in a caravan. However, I left on good terms and have very fond memories of the time I spent on the farm. I was grateful for Jim giving me the job, and especially for the time I spent with Mrs. Jorgie who was very kind to me and made my life bearable. I did not know at this time that the path I was to take from this time would be more adventurous; seeking something that I had not yet found.

I ended back in Alexandra Headland at home for little while. I had decided to sell my 21 acres of land, with the Sugar Shack at Buderim. I was paying the land off – so much a month and with poor paying jobs, travel, and unpredictable life it had become a burden. It was a mistake to sell the land, but at the time it seemed right. In 1967 it only cost me $1,200 and is now many years later an extremely exclusive residential area. Oh, for hindsight. But in any case, no use thinking of what could've or should've been. I sold it and that was that. I think I got what I paid for it. After selling the land, paying off the bank, I had enough money left to buy a grey Falcon sedan. I was now free to go wherever I wanted and do whatever I wanted.

But where did I want to go and what did I want to do?

Chapter 13
Shark Bait

It was 1968. History would record that:

...*1968 was 'tumultuous' in the world beyond Australia. Student riots in Paris almost pulled down President de Gaulle; demonstrations in Britain, Italy, Japan, and Mexico also threatened the established order.*

In Australia...There were increasing number of soldiers being killed in Vietnam and the Government was looking for an honourable retreat and consideration of post-war South East Asia – one that America would be involved. ... The Government outlined the broad principles of Aboriginal policy of which 'assimilation' was one and Lionel Rose won the world bantamweight title....Twice daily suburban postal deliveries were abolished; the standard gauge line from Perth to Kalgoorlie was completed; the first section of the Tullamarine freeway was opened; a referendum in Tasmania approved the proposed Wrest Point Casino; and Joh Bjelke-Petersen became Premier of Queensland. ...The Graduate, To Sir with Love, and Guess Who's Coming to Dinner, were the movies in demand. The Pope declared that Catholics should not use the Pill, the Australian Methodist Church agreed that women could be trained for its Ministry, and the Mayor of Brisbane, Clem Jones, announced that theatres, theatre restaurants, cinemas and drive-in cinemas could open on Sundays....A Sydney University survey found that 66 per cent of young people believed in God; and a Gallup Poll found that 40 per cent of respondents favoured Australia becoming a republic, up from 28 per cent in 1966. John Laws announced that he was making more money than Graham Kennedy, Don Lane was still king of TV vaudeville, Courage beer joined the market, and Americans on R&R began arriving in Australia....Old Australia was unrepentant. Billy Snedden, the Minister for Immigration, said that Australians, and certainly the government, did not want a multiracial society. Sir Horace Petty, the Victorian

Agent-General in London, explained that 'the trouble comes when a black man marries a white woman. No one worries if a white man is silly enough to marry a black woman'.

I had just returned to Alexandria Headlands after living and working on a dairy farm in Maffra for some months. I had sold my land and Sugar Shack at Buderim, Queensland. I had no shackles. After doing a few odd jobs around my parent's home, I said goodbye to them, and took off in my Falcon car towards the Gold Coast to see what was going on that way.

I had momentum, the car was driving well, and it was a good highway. I didn't have to think about what I should or could be doing when I drove. I enjoyed the countryside and pleasure of driving especially when there are blue skies and green lights all the way. It's only when you stop that reality and doubts creep into your thoughts.

I ended up at Tweed Heads, almost on the border of Queensland and New South Wales – well past the Gold Coast where I thought there was not much happening apart from a lot of high-rise buildings going up altering the landscape forever. I needed to find work quickly as my meagre savings would not last long. I'd heard about the prawn boats in Tweed Heads – how they come in and load up with ice and other supplies before going out to Moreton Bay to catch prawns and of course, the famous Morton Bay bugs. 'On the spur of the moment', I turned the car around and drove to where I could see boats moored. I got out of the car and walked along the jetty.

It was still early in the morning and I hadn't eaten. I stopped at a prawn boat where the delicious smell of bacon and eggs being cooked, was coming from, and thought, 'God, I'm hungry'. I bent down to look inside the boat and looked straight into the eyes of a wrinkled old man. I quickly said, 'how 'ya' going mate?' To my surprise he said to me, 'Are you the new deckhand?' Made reckless by my hunger and need for work, I quickly and confidently replied, 'Yes, I am'!

What did I know about boats and prawning? Absolutely nothing! But my instant reasoning was that I could be a deckhand and was very happy to be if it meant a job and more importantly some food. The man – the skipper continued: 'Well you'd better come on board. We're going out in a couple of hours, and you've got a bit to do, and we've got to go just up the spit there to get some ice to put in. Another 'fellow' is coming as well, so it'll be a couple of you. I've got a crook back, so I can't do much this time, but you should be right. You want to come aboard?' 'Yes, yes, thanks mate' I replied and went on board, hoping that the real 'deck hand' he was expecting, didn't turn up and blow my cover. Once on board, I was offered a cup of coffee, but no eggs and bacon – they had all been devoured. This should have been an omen to me as to what may come.

But before I really knew what I had signed up for, the second deckhand arrived and the Skipper immediately casted off. He steered the boat around the spit to where we loaded the boat up with ice. At this time, I thought, 'No problems, everything is going all right, I can do this. I became 'cocky' – I was beginning to think there really wasn't much to this sailing caper.' I would be proven wrong – very wrong.

With the ice loaded it was all hands to the deck. To get into the open sea, the boat had to go over the bar – not a pleasant thing to do as it is particularly rough in a small fishing boat. And, on this occasion, it was very, very rough – extremely rough. I thought, 'Just as well I didn't have bacon and eggs as I wouldn't have kept them down at this rate!' We were just about getting to the bar, and I was staggering a bit on the deck when the other deckhand said to me: 'Hey mate, have you ever been a deckhand before?' 'Oh yes', I said trying with all my might to convince him – 'I've just got to get my sea legs.'

I made my way into the wheelhouse and the skipper said to me, 'Can you make us a cup of coffee. There's the fridge.' I said 'okay, no worries', with all the enthusiasm I could muster. I opened the fridge and managed to stagger around and make the coffee. But I didn't latch the closed fridge, to ensure that the door stayed closed. It's common sense really to latch the fridge – when the boat is lurching from side to side, the fridge door will be thrown open, and everything will fall out. And that's exactly what happened. Well, the skipper was not happy, and said to me, 'you stupid bastard! You should have put the latch on the door. What's wrong with you?' I said, 'I'm very, very sorry' as I scrambled to put everything back in its place, which really wasn't much to feed three people, and then latched the fridge.

The boat continued going over the bar and it was still unbelievably rough. I sat on a bench running along the back of the wheelhouse and did something I never had before and never have since – I broke into a cold sweat of fear! The water literally poured out of my forehead! I thought, 'I'm never going to do this again!' And this was on the way out to sea! I had hours and hours to go before we would return to shore. I thought to myself: 'this is it. I've bitten off a bit more than I can chew with this one.' I didn't know at this stage, and I am glad I didn't, that considerably worse conditions were to come, and the torturous hours would turn into risky and dangerous days. And this, I had gotten myself into, just based on hunger and a whiff of bacon and eggs!

I returned to my post still feeling incredibly queasy and it was getting worse. My fellow experienced deck hand, kindly said, 'I'll give you a hand. It's easy. You just need to do this, that and the other. It takes a couple of hours to get out to the dredging site, so you might as well go and lie down and have a rest.' I said, 'thanks mate – that's a good idea'. Well, my bunk was by a porthole and as I lay down, I could see the water going up and down, up, and down. I thought, 'oooooh!' and with that, got up quickly, because I was sick-as a dog! After about three hours I felt no better but had to go up to the deck and do some work.

I spent the best part of a day trying to do my work in between bouts of vomiting into the sea before I got used to it and wasn't sick anymore. I also managed to walk reasonably upright which was good. And, of course we had prawns to eat, which was just as well because we had no other food on board to speak of. I dread to think how we might have managed if we had failed to catch any prawns.

The process of trawling for prawns continued. We lowered the nets and after three hours we brought them up. In between we slept or rested, and this went on all through the night.

My next ordeal was managing the two big booms that had wooden floats that support the nets either side of the trawler. Now, imagine the trawling net like a big shopping bag except it's all fine rope net. The handles are two big steel ropes that go either side of the ship, over the boom and the winches operate the net. The net is winched up high so that the bottom of the net ends up over the secured sorting table – about the size of two kitchen tables with a raised edge and some gaps to separate the by catch from the prawns.

When the nets are being hauled up you lean over the side of the boat to guide the base of the net onto the boat. And I mean lean over – a one-foot rail, and it's dark, the boat's lurching and bobbing up and down and it's cold and rough. Bits of net are catching on the side of the boat as the winch is hauling it ever higher. Eventually the net is as high as it can go and tapers down like a funnel. The rope securing the haul is released and swoosh, whatever is caught in the net comes out – including little sharks, sea snakes and other weird and wonderful sea creatures. God knows what's down there but there certainly are a lot of strange looking creatures in the sea! They all come out – splat – onto the sorting table. Then, with wooden paddles we scooped all the things we didn't want, in fact, anything not a prawn, into a basket under the table. Then, everything in the full basket is tossed back into the sea, and the separated prawns transferred to ice within the boat.

We were never alone in the dark of the waters. In the distance we could see small flashing lights that signalled the presence of other prawn boats. In all I counted ten boats out 'prawning'. Beneath the sea, there was more company. Attracted by the unwanted creatures and bits thrown overboard every three hours, sharks circled, looking for an easy feed. No, we were never alone in the dark of the waters.

The Skipper was all too aware of the sort of danger that lurked in the dark sea. My survival instincts kicked in and I gingerly edged forward to the side of the boat to do my job. The Skipper shouted at me – get closer to the 'bloody' edge – you'll never do any good there! You need to lean over and grab it! I did as he said and immediately became perilously close to toppling over the almost non-existent guardrail into the dark, threatening sea. Behind me, I heard the Skipper's advice:

Well mate, if you fall over, it's no use us stopping for you and I'll tell you why. One or two things could happen. If you're lucky, the sharks will get you straight away... and if not, you're going to be sucked down the net and drown. And it's no use you trying to climb the steel rope that holds the net in the water because they're all oiled and greasy, so they don't go rusty which means you'll just slide down again until, finally, the sharks will get you! My best advice is don't fall in will you mate, because you've really had it if you fall in.'

I didn't reply – I couldn't – I was concentrating on the task at hand with his words ringing in my ears!

Once, after lowering the nets, the skipper asked me to come to the wheelhouse to steer the boat for 3 hours while he rested. He said to me 'it's easy – we're trawling down this gully in the sea. On the echo sounder there is a green button beeping on this coordinate. Make sure it stays in this line. You'll be right. There are plenty of other ships in the area – you can see the blinking of lights. The experience and responsibility exhilarated me. All went well. I had survived the first day! But worse was yet to come.

Suddenly, a huge storm blew up. The waves crashed into and broke on the stern and the wheelhouse. The boat bobbed around like a cork and the rails on the side of the prawn boat were no more than a foot – 12 inches high, and that's a generous estimation! And in this environment – without a life jacket or safety harness, we continued to work and try not to be washed off the boat!

The storm increased in intensity, and we all retreated to the wheelhouse and watched the waves go over the boat. An alert from the coast guard demanded all boats to return to port given the severity of the storm and what was to come. My Skipper ignored the order and did not respond to the coast guard. His reasoning? He needed a full catch – he'd had a bad back, and he was short of cash. Therefore, he told us his boat would not return to port as ordered but would stay to get a profitable catch. This obviously meant his two deckhands would also not only have to weather the horrific storm but survive!

The small boat continued to roll precariously from side to side as the wind, waves and rain battered it, and we hung on for dear life. I shouted loudly to the Skipper through the noise of the wind and waves, 'Are you sure we'll be all right? Are you sure we should be out in this storm? His response: 'it's all right. Don't you worry mate. This old tub won't sink. It's been out in worse.' So, there we were, in an old leaky tub with no guardrails to speak of, no safety apparatus, and the boat's bouncing around like an unrestrained cork. I slept and spewed, slept, and spewed. And prayed that we would get through this. When I woke it was dark, but we had spotlights on the sail.

Somehow, divine intervention or, more likely, dumb luck, kicked in and we didn't sink. The storm abated. We were exhausted. The Skipper said, 'we'll go into a cove off one of the small islands in Moreton Bay and drop anchor and have a rest before heading back to port.' It was at this time the Skipper radioed back to let the coast guard know we were okay.

We fed on prawns, as that was what we had in the fridge. I peered down into the bilge, a dark black hole at the bottom of the boat, and all I could see was water sloshing around. When I raised the alarm the Skipper said, 'Oh the pumps will look after that. Don't worry.' But his words didn't give me much comfort and I did worry. We were a long way off course and a long way from home. We eventually set off and continued to trawl for prawns as we headed back to port. The catch increased, but not to the size the Skipper wanted.

When we arrived into port, an ABC news team – a Reporter and TV cameraman met us. The reporter asked, 'Are you all, right?' 'Yeah' we replied. The reporter then said, 'we were very extremely worried about your safety because the storm in Moreton Bay, was very severe and every other boat returned, except yours. We thought you had disappeared.' I said 'Tell me about it! I did not elaborate – I would like to have said something like 'only the sensible prawn boat Skippers returned to port!'

In the end it wasn't a very profitable venture for me. The Skipper said 'Look, sorry mate. I haven't any money now. Can I owe it to you? Take some prawns with you.' I said, 'that's okay mate – the prawns will do'. I genuinely figured my reward was to have my feet on dry land and not having ended up as a shark snack. He gave me a few 'bobs' for the petrol to get back to Brisbane. Luckily, my car was still parked at the docks at Tweed Heads on return. I gathered up a bag of prawns and drove to Wynnum a suburb of Brisbane where I stayed with Tony and Helen for a few days. And you can ask them – I walked sideways for a while because I got so used to walking for the last three days on a ship that was far from stable!

But it was a great adventure – a terrifying one that I vividly recall over 50 years later. It is however, one that I would never like to experience again. What did I learn from this experience? I learned fresh prawns are a *really* green colour, the sea is full of incredible sea creatures and the prized Moreton Bay Bugs are strange things that keep flapping. Most importantly, I learned never, ever to go out on another prawn boat even if I am starving!

My land legs were back again, and I needed to find work. I was still broke. I returned home to Alexander Headlands and spent a few days relaxing and swimming in the sea then took the first available job I could find.

I worked as a kitchen hand in a hotel at Noosa for a couple of months. It wasn't the greatest job, but at least there was some money coming in. Noosa was a very popular hippie destination. It had an alternative, free, relaxed lifestyle, and was a famous surfing destination. In fact, in the 1960s most of Queensland was still considered a wild frontier of bush, beaches and dirt roads. A lot of Victorians also spent their time at Noosa. Queenslanders often referred unkindly to Victorians as 'rubber necks' or from 'south of the border'.

All the time I was working at the hotel, I was thinking about 'where to and what to do next'. On the-spur of the moment, I decided. I would reverse the trend of Victorians moving north – I would move to Victoria again.

Winter was coming. I had no distinct plans. I was going to 'play-it by ear'.

Chapter 14
Aussie Life

It was May 1968, and I was heading towards twenty-six-year-old. I left Maroochydore by bus for Brisbane and then boarded the train to Victoria. My tape recorder was beside me, ready to record the adventure.

...We're just passing through the upper somewhere or other, still going out of Brisbane, passing all the sidings on the way, and going under the bridges. We have been travelling for about half an hour and have reached the rural parts of Brisbane....

...As the Great Brisbane Express noses its way into Pitt Street Station, Sydney at 08:45, I collected my cases, made sure I didn't leave anything behind in the cabin, put a firm smile on my face and walked the length of the platform to the cloak rooms. I walked up to the counter at the end and put my two cases into the luggage compartment and set off to explore Sydney before catching the train to Melbourne a few hours later.

... I looked up and down Pitt Street and the surrounding area then it was time to make my way back to the station and boarded the train. There are a lot of students.... I settled back and enjoyed the trip, looking at the towns along the way. We pulled into Melbourne – I stayed a night, and it seemed big and noisy.... I went to the movies – saw Bonnie and Clyde, and by the end, I had decided to jump on a train going back to Albury – a town I had noticed on the way to Melbourne.

...But, when the train pulled into Benalla, before Albury, I thought, this small town will do. I got off. Benalla is near the border of New South Wales it's quite a small place where not much goes on. I'll have to see how I get on. I booked into the pub – the Commercial Hotel in the main street and looked forward to my first night's sleep for two nights. But before this I went to the bar for a meal

and in the hope of meeting a local who knows the town and if any jobs are available. I was in luck – the old man perched on the bar stool replied to my question – 'go to the Army camp – it was once a migrant camp and was taken over by the Army to train cadets about 15 to 18-year-old. They're putting people on there.' So, if I am lucky, I might have a job lined up for tomorrow.

... Today is Friday, and this morning I went up to the Army Camp at 8:00 and saw Sgt Mackenzie. Unfortunately, there weren't any vacancies as they'd just been filled. However, he said they might have a few vacancies on the 10th, which is in another week. I don't know how I'll manage until then. I booked in tonight again at the Commercial Hotel here in Benalla, which incidentally is about 120 miles from Melbourne on the Hume Highway going towards Sydney. If I don't get a job here, I shall probably end up going to Albury, which seems to be quite a big place and on the border of New South Wales and Victoria where it might be quite possible to get a job.

... I spent most of this morning talking to the employment officer who is the agent for the Commonwealth Employment. He also runs a tourist bureau at the end of town here. He was quite an interesting man to talk to, so I yarned away a few hours. Since then I've walked the main street, and that's about all. ... Benalla really is a one-horse town.

I went to bed despondent. But early next morning, there was a message for me: someone had dropped out from the Army Camp and I had the job that started immediately and would last a week. I now had a job and accommodation and food at the Army Camp. Along with all other workers I was issued a pillow, sheet, and a blanket. About 20 of us slept in a big shed. My job was to help feed the young cadets. I worked in the kitchen, and 'dolled' out food to them, which was basic. It wasn't very hard work.

Everything you do teaches you about life, or yourself. Whilst the job in the army camp was only for a week, it taught me something I would repeatedly draw on over the next few years. That is a job –one that includes accommodation and food – all 'perks' for a Drifter, is prized, particularly in winter. It would be this type of job that I would continually seek out in the future.

During the week, I got friendly with Jeff, about twenty-years old, and a local. who also worked in the kitchens at the army camp? Jeff was a bit like me I thought. He was quiet and 'picked up' work where he could. One night he said to me, 'Why don't you come home and meet the folks. They live here in Benalla, and I think they'd like to meet you.' I jumped at the chance, saying, 'that sounds great Jeff. I'd like that. Thank you.'

Little did I know at this time that this invitation from Jeff would lead to a long association with his family; and that I would learn a lot about Australian life, close family ties and living in a small Aussie town in the 1960s. They are memories that I cherish to this day.

Jeff's family house was in Railway Crossing, Benalla. Just across the road was the train station, and you could hear the trains being shunted. It was an old pokey house, with many peaked rooves indicating the old method of adding rooms over time, but it was very clean, warm, and homely. The kitchen stood away from the house, a sort of a lean-to and was only connected to the main house via a small pathway. Something resembling a bathroom was tacked onto the side of the house. By the bath, there was a wood stove. I got to know later that to bathe, woodchips were put in the stove to heat the water, and because it was so difficult, and water was scarce, everyone tended to have one bath a week.

Jeff introduced me to his happy family: Sid, his father, about 40 year old, who worked for the Main Roads Department as an operator of heavy machinery repairing roads; Jean, his mother, a bit younger than Sid, and a motherly housewife who looked after everyone; Janine, his sister about 17 year old, dressed in a crisp white shirt and black mini skirt as she worked at the local Coles Supermarket on the checkout; and finally his brother Rob, 21 year old, who was a plumber's apprentice. Lorraine, his elder sister, and her husband Ron lived close by and 'popped' in to see the family all the time but were not there on this day.

I had a great night that first night I spent with Jeff's family. We all had a few drinks and sang a medley of old Australian songs. It was the happiest I had been for some time and the family made me very welcome. Jeff and I didn't get back to the Army camp until quite late.

Too soon the time came for the army cadet camp to pack up. I said goodbye to Jeff and Jeff's family, and got a lift down to Melbourne on the back of the canvas covered Army truck. It brought back memories – this army truck was like the one that I stowed away on to go to the pictures when I was a boy at boarding school.

I was hoping to secure more work in another army camp, and to see if this was possible, I had to go to the Victorian Barracks on Swanston Street, Melbourne. Frank and Ray, a couple of cooks I had seen at the army camp in Benalla were sitting next to me on the long seat, and we struck up a conversation that passed the time. We eventually arrived at the Victorian Barracks, but no jobs were available for me. Here I was again in Melbourne, with no job or accommodation. It was getting late in the day.

Frank said to me, 'Are you staying anywhere now?' I replied, 'no, no… I've got to find somewhere to stay.' 'Oh,' he said, 'you might as well come back with Ray and me. We've got a room in a rooming house. We can put you up for a few nights, then you can decide what you're going to do.' 'Okay. I'll be in that,' I replied, relieved.

I went back to their digs with them – a very small room with two single beds. Frank said, 'you can bunk in with Ray. He won't mind. So, I did what he suggested… but in the middle of the night, I woke up very suddenly and 'shot' out of the bed like a 'rocket'. Ray had gotten too close to me for comfort! I ended up sleeping in the other bed where Frank did keep his distance. I didn't sleep well and was glad when morning finally came, and I looked forward to breakfast. I should've left then and went my own way, but where was I to go? I was at a loss as to what to do and thought at least I know someone in this city – even if I have only just met them, and they are not the most desirable company! Being positive, I thought that today was another day.

When Frank and Ray woke up, Frank said, 'Let's go and have a beer, and we can have a talk about the future and see what we can do.' Having no other plans, I said, 'okay, I don't mind, I'll go and have beer'. I really felt I needed a drink after the 'close-call' during the night.

We went to a hotel close by, had our beer and then left. Ray said he would head off back to the rooming house. Frank said to me, 'I just want to call into this shop first and buy some clothes.' 'Ok' I said, 'I'll just hang around and wait for you.' We entered the store together. Frank went to one side of the store to look at some clothes and I went to the other side, where the shirts were, browsing.

Well, bless my soul, next minute, two coppers were either side of me and promptly marched me out of the store and shoved me into a waiting paddy van, and slammed the door. It happened so quickly – I was confused and protesting loudly! 'What's up?' I said. The response chilled me: 'You'll find out soon enough son, you'll find out.' The police took off in the paddy van like a 'bloody rocket' – round the street corners at such a pace I reckoned they were going around the corners on one wheel. All the while I was lurching in the back – forward, backward, and sideways!

The paddy van ended up at the police station and I was marched inside to a small room where I was interviewed – no not interviewed… really interrogated. One policeman said, 'Now what were you doing in that shop? Before I could answer him, he said: You came into the shop together and you were acting as an accomplice, weren't you? You were distracting the salesman while your mate stole all the goods.' Astounded I said, 'what mate? I only met him a week ago at the Army camp, and he just asked me for a beer and wanted to go into the shop.' They were obviously not convinced replying, 'Oh that's a likely story. How long have you been here (in Australia)?' 'Not long' I said. 'Oh yeah…. Pommy, are you?' they asked.

The police grilled me for three hours. They kept saying to me, 'I was 'in on it''. I kept denying 'it'. This was repeated time-and time again. All the time I had a knot in my stomach and thought that this situation might not end well. At one point I said, 'I'll be glad to get home tonight and have a shower'. Their response heightened my concern: 'Mate, you'll be lucky to get home and have a shower at all; the way you're going!'

During the three hours I was held there were great lapses where I just sat there and thought, 'Now what's going to happen?' Suddenly, the door opened, and the police returned, and one said abruptly, 'Right, you can go. Your mate owned up that he did it all by himself, and you weren't involved.' A wave of relief washed over me, and I thought to myself 'Thank God for that'. I got up and was escorted out the side door of the police station. I did not look back.

Outside I met Ray who was standing in the street. It didn't cross my mind at that stage as to how Ray knew where I was and what had happened. I was still confused and reeling from the experience of being arrested and just so thankful to be let off and out of the police station. It was only much, much later that I could think clearly and realised that I had been set up and used as a decoy for Frank to go on a stealing spree in the clothing store. Ray said to me, 'It'll be all right. Frank will be out on bail tomorrow and we can take off to Western Australia. They'll never find him out there'. Let's go and find somewhere to stay tonight.

Still shaken, I followed him to a hotel where Ray said, 'We'd like a booking for the night.' They said, 'single beds or double bedbeds?' 'He said, 'We'll have a double bed, won't we?' This response jarred me and snapped me out of my haze of reflecting on my close call with the police. With Ray's comment coupled with the previous night's experience I thought, 'like hell we will'! So, while he was busy booking in, I said I needed to get something from the Milk Bar next door. I walked straight out of the Hotel, cleared off around the corner, jumped on a tram to Spencer Street Station and caught the train back to Benalla. I thought, 'What am I going to do now?' Then, I thought, 'I'll go and see Jeff's family and tell them my story.' I was a bit shaken up by my experience in the police station.

I got to Jeff's family home at about six at night. They were all there and asked how I was. 'Oh God' I said, 'I've had a hell of a time'. 'Oh, come and tell us all about it.' So, they cracked open a couple of bottles of beer and I told them everything that had happened. I must admit they had a good laugh at certain points but did show some much-needed empathy… 'Oh that's terrible. Oh dear, oh dear. You'd better stay here the night.'

The next morning, I got up and Sid said to me, 'Well what are you 'gonna' do now?' I said, 'well, I don't know really'. Sid said, 'you can board here if you like, but you'll have to pay rent. I can't keep you for nothing.' I agreed, and he said, 'How about 10 dollars a week, and you'll have to pay promptly or else you'll be out on your ear. You know that don't you?' I said to Sid, 'that's great no worries at all. That'll be good.' Sid replied, 'All right then, that's a deal.' I was so relieved. A mattress was put in the passage for me to sleep on.

I only stayed for a short time, but it would be a place I would return to off and on over the next 12 months or so.

Hunting at the weekends was a common practice – mainly rabbits and ducks. Jeff had a pet ferret that we put down rabbit burrows. We blocked all the rabbit warren holes except one that was covered with a net. The ferret went down the open hole seeking the rabbits, and they would come scurrying out and be caught in the net. But half the time the ferret simply stayed underground and ate the young! When that happened, it took us a couple of hours to dig out the ferret! When we did catch rabbits, Jean assumed chef duties. Rabbit is a lot like chicken if you cook it nicely.

Once we went away for the weekend to Cobar in New South Wales and stayed with one of Sid's relatives – an old Trapper, who lived in a small shack on a block of land. Sid and Jean sat around with the Trapper, drinking and yarning while Rob and I went out shooting ducks and trapping rabbits to sell.

There were small holes in the fences where the rabbits had pushed through the wire netting, and we put a wire with a slipknot on it, so when the rabbit ran through the hole, the slipknot tightened, and it was caught. If you were lucky, you could pick the rabbit up the next day if the foxes did not get to them first! It was big business and quite profitable for those who were successful – about $1.60 dollars a pair. Buyers with freezer vans would buy the pairs of rabbits to sell in the towns and cities.

One day Sid, Jean, Rob, and I went to Mansfield to the ski slopes. We left early in the morning and returned late at night after spending most of the time frolicking in the snow. It was a good day.

We – the family, naturally had a few arguments because drink always starts arguments. We either drank at home or at the local pub. The family started singing every time they drank beer, which was often. I joined in as well, and at the same time recorded the family singing and then played it back to them. They loved it – it was a novelty. They would listen to themselves then have a couple more swigs of beer and start singing all over again – all the old Australian songs. Jean particularly loved singing 'Your Cheatin' Heart.' All she needed to get started was a few drinks. Sid had a favourite one that he used to break out into: 'When Shep was a Pup and I was a boy, we grew up together this way....', and 'Bridle Hanging on the Wall.' We all joined in to sing the chorus. It was good fun.

A few times Sid drank too much and 'carried on' a bit. At these times it was obvious that he didn't like Pommy's, and he would often have a go at me. I concluded it was the drink talking and never responded or challenged him. It was also at these times that Jean and he argued. They shouted at each other, and slammed doors, but there was no physical violence between them. They obviously loved each other, and their children, and had brought them up well principled.

However sometimes Jean couldn't stand anymore and said she had 'had enough' announcing, 'that's it, I've had it, I'm leaving'! When she left a sombre mood came over the house. But it always amazed me as she'd leave one day at the weekend and as I understood it, go to her sisters' house. But by Monday morning without fail, she was back at the home rising early to make the lunch for us all to take to work and everything was back to normal – until the next time.

They were a *really,* good Australian family. They enjoyed family life. One, sad to say, that I had never experienced. Being part of their family for a short time before going to Seymour to take up work in the Army was something I treasured.

...The date today is the 27th of May 1968. Here I am at Puckapunyal Army camp, seven miles outside Seymour. I managed to get a job here as a steward which means looking after the officers who eat in the officers' mess. There are two other stewards besides me. One's Italian, and one's Polish. There are a few Englishmen here working. I get 20 pounds a week, and I think it costs me 3 pounds a fortnight to live. Good food, as much as I'd like, and I have a small room here.

...My room is about 12 yards by 10. There is a desk, two wardrobes, chest of drawers, a bed, reading lamp over the bed, two windows with curtains, and a strip of carpet about a yard wide and three yards long on the side of the bed. The television room in the big army hut is partitioned off and I can watch TV there whenever and the duty room is next door.

. It was here that Jeff and I, along with heaps of other civilians and soldiers watched history being made – that is, we saw *Lionel Rose* win the world bantamweight title.

...I get four days off every fortnight and all my clothes and uniform are provided. I have to wear black trousers with a red stripe down the side and a white coat with silver buttons, the perfect attire for what was, in essence, the ideal uniform of a professional waiter. I have to lay a full table for them every day. Two knives, two forks, bread and butter plates, cups, saucers, pot of cold water, pot of tea, solid silver teapots, incidentally. They really live well here. I managed to get Jeff a job here. I know Jeff quite well from the time I spent with him in Benalla and his family. It was very lucky really, because most of the people working here seem to be Italian. It's like when I was working at Benalla for the 23rd Battalion Army Company stationed in Melbourne. I enjoyed working there, and it was great fun looking after all the young cadets. I wasn't in the Officers' Mess, but in the General Mess, which was a true mess after the children had finished eating! We used to have to clear up for about 300 of them – wipe the tables down and serve the food.

...Today I went into town as I was on the shift six to three. I hitchhiked in at four. It is quite easy to hitchhike. People were very willing to stop for me. I bought a pair of black shoes and had my hair cut. They stipulate you must wear black shoes, so I bought a pair, for 2 pounds 10 – quite a nice pair and quite comfortable.

...A lot has happened since the beginning of this tape when I came down by the sleeper from Sydney. I told you I spent some time in Melbourne back on the 22nd, and I went to see Bonnie and Clyde, which was quite a good movie and if it comes to the drive-in, maybe you'd both like to go and see it. As I say, it's a very good job here, and I think it's about 18 pounds a week clear. That's keep and everything, and it's only 9 hours a day starting from six to three, and then the 11 to 8, night shift. So, every other day you are off from three in the afternoon

until 11 the following morning. And every 10 days, you have four days off. I think that's pretty-good, really.

...I'm still getting used to the clothing I wear and having to always serve on the left-hand side and take away on the right-hand side also took some getting used to. In the morning I light a fire for the bath. We have a billiard room as well. I have until about 10 to take them their morning tea that consists of toasted sandwiches and, of course, tea. I can choose what I put in the sandwiches. As well as tea they have soup, two ladles of it, and I take the cups and saucers out and take their pot of tea in. And then about 11 we take it all out again. They have dinner at one where I wait on the tables. After dinner, I take the remains, the bowls, and plates, on a trolley into the back. In the afternoon, they have tea at 3:15, which is usually only biscuits or maybe some toasted sandwiches sometimes. At five I take in gherkins, onions, and cheese biscuits. At about half-past six, they have their evening meal. So really, they're looked after damn well, aren't they? Join the army and get fed. Mind you, this is just the sergeants' mess and in the officers' mess, they have wine with their evening meal.

... We still cut up three plates of sandwiches, in the afternoon. The women – wives of the sergeants have a game of tennis Tuesdays and Fridays and expect a cup of tea and sandwiches at about half past three. I did cut the sandwiches for them this afternoon – I just gave them cheese and tomato.

... I'm leading quite a social life really. I go into the pub and have a few drinks with Bill who's one of the cooks and it is where I see the sergeants and talk to them. And then I go up to the barracks, where the troopers stay. I went up there the other night. There's a pub there, and I sometimes go up there and have a few drinks with them. They've got all brick buildings, a beautiful canteen and television room, billiard room, table tennis room and a nice bath.

... Just down the road from here on the way to the barracks there is a big tank factory. They call it a 'tank workshop', where they repair all the tanks, and I believe they probably make them as well. It's quite a big place, as big as your factory at Talke and quite a lot of people work there. When the tanks go out on the ranges, and return without a tread or runner, they repair the tank there. It is the only Army camp in Australia that has the Tank Corps in it. So, all the training done here is for Vietnam and that's why they go out when it's raining, and they have night practices. I think I must have told you on the other tape that they fire at old cars they bring from the wreckers and put down the hill. I understand it's

quite spectacular when a direct hit occurs because the car just disintegrates. There are quite a few bits and pieces of broken cars lying around.

... Well, do you know Tony Hancock's dead? I heard on the News at dinnertime when the sergeants were looking at the television. He was found in his underclothes lying on the bed with tablets beside him. A few weeks ago, he was informed his wife had divorced him. I used to enjoy listening to him, didn't you? And President Kennedy has been assassinated. They're tightening up on firearms in America, aren't they? It's a good thing as well. I don't think guns should be allowed to run around a country like that.

... A soldier was showing me the other day how they stick bayonets into people. They ram them into their stomach, and twist the bayonet and pull it out again, so they break the rib cage as they pull it out. Then they push it up under their ribs to get the heart. Don't think I'd make a very good soldier.

... The average tank now can go through I don't know how many inches of solid steel. And the rifles they use now, if you hide behind a tree, say, about 4-5 foot-wide, the bullet will go straight through the tree. So, I don't think it's much use hiding behind a tree these days if you get shot at. I think these rifles fire about 20 bullets, one after another or singly. Oh, and the bullets now, they enter the body in one little hole, and as they come out the other side they explode. So, you've got a little hole on one side of you and about a 3-foot hole the other side of you. So, wherever they hit you really, you pretty-much die. It just doesn't go through like it used to in the old days – things are a lot more effective now when it comes to killing.

... What else can I tell you about the Army? We'll be going up to Jeff's place again on Friday and stay there for the weekend and probably going out in Benalla. He's quite easy to get on with is Jeff.

... Most of the troopers walk around in their tank suits during the day. They're like a boiler suit, but different. They are green, and they have a strap inside from the shoulders going down to the waist that fixes onto another belt inside the boiler suit, not on the outside, and an ordinary belt that buckles around their waist. The reason is if they're in battle and the tank is burning and they want to lift their mate out from the seat, you've got to pull them upwards. And if you didn't have the shoulders supported by the belt around your waist, it would be very uncomfortable for you and you would probably do yourself an injury. That way you can lift a person up by the shoulders without undue discomfort. That is called the tank suit. Then they have their ordinary khaki drill uniform *that they wear in the evening or if they're going out somewhere. But they're allowed to wear civvies quite a lot now.*

... I'll tell you a funny thing that happened today in the lounge bar. You know there's always a roaring fire in there that I told you about earlier. I was on the early shift this morning, so I made the fire and put the guard in front. Well, about 11 I asked why we had three chairs missing, I reckoned they went over to the officers' mess after they had a party. I always check up on these things and the teaspoons and everything else whereas the others don't seem to bother so much. I walked into the bar to see the barmen, Ray and Barry. As I walked in, they were playing billiards in the billiard room and there was nobody in the bar. And on the carpet was a big piece of wood that had rolled off, and the carpet was alight. I told them, while you're playing the house is burning down! We managed to get it back and put out the fire, so everything was under control. Now they've put a big piece of carpet in front of the fire to hide the hole made by the burning log.

... Getting back to guns and the tank corps. I asked a medic does anybody get seriously injured with shrapnel when they're blowing up cars and God knows what else? He told me the only accident is when they squash their finger as they're pushing the bullets in. There's nothing ever very serious. I imagine they wait until they go to Vietnam before they get hurt. All of them from here go over to Vietnam and quite a few come back here again. They told me that they're only allowed to stay over there about nine months because the continuous fear affects their health, and they could develop mental problems.

It was a dangerous time to be a soldier in Australia. There were increasing number of soldiers being killed in Vietnam. Whilst it was reported that the Government was looking to retreat from the war, it had not yet occurred. Public protests continued.

I would not like to be a soldier.

Chapter 15
Aussie Mates

Jeff and I left the army camp at Puckapunyal after a few months. We decided to apply for work on the railways around Benalla and headed down to Head Office, Melbourne to sign up.

We were assigned to the labouring gang that was replacing the rotted sleepers along part of main Melbourne to Sydney railway from Benalla to Albury. The gang of about 10 people slept in 'bug huts' – railway carriages made specifically for housing gangs working on the railways. They were positioned on the sidings of the railway line. The 'bug huts' were named because of the variety of bugs they contained. They had four bunks and a cooker that was an old-fashioned stove with a chimney. The wood was thrown off to the bug huts from trains passing by. There was normally a cook who doubled as a camp orderly to look after the possessions whilst the gang was out working. We lived reasonably well, but it was really hard work laying the sleepers.

There was no machinery with automatic jaws and hydraulics that pull out the sleeper and put in a new one. The gang used brute force using a pick, shovel, hammer, and a crowbar with a forked end. Two people worked together to remove the sleeper. The big crowbar was used to shove under the bolts – two bolts each end of the sleeper [called 'dogs']. The crowbar prized the bolts up, and then with the shovels we removed the gravel from either side of the sleeper before using a pick, and with one mighty swipe stuck the pick into the old sleeper and heaved and pulled it out. Then you cleaned out the bed where the sleeper lay so you could slide the new sleeper in. Once the sleeper was in, you used the auger to drill two holes in either end of the sleeper and then belted the bolt in. After this, you replaced the gravel either side of the sleeper before going on to the next sleeper. The good part was when the train was coming through – we had to stop work and take a rest.

You might say how did we know a train was coming? Well, we weren't going to be run over – we were smart on the railways! The foreman of the gang clipped three small round detonators to the line at intervals so that when a train ran over them it caused a small explosion that slightly shook the train. When the train driver heard three explosions in quick succession, he knew that a couple of hundred yards up the line there were people working. As well as this, we knew the timetables of the train. If all that failed, you could hear the train rumbling towards you, and you would jump to safety.

Sometimes Rob and I got weekend work that consisted of carting lengths of rail on a long, flat bed train truck with cranes, and dropped them off beside the track for the specialised gang of men – welders and fitters to lay the new tracks during the week. We travelled quite a few miles with these flat railway trucks.

The old gauge railway lines were very short. When you went on a train you heard clickety-clack, clickety-clack, clickety-clack every time the train passed over a joint in the track. There were songs written to match the rhythm of the train tracks. It was quite a romantic sound and experience when you went on the old steam trains and heard the whistle blowing and saw the smoke and the soot going past your window. If you were adventurous and opened the window, the 'smut' from the engine would gush in. Railway stations were covered in soot and grime, unlike the sparkling railway stations now. Now when you go on a train, you hear no clickety-clack because the railway lines are quite long, and where before they were simply bolted together, they are now welded tight.

Our hard-working day was punctuated with lunchtime and 'smokos'. A good day was when it rained, because we didn't do anything except play cards. Even though we were paid for sitting around, it wasn't profitable for me. Because when it rained, we scrambled into the truck that had driven us to the site we were working and played cards! Mind you, we didn't bet big, more cents than dollars, but in the-course of a day if you weren't very lucky, you could lose quite a lot of money. So, I'm glad that it didn't rain much! Playing cards in wet weather was common – I did this also in England when I was working for the council laying sewerage pipes.

Jeff and I returned to Benalla at the weekends. Usually the whole family went to the local pub and had a sing-along and a few beers, and then 'kicked on' at home after closing time.

We continued working for the railway and completed 20 or 30 miles along the rail track, and then, the gang in another town took over and did the rest. Jeff decided to move on, to other work. I was offered some fencing work with the railways and decided to stay on.

Three years earlier, in 1965, Violet Town and other areas of Victoria had a lot of very bad fires. All the fencing along the track I had just worked on replacing the old sleepers had been destroyed during these fires and had not been replaced. The old sleepers I had prized out, now had wire run through them and made into a fence. This fence was between Longwood and Violet Town.

Charlie was the other fencer – only two of us. We shared a 'bug hut' at Violet Town – there was no cook allocated for this type of job. The way we got the provisions was via the 'tea and sugar train' that came once a week. This train pulled up at the station sidings all along the railway line and people came to greet it, so they could buy eggs, flour, and other basics. It was really a grocery shop on wheels. We had to cook our own food, but there again, the firewood was dropped off to us.

Violet Town had quite a big train shunting area and we watched these being shunted – it was good fun. We watched the great lengths of goods trains that were parked there for days and then, suddenly they disappeared. It was a quiet existence, apart from the trains. We stayed in the 'bug hut' during the week, and both went to our respective homes at the weekend.

It was a monotonous sort of job, really. We had a tractor and a posthole digger and a heap of sleepers. We used the posthole digger to put in the sleepers, and then with a brace and bit we drilled the appropriate holes. We ran about four plain wires in and out of all the sleepers. We did 10 or 20-meter lengths at a time, and we put barbed wire on the top row. We did that day in and day out and covered quite a distance.

...The scenery around here is very nice. The hills have a lot of trees. I can imagine, especially around here, what a devastating effect the fires must have had. But other than a few scorched trees here and there, the countryside seems to have picked up quite well. Victoria seems to be a very advanced state.

...I hear that New South Wales is having a little bit of trouble as far as its bush fires go. It's very early to have fires up there in New South, but I was talking to somebody the other day, and they were telling me that it's very dry in New South Wales. You never know, the tables might be turned this year, and the farms up there will be sending their cattle down to Victoria for agistment like we had to do last year.

... I might be a little bit biased in saying the train service here in Victoria is excellent. However, the New South Wales railways are quite good. We have the Spirit of Progress and all the other ones that go straight through to Sydney, and they're quite nice. I come by train every week from Benalla on my rail pass, which is worth about 25 shillings because it's 40 miles away from Benalla. I usually have a quite comfortable trip down. I catch the 8:43 train on a Monday morning and hitchhike back on a Friday night.

Despite having a free railway pass, I hitchhiked back to Benalla at weekends – I couldn't be bothered waiting for a train, and hitchhiking was simple, and people were willing to stop and give a lift.

... It's a wet windy day and we can't work when it was pouring with rain. I have just got my recorder back from being fixed and am taking the opportunity to start a tape to you as Charlie is not here. He went home last Thursday with a bad back, and he hasn't turned up this morning.

... I'll tell you what we did this weekend. Maybe it accounts for Charlie not being here today. Charlie was 21 last Wednesday so we had a couple of beers. Thursday, he went home, and he invited Rob and I to his 21st on Saturday. We went, but I must admit, it was a very weak 21st. It was more like a family gathering than a party. But Charlie hasn't turned up today...so maybe the party took on a different atmosphere after we left!

... He's always been a bit strange, very quiet, and we never share our food – I'd like to, but he doesn't seem interested. He does his own cooking and I do mine. But I've been all right. I've been doing a bit of work by myself, and I've been thinking of ways of how I can make some more money.

I had a lot of fun on the weekends when I returned to the family. I did a lot of things with Jeff and Rob initially, and then mainly with Rob. My tape to my parents outlines life and ventures to establish and get on, and the rivalry and different approaches between us – even in relation to tax paid, or not, as the case may be.

...I've no doubt told you before about Jeff's family. ... Sid –his father – not a bad fellow – he drinks a bit, but he's not that bad if you know how to understand him and Jean his mother who is a very nice woman. Then there is Janine his

younger sister who is quite a nice girl and has a friend named Jean who is English. They're about the same age and go around together, to the dances and everywhere else. Jeff and Rob – you've heard a lot about them, and then Ron comes into the picture because he married the older sister, Lorraine. ... Ron, the brother-in-law bought a truck and he and Jeff were chopping up wood and trying to sell wood around the town. But Ron is making the same as I am in my rail job, but outlaying a lot of money, I think 400 pounds or something for the truck which he's paying off, and the saw and everything else needed for this wood-chopping venture. I don't think they're going to make a terrible lot of money out of it. I said to Rob 'what you want to do, is make money without outlaying any.'

... I'm on a campaign to make money. I want to buy a Falcon car when I come to see you in Queensland, and then travel to Western Australia – I haven't been there yet.... The last two weeks I have had an ad in the local newspaper for weekend work. I think it goes something like this, 'two young men require weekend work gardening, land clearing, and experience in dairying'. Rob hasn't had any experience in dairying, so I put down I've had eight years' experience, and he's had three. I told him he could bluff it out. We got a reply this week, and we did six hours work on Saturday and we made 4 pounds each which was very good.

... Ron said he wouldn't lower himself to do gardening, but as I told him, the money is the same colour, and he must take into consideration that the money you get from gardening is free of tax. And where else can you work for 15 shillings an hour and have a clear profit? If you do overtime on the railways or anything, you're taxed on it – the government still has their share of it.... Rob and I are the doing the gardening. Jeff doesn't drink, and Ron doesn't drink much while Rob and I both like a drink. It gets us into more strife than not. But we're not drinking half as much now. We've 'turned-over' a new leaf now that we're doing the gardening. I think that's how drinking less came about. Rob's a very good worker. He worked very hard when we did the gardening this Saturday. In fact, he works as hard as I do. You see we both play hard, and we both work hard.

... Strangely enough, Rob's very quiet, really. He listens to me rave on every so often. I can never argue with him because he just doesn't answer back. If I ask him something, he'll say maybe, perhaps, could be. He never gives a direct answer. He reminds me of Tony in that respect, because with Tony, any question and you will never get a straight answer. We get on all right, though, maybe

because he's quiet and I'm noisy, but both shy. The only time we start chasing after girls is when we've had a few beers. We went to Euroa last Sunday and on the way home from the pub, started talking to a couple of girls who were riding horses beside the road. Trouble is they were only about 16, which is a bit young really, isn't it, but they were quite nice.

Rob and I roamed around and went to all the local pubs – Euroa, Benalla, Winton, and Glenrowan – Ned Kelly country. We met a couple of local Euroa girls – Glenda and her friend. I took Glenda, an office worker out a few times and even had Sunday lunch at her parents, after which time we watched the 'footy show' on television. Never a sports fan, this was boring to me. Glenda drove a mini-minor car and we went to a local drive-in. We also 'necked' in the surrounding bush – at a favourite spot like a lot of other courting couples. We were kissing and cuddling, and the car was shaking a little, and suddenly, someone looked in the window! We got embarrassed and moved to another spot. Once, her father, a farmer, said to me, 'the mini is a bit small to go to the drive-in, here, take my car'. We did, and I thanked him, as it was a very nice gesture. Her mother and father encouraged the relationship. Tony was also thinking that I might finally be settling down and bought a wedding present! But I was not ready for any commitment and backed off. The relationship fizzled out and I continued to roam around the area. But Glenda and I would catch up with each other again – later.

The Glenrowan pub had a large painting of Ned Kelly, the famous bushranger on the wall. Ned's image in his armour had been painted *directly* onto the wood inside wall of the pub. Many people came to the pub to see this this unusual 'painting'. It was after drinking in this this pub that the following occurred. So much for my campaign to make money – It should've included a campaign to retain money!

...I was driving Rob's car one night coming back from the pub, and I sideswiped the car, taking off the passenger door...it didn't help my expenses, and Rob was not happy with me. But I was very lucky in a lot of ways. The car cost me quite a lot of money but that was through my own carelessness. It's the first accident I've had, so maybe I can be excused this once seeing I was the one who suffered financially because of it. In any case, it's no use talking about spilt milk, and I expect a lot-of-things have happened in both our lives where we can

say well, if I hadn't had done that, things might have been better. But that is done and in the past. Now I've settled the bill and ready to start off from scratch again.

... On a lighter note, last week Rob and his friend from his school days and I went down to the Melbourne Show. I'd never been to the Melbourne Show, and Rob and his friend hadn't been either, so we decided we'd go and see exactly what goes on there. I'm afraid I was a bit disappointed, and it didn't come up to the standards of the shows at home. I still think the Staffordshire was a very good show. In any case, we got up at six in the morning and arrived in Melbourne at about nine. We stayed at Rob's relatives place for the night, which saved us a night's lodgings.

... We went into the show and got there about noon. Like Lunar Park, they had big wheels and big dippers and the mad mouse, which I braved again. I'm sure I must have been a fool because I closed my eyes all the time and wished for it to finish. Then I went to go on another ride that you go right up in a cage and a big wheel sort of thing, turns it round, and that's where I really had to draw the line. There are some things I won't do. But I looked round for the dairy section, and there wasn't a very big one, and there weren't any dog trials which I could see there. We did see the wood chopping. We had a quick look at the dairy section, and really, that pretty-well covered it.

... We returned home on Sunday night. This week I've been fencing down in Longwood still, putting on the droppers, the pieces of wood that you put on between the posts.

... Quite a lot has happened. About three weeks ago we went out trapping, Rob, and I, and we caught 14 pairs of rabbits. We stayed out all night. It was quite an experience setting the traps. As you can probably imagine, the bit I didn't like was going around in the morning, catching the poor rabbit, and wringing its neck. I'm a bit of a coward when it comes to killing things, being a peace-loving person at heart. Rob said to me, 'Get hold of their neck just between their eyes. Put one finger either side of the eyes. Twist the neck and pull down and it breaks their neck.' The first one I did, I almost pulled his head off his shoulders!

... I really don't like killing things. It brings back the memory of the time we tried to kill the ducks in England. That was years ago... I only hope Rob will never ask me to gut them, because I couldn't possibly do that.... But when the killing was done, Rob said, 'Right, you've got to gut them now.' I won't go into that, but I thought if he can do it, I could do it. So altogether, I gutted 28!!... But *the ferret is quite a funny thing. You put the nets over the holes and then you send the ferret down. You have to-be very quiet and nobody speaks a word. A rabbit pokes his head up, and it's a race to see who gets there first to catch the rabbit. It's fun trying to catch the rabbits... We seem to eat quite a lot of rabbit. I suppose all the rabbits that had been caught have to be eaten, and on weekends we've gone out rabbiting we've caught a lot.... But I found that by the time the family had the rabbits, and we gave a few away, it wasn't all that profitable, so we decided to put an advertisement in the newspaper....This week has been good because we managed to do a little bit of weekend work that keeps us both out of trouble. I will put the ad in again this week and see what happens.*

... I suppose I'd better start from the beginning...I put in for a transfer onto another railway gang where there were more people, but I didn't get it, so I decided to give it away. In any case, it's not the best job. It was an easy one, I didn't have to work very hard.... I hitchhiked back to Benalla. I asked the driver who picked me up if he knew of any hay carting or any other work around. I was

in luck – he put me in touch with one farmer that had 25,000 bales to cart all in one go which is a lot, isn't it...? I got the job and was paid a cent and a quarter for carting the hay bales that works out I think to about 6 pounds to 1,000. Yesterday we managed to cart in 1200 bales working 12 hours from six to six. The haymaking is different when you're doing it as a job to the haymaking I remembered doing back home. There you had a load come in and sat on the stack for about an hour drinking tea and biscuits. Here we have to go flat out and every minute lost is a penny lost sort of thing. It's hard work but I hope it will pay dividends in the end.

... The farmer is getting one of these new-fangled machines on Wednesday that makes large rectangle hay bales. I'm working with Ray, about 18 and Tex, about 27, whose real name is John, but they call him Tex because he dresses like a 'cowboy'. He goes around to the rodeos off – hay making season and rides everything in the rodeo. He's a very interesting person to talk to. So Tex and Ray and I are teamed with a truck and a driver. Tex is on the truck's tray and Ray and I walk alongside the truck with a pitchfork and throw the bales up to him. We get about 110 on a load and bring it back and put it in the hay barn. Some of the bales were heavier than others, and in this case, two people needed to work together to pitch it up.

After this hay carting job, Ron, Rob, Jeff, and I teamed up – one driving Ron's truck, one stacking and two pitching. We split the amount we were paid five ways and included the truck as an extra 'fellow' as we had to put petrol in the tank and pay for wear and tear. The farmers paid about nine cents a bale, and we carted three or four loads a day around Benalla. It was quite good money. Sometimes when work ran out for our team, I went hay carting for other people.

At some farms I worked, there was a hay sledge pulled behind the baler that collected 4 bales before releasing them. This made it a lot easier because the truck just drew up to the four bales and we pitched them onto the truck, before moving onto the next heap of bales. We had to make sure the bales weren't pressed too tight or wet as this made them heavy. All we had for tools was a pitchfork that we'd push into the bale then lift it up over our shoulders and push it onto the stacker. We took turns in stacking and turns in driving the truck. When we got to the hayshed, it was a lot easier if there was a conveyor to take the bales up to the levels to stack.

I had a bit of bad luck hay carting:

... I got a hayseed in my ear. I'm not joking, it was as if someone was playing a violin in my ear but without the pleasure associated with listening to a fine violinist. It kept twitching and was so annoying. I tried to get it out with a cotton wool bud, but it wouldn't budge. I had to go to the doctor, and with a pair of

tweezers, he managed to get it out. But it was no fun having a hayseed in my ear!... You know how the husks of hay stick out? Well, I scratched my eye on one. It was very sore, but I kept working. Then, my vision went fuzzy. I wouldn't have cared if it was my 'bad eye', the one with the poor vision, but it was my 'good eye'. I thought there was something in my eye as there was in my ear, so I went to the Benalla hospital. The doctor couldn't see anything, but said, 'you've scratched the cornea of your eye' He gave me a prescription for some golden eye ointment, and I had to put a large patch on it for a few days to keep the light out and stop any infection. I asked him, 'Can I go to work'? He replied, 'you'll be a bloody fool if you do. You'll end up having a great scar on your eye if you don't look after yourself'! So, I didn't. It was a Saturday and I had to pay $3 for the visit to the hospital.

The hay season ended, and we all had to look for something else to do. The end of the year was coming, and it would soon be Christmas.

... *About a week before Christmas, Jeff, Rob, and I were all out of work. We were talking to someone in the pub, and by chance, we all managed to get a job on a building site – a motel was being built at Winton, about 7 miles outside Benalla. We worked there for about four days, right up until Christmas Eve. ... The builder was Sam McManus, a Scotsman. Well, you know, Scotsmen are noted for being tight-fisted, aren't they? But, on Christmas Eve he put on an eighteen-gallon keg for the men. Jeff didn't go because he doesn't drink. Rob and I went out there, and started drinking, and the next minute the Scotsman's mother and father drew up with chicken, salads and a real feast followed. We didn't feel all that hungry because we'd just had a feed. Sam said, 'you've got to eat it. If you don't eat it, the flies will.' So, we sculled the keg and on top of that we had chicken and everything else. He was the first boss I've ever worked for who's given me something for nothing. We only worked for him for four days, but he was a really-good boss.*

After the keg had finished, Rob and I went back to the pub in Benalla and continued drinking. We both had way too much to drink – I was happy, but Rob became 'stroppy' with a fellow on the footpath outside of the pub after closing time. I could see that Rob was getting serious – way more than I had seen him before. He took off his coat and asked me to hold it for him. But I was carrying on 'like a two-bob watch' as well and at the same time saying to Rob, 'just let it be'. Then, suddenly, out of nowhere two policemen appeared and when I looked around, Rob and the other fellow had disappeared! I was left there, singing loudly, and holding Rob's coat. I had not seen the police arrive, or the others disappear.

The next thing I was bundled into the paddy van and I ended up in the lock-up – still singing. The police told me when they let me out the next morning, Christmas morning; I was the happiest drunk they had ever locked up! They said to me, 'Do you have the money for the fine? 'No', I replied, 'I spent it all last night'. 'Alright' they said… 'We'll take you home and one of your friends can pay the fine for you.' This they did, and I paid them back. Luckily, I never had to go to court. On the sedate tape I sent home describing Christmas to my parents I simply said: *'Christmas Day was a quiet one. We had Christmas dinner and pudding. I think the meat was chicken.'* Some things were best not shared.

Selecting stories to record on tape to send to my parents was repeated time, and time, again over the next few years. For example:

… I'll just go to the post office to see if there are any letters from you.… It's nice to know that you are 'chugging' along all right in Queensland. Tony told me in a letter that your home renovations are now finished, and it was nice to see all your ornaments around.…Thank you for my birthday present. I am glad you got the Bentley fixed – it's about 30 years old now, isn't it?… One day I will have to go back to the old country to see what is going on there.

But some things shared were poignant:

… You're a little bit better letter-writer than I am; but I hope that you don't think that I will forget you down here. I like to think that you will always be there for me to go to…. Somebody said to me, 'it's funny you never talk about your parents or home or anything'. I had an answer for them… 'I never talk about things that are closest to my heart.' It is something that is mine, and I don't want to share it with anybody. It's one of the things that I want to hang onto.

And this, a reflection on possibilities for the future:

… I must write a book one day about my experiences, it might be a best seller! Ha, ha [laughed on the tape at the thought of this]!

I didn't know at this time that the path I was following – hard working, hard playing, hard drinking and having an occasional 'brush' with the law would become a pattern for me and intensify over the next 5 years.

Chapter 16
Bright Lights

1969 was looming. Official records of that year list the following occurred:

...Moon walking, Johnny Farnham declared 'King of Pop', Lionel Rose made Australian of the year; the nudity in the musical 'Hair' offended; a number-of people died in bushfires in Victoria; the Southern Aurora crashed head-on with a goods train at Violet Town and nine people died. Lang Hancock announced that colour television produced far more dangerous radiation than any nuclear device, and the government decided that an Australian would be an 'Australian Citizen' rather than an 'Australian Citizen and British Subject'. A Glenrowan publican said that bringing Mick Jagger to Australia to play Ned Kelly was like sending Normie Rowe to England to play Robin Hood except that Normie was a decent bloke. And the Vietnam War was 'inevitably moving towards an unpredictable end at an indefinite date'.

Sydney is a long way from Benalla. Rob and I did not intend to end up there when we set out for a drive on New Year's Eve 1968. But end up there we did, with dire consequences when we got there.

...I'll have to tell you how we got up to Sydney. You know whatever we do, we do on the-spur-of the moment. Rob and I were both at home in Benalla and decided we'd go out for an afternoon drive as we've done many times before. It was New Year's Eve.... We decided to go up to Albury and let the New Year in with Sid, a good hay-carting mate who worked on the Country Road Board and drove one of these big graders. His camp was about 15 miles this side of Albury near Coburg. He wasn't there, so we stopped at the nearby pub. It was a very dusty day and very, very hot. We washed the dust off and decided to head for Tarcutta. We kept stopping, and when we got to Tarcutta, we filled up with petrol

and kept going, and soon it was 10 to 12 midnight. Well, have you ever heard of anybody driving through the New Year? No, you haven't. Most people celebrate or sleep through it but not us.... We stopped at a nice little pub – somewhere on the main road. Rob said we could afford $2 to see in the year. I hope next year is a bit better. We had a few beers with the fellows. And it was very good because you can kiss all the girls at New Year! It's the only time you can kiss them all... ten minutes after New Year, they slap you in the face when you try to do the same thing!

... We stood out in the main street and sang Auld Langsyne and then we went in and had a few more beers. It was a real 'beaut' place and the publican put on quite a feast for us. We were glad about that because we hadn't any money to buy any tucker, so we both tucked into what was on offer. We left about two, a bit happier than when we got there. By this time, the $10 was out of my boot.

... We forgot all about Rob's family at home in Benalla. I then remembered I had a brother in Lismore and thought I ought to go and see him. It's his birthday tomorrow. But we didn't, and I forgot to call him for his birthday.

... Anyhow, we only drove about 5 miles down the road before Rob said I think we might as well have a sleep. Fair enough I thought. He pulled the car over and slept. He sat on one side, and I on the other. The next thing it was seven in the morning. It was the best night's sleep I've ever had in my life!

... We discovered we were 140 miles this side of Sydney. So, if you know a little town, 140 miles this side of Sydney, that's where we stopped. When we got into Sydney, we decided we'd better make a phone call back to Rob's family in Benalla because they still thought we were out for an afternoon drive! When you don't turn up by seven the next morning after being out, people are just liable to get worried. So, we stepped into a phone box for a 'quick' call that took us half an hour to make! In any case, we wished the operator a happy New Year and had quite a chat and we wound up sending a telegram, which cost 80 cents or something, just for a telegram!

We got to Sydney and found Rob's friend's house and he offered us accommodation for a couple of nights. Then, of course, we all went out to the pub. Rob was driving the car and we'd had a few beers to celebrate New Year.

... Bill is an old friend of Rob's. We used to go trapping up in Nymagee together. He's married now, and he's got a nice son called Shane. We stayed with Bill and Ann, his wife, and his parents while we were in Sydney. It's very nice having a place to stay. It is in a suburb called St. Peters, about 4 miles outside Sydney, on the Melbourne side.

... Sydney isn't a place where you want to start 'stirring the possum' because they're not at all friendly. Not like the friendly police in Benalla or up in Nymagee which was where we were heading and hoping to get work before we ended up in Sydney. We had an advantage – Rob has a car, so, you never know where we might end up. But unfortunately, the trouble we got into cost him his license.

On the way back to Bill's house after having a few beers, we heard police car sirens go off loudly behind us. Rob pulled over. The policemen said, 'Wind down your window please. We've been following you for a few miles, and we see that you keep veering into the other lane over the white line. Would you mind getting out of the car and having a breathalyser.' Rob blew into the breathalyser and, he was well over .05. 'You'll have to leave the car now and come to the station with us – you're over the limit here in New South Wales.' Before we knew where we were, Rob was at the police station being charged with drink driving and he was locked up for the night!

Suddenly, the New Year of 1969 had taken a very bad turn. I asked the policeman, 'How can we get him out?' He replied, 'You have to pay his bond, which is $100.' I queried, 'Why do we have to pay $100 – so much? He hasn't even been charged?' They answered, 'He's an interstate traveller that's why – we might never see him again once he's let out. So, pay up or he'll stay in gaol.'

I couldn't leave Rob in gaol – I wouldn't be able to face his parents. But we didn't have any money between us. So, I made a call home to my parents and asked them to lend me $100 and I would pay them back. They deposited it in my bank account, and I paid the fine and got Rob out of gaol, but by the time this had happened, Rob had spent two nights in gaol. $100 in 1969 was a lot of money. It bought Rob freedom for a short time, pending summons.

... With all our trials and tribulations, Bill and his girlfriend put us up and fed us and gave us a bed, and we were there for about a week. I don't think I'll ever forget St. Peters or Newtown. Newtown reminded me of the TV show Z-Cars. The police station there was called Newtown. They say that these coppers on the TV act the same as those in real life. No, it wasn't the same. They're a lot rougher in real life.

... Luckily, Rob only spent Friday night in gaol, so Saturday we could go sightseeing in Sydney. We went to Bondi Beach, which is quite a famous spot. As Bill said, all the film stars go there, although we didn't see any film stars when we were there. We got there by about eleven and spent an enjoyable three hours frolicking in the surf. Just like old times as far as I was concerned. It was a nice day that we spent at the famous Bondi Beach, despite the absence of any movie stars.

... On the way back, we watched the Opera House being built and marvelled at the size and shape of it. There was a lot of controversy about the building and

the cost – well worth the expense I thought. We came back, and tea was waiting for us. So, we had tea and a good sleep. Sunday, we spent a quiet day at home looking at the telly and doing nothing much, which makes for a good life, I suppose. Monday Rob had to appear at court at ten where the judge passed his sentence. Rob had his license suspended but he could return to Victoria where a summons would be sent to him to attend court there.

... Tuesday, which brings us up to today, we left this morning about nine heading towards Bathurst that, as I said before, is about 143 miles inland from Sydney.... We're at a little place called Orange at-the moment. It's a funny name for a place isn't it, Orange? You'd think they grow tons of oranges here, but they don't. I haven't seen one orange here yet. In any case, we thought we'd get a good night's sleep and book in one of these pubs around here. We went to all the pubs. The cheapest one was $5 each. We decided that was too much for even the best of us, and we slept in the car that night.

... I expect if you have the map of New South Wales there, you can probably find it. You've probably got more idea where Orange is at-the moment than I have. We had good intentions tonight. We've had a good meal, and we stopped driving and parked the car and went off to find the employment exchange. There was nothing there, so we forced ourselves to go into the hotel and hoped that in the morning we'd find a job at the slaughterhouse. I hope it's not killing the poor old cows that I've tried to keep alive for so many years, but if it is, I guess I can turn my hand to it.

... We had a swim at Orange, a very good swim in a nice swimming pool. We bought a pair of jeans, a 'T shirt' and a pair of swimming togs because we needed to get clean and couldn't find a shower. So, we thought the best thing to do would be to go for a swim. We didn't leave Orange until about eleven and kept heading west.

... After leaving Orange, we kept going and went through a couple of small towns where we had a little refreshment, and we ended up at Wellington. The next day there was nothing going on at all, so we decided to keep plodding on. We stopped at another little town between Dubbo and Orange and had another swim. Last night we ended up at Dubbo and slept in the car again. This morning we kept heading further west because there's no work wherever you go. So, we kept going through to Dubbo along the same road, through Warren and Nyngan. We could see where the bushfires had been up in the hills. After Nyngan we had the choice of going either to Bourke or Cobar. We know Cobar, so we ended up there about ten this morning. We had a few beers in Cobar, and they told us there was no work there. We then decided to go to Nymagee because we both had a good time in Nymagee trapping rabbits about three months ago. I must say it's better than staying at Sydney. You might have dirt roads, but you've got a little bit of country around you, and it's better than having cars zooming past you, which they did in Sydney.

...We met quite a good fellow, called Jim. We had a few beers with him at a little place between Cobar, just off the Cobar Road. On the way to Nymagee we had a few more beers there and met another nice person, and we had another few beersbeer with him. That's the trouble when you're in the country. You meet so many friendly people, and you just cannot help stopping and having a few beers with them.

... They wouldn't know if you have a license or not here in the country. It's the best place to be, I can assure you. As Rob just pointed out to me, we're near Rankin's property, which is about 15 miles square. It's a great, huge place, really.... We have good intentions about getting work and will probably have to follow the coast again and go down to Warren, but who knows when you get this far up country what you're going to do? We might get a license and go roo shooting, which is quite probable. I suppose now we're about eight miles from Nymagee. When we get there, we'll go and see Rob's Pop – the Trapper who I told you we met before.... Maybe tonight we'll find a bed at Rankin Farm. Like most of the properties out here, they're big. There are plenty of rabbits. You'll never go hungry out here if you've got a gun.

... We went up to Nymagee. We only stayed there a couple of hours and then decided we would hit the road again. We got about 20 miles the other side of Nymagee where we spent the night in the car again, and then set off for Katoomba which is on the way to Griffith. Katoomba is quite a big place. We didn't get any work there. We went in for a swim like we did all along the line. It's a nice way of having a bath, isn't it? I don't think I ever told you. We went to Bondi Beach when we were in Sydney. There are a lot of people there. Any case, we got in and had a swim. We were there for about three hours. Maybe I did tell you about that, now that I think about it but, in any case, I've now told you twice!

... After going to Katoomba, we decided we were going to head for Griffith, which is a bit further than Sydney. It's still inland a lot, and we went through West Wyalong. We ended up at Griffith at four after looking for work all along the line. I must say of all the places we ended up at, this seems to be the most hopeful place for finding work. There are big orange groves here, and there are apricots and grapes and a lot of other things. When we got to Griffith, we decided there is no use sleeping in the car because we've slept in the car already four nights and we were determined to find a bed no matter what. Well the same old story. We went to several of the hotels and most of them were about $9 for the two of us. So, we decided we'll go to a motel, which is cheaper and that is where we are at-the moment – a motel in Griffith. It's a very nice place. I wish we could live like this all the time. We're in one of the suites here. Carpet on the floor and two nice twin beds and air conditioning. We had a meal this evening. The T-bone steak covered the plate. At-the moment we feel pretty good and especially after the experiences of the past week which seem to be way behind us, and we hope we'll have a good night's sleep.

... We booked in here about 6:00 and had a shower and shave after which we felt a lot better and washed some of that Cobar dust off us. We went down to have a meal in the dining room, and decided we'd go along and have a couple of beers at the hotel. We went there and asked if there was any work available. The prospect of finding work at Griffith seems to be pretty-good and we certainly hope we'll get work. I suppose we haven't had a holiday for a while. But we've seen a lot of places. As you know, we've come right up through Albury, Goulburn, right up to Sydney. From Sydney to Katoomba, Katoomba to Lithgow, Lithgow to Bathurst, Orange right up then into Dubbo, and then across to Cobar that is really in the centre, in the heart I suppose of New South Wales.

... Just as well we didn't go up to Burke – we did think about it – or go to Broken Hill. But then we were thinking about going to Tasmania and even Mt Isa. But somehow, we're heading down again. It would be interesting if you got a map, and you could see the route that we did take. All these little towns are quite big, but there's been no work right through. We must have covered about one thousand miles in the trip that we've done.

Unfortunately, we never did get any work on our trip around New South Wales. We had a great holiday, though, and saw a lot of places that we hadn't seen before, so it was well worthwhile going. And, we had some adventures in Sydney. Unfortunately, it didn't turn out that well for Rob in the end. The summons came, and Rob attended court but was sentenced to gaol in Melbourne for a short time. Rob's parents were very unhappy at what happened, and that Rob was to spend time in gaol. They blamed me as they thought 'I was a bad influence' on him. Rob was never the same after going to gaol. I don't know why; he just wouldn't talk about it. Perhaps something happened to him in gaol? Perhaps he thought he was always beholden to me because of me paying the $100 – but he wasn't, as far as I was concerned, because we had a good time. And that's what mates do – bail each other out when they get into trouble. That was my philosophy at that time.

We settled down again in Benalla and continued the same familiar pattern – hard working and hard playing. However, the tape I sent home to my parents at this time does indicate confronting reality after the trip to Sydney in early 1969.

...Dear Mother and Father... I haven't been working for a while and I sort of had a bit of a holiday and I've got to get back to work. You can't take everything out of life and put nothing back, so that's why I signed on for this job as a labourer here at the Benalla relay station. There is a lot of digging and concreting going on for the underground ducting for cables. The overtime will last for a couple of months, and I should be getting about $50 or $60 a week, which is good money. The thing is I really want to pay off the loan of $100 that you lent me, which was supposed to happen by February. We're nearly in March now.... It doesn't sound very good when you go away for nine months, have a good time and drink pretty-heavily and spend pretty-heavily and then when everything turns out wrong, you turn back to your parents for help... it's not right, it's a defeatist attitude. I'll wait two months and I'd love to come and see

you. Maybe a few years ago I would have gotten a pat on the back and been told never mind dear, everything will be all right and go on my happy way. But it's no good, life isn't like that, that's why I'm still down here working as a labourer. ... I record music on tape, and we all have a singsong at the pub. Of course, they all drink too much, I had my fill of beer, but you tell me an Australian who doesn't drink too much? Every Australian drinks too much I think, either that or the opposite – and the opposites are worse. Oh well.

The work ran out at the power relay station and the money ran out. Rob and I decided to go to Melbourne looking for work. Rob was going to stay at his elderly grandfather's place in Clifton Hill. Rob told me his grandfather didn't like Poms, so I could not stay there. I had to make alternative arrangements. This I did – of a sort.

Here I was in Melbourne again. This period was probably one of the lowest points of my life to date. It was a time when I was not as one with the world and this sense of disorientation and hopelessness is reflected in my recollections of the time. I was, broke, homeless, 'down and out', and friendless.

It's hard to get yourself up when you are *really* 'down and out'. I know. Thank goodness for my trusted reel-to-reel tape recorder which would soon become much more to me than a means to communicate and record my stories.

Chapter 17
Sleeping Rough

It was February 1969, and I was in Melbourne. Since leaving Benalla, my life had spiralled out of control and become disjointed. These were not my finest hours. I went between being homeless, hungry, and down and out, to having a job and room in a boarding house. Again, I only communicated with my parents when I was 'on the up and up'.

... Hello Mother and Father! How nice to be able to talk to you again after such a long time and it was nice having that phone conversation the other night.... Well I managed to get the tape recorder back tonight from a pawnshop which I pawned last week for $30. It was funny because I'd never pawned a thing in my life but then I suppose some of the Thompsons have... the ones we don't talk about.... I expect Uncle James – the one who always roamed around the world... I expect he did. In any case I went to this place, and said 'excuse me can you tell where there is a second-hand dealer'? He looked at me and replied, 'you want a pawnbroker mate, go down the road to Tilly's, get a good price as well if you've got something to pawn.' 'Thanks a lot' I said, I'll go down and see what they've got to offer.'

... As I said, I've now got a good job here and I worked overtime this week and earned $70 but by the time tax and everything was taken off, it ended up at $58. It's Thursday today, Thursday 6th February 1969, is it 1969, dear oh dear I don't know, I think it's '69 isn't it, it must be '69, yes, fancy that eh. There's such a lot happened, I'm not quite sure of the days.... It was lovely to hear you both. I've only heard the first side of the tape now where you had a nice, homely talk with me and what you say is very true and it was lovely to hear you after such a long time. I really felt as though I was at home. Unfortunately, I'm not; I'm here in Melbourne staying at Clifton Hill.

... The first couple of weeks were a bit hard. I slept in the park a couple of nights, and at the Salvation Army... Salvation Army for unwanted men or something. It was a terrible place where all the drunks and the people who broke out of gaol were there too. I will tell you more about that later. You can get a bed there for 4/6d and if you don't have that you can get one for nothing, which is very good....

I lived on milk a lot but, in any case, that was the past. I managed to get the milk on credit, $5.50 a week, which is a bit dear. I couldn't get a sub – an advanced wage at work; but luckily, Mick the supervisor lent me $2, and I thought I'd struggle through one way or another.... I thought life's funny...you help all these people to get out of their troubles but when you're lying on the ground with no bed and $2 in your pocket nobody is there to help you – well, somebody's a bloody fool around here aren't they? Because it's the first time I have really hit bottom in the middle of the city, and I thought... I thought well no, never again, am I going to help anybody in my life! And, I don't think I will because it's a horrifying feeling being down and out, and you think less than a month ago that you helped somebody keep out of gaol and now you're pretty-well in a worse position yourself and when you have to scramble up, there's nothing, no-one – just beg and ask for credit, get turned away and go into places where the lowest of the low hang out. It's hard to rise from that but I did, and I retrieved the tape recorder and bought a radio for $4.

... I got the tape recorder back with last week's wages and paid more-or-less $10 something for the room, but in any case, that's enough about what has happened and what I've gone through. As you say, it takes more for a Thompson to go under however low he gets. I'm glad, Tony, you didn't see me, that's the main thing. I would have hated you to see me, in such a perilous, bedraggled way with the down and outs of Melbourne, but even then, there are some stories to be told but I'm afraid I can't tell them. There are some funny people around – that's for sure.

... I slept under a bush in Clifton Hill Park. And about eleven at night, somebody woke me up and said concerned, 'are you all, right?' 'Sorry,' I said, 'I must have just dozed off. I'll go home now.' I jumped up and walked off head held high – the direction didn't matter...and when there was no one around again to see me, I quietly returned to sleeping under the same bush. You had to be very careful sleeping out otherwise you will end up in the 'nick'. I wasn't concerned about getting bashed or robbed, just ending up in the 'nick'.

... I queued up to get a bed at the Salvation Army about ten – it may have been half past eleven. If you sleep out, the chances are the police will pick you up and if you haven't any money or address, they probably will nick you and when you're behind bars, I'm not quite sure when you would get out. In any case I queued up in a long line of people waiting to get in for the night. Of course, standing there, everybody says: 'I don't know, it's not like me really… I don't know, I don't know how I got here.' There was this large fellow slouching around – he had a crew cut and he said to me 'it's better than being in the nick, isn't it?' I don't know, maybe it is, but gee you get to see people. I think there is a number of floors, all crowded with people – the place is full.….I said, 'have you got a bed for me tonight?' 'No mate, we're full', was the reply. 'Oh gee', I said, 'I don't want to sleep outside again.' Maybe sensing my extreme desperation, he then said, 'okay mate… if you want to sleep under the dryer in the laundry in the

basement, you can...and you can have breakfast.' Genuinely relieved I said, 'thanks a lot mate, I really appreciate that.'

The food wasn't bad. I always had breakfast before I left ...that's why I always give to the Salvos because they're one of the few people in my life who have helped me when I was really-down and out. Years later, on my travels, I became friendly with a Salvo who used to come into the pub in Darwin where I was drinking. His name was Steve, and he was always smiling. I'd call him over and offer to buy him a beer as if to repay the debt I felt for the help I had received in Melbourne, but anyone who knows the Salvos, knows they are teetotal, and he always refused my offer of a beer and sculled instead a glass of lemonade. In my half-charged state, I would gently mock his refusal of a glass of beer. I did not appreciate then, that some people who joined the Salvos did so from a background of alcoholism. Steve always replied with a smile and plenty of good cheer that he wasn't reliant on the 'demon drink'. I admired him.

I was desperate to get a job – I never wanted handouts, even in my darkest times.

... I had enough money for the bus fare to the employment exchange. I went to the exchange and I know for a fact that if you keep trying you won't starve in this country... there is work around... I don't think you can starve. I told the woman in the employment office, 'I've got to get a job... I don't care what I do, I've just got to get a job.' She asked what I did, what do I do? I said, 'I'm in Melbourne now but I spent nine months pulling out sleepers in the bush on the railways' and told her all the jobs I had done. I mentioned farming but there weren't any farm jobs in Melbourne.' In any case, she could see I was desperate and said, 'I think there's a job for you... you seem to have had a varied life'. She sent me out to Brownbuilt, a big factory at Northcote on the Thursday and I started work the next day on the Friday. As luck would have it, they wanted me to work all day Saturday and Sunday, double time and time and a half! Then, last week I worked Saturday morning and two nights, so the wages have been pretty-good and, as I said, I got $58 this week and I've still got $58 now, fortunately.

... My job is to assemble the office furniture – like the lockers when you go down to have your game of golf. If there's Brownbuilt written on them, I made them! Just like Meccano. I'm in the assembly lot and I assemble it. It's surprising

all the people I've met in the short time I've worked here.... Being down here in the city, the first week I thought I'd end up being run over or something would happen to me when getting on and off trams. I couldn't remember where I was going when I got on it. Even now when I go to work, if I miss my stop, I keep going straight on and I get to the end and they say, 'we stop here'. Oh, I say, I must have passed my stop. Yes, we go back again in five minutes if you want to stay on. Thanks, I'll have to go back again!

... I've got this room and had a few decent night's sleep. I had a few beers with various people, but the trouble is it is costing me too much to live. What I need is to get into a good routine. I suppose Tony did that when he was in London when he did everything by the clock? I do nothing by the clock.

... I have my routine now.... I get up at quarter past six, am out of the house by half past six, catch the tram at twenty to seven, get to Durban Road in Northcote at seven o'clock and then walk a mile down the road. About half a mile down the road there's a milk bar where I call in, get the paper, buy a bottle of milk and get a ham roll, continue the walk to work, get into work about quarter past seven, sit down, read [look at] the paper, clock on and go to our table to start work at half past seven. The table is about the size of a bed and there are two of us working on the table. Overhead there are two-rivet pop guns that 'pop rivets' into things.

...The bell goes at 10 o'clock, for a tea break. The tea ladies come around with a trolley with cups of tea on it and you can stop for about 30 seconds, almost. Well I suppose more than that.... Then six minutes after 10, the bell goes again, and it's time to start work again.... They won't let you leave the bench until lunchtime.

... At twenty past 12, the bell goes for the dinner [lunch] break – 30 minutes. There's a canteen from which we can buy dinner for three 'bob', or three shillings, and I go up there for a feed, and buy a dessert of peaches or something for an extra 10 cents and I get a bottle of milk as well and that's my dinner.

... At three o'clock the trolley comes around again, and I buy a bottle of soft drink now that I'm financially on the up and up. Well I couldn't go any lower than I was, so I have to rise.

... At precisely six minutes past four the shift finishes and then you clock off. I catch the quarter past four buses back to Northcote and start all over again the next day! Very orderly indeed!

...But I tell you what really upset me the other day... these two people came around to my table. One had a clipboard in his hand, and the other fellow had a time clock. One said, 'We just want to time how long it takes you to pop rivet one of these filing cabinets, so just tell me when you're ready to start, and we'll start the timer off.' I thought that's bloody-annoying having to time us how long it takes us to do it! At the end, they said, 'so then, we anticipate you can make about 20 or 30 of these in the eight hours. Is that correct?' 'Oh probably' I said. So that really got me annoyed because it was such a monotonous job working opposite this one fellow. We didn't talk much because he was Italian. Nice fellow, but it was a boring job.

... It's not a time of joy but it's a life that I can adapt to, as I've adapted to everything. I've adapted to being a pauper, but, then it's funny you know, I'm down and out but I can still mix with the big guns. I mix with the downtrodden as we queue in the dosshouse. Then, later, on the up and up, I sit in a smart restaurant ordering a bottle of wine and liqueurs. It's really a very funny combination. It's the spice of life, I suppose, but when all is said and done, I think what I'd like more than anything now would be to settle down with a nice wife and have a few children. But there again... I wouldn't mind going on a boat as a steward, not a steward, but a purser ... I'd like to do that. It's hard to know what to do... but-in any case I know things are straightening themselves out....

... I was sitting in the park the other Sunday talking with a fellow from the rooms – a Mavis Bramston sort of fellow. Next time you see the Mavis Bramston Show think of me. We talked about the weather mostly I suppose, then I met another fellow, who told me about another boarding house – a nice boarding house for $12 a week, full board. He told me, 'She does your washing for you, and you can watch television at night.' I'm going to move there – it will be much nicer than where I am.

It was a good place, right in the middle of Clifton Hill. I just go up the road to the United Kingdom Pub. Just beyond that there is a nice park, and I could walk down the main street of Clifton Hill. So, it was very central. Especially at weekends, it was good. It was close to the tram. I enjoyed staying there, and stayed there quite some time, even when I left Brownbuilt. It was a lot cheaper living, especially because I had all my meals given to me as well.

… I shared a room with one other person at the boarding house. He snored sometimes which was a bit of a nuisance, but he was a nice enough chap. And, we had all our meals cooked for us. We go down to breakfast in the morning and have a cooked breakfast. And she used to make me sandwiches for lunch – usually baked bean sandwiches. That was another bonus. And in the evening, we would have dinner – main meal and then sweets. Once she asked me, 'Would you like some more sweets love?' I quickly said, 'Yes please'. As she handed the plate over to me, my right eye went off-centre, and drifted into the corner of my eye. 'Oh my God,' she said, 'what's happened to your eye?' It quite upset her! The people in the boarding house were like family and we all helped with the washing up and drying, when the meal was finished.

… I was becoming a regular commuter to work on the tram, and even got to know a few people. One was Tom. He said, 'I know you. You live around here, don't you?' I said, 'Yes, I've got a room down the road there.' He said to me, 'you're the fellow I always see running alongside the tram trying to catch it!'

… Dear Mother and Father… I hope you received the telegram I sent a little while ago asking you to take the tape down to Helen and Tony. I'm sure you will do. In any case, I'd say on this side of the tape hello to Tony and I'm sorry that I've been out of contact with you for a few months and when I did phone you up it wasn't the best conversation. In any case I'll fix that up with you later-on. I did have full intentions of coming up to see all of you but as Mother no doubt told you, I got caught up in Sydney. It was my fault really.

… It all started when we went to Sydney and we met up with Rob's friend and stayed at his place and we went out to the hotel to celebrate. On the way home there was a police car behind us, and they stopped Rob and said you're over the white line a bit and had him up for drunken driving and the next thing they locked him up and they wouldn't let him out until we paid $100 bail and I thought, gee, his parents are going to go berserk if he's stuck in Sydney. We didn't want to stay there for weeks so I paid the $100 to get him out of gaol and I never got it back either.

… I have just been recapping how good it was a few weeks ago and how bad it became, but, in any-case I have picked myself up and I'm on top of the world again.

… It's 1969 and I'm a little bit wiser I suppose, maybe a little bit more wary towards one's fellow man. I think that's what separates an adult from a child, where children play together and accept people as they find them, an adult eventually becomes embittered of one's fellow man, but that's just the times we

live in and we have to learn the lesson. However, it's taken me a long time to learn that hasn't it?

... In any case I was very pleased to hear about your boat and it's good that it doesn't leak anymore. When I come back, I'll get into your garden and get it all nice and tidy for you and it won't be long, I promise you it will only be two months, just long enough to get me on my feet again so I can come home and hold my head up. You surely can understand that can't you? No Thompson has ever come limping home and I'm not going to be the first. Where I work now, they said they've got a banking system so I'm going to ask if they can take $20 out of my wages every week and put it in the bank and that will put a stop to my larking around.

... I'm not in the big factory, I'm in the assembly lot and we assemble it and bend the sides – Father you would understand all this. You tell them all about it because I can't explain it in any case. It's a very monotonous job that drives me round the bend. It's just factory work, but it's good money. They're all Italians here. I told them before I leave this place, you'll end up talking English and I'll end up talking Italian. Some of the Italians are all right, really, it's surprising how they get on. I'm thinking they're really, all right to work with. I'm thinking I might get a part time job, do four hours on a Saturday morning or something at the petrol pumps. There are a lot of jobs going in Melbourne, two hours a night or something. I knock off at four o'clock, and I'm home about five to five. I should really work till about nine and earn 20 quid a week or something extra. I might look into that, to see what I can do there.

... Well it looks as though the tape is coming to an end, and it has been nice talking to you all, Mother, Father, Helen, and Tony. This is Christopher signing off until we meet again.

Rob and my friendship had waned since moving to Melbourne and we had both gone our separate ways. At the weekends, I sometimes went into Melbourne to a pub that had a piano and a sing-along. Sometimes Rob and I would explore Melbourne together. We went to Luna Park, and many other places. Occasionally I bumped into Rob at the United Kingdom Hotel in Clifton Hill. I was a regular there, but Rob only used to come in every so often to get his grandfather a small bottle of whiskey and have a few drinks.

Roaming around the streets one night together, we heard music and the sounds of a party going on upstairs. The front door was open, so we went upstairs. No one noticed us enter as they were all 'carrying on'. We saw one fellow pour a bottle of red wine over another fellow's head. We looked at each other and thought they must all be high on drugs, so we left. It was the swinging sixties, but I never got into the drug or sex scene, rather just alcohol and all types of music. My belief was that with alcohol, you would wake up with a sore head the next day, but with drugs you may not wake up at all.

One weekend, Glenda and her friend from Euroa came down to Melbourne and Rob and I met up with them. We all went to Lunar Park and then the Myer Music Bowl. We had been told –rather crudely by some other fellows who professed to know how to approach things, 'you want to give them a couple of glasses of gin. It's a real leg opener.' Forever naïve, we thought that sounds like a good idea – we might be able to have a little bit of 'you know what'. So, we went to the park with the girls and the gin, to try out the theory. But, as you could guess, these nice girls from the country weren't interested in drinking the gin or anything else for that matter! So, Rob and I ended up drinking the gin and then danced and pranced around the Myer Music Bowl making fools of us! There was no 'you know what'… *we* got drunk, and the girls took us home! Obviously, Rob and I had a lot to learn about 'wooing' the opposite sex!

… Once Rob and I were out drinking and stopped at a hotel in Carlton. We were both drunk. We saw a number of scantily clad girls in various poses and embraces with a number of men. Two of the girls came up to me and said, 'come on love, come with us.' I turned to Rob and said, 'Let's get out of here – it's a bit of a dive – they're all whores.' Oh God, with that comment, didn't all hell break loose! One of the girls got hold of my jacket from behind and ripped it apart at the seams – right up the back – split it in two! At the same time, the other girl started belting me on the back with her stilettos! I was lucky to get out of there alive! I staggered out of the hotel and onto the tram and went home, a lesson learned.

I regret my statement. It wasn't the right thing to say, and I should have apologised, but I didn't get the chance, as I was too busy dodging their blows!

… It is about April now and I have left Brownbuilt because I got sick of making office furniture and sticking in rivets in holes. I am still staying in the nice boarding house. But I managed to get a job at Stephen King Wine Merchants

in town, which was a lot better job, surrounded by drink. My job, with about five other people, was to make up the orders to go to the various hotels in town. I was there a few days, and this old fellow came up to me and said, 'would you like a drink mate? Do you drink at all?' I said, 'I don't mind a drop occasionally.' 'Come with me' he said. We went right to the back of the warehouse, and there were all these boxes around making a nice wall. Inside the boxed wall, it was like an Aladdin's cave, full of every type of drink you could imagine. He said, 'If you feel like a little nip during the day, just come around here and help yourself.' I said thanks for that mate. It was the happiest job I ever had. The orders were still going out all right because I didn't get myself 'sozzled'. But everybody around seemed to be very happy – they all knew about the Aladdin's cave! I enjoyed that job.

Things were going okay, but one night, Rob and I were talking in the pub and decided that we should get out of Melbourne – it wasn't the place for us. We decided to head to Western Australia as neither of us had been there.

Chapter 18
The Nullarbor Plain

...It's May 21st, 1969, and we are at Kunundah Sheep Station, eight miles from Naretha Railway Station, which borders the property. No trains ever stop at this station unless like we did, coming for a job. We had to get special permission from the Western Australian Railways for the main Perth to Adelaide train to stop to let us off.

...Rob and I left Melbourne on the Pioneer Coach to go from Melbourne to Adelaide, the first step of a 2,000mile journey to Perth. We boarded the coach about 8:00 Tuesday night and had a very good trip – most of the time we spent talking to the driver, and each other. It did help that we smuggled a small flask of Scotch on the bus, so we had a swig of that every so often. I think the driver was unaware of it, thank goodness. Probably we did sleep a little bit as well.
... The driver stopped the bus at the border town where we could get out, stretch our legs, have a cup of tea, and go to the toilet. Appropriate name for the town, Bordertown, because it's on the border of South Australia and Victoria.
... We arrived in Adelaide about half-past 8 the next morning where we got out and walked around as we had the day to fill in, before the rest of the trip to Perth. We had breakfast at Adelaide in the cafeteria, and then we set out and walked around the town. Adelaide is a very nice town, a quiet town and well set up, and I rather liked it. Not that many high buildings: a very nice, quiet town similar to Canberra. The day passed, and we walked around the shops and streets and had lunch at Coles. Then we decided that we'd have a shower.
... We went to a Turkish bath. We didn't want a Turkish bath but were told we could have a shower for 50 cents each, which we did, and came back to the Pioneer terminus, which left at night. We paid the extra $35 fare to get to Perth, which was the start of a three-day trip. We boarded the coach, and our seats

were just behind the driver, which was good, because as the journey progressed, we talked to the driver, and he told us all the landmarks as we were passing through the various places. We went through a lot of small towns before we got to the Nullarbor Plain. It would be around two and a half full days of travel before we would reach Perth.

... The town of Ceduna is at one end and Eucla at the other end of the Nullarbor Plain, which is a dirt road for about 500kms right through the plains. There's just nothing either side of the road. The Nullarbor Plains have always conjured up a vivid imagination of desert or shear wilderness. I suppose it's a bit of both really. It's not barren; it's just not populated. It's very flat and there's a lot of salt blushes or blue bushes – mulga. There's just space, wide-open space, and this dirt road going through the plains and a coachload of people.

... You have to be very careful when you're travelling through the Nullarbor Plain because there is a lot of 'bull dust' on the road – where the potholes in the road are filled up with this dust – and you just can't see them – especially in a car. You could quite easily run over the potholes and do an axle or exhaust or anything. This was apparent, as there was a number of burnt-out car bodies alongside the road that had fallen prey to the treacherous potholes filled with bulldust. Before I knew this, I said to the bus driver 'why don't you go on the side of the road a bit'? He said, 'we can't do that mate. I have to stay straight in the middle. Anything happens to this bus and I veered off a bit, I would get into big trouble.' I said, 'Yes, I suppose I can see that.'

This knowledge about the infamous 'bulldust' would stay with me and be very useful when I drove my car through the Nullarbor Plain on more than one occasion in the future.

... We veered off the Ceduna to Eucla road and stopped at the Nullarbor Station, which is a sheep station in the middle of the Nullarbor Plain. We bought a bottle of Coke each from the shop and looked around the station. Here we saw a camel, and then later, a lot more. Camels were imported many years ago as the early outback settlers used them for transporting goods, as the camels didn't need much water to survive. We continued speaking to the bus driver and wondered what would be at the end of the journey. You would appreciate, that right now, I must be about 3000 miles from you in Queensland and 2000 miles from Melbourne.... Finally, we arrived. The journey started on Tuesday and eventually finished on Friday morning when we arrived in Perth – it was May 17, 1969.

In 3 days' time, we retraced some of our journey by train to reach the outback Station we would work on for the next few months.

... Perth is a beautiful city and the capital of Western Australia, inland from Fremantle, and it's got the Swan River that winds its way through Perth and Kings Park as well which is up on the Headlands. It is a beautiful city after a 2,000-mile trip from Melbourne.... You'll have to look it up in your geography books. On either side of the Swan River, there are great expansive spaces and lawns. It's not a crammed city at all. It's nice, clean, and fresh. The people here are very nice, very hospitable people.

... We didn't know anywhere to stay when we arrived, so we asked the Pioneer Bus to people if they knew of any cheap hotel, and they booked us in at the Forest Hotel, which is quite a nice private hotel in Perth. The problem was that it was $5 per night, which wasn't very good because neither of us were that financial that we could afford luxury! However, seeing that we'd spent about three nights on the coach, we decided that we would. So, we booked in a room that had single beds and a nice view over the river. We had a three-course meal – soup, a nice piece of lamb, carrots, potatoes and custard and jelly. It was better food than that at the boarding house in Melbourne. We bought half a dozen bottles of beer that night and we had a few beers and spent a very comfortable night.

... The next morning, we were woken up with someone bringing us a cup of tea... very nice! Then we went down and had a smorgasbord breakfast, you know, the usual bacon and egg and everything else. Then we decided we'd better have a look around Perth and see what's going on and more than ever, see if we can get a job. And what better place to start than the employment exchange?

... We went to the employment exchange and asked what work was available. We were told that we had just missed out by a day of a job at Port Headlands, $90 a week for concrete work; and there wasn't that much going on in Perth. We both decided then that we weren't really born to the city and the city life wasn't quite what we wanted. We're both very good in the country, but the city mesmerizes us.... So, we decided to go to the various agencies that deal with station vacancies. We eventually ended up at Hamilton Stock and Station

Agency. We asked for a job at a sheep station for the two of us because we'd like to be together on the property. No use of us coming all this way and being 100 miles apart. We were told there was a job out at Naretha for two station hands. We decided that we'd take it for $29 per week, with $9 taken out for keep. The size of the property is pretty big in anyone's standard I would imagine. I hope you believe me when I give you the figures because it's true. Three million acres and just under, 4,000 miles square!

But where was Naretha? We didn't know, didn't have a clue! We just knew it was in the middle of the Nullarbor, somewhere. We had a job, and that's what mattered. Someone told us that Naretha was an aboriginal word meaning saltbush.

... After getting our jobs, we decided to look around Perth. We must have walked up and down nearly every street in Perth. Of course we had a good time window-shopping, deciding what clothes we'd buy and what we'd do if we had the money, which we haven't. We both decided we'd buy a brand new suit one of these days and try to prove to you all that we're not so hopeless.

... We called in at a few hotels around the place and chatted to a few more people – all very nice. Several of them showed us around. We went to Kings Park and had a look around there. We went to a dance on Saturday night with somebody we met named Eddie. He'd just come down to Perth on holiday from a sheep station. So, we went to the dance, and I had a dance with one or two girls.... It must have been about 3:00 in the morning after the dance and we were still roaming around. We decided that neither of us had ever been to a nightclub and we should go. We didn't know which one to go to, so we hailed a taxi and said, 'take us to a nightclub'. We ended up at the 'Zanzibar' – a fitting name for a nightclub. I'm not going to tell you how much the cover charge was! Anyhow, we went in and we, of course, wanted a beer and got one for 80 cents a bottle – a bit dear.... Just after sitting down, two very glamorous looking girls sat next to us and said, 'hello darlings. How are you? You 'gonna' buy us a drink?' We said, 'Sorry, we can't do that'. 'Well why don't you have a dance with us,' they said. We got up and danced with the girls. Then the one I was dancing with said, 'it'll cost you, but do you want a good time?' As neither of us had any money to spare for this 'good time' and we couldn't afford any more drinks at the price,

we retreated saying, 'No thanks, we have to go now'. We didn't stay that long at the nightclub, but we had a very enjoyable evening!

... We found a cheaper guesthouse to stay for 3 nights called the Cloisters Guesthouse just over the road from the Forest Hotel. Here we could get a bed for $2 a night, which was quite reasonable taking everything into account, including the need to buy a sleeping bag and ground sheet for our job. You use the two together – do your sleeping bag up in a ground sheet folded like an envelope and sleep in it, and it's quite warm and comfortable when we have to go out camping which will probably be quite frequent in the next few months, as lamb marking, and shearing will be coming very shortly after we arrive.

... We went to Freemantle one day. I was a bit disappointed with the town, because I thought it would be a lot bigger. It's only a small place. We went to the docks and took a couple of pictures. We went into a pub where we heard a jukebox playing. What I saw in the pub was 'bloody amazing'! The jukebox wasn't just playing a tune; it brought up a film clip on a screen! So, when you chose a song to play, you could see the actual artist singing it – it was amazing and the first time I had seen this happen. You put your money in, and a colour film clip came on the screen! Different from the older jukebox where you pressed the button to choose your record and the lever came down, tipped it over, put it onto the turntable and it played. That didn't happen with this one. I believe it is the only one in the country at this time.

This *Jukebox and colour film clip* – a brilliant 'video jukebox' was imprinted in my brain. I didn't know it at the time, but it was the 'dawning of the electronic age' for me. But, not recognising the impact and opportunities for me for the future at this time, I simply wandered off to work at an outback sheep station where I would have little exposure to anything else except sheep and the outback for the next few months! It would be some years before my fascination and attraction to this media would be sparked again; and this time it would be on a remote Aboriginal settlement in the Northern Territory. But this is some years off.

The bright lights of Perth faded. To get to our job at the *Kunundah Sheep Station* we had to travel many miles, in fact retrace part of our footsteps when we travelled from Adelaide to Perth! The difference was that we now travelled by train, not bus, and we had to get special permission from the Railways, for the train to stop at Naretha, the name of the tiny little station. We were going to be working deep in the outback.

... Naretha is about 500 miles from Perth going east towards Adelaide so only about 2,700 miles away from Queensland, as the crow flies. There's a time difference in the West from the East of Australia of an hour and a half.... The railway was first put through here in 1917. Commonwealth Railways it's called, not Western Australian Railways. The Commonwealth Railway was first laid to Kalgoorlie in 1917. Now it's the Transcontinental Railway Line, that links up with the rest of the country.

... We got on the Westlander train at about 4:00 in the afternoon. I don't know if you've ever seen any old trains that you see in westerns or the silent movies where you go out on to sort of balcony before crossing over to the other carriage – the really old ones with a little canopy. It was one of those. It tickled me pink going out the door across this little balcony to the other side. I really expected the Indians to come pounce on me at any minute! It was a sleeper train. There were two bunks stacked on top of each other, two either side of the carriage. You couldn't sleep, the train rocked that much. I think it cost us about $18. We had a nice meal though – very nicely served in the buffet carriage, which also had a gas heater in one corner. All-in-all, a very old-fashioned carriage and where we also had breakfast in the morning.

...We had to get special tickets so that we could get to Kalgoorlie on the Westlander train, change and board the Overlander train that would return to Adelaide, but make an unscheduled stop at Naretha on the way for us. When we handed these tickets to the conductor, he looked at us and said, 'Are you sure you want to get off there?' 'Oh yes. That's where we've got to get off.' He replied, 'That doesn't really happen very often because it's the main line express train to Adelaide.'... There was one hitch. I don't know if you remember, but the Western Australian Railway decided to go on a 24-hour protest strike, and our trip would be affected. I think New South Wales joined in as well. They usually do join in these sympathy strikes, don't they?

... Anyhow, we arrived at Kalgoorlie, which is about 300 miles from Perth, about half-past 7 and we were due to leave at 8:00 on the Adelaide to Kalgoorlie Overlander train when it arrived. Kalgoorlie is as far as the Overlander train from Adelaide goes into Western Australia, because that's as far as the standard gauge goes.... When we were waiting to board the Overlander train, we thought it would be a good opportunity for us to look around Kalgoorlie because as you can see on your world map, it is marked as quite a big place. But it's not all-that big really. I suppose it's about as big as the main street of Nambour. It's got a Coles and a Woolworth's and about four or five pubs. It's mostly noted for gold mining country.

... When we got back to the train, the person who was sharing the sleeper carriage with us was an Englishman who had just come out from England, about three days ago. He was intrigued with everything. He even asked me if Sydney was in Victoria, but I didn't tell him it was. I should have done really. We talked with him for a while because by this time we were flat broke, and it was a good way to pass the time. By the time we had paid for the train fare and everything else to take the job, we were pretty-short. But we have a nice sleeping bag and ground sheet to show for it.

... Eventually, after looking around Kalgoorlie and getting back to the train, we pulled out of the station at about 12:00 instead of leaving as planned at half-past 8 to conclude our journey. It was about another 200 miles in outback bush country. As I said before, we'd run out of money. On our ticket it had meal paid $1.70 or some ridiculous price they charged us for a meal. Most meals we had in Perth cost us about $1.50 for a steak or something and we went to a Chinese restaurant quite a lot and had those takeaway Chinese meals; and we drank very little really. We walked around the shops.

... We were hungry on the Overlander train, so we talked to the conductor saying that we hadn't had our meal due to the strike and everything, so we managed to get a midday meal on the train. This Overlander train was a big contrast from the old Westlander; it was a much better train. It was air-conditioned and had nice sleeping carriages, but we weren't allotted a berth because we were getting off at Naretha station. We sat in the lounge and bar area all night – lounging in the easy chairs and had a drink. There was piped music and all the 'works' – very nice and comfortable.

... The train rolled on. By this time, we were both wondering what we were coming out to. Had we made the right decision? We thought for the last 400 or 500 miles all we've seen was the Nullarbor Plains, which we were going to be working in the same location on the station.

... We got talking to a few people. After lunch, about half-past 3 or 4:00, the train suddenly pulled up and stopped. I looked out the window and saw a little wooden hut that had Naretha written on the side of it. We stood up with our bags and people in the train said horrified, 'are you getting out here?' 'Oh yes', we said, 'we like the quiet life.' We clambered down the side of the train. There was nobody to meet us. There was just a barren desert with this very desolate looking hut with Naretha written on it. The porter said, 'Have you got plenty of water?' We said, 'yes' but didn't have, as we could see a water tank on the roof connected to this small hut – we hoped it had some water.

... We waved as the train sped away into the distance. Then, we looked at each other, and neither of us said anything. Where were we? Kalgoorlie to Perth is 372 miles, and from Kalgoorlie to Adelaide is 1,381 miles. I suppose we're 200 miles from Kalgoorlie, so that would make it 1,181 miles from Adelaide.

... We talked – why are we here, there is no one around, what is going to happen to us. I took a photo and we walked into the shed and saw names inscribed on the wall. So, with our penknives, we very quickly put our names on the wall amongst the others. What is going to happen to us? About an hour later, in the distance we saw a puff of dust and I said – 'I think there might be somebody coming for us. Then we heard a car approaching, and we both gave a big sigh of relief. Sure enough, it was Mr Swan the Kununda Sheep Station manager, with a car full of children. The three children were very excited to see us. The car pulled up beside us – it had a great antenna sticking out of the front and a radio inside. He said, 'Are you the two fellows which have been sent out from Perth? Robert and Chris?' 'Yes', we said. He said 'we didn't think you'd come today because of the train strike. Just as well I was passing, wasn't it! You might have spent the night here.' So, with that, we all clambered in, and our expectations turned into reality. We headed off to the station wondering what would meet us at the end.

... After quite a bumpy ride over the eight-mile stretches and chatting to the boss, we arrived at our destination. We were given a nice meal and shown to our room. The room was a nice size room with two single beds in it, and the mattresses were quite comfortable. We slept heavily, after the long journey.

... The date is May 30, 1969. I am speaking to you from Kununda Sheep Station, 500 miles from Perth, which is three million acres and 4,000 miles square. A big place indeed, and I don't believe that every part of the property has been explored yet. It's one of the four biggest stations in Australia and is owned by wool brokers in Adelaide. Mr Swan is the manager on the property here. We're 200 miles away from any town. We're not that isolated because the Flying Doctor calls here once a month and treats any ailments that we have. In emergencies, we've always got the radio, and we can always contact him by that.

... The manager is a family man, and the eldest children go to boarding school in Perth. The young ones listen to school of the air every morning about 8:00 that is relayed in the transmitter receiver set, which is situated in the schoolhouse. So really, it's like a real school – the School of the Air. It's quite a big room as well where they show picture shows to us once a fortnight. Pretty-old pictures, older than the ones you see on the television. But they're good to look at. We appreciate the transmission to listen to the radio and the pictures when they come.

... The property is situated on the edge of the artesian basin, so half the property we can get water by sinking bore holes, but the other half is supplied by huge dams, we have around the property. The dams are about half a mile wide and a huge catching area going into it.

... Life carried on as usual – a very civilised community considering where we are, so far from civilisation. The community consists of a mechanic, and an overseer, who each have their own house and live with their families. Dozy, the dozer driver maintains the dirt roads around the station with one of these big Caterpillar dozers that are in the workshop at the moment being overhauled. Dozy and his wife pull a caravan behind the dozer and they go around the property making new roads and maintaining the old ones. Then there is Charlie the trapper who lives in a caravan. He has a full-time job trapping dingoes and keeping the foxes down, and camels as they break down the fences and do a lot of damage. He has a caravan too.

... Then there are those that live in the worker's accommodation – mainly the station hands. I'll try to explain to you a little bit what the building looks like that we are living in. It takes a while to get used to being out here, but we seem to be settling in.... There is a sort of long building which either side of the building there are rooms. They are quite big rooms, about 12' by 8' wide with two beds in, and they're about four of these rooms either side of the building. At the end of the building there is the dining room, and at the end of the dining room is the cookhouse. Rob and I were ushered into one of these rooms we are sharing. In the dining room we have darts and a dartboard, and sometimes we play cards and talk. Usually we go to bed about 8:00.

... Dave, a Queenslander comes from a Queensland Station and has been here for about two years. Then there's Butch who is sub-overseer. He's 22-year-old and been here 18 months. His brother Tim, a jackeroo isn't very old. Tony is another jackeroo and Arthur is an odd-job man – just does odd jobs around the place, and Bruce who is a truck driver – drives a big five-ton Bedford truck only 18 months old. Bruce carts water and posts around and anything else that wants carting around from place to place. Then there is Helmer, the yardman who only has one eye. He kills the sheep and generally maintains the yard immediately around the homestead. Then, there is Rob and me.

... After arriving and settling down on Thursday, we had a pretty-easy job on Friday. Rob and I went out with Bruce the truck driver. About 35 miles out to roll up some water pipe. We went past windmills where there are big tanks of water pumped into big high storage tanks and gravitated down into troughs, and there's a system right through the half of the property, I suppose about 1,000 acres of it. There are a lot of pumps, pumping the water from here to there, which is very expensive. The property isn't making money at the-moment, and the company owns other stations in South Australia.

... Saturday we didn't do much, just wandered around the yard and in the afternoon, we did our washing. On Sunday, we drove 16 miles out to the drilling rig, used to sink boreholes, to find water. By the time we drove out there and drove back in, it was 12:00. We only worked half a day Sunday.... Monday was when we were going to get our first experience of camping out in the bush where *our $18 ground sheets and $9 sleeping bags began to come into their own. Yes, we had to go out to cement a couple of spillways down the side of this dam to stop the water when it rains from eroding the dam walls as the water fills it up. Where we went was about 60 miles out, and there was Rob and me and Butch, sub-overseer, and Tim, who is Butch's brother. We spent four days out there camping and working pretty hard in the day and collecting wood at night. Sitting round the campfire watching the flames flicker at night and then eventually going to bed is an interesting experience, and wasn't so bad, and the nights were warm. We came home Thursday night.*

... Rob, Tony, Dave the overseer and Bruce the truck driver, and I went out about 60 miles away, and cut down some lumber posts, which will be picked up tomorrow and left in a distant corner of the property ready for when mustering starts next week. On the way out, we saw literally 50 kangaroos hopping around everywhere. There were little joeys and kangaroos in mobs of 10s and 20s. It was really good to see them in such large numbers. We had to be careful not to run them over.

... There are quite a few hawks around, and there's a lot of rabbits and, a lot of dingos. I think you have dingos in Queensland as well. That's why Charlie the trapper goes around trapping the dingos, baiting with strychnine. Being a lot of sheep around, the dingos attack them and kill them. I've been told there are a couple of camels around on the station, but I haven't seen any here yet. But I've heard that camels have been pretty much wiped out because they're a menace because they break down the fences.

... Today is Saturday and we've been working all day. Something I forgot to tell you what happened yesterday on the way home from cutting the posts. We stacked the posts ready for Bruce to collect them this morning to take up to the site where they're building holding yards for the sheep. On the way back, we called in at an old lime quarry, which hasn't been working for several years. They showed me the old kilns and how they used to put the limestone and a layer of wood and then some more limestone and more wood and fire it, and that broke down the limestone, and they used to shovel it up and sell it. Around here on the Nullarbor Plain, there is supposed to be some of the best quicklime in Australia. But the quarry closed. I don't know why. Now it is a derelict site. I suppose there were about 12 or 13 kilns and some sort of squatter's dwellings there. Very primitive – it was interesting to see.

... Probably Monday we'll all be going again when we start lamb marking – a few thousand of them. We muster them all on horseback or motorbikes, so I expect we'll be busy. We'll only be camping about 12 miles away from the homestead.

... This morning, I was on the saw bench sawing up campfire wood with Tim which we'll have quite a heap because we're going out mustering and marking on Monday and all 14 of us will be living under the stars for at least a week. Preparation for moving to the camp is well organized. This afternoon I was in the bridle room oiling all the saddles to be ready when we have our taste of horse riding which will probably be on Monday. This morning it was very misty outside, and I wouldn't fancy sleeping out somehow.

... Most of the people here are very easy to get along with and very good to work with as well. Really, it's a happy self-contained communal life out here – I suppose like most of the properties around here. I expect you wonder how we get power to light the place. We have our own large generating plant that provides power for the whole homestead and buildings – I expect like most properties around here. Of course, we have tank and bore water. I am getting used to sleeping in a sleeping bag now because that's all there is to sleep in – in the bed at the homestead and sleeping bag when camping.

... Periodically they show movies at the station. There's a picture shown once a fortnight free. Last week it was quite a funny one – a comedy. And then there was one with the Marx Brothers. There was another one that brightened up the weekend considerably and I didn't go to bed until 12:00. This week there won't be one. There'll probably be one next week. ... We're allowed to have two bottles of beer a day, which limits our drinking habit, and most days I don't have any. Rob and I usually have a couple of bottles Friday night and Saturday night. That's all we have during a week now. So that's good, isn't it? Better than going around to the cities to the pubs and leaning on the counter like a lot of drunkards. This is a lot better life. I am a lot more contented.

... Being in the outback – way out in the bush with a campfire is peaceful. I think you get your perspective right in such a place. The nearest town is 200 miles away, which is quite a way. It's funny, at night, about 12:00, the train used to come through. I was sitting in the car waiting for a shearer that was coming on the train, and sort of nodding off. And all of a sudden, I saw all these cars just going past. I thought what's happening? And it was all these cars on the flat top of the train. You had the carriages, and then you'd have had 8 or 9 or 10 carriages of just trucks and cars.

... You spend very little money here, and I have saved quite a lot. You get paid once a month, and you have a statement. I expect I'll be getting about $80 or $90 a month clear which I'll save. Food and entertainment are provided – pictures once a fortnight – very old pictures. And you have beer, a couple of bottles if you want it. There is a shop here, surprisingly enough, where you can buy toothpaste, shaving stuff, cigarettes, sweets, anything like that. Really, it's very interesting as was the trip to get here. It's surprising that the eastern part of the world [Australia] doesn't really know much about Perth and Western Australia.

... Later on, I hope to go up to Port Headland and Darwin to see what is going on there. If you are coming across the Nullarbor Plains, it would be advisable to take plenty of water and tin food in case of breakdowns – although halfway across the Nullarbor Plain there is a big water tank, so you can fill up with water – but this depends on the rain of course.

... We have a sugar and tea train that comes from Kalgoorlie twice a week to the Naretha station. The train is very similar to the one that I used to go and get stuff from when I was fencing down in Victoria. This one, I think, has a little bit more on board than that one. It's just like having mobile shops go around the outback. There is a butcher's shop with a butcher on the train and you can buy all sorts of cuts of meat. You can buy butter, tea, sugar, and all the essential foods. When I first arrived at Kunundah Sheep Station, I ordered a decent pair of boots to wear which were sent up from Kalgoorlie on this train, as arranged by Mr Swan.

... There are quite a few squatters around, especially on the Crown Land, which is about 100 miles between here and Kalgoorlie where anybody can just stop or settle if they want to farm it or anything else they want. The tea and sugar train are essential for them because that's the only means they have of ever getting their supplies. If they can get to the railway line, they're all right.... Of course, the main thing here is water, which is essential. That's why they're building four big dams on the property. The dozer driver makes a good job of them as well. They really look professional, and they hold a few million gallons of water I imagine when they fill up. The same as in Queensland where there have been droughts. I think Queensland has the three biggest cattle properties in Australia. They do have water problems, so we have as well. I expect when we have shearing and lamb marking, the rains will come and wash us out!... When you're making your swag, you go to the highest ground, burrow out a slight dip to put your hip in and fold it up like an envelope with a flap that folds over your head, if it rains. Even if the rain comes you don't get wet – and because you're on high ground, you won't start floating away!

... We stayed out camping for over a week, lamb marking. Lamb marking is where the lambs are put in little pens, and we had to catch them, hold them, put them on the rail, hold their legs apart while the vet or somebody who knew what he was doing, nicked them and took the testes out and threw them to the dogs that circled, while we threw the lamb back over the side of the pen. The flies buzzed, and blood constantly kept flowing all day over our hands ...I didn't realize that blood dries out the skin so much. But the evenings were good because somebody had a guitar, and we sat around the campfire and had a singsong. But, at the end of the week, it was so nice to get back to civilization, as we called it, and have a shower.

...Then, the next thing, we had to go droving. And they did ask me had I ever ridden a horse. 'Oh', I said, 'Yes. I used to have a dairy farm, and I used to ride the horse to get the cows on the dairy farm.' I did forget to tell them that the horse was blind and had pink eye. 'Oh well', that's good. 'We've got a horse here that you might as well give it a go and just go up about seven miles and we'll see how you go and come back again.'

... Apparently this horse named 'Flyaway' won a place in the Gymkhana a couple of weeks before. But I didn't know this at the time. So, I got on the horse and they gave it a pat on the back, and it shot off like a rocket. It must have been galloping 80 miles an hour! Forget about turning left and right and opening the gate and doing all the rest of the things, I just kept going until it slowed down. I don't suppose I went more than 20 miles, but I could have gone a lot farther seeing the size of the property! Eventually I came back on the horse. 'Oh', they said. 'That's good mate. You've come back in one piece. That's a good sign. You'll be able to ride him on the sheep drove that you're going on shortly! There're 6,000 sheep we've got to take upcountry, so you'll be right on that trip.' Of course, it is important how you get on a horse. You sort of get on him sideways, and the horse has-to bend into you. You put your right hand, so you don't change hands halfway, otherwise you will fall off.

... One horse I rode, every time I got on it, he used to turn around and try to bite my bum. Cheeky bugger! Another time we were in a paddock mustering some cattle. There are about four of us on horseback and you're just in sight of each other, as you comb the 100-mile paddock. You just push everything in front of you.

... I was talking to a fellow drover and he said, 'I was stealing cars in town, and I came out here to get away from everything. I think there's still a warrant for my arrest. But they don't bother about you out here at all.' And that is pretty true because if you want to get lost, don't try and get lost in the outback. If you want to get lost, get lost in the middle of the city. The police used to phone up the sheep stations and ask, 'who have you got working there now...? All right. He can stay there. We'll pick him up when he leaves. Just tell us when he's leaving.' And that's what happened.

... So, if you want to break the law, don't go onto a sheep station. But Rob and I were all right. We were pretty honest people, so it didn't apply to us. And we kept pretty sober because we were only allowed two bottles of beer at night, and we weren't allowed to stash them under our bed and have a great booze up at the weekend. They used to make sure that the bottles you did get, you had to drink at the time that you got them. So, there were quite a few ground rules that you had to abide by, and it was pretty good. As I said, we were a happy bunch, 14 of us, all living together, and we all lived quite amicably.

... I was driving the truck with this tank of water and taking it up to the various tanks. They're very short of water here at the moment, and they're having to cart it from one end of the property to the other. It is a very serious situation. ... The track that we took was an old camel trailers track. In the old days, they used to have these camels instead of horses and hook them up to the great camel trucks. There are still a few camels up there, but I haven't seen any. I saw a couple of carcasses of camels. I could tell it was a camel because it had a hump.

Now camels aren't being used at all, and they're still breeding, so now they are causing a bit of a problem in the desert.

... The other week Rob and I, and Dave the overseer went out checking the windmills and water tanks. After shearing, we're going to have to make a few concrete tanks. They've got quite a complicated system of tanks and water and pipelines going 40 miles. Various tanks. One tank fills up and overflows into the other. There are only a very few bores around because they're just on the edge of the Artesian Basin. They get the water from the Artesian Basin and fill up the tanks and pump it out.

We haven't gone over to the other side of the property – over to Pinjarra. This is two blocks of land because by law, you're only allowed to own so much one person. But these are brothers. One brother owns one half, the other brother owns the other half, and one manages the whole lot.

...I haven't really told you about the last trip when we only drove 4,000 sheep down to be shorn – the same old crew – Rob, myself, horses and the sub-overseer. This drove went very well apart from one hiccup. Fynx is a beautiful horse – like driving a Jaguar car. Fynx threw me three times during droving the sheep back to the station to be shorn. The last time he threw me was pretty bad. I landed right on my hip. I blew my nose – bad idea! Blowing one's nose when you're on the winner of the Gymkhana – Fynx! Of course, Fynx reared up, and I landed flat on my back on solid rock. The other drovers were heading off in the sunset, and I thought: if I stay here, they'll forget about me. So, I had to get back on the horse again and keep going. I ended up with a great bruise and I thought I'd cracked my hip for a while. I was limping around for about a week. It was very, very sore.

...Fynx was a very nervous sort of horse, easily upset – very flighty. Once, I got on Fynx, not knowing that she had a saddle sore. Straightaway, she reared up and then dropped straight to the ground. I ended up with one leg trapped underneath her, still in the saddle sideways. I got on her again and didn't have any further trouble. All my bruises have healed up and I'm none the worse for wear except a little greater on experience that is a good thing.

... Another challenge when droving is stopping at night. I never liked this part – because, when we stop, you have to 'hobble' the horses. That was like putting handcuffs on them, so they didn't wander off. Then in the morning, you had to find the horse. But seeing as how their front legs were fastened together, they never went far. Well, I'm not a morning person, and I always found the early morning work a little bit hard.

... We camped along the way. There are no fences, just wide – open spaces. Rob and I rode the horses – he on the tail and I on the wing, and Butch on the motor bike, the other wing and front.

... Charlie 'the Dogger' drove the 'chuck wagon' and was responsible for feeding us on the drove. He drove ahead of us, and at midday, he would stop, make a fire, and bury the camp oven in the ashes, and bake damper – made from *flour and water – bit like scones. This was the first time I had tasted damper. Then, he would drive on ahead to where we were going to camp at night. He would roll out the cyclone netting ready for us to drive the sheep in at night; and then cook the meal.*

... *It's been long days. We get up about 5:00, day after day bringing the sheep down and taking them back. Daylight to dusk, and you really just don't ride behind them, there's quite a bit of riding to do. I'm becoming a quite good horseman now, as Rob is, considering neither of us could hardly ride before.*

... *We passed a few little communities in the distance – aboriginals living in their humpies that were dotted around the outback. I hadn't seen this before ... I should've taken a photo, but I didn't have my camera on me at the time.*

... *I think you have to be very patient to work sheep on a regular basis. Go out one way, and they got out the other way and you have to race and bring in one corner and then the other corner, but you manage. The trouble was with this there should have been five men instead of three. Horses are very good, but you just can't beat dogs.*

... *When I returned, I showed the boss the bruise on the right side of my hip. It was like all colours of the rainbow by now and still sore. I told the boss 'I'm not being paid enough to do this, and I'm not going to ride this horse again or take the sheep back again! His reply? 'But Chris, we value your input, and you* and Rob are the only ones that know the way to take them back... it will be all right this time, don't you worry, you'll have a few days rest before taking them back.' I huffed and puffed, gave a big sigh, and said 'all right'.

... Rob and I will be going on another drove. We seem to be elected as 'horsemen' on the property. We're the only two horsemen they have on the property. All the rest ride motorbikes. Rob got thrown off the horse this time. He got thrown off and the saddle went with him. This was just as we were starting to take the 2,000 sheep by ourselves. It was a successful drove bringing 4,000 sheep in to be shorn.... But when they've been shorn, the sheep seem to rebel and are much more frisky. On the drove back, we had 6,000 newly shorn sheep – the original 4,000 plus 2,000 weaners – which are just a bit bigger than lambs.

... What a drove it was this time! It was really about the 6,000 sheep that got away. Nothing really went right this trip.... I did take a camera along this time and took a few pictures of them at various stages, so I'll send them to you, and you'll be able to see what sheep really look like in the outback!

... Drafting the sheep sorting out the big from the little ones and the various types of sheep for the shearing sheds. Then once they've been shorn, we have to put them through this sheep dip to delouse them, which is like a big 1,000-gallon tank with sprays pointing up, and this big arm goes around on top like a propeller. Once they walk through that, they're really soaked. But it was hot, and there was a drought on. A lot of sheep were very thirsty and started drinking the tank water. When we got up the next morning, there were about 100 dead sheep that we had to gather up and put on the fires and burn. That was a pretty horrific sort of a day.

We were dipping up until about 3:00 and then we drove the sheep on horseback down to the home paddock – the first camp at Naretha, seven miles away and this was the start of our journey back. Butch had left earlier on the motorbike, to get things ready for the drove that started the next day. It was getting dusk at the time. We hobbled the horses by putting two straps around their front legs to stop them walking away. Eventually somebody came and picked us up about 7:00 to go back to the homestead for the night. We closed the gate, but somebody had gone through a gate a mile away earlier on and left it open! So, when we returned in the morning, you can guess the rest... The two horses had gone through the open gate. We spent about an hour finding the horses. We started our drove on Sunday. It's now the following Monday week. ...Most of the drove was up the side of the railway line, which divides the two properties. I got on Flyway, my horse, the fourth winner of the Gymkhana and a more docile horse than Fynx.... The first day's drove wasn't too bad. We were actually able to get over the railway line and knocked up about 17 miles. The next day wasn't too bad either, andor we did our quota of mileage.

...The third day we didn't get into camp until the sun went down. The sheep hadn't had much water – there was very little around and had very little feed – being shut up for two or three days while shearing. And we had to improvise and put a fence up of wire netting. We made a campfire, watered the horses, fed them, and had a feed of mutton, cooked in the camp oven over the fire. We went to bed early, in our swags. About 9:00 we heard this great rumble and Charlie said, 'They're gone'. A dingo was on the flats, and had spooked them, and the sheep – 6,000 of them had bolted right over the cyclone fence! Sheep are very touchy about dingos, and for good reason as many have been taken by dingos.

... There was a mad panic and we all scampered to get them back, in the dark. Butch went out one way on the motorbike. Charlie got Flyaway, saddled her up and went off the other way. Rob and I straightened the fence and made a 'wing' to bring them in. We only managed to corral about 2000 that night. There were around 4000 missing. The next day Rob and I stayed to watch the sheep in the yard to make sure they didn't bolt while the other two station hands combed the countryside and brought most back. After this, we set out again. We covered about 8 miles and made another yard. That was all right. Bruce came up in the *water tanker and filled up the troughs for the sheep to have a drink.... The next day we took them on to water, and then moved them on again. As we were going along a fence, there was no trouble, because the fence ensured the sheep couldn't drift out too far.*

... After about 40 miles down, the fence branched off making it harder to contain the sheep. Adding to this precarious situation was the fact that there had been a fire through this area last year, and there had been a bit of recent rain so there were a lot of nice green shoots. The sheep hadn't had any green feed in I don't know how long. They just went wild. We couldn't hold them. They scattered!

... We camped at this area overnight, and the next day we only managed to muster up about 400 and put them in the pen. The next day, we eventually rounded up 2,000. The others were more widely scattered and lost to us. Charlie, the Dogger, contacted the homestead by two-way radio and told them about the disaster. Butch told Rob and I to take the 2,000 on to the final destination at Duck Dam, which was about 30 miles away. The boss got a spotter plane, to look for the missing nearly 4,000 sheep. Three men off one neighbouring station 180 miles away came to help us. Another station sent their two station wagons to assist. Rob and I arrived back at the homestead on horseback with the 2,000 sheep. We had a shower and shaved off a week's growth of beard; and then went on with other work around the homestead that included driving the 'ute' with the fuel to the spotter plane, to refuel. Eventually, most of the sheep were found over several days, with the help of helicopters and neighbours.

... There's a radio transmitter in Charlie's chuck wagon. There are two crystals to put in it to get various wavelengths– one to let us talk to the main homestead at the station and one to listen to ABC radio. We're way out in the outback. I don't think you can get any more in the outback than the edge of the Nullarbor Plain. We used to hear each day how the moon project was going. It truly is a remarkable achievement, isn't it?

...It's July 21st, 1969, today – a historic occasion really. We've just got back from our drove of sheep, and two people have landed on the moon! The new and the old sort of thing, mixed. When they say you can see the man in the moon, it's really true now isn't it?

It was such a contrast – the moon landing and outback Australia. It brings back memories. I think of my letter writing pad I had at school, at Cloverley Hall.

One page of the letter pad was ripped off and sent home to my parents with my scrawl. Then, several pages were used to amuse myself, drawing rockets and spaceships. I was a fan of Dan Dare, Pilot of the Future, in the Eagle Comic. Now, all these years later, a rocket was now on the moon. Was it similar to what I drew all those years ago? And is the surface of the moon similar to outback Australia? I know that the red soil is often compared to Mars.

... It gets very cold these mornings. When I was sleeping in the swag, I used to really go down into the bottom of it some mornings because it would be very cold. It's not too bad sleeping out. There's usually a good campfire going all night. It never seems to go out until we move because we only stay a day in each place. I don't know where I am – I've slept in so many places in such a short time, a new camp each day. It's very good carrying your bed around. It's like a tortoise. All I have to do is roll it out and get into it. ...I'm flat out at-the moment with the shearing and I was also flat out at lamb marking time. We were camped out then for about a fortnight.

... After our return, we only had about four days before the shearers came. About 30 shearers, and they live about seven miles up the road where the shearing sheds are. The contract shearers are pretty-well a community on their own. We don't have all that much to do with the shearers really, except we have to roll the wool bales out of the sheds and stack them up on the truck. They've got a boom rigged up just outside the shed with a pulley block on the top. It's about 50 to a load that we take down to the railhead at Naretha, about eight miles away and put them in the trucks ready for the train to hook up and take them to Adelaide to go to the wool stores.

... We're leaving here the end of the month and going back down into Perth again. Mr Sinnott, one of the shearers we saw before we came here, started shearing on the 21st of this month. We were to stay with him in shearing sheds until Christmas time, but we decided to leave.

... We stayed at Kununda until they had shorn their 39,000 in the end. We loaded up the wool bales onto the truck to take down to the railway siding, and then we had to load them into the carriages – quite hard work. We put a rope around each bale and then over the pulley over the boom, and one end of the rope was tied to the tractor, and we kept backing back, lifting the bale, and dropping it down onto the truck. We got 52 on each truckload and took them down to the Naretha railway station. It's quite a hard job to get 100 in a railway truck – more than a bit of heaving and grunting.

...At the time we left, a lot of sheep were dying like flies mostly due to the drought. I heard on the wireless that the drought is very severe around Naretha and we were burning 20, 30, 40, 50 sheep in different fires – putting wood down and a bit of diesel, which is terrible really.

... It is a harsh and unforgiving land.

Chapter 19
I'm A Pommy!

It was August 1969 when Rob and I left Kunanda Sheep Station. We returned to Perth for a few days, before starting a job in a shearing shed in Sandstone, towards Port Headland. This job was not a long stint, just a couple of weeks until we headed back to Benalla, Victoria in my car, across the Nullarbor Plains. It would be a journey, and arrival, to remember.

…Hello Mother, Father, Tony, Helen and Timothy and Anne…Well here I am sitting on a great heap of red rock jutting upwards out of a very flat and barren land, looking at the shearing shed and sheep in the distance. Where am I you might ask? Well I'm in Sandstone. I'm sorry I haven't spoken to you for a while. I thought it best to send a tape to you all, as I will soon be leaving Western Australia.

... Anyhow, I'll tell you what we have been doing too now. We left Kunanda Sheep Station and caught the train to Perth again. This time we did not have to change at Kalgoorlie as a compatible gauge had been put through during the time, we were at Kunanda. The train was very nice and modern, and we had a sleeper this time. The sleepers were just little humps jutting out into the walkway either side of the carriage, and there are two chairs facing each other and a basin. There were two additional carriages for a lounge and a bar, a small cocktail bar, and tables and chairs. Nice really, not sitting still in one seat all the time. And there's a proper dining room laid out. It's very comfortable riding in a train now. You can meet all your friends and have quite a social time. I met a lot of truckies and car owners on the train now, all crossing the Nullarbor Plains. They won't bring their cars through because the roads are so bad. They put their vehicles on the train in Port Augusta and take them off at Kalgoorlie – that's the worst stretch. Then, they start their trip again.... I hope that you have a map of Western Australia, and then you'll be able to see more-or less where we are and where we have been. It's very nice weather here in Perth. I imagine it'd be a lot like Queensland weather. Very hot and the land is very dry – much the same as the land around Kalgoorlie way.

... The first week we were in Perth we booked in at the Glen Lee Private Hotel that was $4 a night, which was dear, so we booked in at the local caravan park. We got a two-berth caravan, and we were only paying $21 a week. There was no tucker provided or anything else, so we used our own blanket. This caravan was quite a modern one. More modern than the one I used to live in full time when I was working on the dairy farm at Maffra.... We spent a few days in Perth and had a good time. We went to a nightclub again and drank a few beers and enjoyed ourselves. I bought a new wallet. The same sort that Uncle Horace gave me. It had a map of Western Australia and a kangaroo and boomerang on it. It's very nice.... Of course, all good things come to an end, and we decided that we would have to get work again. We phoned up so many places looking for work, and they all said: 'have you got your own transport'? We decided that it was essential that we had transport. So, we looked in the car ads, and I bought an old Hillman car for $55 – which isn't very much even if it only goes three months! It goes all right, and it's registered up until Christmas. That's a good thing really-as at least we're mobile now. Paying 6 shillings for taxi's here and there, is expensive isn't it.

... When we were looking for a job, we did say we were experienced 'shed hands' otherwise we never would have got a job! When you're out in the bush, they're not going to say, 'you're not experienced so you'd better go back'. I think we'll be experienced after the shed we are going to. Like when we went horse riding at the last sheep station, we said we can ride a horse, but not very well. Little did we know we had to break them in before we rode them! But it's a very exhilarating past time once you learn how to do it. I really enjoyed the sheep station, but in the end, it got a bit monotonous – day after day just droving sheep. The stupid things never went the way you wanted them to, and I think we were all tired at the end.

... I never seem to stay out of work long.

... I think this shed goes until the 29th of August and then we're going back to a shed that's only 60 miles outside Perth. Having the car will enable us to go and see a bit more of Perth when we go back.

...When we were coming up here, we only brought the car for the first 200 miles and left it at a Caltex service station. We just happened to meet Kevin, a shearer there who was also going out to Pinnacle Station in his Holden car. He reckoned that it would be more reliable going through these rough roads with his car, rather than my old Hillman. We agreed, and we had quite a good trip with him. The roads here are just bush tracks, and even the road halfway across the Nullarbor Plain is only a dirt road, and very rough. I just hope my car is there when we return. The owners said, 'just put it in the corner, over there'.

... We travelled north from Perth up the coast road but inland a bit, until we came to a place called Sandstone – a small town in the Midwest region of

Western Australia, 157 kilometres east of Mount Magnet and 661 kilometres north of Perth. And just a little way from Sandstone, well 150 miles in fact, is where we are at Pinnacles Station, where the shearing is. Pinnacles isn't a big station, it's only 1,000 acres.

... It's very isolated out here. I suppose a lot of Western Australia would be. It's just not very densely populated. Looking around from up here I can see rock, scrub, and a great plain of bush all around me. But there's not as much saltbush as there was at Kununda.

... The shearing team has ten shearers. Rob and I and another person are what they called 'roustabouts.' There was a 'penner up', and there was a 'presser'. Chris is the name of the wool classer. When he was driving up to this shed, he put a hole in his radiator.

... We're sleeping in old shearing quarters with old wooden floors. It's lovely weather we're having. Sleep with no top on at night and with the door open. There is a cookhouse and a dining room, which is just a tin building, with whitewashed slats on it. It conjures up a lot in the imagination.

... The sheep here look a lot healthier and a lot fatter than the ones at Kununda that were very skinny, poor looking sheep and you could tell the wool on them wasn't that good. Here, the ewes, lambs and wethers look a lot healthier, and its nice wool. At Christmas time some of the best wool in Australia comes from around here.

... Rob is on the 'board' picking up the fleeces when the shearers shear them and then puts them by the table, and then sweeps up after the shearers. I throw these fleeces – they have to land nicely on the table so that you can 'skirt' around the outside picking off the wool with stains and take the 'back' off and throw it to the side. Then Chris comes along and decides if the fleece is good wool or poor wool. The good wool, which is a higher price, about 50 cents a pound. Some of it is very nice wool. Seeing it on the skirting table, it's surprising how many sorts of wool from the sheep you can see. The wool classer has quite a task ahead of him grading all the different wools and textures. I also spend some time pressing the wool, on the wool press – quite a manual job – it's not electrical – you have to pull the lever down.

... At the end of each day, we have to move the bales around which are quite heavy. We have to stack them in heaps depending on the grade of wool. There are about 300 weights in each one. Pretty heavy, especially when you have to move them around.... We've been doing wethers today. That's the big ones. We

were on weaners yesterday – they're a year old and have quite small fleeces.... Today we had a break for an hour because the engine broke down. It was very good. I hope it breaks down again tomorrow.

... Usually, when the bell goes and the shearer's stop, they let you just finish the sheep off. It would be interesting to learn – I would like to know how to shear. I might even end up a shearer.

...Today I had a go at shearing. I didn't do a very good job of it, but I did half a sheep before the bell went for the shearers to start. Phil showed me how to do it, and he said I got a fairly clean cut.... At least I have shorn a sheep, a bit of a one.... It's quite interesting the shearing and learning about the shed. I told you that we'll finish this shed on the 29th, and we hope to get into another one, although we're not all that experienced. At the present, we have done 4,000 sheep in this shed, 4,000 a week. The average shearer seems to shear about 130 a day. The foreman was very upset one day and the reason was that his best shearer – an aboriginal, went 'walkabout' and he did not come back for several days.

... We have Saturday and Sunday off from the shearing shed, which is very good. The trouble is way-out here, there's not much to do. But I suppose it's worth something to have the time off. We work pretty hard in the sheds. Yesterday we went out in the afternoon. One of the shearers was going into the township, which is about 70 miles away. Leonora. All it consists of is a pub. So, we went out for the afternoon, had a few beers at the hotel and came back again. This is where I phoned you.

... The countryside here is very similar to around Naretha and Kalgoorlie way. If anything, I'd say it was a bit better, more open. There are still lots of kangaroos – 'reds', around here. We've got three New Zealanders here, and last night they went out shooting. They shot quite a good red roo and skinned it. It would be nice to have a roo skin, I think. I have shot a couple of 'roos, but I'm not a very good shot. There are quite a few rabbits around, and we saw a whole herd of emus on the way up to Pinnacle Station. I haven't seen any snakes yet thank goodness, but I suppose they're around here.... We're seeing a bit more of Western Australia here.

... All the people here in the shearing shed seem to be decent enough fellows. They seem more of a 'happy family' that at Kunanda. I suppose it's got a lot to do with whether you're getting good money and good tucker. The food's a lot better here and the money is good – I get about $45 a week clear. That's tax and food taken out. Oh, I must tell you – the food is good here, but one day we were having cold mutton and salad. I saw maggots wriggling in my meat. Horrified, I turned to my mate next to me and said, 'There's maggots in my meat'! The response was 'don't worry mate, they won't kill you'. I picked them out and pushed them to the side of my plate and continued eating. Blowflies are rampant here, around the sheep.

... When we go back, we'll pick up the Hillman at the service station and continue our journey. We hope to be in the next shed. It's Thursday today – near the end of the week, and 'cut out'. Everybody's getting ready to pack up and go down to Perth. The lucky ones will get a job at the next shearing shed.

... We picked up the car successfully and drove towards Perth to the next shearing job. On the way, I saw a dead roo on the side of a road, with a joey next door to it. I asked Rob who was driving to stop the car, and I got out and picked up the joey and put him in my jumper I was wearing, with his head sticking out. We continued, and after a while, the joey turned around, and went to sleep. We stopped at the next roadhouse and I gave the joey to the owner as he said he would give it to the ranger that was coming in. We went on our way.

... I would never attempt to drive through the Nullarbor Plains. If this car drives all right, I'll put it on the train, and then I'll just drive it as far as I can until the damn thing conks out, take the plates off, and there won't be any loss.

... I always had a carload of people. I always seemed to have a lot of people around me when I had a car and a recorder. People who drink always seemed to have a lot of friends. I remember somebody said to me: I like you Thomo because you'll always come and have a drink with us. Which probably won't do my liver any good in the end, but still.

... I was out with a few friends I'd met in the shearing shed. I was driving along, returning late at night after having a good time in a pub and had been drinking quite a lot. I hit a kangaroo that jumped out in front of the car, which isn't a good thing but quite common, especially in Western Australia. I did the car radiator in, so the water started leaking out. Luckily, we weren't that far away from a farm, and the car managed to 'limp' into the farmyard. We all got out and were hanging around the farmyard looking at the car, and thought we'd better not wake up the farmer.

... We decided that we'd stay there, in the farmyard for the rest of the night. One of us said, 'I'm cold, we'd better light a fire'. I said, 'We have nothing to light it with'. 'Oh yes there is. Look at all those posts over there in the corner.

We could use a couple of those. He'd never know there were a few posts gone. They don't look that good anyway.' 'I suppose so. I suppose we could.' So, we lit a roaring fire with the posts in the middle of the yard. After we'd all warmed up, somebody said, *'I'm hungry. I need something to eat. I haven't eaten all day'.* A bit further along the farmyard was a chook pen. Well he wouldn't miss one chook in amongst thousands in the pen, would he? So, we went around the back of the chook pen and the chooks were all dopey because they were half asleep, and somebody caught one. We sat in a circle, in the yard with the fire in the middle and a live chook in hand. So, all we've got to do now is kill it, pluck it, put it on the fire, and we'll have a meal. One of my friends said, *'I know how to put them to sleep. You just get a hold of her head, and put it under her wing, and she will go to sleep.'* I said, *'Well, who's going to kill it? I don't want to kill it.'* One by one, each of my friends said the same – *'No, not me. I don't want to kill it.'* We then decided – all right we'll just *'put it to sleep'* and think about it.' So, we tucked the chook's head under her wing, and she went to sleep. We all laid back thinking about how we were going to kill the chook and pluck it. The fire was burning nicely, and it was warm. We all went to sleep with the chook next door to us!

...Early morning, we woke up – it was a very hot even at this time. The chook was wandering around scratching for food and there was a heap of cinders in the middle of the yard where the fire had burned down. I said, *'I know what we can do. I've heard you can cook an egg on the bonnet of the car in this sort of heat.' 'Can you?' 'Yeah, all you have to do is crack and egg on top of the bonnet, and you'll have a nice, scrambled egg.' 'That sounds a great idea. Give it a go'.* So, I broke an egg on the hot bonnet of my car. It did go white and yellow – just like a cooked egg; but it was all over the bonnet, not in one spot!' There was a lot of laughter and comments at this time, and the farmer came out.

... *'What the hell are you all doing here,'* he said? I told him the story – *'We're sorry, but we hit a 'roo down the road, and it did the radiator in... we were going to wake you up, but we thought it was too late and you were asleep, so we just stayed here.'* Angrily he said, *'what have you done with my fence posts? You've burned half of them.'* I replied, *'Yes, well, we got a bit cold.'* He went on, *'And what's this chook wandering around?'* In any case, after a bit of altercation, he sort-of calmed down, and we paid him some money for the fence posts. He felt better after this, and because we said we couldn't go anywhere because the radiator's gone he managed to patch up the radiator with his welding set and other tools. We put some more water in the radiator, paid him some more money, and thanked him very much. We left as he was muttering, 'I'm not happy. My fence posts. I'll have to make some more now. I'm not happy.'

... We finished in the shearing shed and decided to return to Victoria. We spent a couple of nights in a hotel, and at this time we decided it was going to cost a lot of money to put the car on the train plus the train fare and everything else, so we decided that we'd drive back through the Nullarbor in my Hillman car. Well, in hindsight that probably wasn't such a good idea, but it was only a cheap car in any case.

We got about halfway through the Nullarbor Plain and I said to Rob, 'Can you smell petrol?' 'Yeah, I can' was the reply. Mind you, we continued to smoke! I had driven over a pothole that was covered by sand and the bottom of the petrol tank had been sheared off and all the petrol had run out. The rocks are very sharp, and the bull dust just disguises all these holes in the road. The corrugation is terrible. The graders come along and try to grade the roads, but anywhere in Western Australia or South Australia where you're going on the dirt roads, the corrugation, you don't know whether to go fast or slow.

... We came to a grinding stop when the petrol ran out. We didn't know what to do. We just sat there. Luckily, somebody came past, stopped, and said, 'What's wrong mate?' I said, 'Look, our petrol tank's been punctured, and we can't go any further.'

... 'Well,' he said, 'about 20 miles away I know there's a sheep station. Have you got a rope? We can tow you to the sheep station and maybe they can fix it, or at least you're not going to starve on the Nullarbor.' We said, 'that's very good of you mate. We really appreciate that.' So we got towed to the sheep station. Just 'plunked' there.

...The owner of the sheep station came out, and we had a chat for a while. He said, 'What sort of car have you got?' He saw I had a Hillman. He said, 'that's good because you've got a pump. It's not gravity fed. The pump is in the front of the car, and all we got to do is put a pipe from the pump, and we've got an old five-gallon drum you can have – that'll help. If you put that in the boot, it should suck up the petrol and get you at least to civilization'. We thanked him profusely and gave him some money.

... Everybody's so generous. Especially when you get into the outback, you have to help each other. It's a sort of camaraderie that is expected, and it is nice.

Not like the city. In the city you can have a heart attack on the pavement and people would still walk past you. But it's not like that in the country, luckily.
... So, we started up the engine like he said, and we put five gallons of petrol in the tank, and off we went. We had to stop at a few roadhouses because there was still quite a way to go, a few hundred miles to go. Everywhere we stopped, we had to get out our five-gallon drum out to be filled. We just opened the boot, pulled the hose out, put the nozzle of the petrol in, filled it up, put the hose back in, closed the tank and the boot. We could smell the petrol all the way, but we kept having a couple of beers and smoking in between and went on our merry way. It turned a lot of heads and we told our story about the treacherous road going across the Nullarbor Plain. Luckily, we got to the roadhouse at Eucla, where we filled up again with petrol. Eventually we got to Adelaide. We went through Adelaide and the suburbs, slept in the car one night, drove through Melbourne and ended back in Benalla. The car was a wreck. I handed in the number plates.

It was October 1969 when we arrived in Benalla, and a surprising thing happened. I was thinking about going to see Glenda, in Euroa and all-of a sudden,

Janine, Rob's sister who was much younger than I decided that I wasn't such a bad sort of chap. We became friendly but did not go out together at this time. However, the family disapproved of the developing relationship between us. The long-term friendship with the family was being stretched in several ways.

Rob and I had argued coming back to Benalla from Western Australia. So, things weren't as good as they used to be. We'd been knocking around together for about 12 months, and I expect Rob wanted to just settle into his home life again without any conflict. Both Rob and Jeff did not want me to be around Janine, both reminding me: 'She's not going to marry a Pom. We're not going to let it happen.'

One night after the family and I had been drinking, things erupted. Rob and I got into a fight, over Janine, and things turned nasty. Punches were thrown. I packed my case and walked out. Where I was going, I did not know. I decided to spend the night in their old house, which was now deserted as the family had moved into a new house. As I lay on the floor in the old house feeling dejected, I realised a big part of my life had ended. I had become attached to the family life I had experienced over the last few months, but it was now finished.

However, a ray of hope came the next day. Ron and Lorraine came looking for me and found me in the old house. They said, 'you can't stay here, you'd better come and stay with us, we'll sort something out'. On the way, Lorraine said, 'it'll calm down, and we'll work out how you can see Janine. She's fond of you – it's a shame for you to break up.' She then said, 'how about if we take you to Wangaratta and we can bring Janine to see you and carry on like that for a while.' I agreed. I expected I would see Janine infrequently as I did not have a car.

Ron and Lorraine drove me to Wangaratta – about 45 minutes' drive from Benalla. I found a good clean boarding house with a friendly atmosphere. The people in the boarding house told me about the dye factory where I might get work – they were always looking for people, and it was within walking distance. I had a test for colour blindness, which was okay, luckily, otherwise, I'd be dyeing pink things blue, and blue things pink! There'd be a terrible mix up in everything! 'Yes, we can give you a job' they said. 'Come and see us 9:00 Monday, and we'll start you off.'

It was quite an interesting job and not hard. I wore white overalls and operated an industrial sewing machine, sewing the large lengths of cloth into a ream. The cloth sewn into continuous loops was inserted into vats – each a bit bigger than a bath, and about 4 or 5-foot wide, and they held different colour dyes. I also worked in the storeroom filling orders – so much cloth of certain colours, to be dyed and then dried. Day after day I did this… I recall during this time that there were festivities shown on television, with re-enactments of landing on shores. I remember there were boats in the harbour.

At the weekends, on Saturday, Ron, Lorraine, and Janine came to see me. Janine and I would walk around the park and kiss and cuddle. During the week, Janine and I wrote to each other – not sure if she understood what I wrote, but her letters were heavily perfumed, and at the bottom of the envelope, in very big letters 'SWALK – Sealed with a loving kiss' was written. When these letters arrived, everybody at the boarding house used to say, 'Oh Chris. You got another letter from your girlfriend.' It was very embarrassing!

But these secret meetings couldn't go on forever. Did the rest of the family know? It was not a good thing, and doubt, guilt and restlessness set in. Ron and Lorraine were driving to Wangaratta every weekend with Janine, and this could not continue. I was staying in a boarding house and getting tired of dyeing cloths. I realised I was not fully committed to the relationship. Knowing that there was a big age difference between us, and her very protective brothers and father were adamant that a relationship between us 'would not happen', I decided I'll have to tell Janine that the relationship was not going to go any further. But how do I tell her? I thought a letter would be the best way – a very brief letter given my abilities in this area. So, I wrote to Janine saying something like, 'I'm sorry. I'm moving on – it's for the best. I wish you all the best for the future, and I am sure you will find somebody else who will fit in to the family and your life better. And with that brief message, it was the end of a perfect friendship with Janine and her family.

It was not a good time. But, in all honesty, I know our relationship would not have blossomed even if the environment and family circumstances were right, and supportive. To the family, I know I would always have been a Pommy, not worthy of their daughter, or sister. And perhaps I was a 'Pommy bastard' whatever that means, and perhaps I was not, at that stage, worthy of their sister and daughter. What I do know is that I would've fought hard if I was committed to the relationship and saw a future. I didn't see a future for a range of reasons including an obvious cultural gap between Janine's and my family.

So, just before Christmas 1969, I had a few drinks with mates at the boarding house and said goodbye. I left Victoria with a clean 'slate' and without looking backwards, I moved on. I flew home to Maroochydore looking a million dollars and had Christmas with my parents. The joke of the time was that prior to coming home, I had broken up with Janine, and dyed*!*

... I think it's a lot of rot the way this Pommy business is carried on, but in Victoria it seems to be a lot and I get a great deal of it at work and everywhere else. Once I was almost ready to pack up and go back to England, but I thought all in all, living would probably be ten times worse in England. It did annoy me though and got me down at times constantly being ridiculed:
'Come here Pom, or
You're a Pommy bastard, or for a
Pommy bastard you're not bad, or all you
Pommy bastards are a winging lot'.
Once I imagined how nice it would be to go back to England, stand in a pub and shout at the top of my voice, 'I'm a Pommy'!
I imagined everyone cheering me loudly as they also would be Pommy's!

Anyhow, enough of the winging and self-pity – it was all a very long time ago.

On Jan 4th, 1970, Father dropped me off in Brisbane. My intention was to get a job in Brisbane and stay around home for a while. I roamed around a bit, and then went to a few pubs in Fortitude Valley to see if there were any jobs around. I got drunk – very, very drunk. Late that night, I was staggering along the street wondering where to sleep when the police picked me up for being drunk, and without a fixed address.

I ended up in gaol, in a cell with bars at the front and enclosed concrete walls on the other sides and usual stainless-steel toilet in the corner. There were about 12 other fellows in the same cell, all slouched around the place and like me, all 'sozzled'. I sat on the concrete bench that went right around the side of the cell, put my head back on the wall and slept. Sometime during the night, there was a commotion and I stirred. I kept my eyes shut, just opening one slightly to check out what was going on. I saw a naked man, being thrown into the cell with us. His clothes were thrown in after him with the words from the rough policeman, *'here, take care of your faggot mate.'* The unfortunate chap cowered to the side of the cell, water dripping off, him. I thought, *'don't get involved... this is a good time to pretend to be asleep, and I dozed off again.'*

The next morning at 6.30 we all lined up to get our meagre belongings. I saw one of the men from the cell with his arms around the so-called 'faggot' and heard him saying to him, 'it was terrible the way he had been treated last night and that he would look after him.' They went off together.

It was a new day. I realised Brisbane was not the place for me and made my way to the highway that headed north. I started hitchhiking – anywhere. I walked for quite some time. I turned to face the approaching cars with my thumb out. It took me several tries to get a lift, and when I did, the ride was short. 'Where are you heading mate – I'm going 10 minutes up the road, will that help? Another, 'Hop in – but I'm just going to the next town.' I kept walking and thinking, 'It's hard to hitchhike.' Eventually, a car stopped, and the driver said, 'I'm going to Townsville'. 'Great' I said, 'So am I'.

I managed to get a job in the Townsville Abattoir where I made blood and bone. It was one of the worst jobs I'd ever done because the smell was absolutely, horrendous! I worked in a very thin room – like a large passageway that had about six heated spin dryers. All the animal guts, bone, and everything else came down from the boning rooms and went into big spin dryers. When they spun, the blood would run out. I dried the offal and then placed it on the conveyor. It was a terrible job.

The 'saving grace' was working in the other building where the blood and bone was bagged. By the time it got there, it just smelled a little bit. It was an awful job. I remember once I sat on the steps outside the abattoir and thought, 'I don't know what to do. It's just too much.' This job always conjures up memories of one of the worst jobs I ever did, not because of the work, but because of the smell. It was worse than working on the night cart. I left this job as soon as I could and hitchhiked back to Brisbane.

I got a lift with one fellow and it was an amicable trip. We stopped off at various roadhouses along the way and I contributed to the petrol, as it was a long drive. Getting towards Brisbane, he asked me to keep going through to Sydney with him, where he was headed. I had already had a few tastes of Sydney that weren't very successful, so I replied, 'No mate, it's been a good trip but just drop me off in Brisbane.'

I headed back home to Maroochydore and bought a car.

Chapter 20
Coral and Grit

It was around April 1970 when I headed up the coast of Queensland again in my newly purchased second hand grey Falcon sedan – a very nice car. I had no specific purpose and did not know where I would end up. History records the following would occur in Australia in 1970:

... Australia would achieve its peak post war migrant intake, double-deck, air-conditioned electric trains came into service in New South Wales, seat belts became compulsory in Victoria, padded post bags went on sale, Western Australia was linked to the national telephone network and nationwide TV relays were now possible. An international terminal in Sydney, and Tullamarine airport in Melbourne were opened; Bass Strait oil and gas field came into operation; nine Australians were killed in one incident in Vietnam, 35 workers died when a section of the West Gate Bridge in Melbourne collapsed; and 13 people died when Cyclone Ada damaged the Great Barrier reef in January 1970. The Queen arrived to open the Captain Cook celebrations, Pope Paul VI visited, Germaine Greer published 'The Female Eunuch' and the Beatles song, 'Let it be' topped the charts....

I had now been in Australia for 6 years and spent most of my time drifting from one place to another. What would the year 1970 hold for me?

... I passed through Maryborough and drove onward to Gin Gin where I thought I would spend the night, but I arrived early, was not tired so I kept driving, stopping at a motel between Gin Gin and Gladstone. It was only $5, and I had a very good breakfast this morning. Last night I had a meal for $1.60. It was a huge piece of steak that almost covered the plate with onions, potatoes

and all the rest of it. I got up about half-past 7 and had breakfast. With that I paid the bill and set off to Gladstone. I felt refreshed – thank you for the money for the motel. Normally I curl up on the back seat and think of the good times as I think it's silly to spend my dollars on a place to put my head, every night.

... I arrived in Gladstone about half-past 8 in the morning it's not a terrifically big town. Driving on, the scenery changed. There is just a little bit of very light, sparsely populated grass, and mostly undulating land either side of the road with a few broken fences as well. No signs of any cattle or much life at all as-yet. The road is still excellent – it's remarkable how they can make the road so straight for so long. It can be dangerous too as you don't have to think too much and could go to sleep with the sound of the tyres on the road, the lack of twists of turns in the road. The Romans would be proud of the straight road. I think I can give the Queensland Government credit here for keeping the northern road in very good repair. Further back along the road, there is quite a lot of roadwork being done where they're improving the road all the time.... I noticed a Stock Crossing sign so there must be stock somewhere and there is a bit of burning off along here near the railway line. A little bit of ring barking has been done on the trees.

... What are my plans for-the future? I don't know.... I hope to get as far as Mackay or maybe a bit higher up. I found out when I went to the employment exchange in Gladstone that Mackay is supposed to be a 'boom town', but due to the shortage of steel, they haven't been able to start all the projects that are supposed to be going on. So, there's not much work there at all, but he did volunteer some information to me that they will be starting cane cutting on about the 9th of this month. That's in about a week's time. I suppose in the mills it's very mechanised, and they don't want many people. He said they still rely on a few thousand people coming for the cane cutting. So that is what is in the back of my mind at the moment to see if I may be able to do something like that – it's quite good money doing that for the time being.

... It's a bit lonely driving by yourself. I'm cruising along at 60 miles an hour. As I was driving along, I saw a hitchhiker in the distance. I thought oh well, I'd stop and pick him up. He seemed to be a young chap. I stopped and asked where he was going. He was American and had actually only been over here about a week. He was making his way to South Molle Island, part of the Whitsunday Islands, Great Barrier Reef to find work. South Molle Island is a very interesting island because they have an underwater observatory. Alex – the American had made inquiries and had been told that he could have a job there, for $50 a week, only $4 a week board. I dropped him at Shute Harbour – the main mainland port for all boats going over to the islands. I drove on looking for accommodation.

... It was clever how this American managed to get to the Island – he had a lot of go in him really. He told the supply boat skipper a story about how he had a cousin on the island, and he hadn't seen him for so long – the skipper bought the story.... Tonight, I'm staying in 'the cabins' as they call them about eight miles from Shute Harbour, and $3 a night. I thought about the conversation I'd had with the American and thought why don't I try something like that? It appealed to me – $50 a week is quite good money, and you would meet a lot of interesting people. Better than in a cane factory crushing cane.

Alex, the American, had just graduated and he had all sorts of good and marvellous ideas. He was confident, knew what he wanted, and where he was going. He was the opposite of me and not like any other hitchhikers I had met in all my travels. He left a lasting impression – even with this passing meeting.

... Celebrations of when Captain Cook landed in Australia in 1770, continues to this day. The 'Endeavour' has come up to the islands here where Cook landed in May 1770, and everyone is having a good time celebrating. There was a party on one of the islands tonight I almost went to, but I thought I'd better not, so I didn't, as I am looking for a job tomorrow. When I was working at the dye house at Wangaratta, I saw the re-enactment of Cook's landing on the TV in the boarding house. At Mackay, there is a small model of the 'Endeavour', and I took a picture of it. It was only a small model but very good – it was made in New Zealand and brought to Australia for the bicentennial of Captain Cook's landing in Botany Bay [April 28, 1770].

... I thought I'd have to have a shower and shave to do any good on the island. You never know what sort of job I might get. I have a job in any case at the end of the week working at the mill at Innisfail. So, it seems hopeful for me at the moment. Tonight, I had a feed, and it was a nice trout. It's a long time since I had some trout. They call it 'coral trout'. It's caught around the islands. It was delicious. I walked over to the communal cabin, set up as a lounge with comfortable chairs, couches and tropical pot plants scattered around and saw 'Bellbird' on the TV. It's all very nice indeed. The cabin that I'm in is varnished wood with a fridge, a sink, and a small grill if you want to do any cooking. The car is still going well but it has developed quite a few noises – the engine is knocking a little bit more than it did before, but there aren't any parts of it really falling to pieces.

... The next day, I got up and went to the pub to find out what was going on in the district. I was having a beer with a fellow at the bar, and he told me how recently all around the countryside was just brown and in the four months since the recent cyclone it has picked up no end. However, 'Cyclone Ada' killed 14 people when it hit Daydream, South Molle and Hayman islands in the Queensland Whitsundays and the damage bill was estimated at $390 million. My pub mate said that he knew that three boats were sunk, and there were winds up to 200 miles an hour and that the islands have been closed since this time and houses were flattened to the ground and still deserted. He told me that Hayman

Island is still trying to recover from the devastating cyclone but was due to open this coming weekend. As we were talking, a lady walked into the pub and said: 'I've got two days labouring work on Daydream Island for anyone who wants it. The boat will be leaving in the next 15 minutes.' I rushed and gathered my gear, left my car in the pub car park – the publican said it was ok for a couple of days, and was at the boat in 10 minutes.

... I landed on Daydream Island. I wouldn't recommend the place myself. It's only three miles by half a mile long. We repaired the damage that had been done on the island by the cyclone. One of the jobs we had to do was get the roof of the motel out of the sea. That was quite a job in itself because Daydream Island is on the coral basin, and the coral is very, very sharp. So, we had to be very careful dragging the roof out of the coral, as you could easily cut your feet. While we were there, we were put up in a motel unit that was quite comfortable, and we ate in the lounge and had nice food. So, we were sort of non-paying guests, being paid – wasn't bad really.

... We had a look at Daydream Island. All it consisted of from what I could see, was a golf course, which pretty-well covered the whole of the island. And then there were resorts where there are nice motel rooms all decked out Hawaiian style. The only way to get to the island and back is by motorboat. I did two days labouring there, and that's where I met Pete, a fellow traveller in the wine bar. We were buying cans for 40 cents a can. We were talking and, as I said before, I don't like travelling around much by myself. It's not much fun. We were talking about going around the 'Top End' after this job, financed by the two days' work of $20. We decided to travel together for a little while, with the aim of reaching the Top End – Darwin.

Listening to this tape nearly 50 years later, my thoughts are a little different of Daydream Island. Oh, only for some vision at the time I was there, instead of my priorities – the price of a can of beer, good food, company, and my next adventure!

... We left Proserpine on Saturday night and drove back down to Mackay because Pete had his gear down there to collect. We spent a day in Mackay and then drove back to Proserpine picking up a hitchhiker on the way. We had a few beers with him on the way to the next town where we dropped him off and continued driving up past Bowen, up to Ingham. We were looking around and talking all the way and having a good time as well – enjoying ourselves. We slept in the car – me in the front, Pete in the back. We went out to the hotel at night and danced with all the nice girls around here. We inquired if there was any work at the mills, and apparently there wasn't. So, we left Ingham and went up to Townsville.

... We spent Sunday in Townsville looking around – it's quite a big place but we didn't think there would be any work for us, and I was not going to work in the abattoir again, so we decided to go back to Ayr as it was more likely we would get some work in Ayr at the mills. There was none. So off we set again, from Ayr, passed through Townsville, up past Ingham to Innisfail, picking up a hitchhiker on the way and went right up to Cairns, where we spent a couple of days looking for work.... I was very disappointed in Cairns. I thought it would be a bigger, more attractive town. We looked at the sights but felt there wasn't much to offer us as far as work was concerned so we decided the best thing to do would be to go back to Innisfail.

... So here we are now at Innisfail. We went to the employment exchange and talked our way into a job cutting cane. A local farmer is going to let us do the season and he's given us $10 sub at the moment until the wet weather stops as it is stopping the mills for starting. Money is short, so we phoned him up again and he said we could have a day's work doing 'the wife's' garden. This we did, and we've been here now for about three days – dug in. I've even learned how to play 'patience' because we've very little money between us now and as I said Pete does shout his fare, on the way we've occasionally got $20 out of the bank, his bank is the New South Wales, and he goes to his and I go to mine and that's how it should be. We've got a bit of tucker in the house, not a bad flat, and we're really waiting to get started on cutting the cane. At Townsville I blew a back car tyre, so it was $20 straight off for the new tyre. It wasn't the best at this present time – more expense, but at least it is fixed now.

... The weather here is very overcast and rainy. The mill was supposed to start yesterday, the 15th, but it hasn't. It's still raining, so we don't know when it's going to start. We hope it starts very shortly because there's not much to do – especially when you haven't any money, and we're just sitting here. We're really waiting to get started now on this cane. Some farms had mechanical harvesters, but the farm we will be working on doesn't.

... We've had a good time of seeing the north coast of Queensland and made a lot of friends and talked to a lot of people. But now I suppose for the next couple of months we'll be settling down to some hard work. Then we probably will go across to Mount Isa, then to Darwin and then onto Western Australia.

... The north coast of Queensland is very nice – Ingham, Ayre and Proserpine. I had a labouring job offered to me at Proserpine and Pete had a job offer in Townsville in a shearing shed as a presser, but we both decided to go a bit further up looking for work. We decided that two travelling together had benefits – there was support and we had more confidence than travelling alone. Two can do a lot of things, whereas one person is sort of meek and mild and doesn't do much. Then there is the expenses side. It's only costing us $5 each per week for the flat. If there was only one, that'd be $10 straight out which is a lot of money.

... The wage is $60 a week clear and this flat is only costing us $10 per week and we have a bit of tucker here now. No hot water and not very good cooking facilities, but we're taking turns to cook breakfast. We'll probably move to a better flat. The reason we went to a flat rather than a boarding house is because of the irregular and unsociable hours – sometimes we start at 5:00 in the morning and may finish at 2:00 in the afternoon, and then return in the evening, to burn off. When you're at a boarding house with these hours you would miss out on a lot of meals and make too much noise coming and going. You have heard my views on boarding houses before, and they're never much good, and the food isn't good – apart from the one in Wangaratta. At least now we can get a decent meal when we cook ourselves.

... We've made friends with the barmaid and a few other friendly girls around the place. I've met a few people along the way that want to travel with me – a lot of funny hitchhikers on the road, there's some queer people about that's for sure. When you have a car, there are always people wanting a lift. Pete and I went out Saturday night to a dance and a good time. Life isn't that bad. I suppose one gets over his bad times. The family in Benalla – I have forgotten them. That's a chapter that's closed, and another one has opened.

... Eventually the rain stopped, and we started our job cane cutting at Innisfail. It was quite an interesting job. Before cutting the cane, you have to burn off the amount of cane that you think you will finish cutting the next day. You have to be very careful when you're burning off. There are 10 or 11 people making sure the fire doesn't get out of hand. We all have beaters –to beat the flames if they go too far. The fires at dusk were a sight to behold, as the smoke and the flames mingle with the setting sun. There are a lot of snakes in the cane *and when the fire is burning, the snakes come slithering out of the cane at a rapid pace, and you have to make sure you're not in the way!*

... We're given a cane knife to cut the cane and it's a bit like cutting kale as I did in England for the cows. The cane knife is double-sided, and it's quite easy to cut the cane if you keep your knife sharp, and because all the leaves are burned. You walk in the middle of the cane rows slashing either side as you walk. You place the cane behind you. You do this row after row. At the end of the day, you gather up all the cane into bundles where you tie it with cord and load it onto the cane train. A bonus is chewing on the cane as you work. It is sinewy, and sweet.

... There are portable tracks for the cane train. You've got the main line to the cane factory at the top of your field, and then you've got portable tracks which you lay at the beginning of the day and load the cane onto the allocated trucks and then push them back to the main line where they are then hooked up to the main cane train and are taken to the cane factory. It's pretty hard work this cane cutting. It's a dirty, dusty job – outside in the extreme heat with a navy-blue singlet, khaki shorts, straw hat and boots. The soot, grime, and dust sticks to your sweat – you look like an old fashioned, chimneysweeper at the end of the day. No masks, no eye-shields.

... Not sure if you received my last card from Mackay? I don't think I'll send cards anymore – I will phone you from Darwin. Life is becoming monotonous – another chapter has closed and another one's open – I suppose it's the way it goes, isn't it?

... Pete's 25 and I'm 28. I look about 50, at the moment – and feel it... Working hard, playing hard, and indecision about the future – is torment. I can't keep doing this.

After a while, Pete decided to work in shearing sheds rather than cane cutting and he did not want to go to Darwin. So, he took off and went back to the job he was promised. I remained steadfast in my plans to visit Darwin. It would turn out to be a memorable trip and challenging beginning to my life in Darwin.

Chapter 21
Three Ways

Life had become monotonous, and I was getting sick of what I was doing, but I still never gave much thought on how to change it other than moving on to another state in Australia. So, I left cane cutting and headed to Darwin via Townsville, Julia Creek, Mount Isa, Tennant Creek and Katherine. There were a few small places in between these major stops. I calculated I should get to Darwin in about four or five days, but the weather was definitely against me. It was raining, and it had been for a couple of days and was coming down quite fast. I managed to get to just outside Townsville the first day where I pulled into a lay-by, rested for about four hours, and then kept going. I turned off at Townsville and headed towards Julia Creek. It was still pouring with rain.

The drive was long and lonely, but I listened to the radio when I could pick up the signal, at other times I listened to music I'd recorded earlier off the radio – the Beatles and ABBA and other hits of the day on my reel-to-reel tape recorder which I plugged into the cigarette lighter of my car, with a car adaptor. This kept me company and awake.

I drove into the town of Julia Creek just as the car generator packed up. There was a large crowd gathered and numerous cars. I asked a bystander why are these cars stopped here at Julia Creek? He replied, 'you won't go any further mate. The roads are all flooded. You'll have to wait until the rain stops and the floods go down.' 'Cor' I said, 'that's no good, is it'? 'No, mate' he replied… 'It happens. You'll just have to wait. There are a couple of hotels here that you can book into. There's the Julia Creek Hotel, which is quite a big one. That's just up that side road. And then, you've got the one here on the main street, which is really, just a pub. I don't think it has accommodation. It only has a couple of rooms, in any case. But I'd go to the Julia Creek Hotel, that's a big one and it's just up there. You'll get in, no worries. The one in the main street's the best one here if you just want to have a drink and have a chat to somebody while your car is fixed.' Okay, all right, yep, no worries', I replied.

I took the friendly bloke's advice and booked the car into be fixed and booked into the Julia Creek Hotel, which was quite a nice hotel, and a reasonable tariff. I treated myself to a meal. I decided to look around Julia Creek walked down the road and found the main street, and quite a popular bar where everybody seemed to be drinking. Well, I thought, why not. I may as well call in and just have a beer and see what's going on in the place. It was reasonably full. Well, when I say reasonably full, there were only about 20 people there.

I put my money on the counter and ordered a beer and struck up a conversation with a young fellow next door to me who was also having a beer. He was a very tall bloke, on crutches, about 25. His name was John. 'Hello, mate, how are you?' I said. He replied, 'I'm stranded – it's a bastard – the road's closed.' I said, 'Yeah – how long do you think it will go on for?' 'Well, I don't know long but I've been told that when the rain stops, we'll have to wait for the river to go down, to get across.' He went on… 'I was going to Darwin on the bus, and the driver stopped for a break. I got off to have a few drinks, and the bloody bus went without me. The bus got through, and I'm stuck here now – waiting for the next one to come through so I can get to Darwin.' 'Yeah' I replied, 'it happens.' I asked, 'What have you done to your foot'? 'Oh, yeah', he said, 'I strained it, and they gave me a crutch so I'm hobbling about a bit at the moment'. 'Oh, well, never mind, it never rains but it pours – excuse the pun'. We both laughed. 'Yeah, that's true', said John.

We had a few beers together to pass the time. I told him that I might see if there are any jobs around here tomorrow to keep me occupied until the river goes down. 'Hmm, I don't give much to your luck, but give it a go and try the local council, they might give you a day's work.' 'Okay,' I said. And with that I said goodnight and walked back to the hotel and slept very well.

Next morning, I went to the Council offices and asked for a job. Luckily, the response was good… 'Yeah, we could give you a couple of days' work just sort of tidying up. This rain made a hell of a mess, and it'll keep you busy.' 'Oh, that's good. Thanks.' So, I started there and then, clearing up the debris in the streets that the floods had caused.

I went back to the pub that night and had a counter meal. Not surprisingly, John was still propped against the bar with a beer in hand. I told him that I managed to get a job – probably not for long but at least it'll keep me occupied.

John asked if I wanted to play a game of darts. 'Ok, but I'm not very good at darts – I'm a bit cross-eyed'. 'Oh, you'll be all right, no worries – just a friendly game mate' John replied. With that, we each put our money on the counter, and both piles decreased as the night wore on.

As expected, John won most games. But there was this one time – getting on in the night, and we'd had a few beers – and really at this stage – I had to prop myself up to the bar to even stay upright – never mind throw a dart straight! John said, 'Here you are, your go'. Well, with that I picked up the dart. I thought, 'oh, this is bloody stupid, this is. I'm never going to get anywhere at this rate'. And I threw the dart. 'Oh, god, Chris, what's happened to you,' said John. I said, 'What do you mean'? He said, 'Have a look'. And I looked. I'd got a bullseye! Well, I don't know who was more surprised, him or I. 'How did you do that?' he said? 'I haven't got a clue' I replied, slurring my words. And it was the only time I had ever got a bullseye – never before, even when I played it regularly in the pub in England. I usually managed to sometimes scrape into the doubles, but bullseye, no way!

The next day I went back to the Council and got another day's work, but after this they didn't think they could find any more for me as the floods had started to go down and life in Julia Creek would return to normal. So, the next day I decided to look around Julia Creek with John who was becoming very efficient on his crutches and his ankle was getting better. It was good to have another young person's company to go around with.

The rain had stopped, the grey rain clouds disappeared, and a brilliant blue sky appeared. Julia Creek was again bathed in sunshine. A sense of anticipation had arrived. I had just collected my car and was filling it up with petrol at the service station and lo and behold, several rally cars drove into the service station. I asked one driver, 'Where have you come from and what are you doing? He replied: 'we're in the Ampol endurance trial and we got held up the other side of Julia Creek due to the flood. We just managed to get through this morning.' John and I walked over to have a look at this amazing scene – deep in the Australian outback, torrential rain, enormous floods, and in all of this, rally cars! It was obvious that these cars had taken a 'belting' on the roads they had travelled to get this far. And … it was obvious that the road was passable!

That night as we were having a beer at the pub, I said to John 'I'm going to head out to Darwin tomorrow. What are your plans? Are you staying here to wait for a bus, or would you like to come with me? It's a long trip to Darwin and I could always do with a bit of company.' 'Yeah, okay, I'll come with you – I'm sick of hanging around here. Thanks, I'll share the petrol costs with you'. The next day we stocked up with some supplies and took off.

The first day we got past Mount Isa, which looked like a typical mining town – a bit gloomy but as it was late at night, we never really got a true picture of it but we could see the mines up on the hill that when set against the dusk sky looked quite picturesque. We called in at the roadhouse at Mount Isa and got a feed of steak, egg and chips and asked about work but were told there wasn't much around. After this, we drove on until it became pitch black. As it was around 600 kilometres to get to Tennant Creek, we decided to kip on the side of the road that night – John in the back, and me in the front. We heard the night noises of the outback and were grateful for my car.

Breakfast was a can of baked beans – always under the car seat, for emergencies, as was the 'Gerry' can of petrol in the boot of the car. I drove onto the Barry Caves where we had a couple of beers and something to eat. We never looked at these caves, but I had seen others elsewhere. I just wanted to get to Darwin. I drove on, only stopping occasionally for a dip in a river to cool off and get rid of the dust, and for petrol at small towns along the way. Interesting, there were no obvious hitchhikers on the road we travelled this trip. But, not surprisingly, I suppose, as it was very isolated.

We reached the Three Ways Roadhouse – a very popular crossing where most travellers and 'Truckies' stopped and only about 20 kilometres from Tennant Creek. It's called the 'Three Ways' as you can drive one of three ways across the continent – north to Darwin; south to Tennant Creek and Alice Springs, and east to Mount Isa, which is where we had come from.

We were ravenous – we'd only had a few snacks and a couple of beers since morning. I walked into the Roadhouse – a wooden shack really, and immediately heard a lot of very 'colourful' swearing. I stopped and looked around surprised, and saw a large green parrot in the corner, in a cage talking rough – like you'd expect to hear on a building site! We laughed – it was good fun and an interesting place.

We had a good feed because the next stage of the trip was long – heading up to Katherine along the 'Beef Road'. These roads were originally built for defence reasons and they're straight as a die, and if you're tired you can easily go to sleep. We decided that we'd have a 'kip' in the car where the 'Truckies' parked before setting off. We slept for four or five hours – making sure that the keys were out of the ignition. We awoke refreshed and started the last leg of the journey, to Katherine.

To me, the town of Katherine never seemed a friendly place. We spent about half a day there and tried to strike up a conversation with people in the pub, but they were wary of us – they didn't like strangers or 'blow-ins' – which we were of course. So, we decided we didn't like Katherine much either so kept driving up to Darwin. On the way, we passed a large crocodile farm. It was a reminder that we were again entering a totally different, and exciting environment. The famous 'Top End'. I couldn't wait!

From Julia Creek to Darwin is about 1,400 kilometres of which there is only about 60 kilometres of dirt road. I did it in a long weekend simply because I was rapidly running out of money.

Chapter 22
The Top End

The car spluttered into Darwin and I dropped John off at his destination. I had exactly $1 in my pocket. I was 'broke'. The first fortnight in Darwin was very, very hard – I tell you. The radio blared: *15th of July 1970. It's 80 degrees, humidity 63%. The time is 8.00pm Darwin, Northern Territory.*

... It's surprising talking to a lot of people how many people do seem to arrive here broke; it seems to be a place where most, sort of head to and some have five or six tyres blow out on the way up. At Julia Creek the generator packed up – it cost $7 to get that fixed but other than that and a new tyre in Townsville I had virtually no trouble at all. It doesn't use any oil so all it does need is just a little bit of money spent on the front of it, shock absorbers adjusting, and a new tyre. It's sprung a leak in one of the petrol pipes – it still goes, but every gallon I put in the car, three quarters seems to water the road! After fixing this, away you go... it would be around $50 I suppose at the most. But all this will have to wait until I get a job and some money.

I slept in the car and showered in the beach conveniences at Fanny Bay, near the gaol situated just back from the foreshore. This gaol was a very old and ominous building with big rock walls towering around it. I pawned my reel-to-reel tape recorder and bought a little Metho stove that I placed on the ground, and boiled potatoes and onions; then piled melted butter on the top. I survived, and after some time got my reel-to-reel recorder back.

... I eventually got a job at Barclay Brothers – a Brisbane building and construction firm that build a lot of offices and are in a big way in Darwin. They paid me a $20 sub, which didn't go very far, but helped. I drive the car to and

from work and work as a labourer building the extension to the joinery shop at the yard. The job varies and is quite interesting. I measure and plane wood, use a pick and shovel, and today I drove a Bedford truck. The fellow at work said, 'can you drive one of these?' I said, 'I think so', and with that, I got in and drove it around picking up the rubbish. And for all of this, I get paid $140 a fortnight – good pay. It costs me $30, a fortnight to live and I spend part of it on entertainment. I think that after this next pay, I'll be able to save quite a lot.

... Where I'm working is right opposite the airport and sometimes, I see jumbo jets land and Boeing 707, Boeing 727 and Fokker Friendships and other little planes that go out to the islands round here. I've been told it is difficult to get on a flight at times, as they are so popular.

... Things are going well for me – I have moved from living in the car, into a caravan park in Night Cliff, about three miles out of Darwin. There is no air conditioning, but I have a roof over my head, and enough food to eat. I got the car fixed and picked up the recorder from the pawn – shop, ready for the next big trip. But this will not be soon as after my hectic life over the last few months, I have to settle down once again to a pretty-well routine way of life after going along the highway and dirt roads.

... Darwin is like a green house, and the caravan park I moved too, is like a little friendly oasis, with palm trees surrounding it. I have the use of a kitchen and stove and it's only $12 a week. Up here in the 'sticks', I'd say the cost of living is considerably dearer than it is down south as a carton of milk and a loaf of bread here costs about 37 cents, 47 cents I mean. The loaf of bread alone is 32cents and the milk is 15cents. The frozen milk is delivered weekly to Darwin from down south. It is very frustrating, as you need to allow the milk to thaw before using. Things are quite a lot dearer here, I suppose that's to be expected and board is terribly dear so I'm very lucky to live at this caravan park.

... The strange thing about being up here is I haven't had a hot shower for months. I have a cold one every night which I suppose isn't actually cold; because the temperature is 80, and this is winter and today has been quite a cool day. So, there's no hot water for a shower. Even on the way here, I stayed in a hotel in Julia Creek and there was only about one cup of hot water and then it started getting cold – the hot water was that already in the pipes that were exposed to the sun. I suppose some of the private houses here would have hot water but there's none where I am. I wouldn't like to be here again in the summer because I think it would be really too hot for me as the locals keep telling me that

February is called the suicide month as it gets so hot and humid.... I went for a swim last Saturday down on Fanny Bay. You've got to be very careful when swimming as there are sea and land snakes and the bluebottles floating around are deadly and they can kill you also if not treated. The locals assure me there are no crocodiles here.

... Darwin is becoming like many other coastal towns – an up-and-coming place. The population of Darwin is now 35,000 and increasing slowly. There's quite a lot of building going on and the place is getting bigger. There's a lot of Aborigines who live here – their homeland. There is a large floating population like many other places – here today and gone tomorrow. There's a 'Gum Banana' pub in town, which is a bit of a rough place and the 'Darwin Hotel' that I frequent. I have met a number of people I previously met on my travels over the years, at this pub. We are a group of people 'floating' around the country, picking up a month or two of work, here and there.

...I have made some good friends up here who live in the caravan park. A few of us meet in a neighbours' caravan annexe once or twice a week and play euchre, crib and 500 and all those sorts of games. At the weekend, I have a few drinks with the neighbours – one who I get on well with is Ken, about 23-year-old, and a kiwi and a carpenter who also works at Barclay Brothers. In case you don't know what a 'kiwi' is, it means a person from New Zealand, a bit like an Aussie is Australian, and a Pommy someone from England. Ken arrived a month before me and told me his friends are still working in Pine Creek, at a uranium mine, further south of Darwin where he had been working for the previous nine months.

... I drink at the Fanny Bay Hotel at the weekends. The choice is Swan beer, Melbourne Bitter, Emu draft, Emu bitter and Darwin Stubbies. I met an old man of about 60 at the pub, who liked talking about old times when he was in the Navy, and how things had changed over the years. I often have a few drinks with him. He seems a very private person, but very interesting and I enjoy talking with him. He showed me where he lived in a large, two-roomed caravan, parked on the promontory overlooking the sea at Fanny Bay. I visited him once and he showed me photos of memorabilia of his past and talked about the war that hit Darwin when Japanese submarines made an assertive attack on Darwin and bombed it severely. It was fascinating, I never knew about this part of Australian history, and I don't recall anyone talking about this when I lived down south. I

expect this is why Darwin is heavily fortified along the coast, as this area is a vulnerable area given the proximity to a range of Asian countries?

... One thing about Darwin that people don't seem to realise is that it is a defence town and has a big air-force and army base, port and the beef roads that are defence roads. There are a lot of radar tracking devices along the coast and abandoned plane runways. The American's have a big defence base outside Darwin, which the locals weren't happy about, as Australians weren't allowed to enter.

Darwin is vulnerable to cyclones – little did I know that within 3 years, the whole town would be destroyed by devastating Cyclone Tracey that flattened most of Darwin, including the Fanny Bay Hotel.

... Television has not yet reached the Top End. They are opening their own local television station at Christmas. People here don't seem to miss TV, but I am looking forward to it arriving. Maybe we'll stop drinking like 'fish', when we have something to watch!... Darwin has a drive in theatre that I occasionally go to you either sit in your car, or a deck chair, and drink 'Darwin stubbies' – only sold in the Northern Territory and are about double the size of a southern bottle of beer!

... There are two flights per week to Brisbane, so distance is not a problem. The only rail line goes to the towns of Katherine and Batchelor, next to the Lichfield Park. Not many cruise ships berth here. There's only one way in and one way out of Darwin – via the Stuart Highway, as you come up the Stuart Highway most towns you go straight through the main street and out the other side and onwards. But, here in Darwin, you drive straight through the main street and straight to the wharf, so you know you're at the end of the highway, and Top End of Australia!

... A lot of the incoming goods came by transport. The locals told me a few stories about this, like the one where air conditioners were being transported in a semi-trailer and due to the corrugation of the roads, the air conditioners were 'shaking' about so much that when they opened the back of the truck, there was just a lot of nuts and bolts! Darwin still has strikes, just like everywhere else and occasionally the power supply cuts off and the water isn't all that good. But the beef is very good indeed and it's lovely and tender. A buffalo steak fills the entire plate!

Time was moving on – to around about August and I was getting itchy feet again. Ken kept saying 'why don't we drive through the centre to Perth. I've got two friends, – MacTavish and Tom, they'd like to come with us, and we could all go together in the car.' 'I don't know' I replied, 'It's a hell of a long way going through the centre…'. Ken persisted… 'we could do it. You've got a good car there, haven't you? Why don't you come down and meet Tom and Mac, and we can talk about it over a few beers? If you decide that you don't want to do it, nothing happens'. 'All right then… 'We'll go down and talk to them and we'll play it from there'.

It was late Sunday night and we had workwrought the next morning, but that didn't deter us. The decision was made – we got in the car and drove the 180 miles and arrived in the camp at about eight o'clock the next morning. Work at Barclay's would have to wait until we returned – whenever that was!

… Mac, Ken's friend came from Ireland, was about thirty-year-old and worked at the United Uranium Mine, Morleen, near Pine Creek. Here they mine uranium and copper although the uranium part had been closed down for about five years and was due to open again in about 1975…. It's fascinating, the whole camp, and the machinery at this mine is well-maintained, but uranium is not something you want to get to close too – apparently what they call 'yellow cake'. I did pick up a small rock that had captured my attention and put it in my pocket. – I think it is a rock – it was black, shiny and smooth. I don't think its lead…it might be uranium. Who knows?

…They even have a pub close by which we went to and had a few beers. During our session, five of us decided to go buffalo shooting the next day, which is terribly illegal, but no one seemed to take much notice of this. The buffalo were only about five miles away out on the buffalo plains, consisting of brigalo and scrub. It's like the song 'home, home on the range, where the deer and the buffalo roam'. We went out in a jeep that had a bull bar and roll bars. Two were in the front, and three in the back – I was one of them. Buffalo are colossal animals. I had a 'pot shot' at them and wounded one and another shooter managed to kill it. I scored a couple of buffalo horns – real beauties out of this shoot. They were about two foot each horn. I enjoyed the buffalo shoot. We had a few beers at the pub afterwards and a few laughs.

We returned to Darwin on Monday to our job at Barclay's – we had been away a week. We were talking about the buffalo horns and Kevin asked me: 'Do you want them mounted?' I responded: 'Yes, that'd be great – how would you do it?' He then said, 'I will mount them with some red felt in the middle, with a crest of Darwin on the red velvet and put a hook on the back so you can hang them up'. This he did, and I paid him $10. ... I might be able to send you these buffalo horns. They're nice, be lovely polished. I don't know what to do with them... I suppose I could put them in a sack or something with the rocks and send home. However, it is illegal to have them. It's a bit 'dicky', you know, to send them.

I decided against sending the buffalo horns. They would travel with me from this time.

... 'I'm going to shoot through. I'm getting sick of Darwin. ...Well, I am.... The prices are always inconsistent and expensive. Darwin is not a big city. After you've driven around it a few times, what do you do? There's no fresh milk; it's frozen presented in large blocks that you could almost build a house with. Life is becoming frustrating. I've decided that Darwin is a terrible place, I haven't fallen in love with the place, and everything is so dear. What really got me, I saw

the bush again and the buffalo. I saw lots of good fellows living in decent quarters.

... I'm not going off on a wild goose chase. No, I'm not.... Mac and Ken are skilled operators, and we are hoping to find work at a mine in Tennant Creek. I went into Darwin and I got a 'C' Northern Territory license, which I sort of wangled it a bit, you know, and got it, which now, enables me to drive anything, even a semitrailer! I hate to think it, but I am now classed as a skilled operator because I have an AWA Union ticket, and have a car, lorry, tractor license, so I can go in as an operator. It's mining work, with these types of licenses, you straightway go up into the high wage bracket.

...Now, if I can get onto a job driving a truck I can save. I can get about a hundred 'bucks' a week, which is pretty good. Ken and Mac are in the 'know', and a lot of people have left Pine Creek and gone down to Tennant Creek. I might score myself a good job to better myself. The mines look after their people well and it is a lot better than living in a caravan. At the mine you get entertainment provided, single men's quarters, good tucker, good pay, meals cooked for you, and you can save your money. You can save because you only get a portion of your week's wages every week as 'booze', drugs and gambling can wreak havoc with wages. Pocket money is doled out for those who agree, and the rest of it is stored up, and when you leave, they hand over the saved money which may be quite a lot and you can stick it in the bank.

Ken and I handed in our notice at Barclays. We were off to Tennant Creek, about a thousand miles away from Darwin. But as it happened, circumstances dictated otherwise – we would not stay at Tennant Creek to work in the mines. But I would do this some months later.

... The car had new batteries, grease and oil change, new plugs, and a tune-up. So now the car is as good as new again. My word, the 'old girl' will get around again, I hope. There are a lot of 'roos' up here. I was thinking of getting a 'roo' guard but haven't, so, I'll have to watch my driving. Hazardous roads, aren't they?

... Ken and Mac are going halves in all expenses for this trip. We're going to Katherine – you know where Katherine is on the map, and then down to Tennant Creek and the Three Ways – the road is straight down to Alice Springs, and then onto Adelaide. I'll phone you tonight, as when you are 'out bush' you never quite know where you're going to end up and what is going to happen.

... They seem to be two 'good sorts of people', from the country and they've already given me $10 towards the 'tune-up' as I had to get this done. I suppose I am helping them as far as providing a car; but I know Ken has enough money to buy one of his own. But it's still good to travel together. I found out travelling here in Australia you don't make real friends; you make travelling companions for one's own personal convenience. So, as long as you always travel on that basis, it's all right, I think ... don't treat them as a friend, treat them as a sort of companion not like friends I've known in the past in England, like, say, Alistair Brown and David Millington. They were real friends.

...Well, I'm sitting here on the beach at Night Cliff once again, watching the sea come in for the last time. I suppose I won't be here again at the Top End of Australia, the northern gateway to the world, as the sunsets over the horizon.

... It's Saturday tomorrow and in the morning, we'll head off early on our trip. We're stopping at Pine Creek to pick up Mac, probably see the fellows there, and then carry on to Katherine. We hope to be in Tennant Creek on Monday looking for a job, it's no use just going as a tourist – one can sort of enjoy life while they're travelling, but one has to get a job very shortly. But for me, I think it will be better off that way.

... On the way to Pine Creek we're going to call in at the crocodile reserve and have a look at the 'crocs' and take a few pictures. I might see if I can get a daring picture taken such as sitting on top of the croc! So, we're going to see the crocodiles tomorrow. What with buffalos and crocodiles, I don't know. Makes you wonder sometimes where exactly you are – you're not sure if you're just stepping out of reality altogether. You suddenly see these great creatures that you've only ever seen on African safari! Oh, it's marvellous really, what you can see around this place, the experiences you can have and the friends and the times you have. Well, it compensates the bad times I think, really.

... I think I'm happier in the bush than the city. One of these days, very shortly, I will settle down and have a family. I'm 28 – nearly 29, so I'm having my final fling now – seeing as much as I can and cramming every experience I can into this short time, and then I shall come and settle down. I have given myself until Christmas, and maybe till January. If I still have a job making and saving good money, I give it four months as I am getting tired of roaming around. A rolling stone gathers no moss.

... Oh well, you never know... one can't make plans for the future, can they?

Chapter 23
The Red Centre

It was Saturday 22nd August 1970. I would soon be twenty-eight-year-old. I was about to head into the Red Centre of Australia, and a unique experience.

... Ken and I got up bright and early and made tracks to Pine Creek where the Moline mining camp is, next to the now Kakadu National Park in the Northern Territory. We arrived there mid-day, and needless to say there was great celebrations going on in the local pub there – a party for Max and Tom who were coming with us.

... We had a few beers with Max, Tom, Ken and Len and a lot of other people. We drank into the early hours of the morning, and the publican, like all these publicans seem to do, gave us a bed to sleep on for the rest of the night. The next morning, we got up and went back to the camp to pick up the gear. Two dogs came bounding up to us. Mack's dog was a half dingo-cross named; 'Mutt' and Ken's dog was an Alsatian called 'Stupid'. Mack and Ken said, 'we have to take our dogs with us'. I said, 'How are we going to feed them?' The reply? 'When we get our slabs of beer, we'll get a slab of PAL for the dogs'. Sounded reasonable. 'Well', I said, 'if you're all taking a dog with you, I want one'. 'No problems – what sort do you want'? I replied, 'a friendly one'.

... Next minute, Ken took off and brought back a dog. I said, 'What's that'? He said, 'it's a whippet – it's yours'. The whippet was a black, long legged friendly dog and I called him 'Whippet the Whoppet' from then on. We finished loading the car – men and dogs – and drove to a clearing on the other side of Rum Jungle, about 10 miles from the camp. We continued drinking and eating.

Many areas have names with 'history' behind them. The naming of Rum Jungle is no exception and tends to fit with what I experienced in the Northern Territory. The story goes that around 1871, a bullock wagon delivering barrels of rum to construction gangs became bogged in jungle terrain. The crew unhooked the bullocks from the wagon and to ease their thirst in heat of the 'Top End' drank the wagonload of rum in a weeklong party until they were rescued! Rum Jungle is also famous as the site of the first uranium discovery in the Northern Territory.

... A latecomer arrived at our gathering and told us that the local Aboriginals were 'hopping mad' as someone had stolen one of their dogs, which sleep with them in the 'humpies' for warmth at night. The latecomer told us that a party from the Aboriginal camp nearby which was next to the mining camp were out looking for the dog, and whoever had taken him. I then realised what had happened. I didn't think of asking where Ken had gotten 'Whippet the Whoppet' from. I assumed it was a stray. But, because I was more than 'half charged', I didn't give it another thought. Perhaps I should've as I had heard a story about a policeman who decided to 'cull' the dogs in an aboriginal camp as he felt there were too many of them. The story goes that the witchdoctor pointed the bone at the policeman to punish him for killing the dogs. A few months later, the policemen became very unwell and had to leave his post.

I thought I might have a bone pointed at me as well. Maybe I did, as two years later I became very ill whilst working on an aboriginal reserve. Anyhow, our party continued until we 'flaked out' in various positions under a tree and had a siesta. The dogs slept as well, full of PAL and beer.

It was quite late in the evening when we woke. The sun had faded into twilight and our mates left for the mining camp after saying, 'see you around'. There were a certain group of people that I met on my travels, that seemed to go around in circles, like I did, and I fully expected to see them again. You meet somebody in Perth, and a bit later, you meet him in Darwin. You just keep going around and round and round. 'We'll catch up with you later'.

... We all 'piled' into the car and started our trip, through the 'Red Centre' of Australia: 4 men, 4 slabs of beer – 24 cans in each slab; and a slab of PAL to feed our 3 dogs: 'Mutt', 'Stupid' and 'Whippet the Whoppet'. We drove to Katherine, taking turns to drive. We stopped there for a while and looked around and had a few more drinks and then kept going. Ken, Mac and Tom paid for the petrol and oil and anything else required as I supplied the car. We got past Alice Springs – it was a great trip up until then, plain sailing on the main highway.

... Then the road deteriorated tremendously, and it was just a dirt track through the centre. We had some water and we bought about a dozen cans of baked beans that we used to throw under the seat just in case we needed them. We didn't. We kept going and sometimes we couldn't find the road at all. Sometimes, there would be a great big boulder in the road, and we thought, 'that's funny...which way do we go? Do we go left or right?' But we kept on going on and stopped at the roadhouses where we played a bit of pool and let the dogs out for a run. We replenished our supplies – dog food and stubbies, and then drove on.

.... We slept on the side of the road. At dusk, we stopped, gathered some firewood – twigs from the sparse vegetation and lit a fire in front of us to keep us warm, as it gets very cold in the desert at night. We had a few beers and talked and listened to the music on the tape recorder. Occasionally we heard a dingo calling in the distance, and we didn't think about snakes or other creepy crawlies. The fire was burning low, and we settled into our sleeping bags, with our dogs to keep us warm – the dogs would head to the bottom of the sleeping

bag and kept our feet warm. We were in a very relaxed sort of state, dozing off because we were all half sozzled, half the time. Then, not thinking, Ken lit a fire behind us, as it was very cold. We all went berserk. We said, 'Light a fire in front of us, light a fire behind us, what happens when the two fires join up? Where are we? In the middle!' Pandemonium – we all put out the fire behind us before anything could happen.

... We were sitting in a roadhouse, drinking, and yarning. Over the top of my mates' head, through the window, I saw five elephants 'floating' past! I uttered some expletives and told my mates that I had just seen elephants going past! They said: 'don't be ridiculous – you must be in the DT's' [delirium tremens]. 'No, I'm not pulling your leg, I did see them'. I rushed outside and saw two semi-trailers – one with the elephants on and the other, with lions and tigers being transported to a circus in Alice Springs.

It was a bit of a worry, especially in the outback, after you've had a few beers and see elephants and tigers crossing the window! You really did wonder whether you should have another one or take it easy! I decided I was perfectly normal, and so resumed drinking with my mates, in the roadhouse. But I did take a picture of this scene because I thought nobody would believe it, including myself at a later stage.

... Little did we know we were making a name for ourselves in the Red Centre. We found out near the end of our trip that one roadhouse would phone through to the next roadhouse to see if the four mad drunk people and some dogs in a grey Falcon car had arrived. This wasn't a trip to be taken lightly and especially by a carload of people that in many eyes, seemed very irresponsible; and, because the road was known to be very, very, treacherous. And it was.

... We saw rusted and burnt-out carcasses of cars left on either side of the road. There were various names of people written on them – I don't know if the names were etched on by those who left the cars there, or those who travelled the same way later. We got about 100 miles outside of Alice Springs towards Coober Pedy and we wiped out a tyre. Not the new tyre luckily, but the one I'd bought in Townsville. We changed the tyre and drove on to the next roadhouse where we pulled in alongside a lot of coaches heading towards Alice Springs. The new spare tyre cost $30 so we all forked about $8 and then got something to eat.

... We drove off for the next leg of our journey. Then there was this stretch of road – about 304 miles of corrugated red soil and the car shook and rattled its way along. There were times when the road was unrecognisable from the vast expanse of nothing – no trees, roadhouses, or isolated outback stations in sight, just dots of saltbush. Luckily, we had a Gerry can be full of petrol in the boot. All of a sudden there was an enormous rattle and clatter, that frightened the life

out of us, and we stopped the car. We could see that the whole exhaust system had ended up on the dirt road. Not just the muffler, the whole lot! Broke off at the engine! There was no use picking it up and putting it on the roof rack or anything. I think we learned that if everybody else can leave wrecks of cars and car parts along the road, so can we. So, we promptly pulled the muffler and tail pipe off the road, got back in the car, wound down the windows and carried on – very noisily, but out here, no matter!

… Outback nothing surprises you – expect the unexpected. We got to the South Australian border, or did we? We couldn't find the border for a long time – there was no sign as somebody had knocked it over. We located it on the side of the road. I stood it up and took a picture. We had arrived in South Australia!

… The next stop was Coober Pedy where the famous opal mines are. Coober Pedy is flat with lots of little mounds of dirt everywhere. Everybody lives underground because it's so hot there. They've all staked their claims for their opal mines. We had to be very careful in Coober Pedy because we had heard that they are a hostile bunch and did not like 'blow ins'. We went into the Coober Pedy pub and everybody glared at us. We gingerly had a couple of beers and got in the car again and drove on to Port Augusta. We had made it! We were at the end of the Red Centre road as from then you hit the main highway. We were so pleased to arrive, and to drive on bitumen again after all the corrugation and dirt roads we had driven.

… We had a quick look around Port Augusta, got the exhaust fixed as it was so 'bloody noisy' and I'm sure some of the fumes were coming into the car –

perhaps that's why the dogs were so docile on the trip down. For $36 I got a new exhaust system fitted and a grease and oil change, which is a lot better value than I was getting in Darwin. I'd paid $8 for just a grease and oil change in Darwin. ... A lot of people travelling to Perth put their car on the train at Port Augusta. But we decided to continue by car because we'd come so far on dirt road through the Red Centre that a bit more dirt road in the Nullarbor Plain didn't really matter.

... We drove the 200 miles to Ceduna, the edge of the Nullarbor Plain an area of 200,000 km. We stopped, had a feed at the roadhouse, replenished stocks and drove on. It was raining – the car skidded in the rain and mud and was difficult to handle. This flat, almost treeless arid land was very interesting, with beautiful scenery – spectacular rocks and rock formations, on top of each other.

...We drove on until the rain stopped, and then made camp. The dogs got out and had a run. They continued to get on well together and seemed to be enjoying the adventure, freedom, and endless food. As we were settling down, I scraped the dirt on the side of the road and saw fossilised shells – not surprisingly given the history of the Nullarbor Plain, which was once covered by sea. Then we carried on to Kalgoorlie where we booked into the corner hotel and had a couple of beers. We went upstairs, had a shower, and made ourselves look respectable,

and we all met down in the public bar again. The night was still young, so we thought we'd go walk around the town and have a look at the highlights.

Hay Street Kalgoorlie is well known right throughout Australia where all the ladies of the night stay. For about 300 yards, there are a lot of little, tiny shop fronts with very nice-looking girls sitting on seats in the window with pink spot lights trained on them. They were seductive, beckoning in those passing by. We thought 'wow' and we went back to the pub and had another couple of beers.

Then Tom said, 'I reckon I'm going to go down there and have a go.' I said 'that's not a bad idea Tom. I think I might follow you.' The others said no, no, I think we'll stay here and have a few beers. You never know what they've got and what you might catch. 'No,' I said, they'll be all right. I said it's a well-known place. Everybody goes there.

So, Tom and I took off opened the door of the brothel and went in. We went from a dusty road into this beautiful, very dully lit foyer with a lot of pink drapes and satin. Half a dozen girls were lounging around in very flimsy negligees.

There wasn't much left to the imagination. The lady at the door welcomed us saying, 'Hello luv. You've come to enjoy yourself, have you? 'Yeah' we replied. 'Ok, we'll see who's about.' She was a nice Filipino, I think. She came up to me and said, 'Do you want a bit of fun with me'? I said, 'Yes, why not'? She took me by the hand, into her room. It had a nice quilt on the bed – and was nicely furnished. She said, 'you can put your clothes on the chair over there'. With that, she dropped her negligee – she had a petite body. She got a little bowl of warm water, washed me, and led me to the bed. All too soon, the Madam knocked on the door and said, 'time's up.' The lady said to me, 'I wish you could stay, but I am only allowed so long with clients.' So, half an hour after I apprehensively entered, I left confidently with a big, big smile on my face. Tom and I went back to the pub, had a few more beers, and slept very well that night.

... The next day we all got up and decided what we were going to do. We went out to all the mines around Kalgoorlie hoping that we'd get a job in the mines, but it was slack out there. Ken and Max got jobs in the railways down in the shunting yards. Tom wanted to go to Perth because his Mother was coming from Melbourne in about three weeks, and he wanted to see her. I decided on going to Perth.

... So, after a memorable trip through the Red Centre, we said goodbye to Mac and Ken and their two dogs. Whippet the Woppett was still with me. I couldn't just abandon him. He'd come a long way with us. So, Whippet the Whoppet and Tom and I carried on to Perth. ... We are now in Perth but Whippet the Whoppet is not with us anymore. We asked the hotel owner if we could tie him up in the foyer and if anyone wanted to give him a good home, let us know. Tom and I then went to have a drink. After a couple of hours, we came out of the bar and asked 'where's Whippet the Whoppet? 'Oh', the Hotel manager said, 'a fella came in and was absolutely wrapped in him and wanted to take him. I knew you wanted to get rid of him, so I said no worries. So, hopefully he has a good home.

... Tom and I were getting low on money and didn't want to waste it on a Hotel. We decided to drive to the sand dunes, just outside Perth where we thought we would be safe to sleep. We found a nice, secluded spot and pulled off the road. Tom got in the backseat and rolled up and went to sleep. I was uncomfortable on the front seat, so I got out and lay down beside the car in the sand, quite comfortable. During the night, I fidgeted, and my legs ended under the car, and

my head sticking out, near the front wheel. I slept well. Around 6 am I had a rude awakening. A policeman was leaning over me saying: 'Son, are you all right'? 'We had a report come in that someone had been run over!' 'Oh dear' I said, 'I must have nodded off – I just stopped for a 10-minute 'cat nap' – I better get going now'. I got up and quickly drove off. We'd only been in Perth two days and we had come to the attention of the police!

...We decided to find a rooming house – $8 a week for a bed. Nice place. This afternoon Tom went to the pictures. I washed the car and cleaned all the upholstery that made a big difference – you wouldn't know that any dogs had been in it now. ... The next day Tom and I went to the recruitment office and then the local barracks in Perth. Low and behold there was an army camp starting on Saturday for two weeks. Seeing that I'd already been at an army camp in Victoria, they said yes, you could start with us. So, we're starting on Saturday. Out in the bush somewhere under canvas. I think it'll be rather enjoyable to camp out with the army.

... Tom and I are looking forward to going to this army camp. It's only for a fortnight but you never know what might happen after that. Saturday morning came, and we got trucked into the bush. It was very good – we got ration packs – and in the army, these packs in the army, are pretty good. The one memorable thing about this job; was the latrines. They were just holes in the ground with tops to sit on all-in-one big row. So, if you wanted to go to the toilet, you had to sit down, next door to someone else who was doing exactly the same thing. I found that a little bit embarrassing, but I had to do it because nature called. Anyhow, we both really enjoyed the two weeks work and on return, we were offered a temporary work in the actual army base in Perth, which we accepted. The work was a lot like what I used to do in Benalla. We were feeding the troops and working in the kitchen. We went to see Tom's mother, a nice lady, and took her out to lunch on a day off and spent the rest of our free time frequenting the high spots of Perth, drinking, and blowing the little money we earned.

... After the army job ceased, we went straight to a job at the Pearce Air Force Base and stayed for some time. We had accommodation again, so we quite enjoyed that. I lived in a room with five other people, Tom and three others. We all got along very well together. Pearce Air Force Base is where the SAS paratroopers, the front-line defence are stationed. If there is any trouble in the world, they're the first ones who go and try to solve it. It was a particularly bad time to work at this Base because they were all heading off to the war in Vietnam.

Inevitably, there were fatalities, which was very sad. The mood at the Base, including my own, changed for quite some time after that happened. Losing mates that you have lived with so closely and trained with is very hard. I feel for them.

... From Perth, Pearce Air Force Base, and the date today is October 27th, 1970. The car is going quite well. I had a tune up and overhaul and the automatic done and the brakes fixed up. So, it's going pretty well now. We're still here now at Pearce Air Force Base and last Friday was quite an exciting day indeed. I don't know if you've heard of the Mirages, the fighter plane, they're next to the F-111. Eight of them came in and landed at 160 mile an hour. That's the speed they land. They came in one after another on the runway, and the white parachute came out as they taxied into the runway. When they land, they land on their back wheels first, so they can't actually see the runway. They have to land by instruments because the nose is pointing up. You know how I love planes.

... Then we have our old Macchi's. We have 36 of those here. These are not really a fighter plane and are used for training, but they could easily be adapted into a fighter. I've taken a few pictures of the Macchi's and the Mirages. And, we have the helicopters and an old Spitfire here but that's not used for much.

... The Hercules is a mighty transport. That was the same one that dropped our ration packs when we were at Benson, the army training camp. It's a terrific, huge thing. It has four engines and has been landing and taking off all day. We had the air display, and all the planes were taken to pieces and we could look at them all, and it was very interesting indeed. That's what happened Sunday. I was

very pleased to be here on our visitor's day. I just wandered around and had a good time. These Mirages are really fantastic. The Macchi's are slow compared to this one. The papers say these can go up to 1,500 miles an hour. But the pilots told me that it could go 1,700 miles an hour.

...Seeing the sound barrier is only 600 mile an hour, it was inevitable during the air display they broke the sound barrier. They shattered three windows in the control tower!

... Have you ever been on an air force base when the sound barrier is broken? We were in this wooden hut when the display was on. When the sound barrier is broken, you can't hear them come and you can't hear them go. You just hear boom all at once. The hut shook. I really thought it's the end of the world. That was quite fun. ... When they talk about these F-111s that we're supposed to get, I can't really see that we need them when we already have such a fast plane as the Phantom.

We were gardeners at the air force – we weeded the gardens, cut the edges of the lawn, swept the driveways, and consistently moved the water sprinklers. In the evenings we went to the mess, had a few beers, played pool, and chatted with the fellows. I used to pop into Perth every so often in the car because we were on the outskirts of Perth.

After being there a few months, Tom and I left Pearce Air Force Base, cashed up. We had quite a good time there, but the job was monotonous, particularly when compared to what was going on around us – the exciting activities of the base.

We again loaded the car and set out – north Western Australia – a completely new terrain and experience was calling.

Chapter 24
Midwest Gold!

The bright lights of Perth faded into the distance as we left Pearce Air-force base and travelled up the Western Australian coast, through the wheat-fields and onwards to Geraldton. From there we drove inland about 300 kilometres to Mount Magnet, about 150 kilometres from Sandstone where I had worked on a sheep station the previous year. It was late 1970 and I would travel, live, and stay in this hot, remote, and expansive area of Western Australia for many months to come.

… We eventually came to a little town called Mount Magnet, about 600 km north east of Perth. We noticed a sign on the side of the road stating Mount Magnet Mines and we could see there was a lot of huts in the mining camp and a couple of pubs in the town, one each side of the road. We agreed that this town looked promising! We followed the sign that said, 'Administration Building and Mine' and asked for work. We were promptly hired and directed to our accommodation – each an aluminium hut, alongside many other huts that the miners lived. I was happy as my work would be on the surface of the mine, and not underground; but this was soon to change. I would stay at this mine for some time and work in the three main areas of the mine before moving on. This was not the same for Tom as we were at the pub drinking not long after we arrived at the mine and a policeman tapped Tom on the shoulder and said, 'Tom, I've got a letter on my desk that says I've got to arrest you for back pay in alimony. I suggest that you're not here tomorrow.' Sure enough, Tom who I had met in the Northern Territory, together travelled through the Red Centre to Perth, worked at the Pearce Airforce Base and then drove to Mount Magnet, had left by the next morning. I had not known his situation until this time.

... I started working in the 'slurry area', on the surface of the mine a white coat job – I was progressing.

... Gold is mined underground. Rock is broken into workable sizes and brought up to the surface on conveyors. This rock is placed in big 'hammermills', huge rotating drums with big lead balls that crush the rocks, which end up a 'slurry'. This 'slurry' then travels down eight or nine waterfalls, and through channels about a metre wide, lined with corrugated mats that trap any little bits of gold in grooves of the mats. Every hour or so, the mats are changed and rinsed in water which ends up in big holding tanks and cyanide is added, breaking down the slurry even more and eventually, this slurry is mixed with mercury, and the gold is extracted in the laboratory under great security. It's no use thinking about taking some of the gold from Mount Magnet – or that nobody will notice it's gone. You can tell the origin of gold, where it has been mined. In Australia, if you steal gold out of any of the mines, they'll catch you.

What did we do in our spare time, apart from drink at the pub? We 'chatted up' the barmaids and waitresses in the camp. No use thinking about getting any ideas, as girls in general seemed to be sparse in this mining town. Anyhow, if you were lucky enough, the only place to take someone out was the pub! And I was not ready to settle down.

So, what did we do? We played pool in the pub, and darts. I was never very good at either; or we bet. We bet on anything. We even bet on how many strikes of a mallet does it take to squash an empty can of beer. Some people read, but not me. I listened to music – mainly tapes I had recorded and spoke on audio tapes to send back home. I took some photographs – mainly of the outside of the mine, and in the camp and mates I met.

Spaghetti bolognaise was always on the menu for lunch on a Saturday. This wasn't a good choice because Saturday was a day of leisure, and my mates and I had been at the pub in the morning. I think the menu was made to show us up – and if so, it was successful! How can miners who have had a few drinks, wrap spaghetti around a fork and find their mouth? I always had to change my shirt after Saturday lunch!

Other challenges included the torrential rain. When it invariably came, the 'trickle' that crossed the road between Mt Magnet the town and Mt Magnet the mine, turned into a dangerous torrent of water! The torrent of water cut off the camp from the mine and town.

Life at the camp was harmonious, despite the number of men, and the monotony of the work. Most of us left our hut doors open during the day, to let the heat out to make it cooler when we returned after work. One evening, a person who I had not seen before at the camp, appeared at the opened door of my cabin as I was listening to my taped music. He said to me, 'I would like to be a friend of yours... I could be a *very good friend to you'*. I thought what a strange thing to say, but as I determined he had just started working at the mine I said: 'Come to the pub tomorrow after work and have a drink with the rest of us if you want – we are all mates here'. With that response, he left.

The strange fellow did not join us at the pub the next evening. However, *he* was the talk of the pub. The conversation centred on how this strange fellow had approached most of the miners in their cabins, offering to be their 'friend', as he had done with me. But the real gossip was how the police had run the fellow out of town. 'Why' I said? The reply? 'He was trying to have it 'off' with the miners. There was a joke around camp that he may have 'got lucky' in finding a 'friend', given the big smile on the face of one of the miners in the end cabin! Anyhow, the story was that the strange fellow seeking a 'friend' was picked up by the police, taken about 20 kilometres out of town, and told not to come back. I did hear that this was common practice of the police managing these and other minor offences in this part of Australia.

Things were going well at the mine, and I had been there for some time. Christmas was coming, and I decided to fly back home for a short time. I flew to

Perth in a 7-seater plane, and then onwards. I stayed a few days in Lismore, New South Wales with my brother, sister-in-law and their children – twins, who both had mumps; and then headed up to Mooloolaba, Queensland to see my parents. It was a good Christmas – I went out fishing with my Father in his boat and drank a glass of whiskey at night with him. Mother fussed and cooked steaks and a roast. My parents mentioned to me at this time that they would like to travel with me in the outback at some stage, but nothing was planned.

After a week, I returned to Mount Magnet. Interesting saying returned, as this is the first time, I had taken approved leave and then, returned to a position; or indeed town, city, or state! Previously, when I left a job, I just left, and never looked back! It was now 1971, and I was returning to a job…was I starting to show signs of becoming a *'regular, normal person?'*

Not long after returning to Mount Magnet, one of my testes got big and sore, and I didn't know what to do. I still worked but I was in considerable pain. So, I went to the hospital but there was no doctor available to see me. I was embarrassed, and with difficulty, I explained the trouble I was into the nurse. It seemed to me that the nurse wasn't taking me seriously or didn't believe me, or found it amusing or I hadn't explained things clearly. So, I took the conversation up a 'notch'. I dropped my pants, there and then, and said: 'what do you think this is, now do you believe me?' She did believe me, and I was immediately admitted to the little hospital, and stayed there for a few days where I was treated for the problem.

Eventually the swelling went down, and pain subsided. I returned to work. I did not know at this stage that this episode of orchitis caused by the mumps, would have such long lasting effects on my life – but this is well into the future. On discharge from hospital I found out that someone else had taken my position working in the 'slurry' whilst I was in hospital. My new job was to work in the assay area, where the slurry went into enormous tanks, cyanide was added, and levels of concentration checked. It was a good job – a white coat job, and I stayed there sometime.

One night I was at the pub drinking beer with rum chasers, with my mates who were all underground miners, and they said to me: 'Thomo, we're going to get you to come underground with us'. I was wary of venturing underground, as it seemed dark and dangerous work, so I replied, 'No, no…I don't know about underground. I'm all right on the surface.' However, the discussion continued, and pressure exerted. 'You're our mate! You've got to come underground with us!' They kept pestering me, and as the night wore on, and the influence of alcohol kicked in, the strong reservations I had about working underground left me. 'Ok, all right, I'll do it!' I said. There was great jubilation in the pub, and another round of drinks were bought to seal the deal!

The next day, a delegation of underground miners went to the mining office and said: 'We want Thomo to work with us – he's a good bloke'. But then came the hitch. Administration said: 'Thomo can't work underground as he has been employed for the surface'. The miners, my drinking 'buddies', persisted and administration relented, with a proviso. To keep things right, Mount Magnet Mines had to sack me as a surface worker in the morning, and re-employ me as an underground miner in the afternoon. This they did.

From this time, my working life became much more dangerous, but at the same time much more interesting and exciting. It seemed to me that people gave you more respect as an underground miner. Perhaps because of the skills required, or because it was well known that underground mining was very dangerous work, and anything could happen at any time. And it did. Just prior to me arriving at Mount Magnet, an underground miner fell to his death when working on a level, deep underground. The police retrieved his body from the depths of the mine. It was said, and I experienced first-hand, that the police seemed more 'understanding' of misdemeanours by underground miners: 'anyone that works underground is entitled to have a few beers on the surface'.

I went underground mining in the miner 'uniform' of the time. A flannel shirt to 'mop' up the moisture, because it gets very hot and is wet underground, work trousers, safety boots, safety helmet with a light, and a battery strapped to my trouser belt to power the light.

I entered the 'Cage' with more than a little apprehension. It would take 5-10 minutes to reach the tunnel I was working, about a mile underground. The Cage is operated from the surface and is supported by metal rope which gets 'springier' the further it descends until it's like a piece of elastic. When the doors of the Cage opened at the bottom, the main tunnel looked like a city street!

The tunnels are huge, and the battery-operated train runs straight through the main thoroughfare; and there are side shoots that go off into other mining tunnels. There are cut outs in the rock at the side of the tunnels where you can have 'smoko' or whatever. You really think that you're at an underground railway station – lights everywhere, people working and lots of activity. The only difference is it's very wet in the mine. Always dripping with water. And there were many levels of tunnels – main and sub levels. It was amazing – a whole community a mile underground!

I started the six-hour shift, along with other miners. In the side tunnel, off the main thoroughfare it was dark, and I could hardly see. I noticed that other miners had a very bright light, and in comparison, mine was pitiful. At the end of the day I said to another miner 'why is my light not as bright as everybody else?' The reply: 'you silly Pommy bastard, you've got it on the safety light. You only put the safety light on in an emergency. Here, flickflicks the switch this way'. Then, the beam of my light was as bright as everyone else's!

My job involved working with the large rocks that had fallen at the end of the tunnel after the 'gun' miners had exploded them from the rock face on the sub-level above. This involved machinery, explosives, and hard, heavy manual labour. I was used to the latter, but not to the other and I learnt a lot in a very short time.

Firstly, I operated a 'Bogger', a piece of machinery like a backhoe, with a bucket on the front to shovel up the rocks that had been dropped from the upper level at the end of the tunnel. You don't sit on a Bogger, you operate the controls at the side to shovel the bucket under the rock, lift it up, move the bucket right over the top of the Bogger and drop the rocks into the little truck waiting.

Secondly, I exploded the rocks that were too big and heavy for the Bogger to pick up. To do this, I placed the small, gel type of explosive, a bit like plasticine onto the rock, put the detonator in, lit the fuse, and 'ran like hell' towards the back of the tunnel and stood, out of danger and rock dust. The explosion cracked the rock into workable sizes so that the Bogger could load them onto the truck.

Thirdly, I manually pushed the truck along the railway track when the truck was full. To do this, you used your shoulder for leverage and to tip the truck up so that the rocks went onto the 'grizzly', a criss-cross grid about 6 feet by 6 feet, with gaps about a foot wide. The rocks fall through the grizzly, way below onto a conveyor that takes the rocks up to the surface – but only if they are small enough to get through. You tip the truck with all your might, and hope that they all fall through, as those that don't, need to be broken down further. To do this, you have to place your feet on the side of the grizzly grids, balance, and remain balanced and at the same time, belt the rocks with a 'spoiler', which is like a hammer, until they break up and are small enough to go through one of the little squares of the 'grizzly', into the very, very deep pit below.

I hate heights. Always have, and probably always will, having the fear instilled into me by my mother during my childhood. But here I was, deep underground, balancing on a 'grizzly', and there is a very huge pit deep below. However, I was not worried. It didn't bother me because I couldn't see how high up, I was, and I couldn't see the bottom, as it was so dark. I resolved, that if the unthinkable happened – that is, I did fall, the conveyor at the bottom would take me up to the surface along with the rocks!

At the end of the day, you rang the bell indicating which level you were on for the Cage to come to your level: One bell, two bells, three bells and so on. Then you entered the Cage and rang the bell for the surface. I often thought what happens if the lift breaks and I am underground? There were ladders all the way up the side of the shaft. I thought God help me if ever I have to climb up the ladder because it would have been a hell of a long way. But luckily that never happened. I never let myself think about worse things than a broken lift – such as the mine collapsing. The conveyor in the pit, or the lift would be no help in this situation! However, I reasoned that compared to coal mining that has poisonous gas around, gold mining is very safe.

I moved to the next level – literally and became 'off-sider' to a 'gun miner' – the person who is actually 'mining' the rock on the sub level. Safety gear added at this level was just a rope tied around your waist! I often wondered if you fell over the edge, if the rope would catch on the rock as the rope was going over and break. I don't know if the rope would have held me. I concluded that it was a bit like when I was on the prawn boat, the sharks will get you before the skipper had time to pick you up out of the water! I was never quite sure about the use of the rope as a safety mechanism.

To get to the sub-level to work as an 'offsider', you had to stand on the side of a 'kibble', which is like a big cauldron, that descends on a slight angle. I felt as if I was literally between heaven and hell. At this sub-level, we worked on a ledge, around 12 feet by 12 feet and our job was to 'peel' back the rock on each side by using explosives. The gun-miner had a sort of jackhammer on a long hydraulic arm, which he used to drill holes into the rock either on the base of the rock or in the front of the rock. In these drill holes, the gun-miner inserted explosives with detonators, and when all wired up, the rock would be blasted off. The rocks fell into the huge cavern below where it was processed and transported by the conveyor to the surface, which was the job I had previously. You can see the strata of 'fool's gold' in the rock. Superficially, 'fool's gold' looks more like gold, than real gold. Real gold looks dull, whereas fool's gold really shines and looks very impressive.

Once, when drilling holes to place the explosives, a big piece of rock overhead, got a bit loose. The gun-miner shouted, 'Hey Thomo, I'd come over here if I were you. That rock looks like it might fall down'. Then… 'You'd better move – quick!' Sensing the urgency, I moved quickly! But, just as I did, the 'bloody' big piece of rock fell catching me on the back of my neck, gashing it open and flattened me on the ground, just like the TV ad, 'Louie the fly'.

Shaken and bleeding I got up dripping with blood. The gun-miner I was working with said to me: 'Here's a handkerchief'. Now you have two options, we either go up and write a report and the ambulance comes and so on; or you could go over to the corner and sit quietly on the rock till the end of the shift and then go up and have a good shower'. I did the latter… I had a smoke, stopped the wound bleeding, and went to the surface at the end of the shift. Nothing was said or done. I returned for work the next day with a large plaster on the back of my neck.

Frank and Ray – the Scottish fellows I worked with were funny people, but likeable. Both were very private, prudish people, who were unusual for a mining camp. Instead of showering at the mines after a shift underground like the rest of us did, they waited to shower until they returned to camp.

The normal routine for all miners was: come up from the mine, take your light and battery off and put onto charge for the next day. Then, except the Scotsmen, all miners got out of their mining clothes and hung them on the allocated hook in the changing room and had a shower – which gave you a slight tingle from electric shock when you touched the hot and cold taps! Then, dressed in your clean clothes that you had left on the peg in the morning, you boarded the bus to camp. All, but the Scotsmen who didn't drink, would get off the bus at the pub in town to have a few drinks before heading back to the camp mess hall to have dinner. So, there we were on the bus – the Scotsmen, dirty and grimy, and the rest of us clean and smartly dressed, all looking like office workers!

I had been at the mine quite some time and had a lot of fun. I was enjoying life, but after the near fatal accident in the mine, my enthusiasm in working underground was dampened. I thought it's no use tempting providence and waiting until something does happen where I might really get injured, or worse. Plus, the aluminium cabins didn't have air conditioning and were becoming unbearably hot and uncomfortable in the approaching rainy season.

I started to think of my future, or more appropriately, I became restless and decided to leave Mount Magnet! I discussed my plan in the pub to travel further up north and look for work at other mines. Ray, an Englishman, and a gun-miner, immediately said he'd like to move on as well. Then, the two Scotsmen I was friendly with said they would like a lift wherever I was going – it didn't matter to them, they just wanted to see as much of Australia as they could.

So, we decided to leave – Ray, the two Scotsmen and myself. But before doing this we needed to do a few things. Ray, who wore glasses, needed to get his eyes fixed. He had been complaining about his eyes for days, and they were very sore and bloodshot. He said he had also had trouble with them when he was in the merchant navy. He was reluctant to seek help, but I persisted and went to management and asked for time off to take him to Perth. They agreed.

I needed to get some new tyres for the car anyway given we were intending to go further north, and I also wanted to find out what was wrong with my tape recorder which had stopped recording my voice but still played music I taped off the radio. The trip to Perth would be a good distraction from camp.

I drove to Perth with Ray and listened to music – the 'hits of the day' all the way. We looked around a bit and stayed overnight at a cheap boarding house. Ray went to the hospital the next day and got appropriate treatment. I bought some new tyres – re-treads – only $36 for three. But there was bad news about the tape recorder. The technician reckoned a transistor had gone in it and it would take time to be fixed. Time – we didn't have. Very reluctantly, I left the recorder to be fixed but arranged with the technician to have it flown up from Perth to me at Mount Magnet.

I would not leave Mt Magnet without my recorder. I delayed the trip. This reel-to-reel recorder had travelled with me for many years. It was much more to me than just a recorder. It was my 'bank' in hard times when I pawned it to survive; it was my company in lonely times when I used it to tape and listen to music; it enabled me to record my stories to connect me with family – particularly when living in remote areas where there was no access to telephones.

The tape recorder arrived by airmail. We were now set to go. The four of us handed in our notice and had a rousing send-off party.

Chapter 25
Pilbara Region

It was early 1971 and I was twenty-nine-year-old. I had lived and worked in remote Western Australia for some months. The weather was hot, very hot, and extremely hot!

My pattern of drifting was entrenched. I worked for a short time and then travelled. Anywhere – not knowing what was around the corner. I was travelling further north into more remoteness and oblivious to what was happening nationally in Australia. History records the following:

...Qantas flew its first 747B jumbo jet and an extortionist tried to collect $500,000 by offering information about a bomb on one of its planes; Ralph Sarich developed a two-stroke orbital engine; three weekly papers – the National Times, the Sunday Australian, and the Sunday Observer (Melbourne) – made their first appearance. Neville Bonner, who became the first Aboriginal person to sit in an Australian Parliament, announced that he was no 'Uncle Tom'. Sir Henry Bolte notched up his 6,000th day as Premier of Victoria. 'Chips' Rafferty died; Sonia McMahon wore a figure-hugging dress split to the thigh to a White House dinner; Bob Dyer announced his retirement from Australian television; 'My Sweet Lord' became the most popular hit; and Johnny Young launched 'Young Talent Time'. The maker of artificial Christmas trees said that his product was designed to fit into the back seat of a Holden car: 'What', he asked, 'could be more Australian than that?' And Malcolm Fraser said: 'Life's not meant to be easy'. Lang Hancock explained how 'the greed of capitalism' was 'the only driving force there is' and predicted that conservation would become a dirty word just like mining was in 1971. In the year when the 'R' certificate for films was introduced, a Queensland Labour MP clearly wanted something similar applied to universities. He wondered 'how much longer must students

have to put up with filthy tutors who seem to believe they are being paid by the taxpayer to embarrass and distress the morals of decent young girls'. The guardians of morality even wondered about the propriety of allowing Michelangelo's 'David' to tour Australia. Margaret Whitlam almost made a surprising revelation when she declared that 'even Gough is getting rather gay in the daytime' (she was, however, referring to her husband's sartorial habits).

Within this environment I headed further up – to north Western Australia, with mates from Mt Magnet. Ray, the two Scotsmen and I, headed to Goldsworthy about 200 miles from Mount Magnet, on the northwest coast of Western Australia. Goldsworthy is noteworthy as the first area where iron ore was mined in Western Australia. We had a very heavily loaded roof rack. Luckily, my reel-to-reel audio tape recorder had been fixed, and arrived just before we left – only $4 for the airfreight.

…The trip was hazardous in places because the great cyclone Sheila-Sophie had hit the area about 3 weeks previously, at the beginning of February 1971, and caused a lot of damage. There were a few rivers flooded, with fast flowing water in some areas where we crossed. The poor old car had to 'hold her nose' while she went through one or two of them! But as luck would have it, we battled on and went through and out the other side okay.… We stopped at Roebourne for a while, hoping that we could get some work there; but there wasn't much on offer. So, we headed to Dampier, which had a reputation of being a marvellous new town. It is not that big, but there is a harbour being built and there are quite

a lot of businesses in the area, including the Hamersley Iron mine and a salt mine in the district. We drove passed a few salt lakes and saw the sun shimmering brightly on them.

Many years later, Dampier was featured in a movie about an infamous 'Red Dog' who roamed this area at the time we were in the Pilbara. The movie also gave some insight into the life of a mineworker at that time, which I could relate.

...We didn't have any luck getting a job at either the salt or iron mine, now both owned by Rio Tinto mines. We headed to Port Headland forewarned that the police in this town were like 'dynamite' the way they cracked down on misdemeanours. We hung around for a few days and then decided to keep moving and ended up in Goldsworthy.

Mt Goldsworthy mine was the first iron ore mine in the Pilbara Region. Goldsworthy town was built specifically to accommodate the iron ore workers. It was a thriving mining town of about 700 and would be our home for a few months. But twenty odd years later, when the mine closed, the town was abandoned and returned to a natural state.

... The word in Port Headland was that Mount Goldsworthy mine owned by a consortium might have some jobs going, so we headed there. Goldsworthy

itself is quite a 'big little metropolis' in the outback. We're 75 miles from Port Headland, and Goldsworthy is bigger than 'Headland' because there are a few thousand people here.... We managed to get a job on the railway 're-sleeping' the line from Goldsworthy to Port Headland, enabling the transportation of iron from the mines to the port. It is similar to the work I did on the railway when I lived at Benalla, some years' prior. We have to change the sleepers, knock 'dogs' [bolts] into them, change the plates, and straighten the line. It's not a bad job. It gets a bit hot – it's about 110 degrees, but it is much hotter than that for us as we are working outside on the line. But the pay is better than I have had before, on average, you make $160 a fortnight; and the food here is excellent – again far better than I have had before in these sorts of camps.

... Arthur, an Australian is the foreman not a bad person, but always dodging around somewhere and I expect he will come and see me at work, before I finish my day. Another Arthur, an Englishman is the leading hand of the gang. I get on well with them.

... There was an accident when I was working on the sleepers. It's always a possibility given the work we do. An oil pipe burst on one of the machines we were using, and a big jet of hot oil sprayed onto the arm of a worker, from Yugoslavia. He reckons he is dying but it looked to me like it was only a flesh wound, but I guess it could've burnt deep inside. The foreman looked after him, while I rushed to the radiophone to call an ambulance to take him to hospital. There was quite a lot of activity and excitement when this occurred, and we didn't do any work for about an hour.

... The train and train tracks are interesting. The seventy-five-mile-long length of track, that joins to the main track is owned by Goldsworthy mines and has nothing to do with any of the state railways. The trains are quite long – about a mile long and usually have about 50 trucks loaded heavily with iron ore. The speed limit is 32 mph. Head office can approximately tell when a train is going to be at a certain place at a certain time.

... I sometimes work as a 'Bridge Guard'. I operate a radiotelephone to direct traffic – quite an easy job, but with a lot of responsibility. Sounds unbelievable, doesn't it – having to direct traffic in the outback? And it is! The roads here just go through the creeks which we found out when we travelled up here from Mount Magnet. Due to the recent cyclone the road got washed away about 20 miles from Goldsworthy. The answer until the floods goes down and the road repaired; is for all the traffic to use the railway bridge, across the *flooded creek. So, the railway line is being used for trains, trucks, and cars at the same time! So, you make sure when the trains come that no vehicles or cars are on the railway line!*

... All the locos and road vehicles have radiotelephones. I just press the button on top of the radio and say to head office: 'VH6PG, the grey bridge. Can you tell me what time the next loco is arriving here?' And head office says whatever time. Then the loco calls and says: 'approaching grey bridge. Everything clear?' I reply, 'Yes'. At this time, I go and close the gates to stop the road vehicles accessing the railway line, wait until the train is gone and open the gates for road vehicles to cross; and ask head office again when the next train is coming, repeating the cycle. It's a very easy job at-the moment. I think this procedure has been going on about two months now and will keep going on until the road is repaired. It's a bit of a boring job really because there's nothing to do in between trains arriving. You can read a book – if you read, which I don't so it is really boring as a train comes through about every two hours. I told them I would do this job for about a week. It will give me a rest from all the other hard work I've been doing. Eventually they fixed the bridges, and I returned to the job of changing the sleepers on the railway.

... Interesting how cyclones and floods alter the landscape and the plans of people who dare to challenge the environment. On the other side of the bridge from where I work as a Bridge Guard, there's a fellow named Joe, and he's been camping there for about a week because the road to Darwin is closed. There's been a lot of rain there, and it's impossible to pass and the road won't be open until about the 16th of April – which is quite a few weeks off.

... Prior to the job as the Bridge Guard, the Scotsmen [Frank and Ray] and myself were recorded as 'A' drivers meaning we can drive company vehicles. So, about every third day we each get two hours overtime at double pay, driving the Bridge Guards to work. Ray, the Englishman doesn't have a license, so he couldn't get the driving job.

... All is well now. I'm as 'happy as Harry' because I'm sleeping well and eating well and getting plenty of money. It reminds me of the railway I worked on in Victoria apart from working hard in intense heat, which is killing me. But I do get a break every so often because I get a turn on as Bridge Guard, which I look forward to even if it is boring, before returning to the sleepers on the railway.

... Poon Brothers have the contract to provide the workers with living quarters and 'tucker'. This company is a very big business concern, especially here in the northwest of The Pilbara. They cater for Hamersley Iron and Newman iron mine, which is not far away from Goldsworthy. The huts were once shared double rooms, but then converted into single rooms. They are big rooms, a lot bigger than Magnet – like a home away from home. There is a desk, an ordinary chair, an armchair, a bed, two wardrobes, air conditioning, lights, and a light over your bed. There is a shower block, and automatic washing machines dotted around everywhere so there's no trouble about washing clothes. The quarters remind me of the army camps I had worked. The air conditioning made life bearable, but it was said that you have to be careful when you're going from your room to outside, and vice versa as you were liable to get a cold – it felt like you were 'going out of a fridge, into an oven'.

... The food is 'something else' – like what you would get at a top hotel! You have choice of variety of three meals every night. You have breakfast – bacon and egg, baked beans, anything you want, as much as you want. Midday we're out on the lines, so we have a salad put in a container where it's kept in a big freeze box on the truck so it's nice and cold. There are two big 10-gallon insulated water containers on the truck, which are full of ice, so we have access to icy cold water all day. We have a variety of food to choose from in the evening – chicken, pork, ham, cold meats, and salad, just as much of anything that you want, set out in a smorgasbord. Usually I have a heaped plate of a hot meal and then go back and have a cold salad and sweets, and a few glasses of cordial. I do like my meal at night, which I suppose I've always been used to. To try and counteract the loss of fluid working in the heat, salt tablet dispensers are provided at the entrance to the dining hall.

... Most nights we knock off work and go to the 'wet canteen', a popular place for most of the fellows here. Then, we shower, have our meal, and then go into the games room and have a game of billiards or darts or watch a movie which brings it up until about 9:00, then retire for the night, wake up about half-past 5 and start all over again. It is quite a pleasant existence, apart from the heat, which is the 'killer'.

... We have pictures three times a week – one or two very good pictures. We saw 'Camelot' the other night and it made me think of Tony's pre-wedding night, when we went and saw it together. There is a free-swimming pool we can go to whenever we feel like it and a games room where we can play billiards, table tennis and darts. It is decidedly better here than at Magnet, as you have something to occupy your time after work, and the longer working day of 10 hours leaves less time to waste. At Magnet, we only worked from 8:00 to half-past 3, and had a lot of wasted time and nothing to do, so you used to trot along and drink. Which is all right in moderation, but it's no use squandering all your money away.

... We do sometimes watch TV in this outback location. Tapes of television programs are sent up from Channel 7 in Adelaide and are put in the recorder in the bar and cabled to the TV in the games room. Sometimes, when you are watching television and in the middle of a movie or something, the tape will run out, and automatically a sign comes up on the screen saying, 'tape being changed'. But then, the barman forgets to change the tape! So, you have to phone him to remind him to change the tape over. It was interesting, but we don't watch TV a terrible lot because, we work long hours, and have to get up early so we go to bed early.

Life continued. Periodically, we went to Port Headland for the weekend. I had sold my car, the one I drove from Mount Magnet to Goldsworthy as it was 'clapped out'. We all put into a 'kitty' and hired a taxi – it was about $70 to get into the Headland. We used to spend so much money at the pub they gave us free accommodation and breakfast for the weekend! We started going into the Headland more frequently, and after about five months, I wanted a change from this life, and decided to look for another job.

In the pub, I heard that there were jobs going at the Headland Power Station. One weekend, I decided to stay on in 'Headland' and try my luck. My fellow travellers and I parted ways – the Scotsmen and Ray returned to Goldsworthy and I got the job at Port Headland Power Station the next day. The job was indoors, shift work, and wasn't a bad job.

... We have accommodation supplied at the power station. There are about 12 'prefab' huts at the back, single quarters, which are very good and similar to Mt Magnet. ... The person who lives next door to me likes white Bacardi rum. Every so often he asks me to come and have a drink with him. We sit outside the huts sipping Bacardi Rum and listen to his records.

... I look after the Mirrlees engines. Big engines. At the end of each engine is a big alternator that generated the power. Usually we get away just using two of them during the day and one at night. My job is to climb up a ladder to get to the top of them and open the big hatches to oil the pistons and the tappets. Another job is to change the oil filters. Occasionally I help the engineer change the rings on the huge pistons. It wasn't a very hard job. The night shift, well really, you slept all night.

... Another job I do is to paint the floor. You have to keep painting the floor all the time. I painted the floor green and the walkways red. There were only two of us there – one was the electrician, he used to watch the dials. It was very important because the power generated by the power station, governs the speed of the electric clocks and you had to make sure the clock kept the right time. Otherwise all the electric clocks in the place would be running out of 'sync'. And, of course, you had to make sure there was enough power. As the power increases, another motor automatically starts. At night you just run one Mirrlees engine that will just chug away quietly and nothing much would happen. Then about half-past 5 or 6:00 in the morning, the power increases so then automatically another engine starts and goes online which generates more power.

...One day the power usage was increasing, and the extra engine wouldn't start to meet demand. If the engine doesn't start, there's no capacity to increase the power and the whole system crashes, and a blackout occurs, and Port Headland is plunged into darkness. Well, within two seconds of the power cut, people phoned up. 'The power's gone off! What's going to happen?' I was on the phone. 'Yes, we do realize that. We're very sorry. The problem will be rectified as soon as possible'. The big thing is the airport. We are responsible, and this was our priority to make sure that the landing lights at the airport stay on. We got a right 'bollocking' from the airport when the power went off, as it had to close until we eventually got the power restored.

...Nightshift started at 8:00 at night. Being Port Headland, I'd always been to the pub during the day. So, half the time went on night shift half-charged, which wasn't very good, especially in a power station. But that's the way things are up here. But, at night you do very little except paint a bit of floor. During the day there is more work as I service the engines. My responsibility is to make sure the huge pistons, are working. I oil the tappets on the top of the piston and change the oil filters at the bottom on the floor. I would have stayed here longer than a month.

This job was quite a good job, but I left because Mother and Father were travelling to Perth to start a great holiday – through the Nullarbor and back to Queensland. I had promised to drive them.

... I left Port Headland on the plane on Saturday morning, arrived in Perth and spent the night at the Forest House Hotel in Perth because I had to get up bright-and early the next day to meet the train that arrived at 7:00. I went to the train station and was told that they would be on time – the train had made up two hours of delay during the trip. As the Indian Pacific train drew into the station five minutes before time, I could see Mother and Father at the window.

The following is Mother and Father's recollections, recorded on my tape recorder.

Mother: 'And what do you think. I said, there he is. And, he had a beautiful beard and side-whiskers and a moustache. Looking very smart then. His best Sunday suit. But we knew him all the same... didn't we...'
Father: 'Yes, he was a surprise with all that bush!'
Mother: But he looked very nice...

We had breakfast together at the Forest House Hotel, and Mother and Father told me all about their trip by train from Queensland to Sydney and then onto Perth. They had not been to Sydney before, and the Sydney Harbour and Opera House was impressive. They had a very comfortable trip, apart from the first night where their cabin was 'just over a squeaky wheel' which Mother thought was going to fall off! Father arranged a change of rooms the next day, and from then on there were no complaints. The food they said, was excellent. They mentioned several towns they had explored briefly when the train stopped and made a special mention of Broken Hill and Port Pirie. They saw emus, kangaroos, and lots of saltbush. The environment was foreign to them, but they embraced every moment. It had been an exciting trip for them, and there was more to come.

We spent a few days in Perth before starting off. Father and I went to the Ford dealership in Perth. I was very lucky the salesman was previously an Officer I knew from Puckapunyal Army Camp. It was great to meet up with him again.

He remembered me well and gave me a good price on the car – a 1966 deluxe model green station wagon with a radio.

We travelled around Perth and surrounding area. We went to Bunbury, the vineyards, Kings Park, and zoo – my parents were most interested and very impressed with the beautiful city and wildflowers. We went to a Chinese restaurant and the new KFC restaurant – a concept that had just recently arrived in Australia. We went to see the very popular film 'Nickel Queen' the Australian comedy film starring Googie Withers and John Laws. The film was shot in Broad Arrow, Western Australia and only just released. The film was more interesting because it reflected Western Australia, was about mining and showed the area that we would soon be driving through.

Eventually, Mother, Father and I, commenced our trip. But there was a slight problem, as I couldn't really see out the back mirror because of the luggage my parents had brought with them! So, we stopped at a Ford agent to get a side mirror to screw on. It was obvious that this was not going to be a trip like I was used to: clapped out car, mates, dogs, and a tight timeline! This was to be a holiday in comfort: nice car, motels, generous parents, and leisurely pace! However, despite this, there was some discord on the trip at times – as would be expected. Most disagreements were over what towns we should drive through and what sights we should see! Mother kept the map and navigated the trip.

We drove around the bottom half of Western Australia to Esperance, and then across the Nullarbor Plains to South Australia and then inland, back to Queensland. The trip took us around 4 weeks – a leisurely pace for my parents who were nearing seventy-year-old. We visited Broad Arrow where the 'Nickel Queen' was shot. We learned that most of the filming was done at the unused train station in the waiting room. A very small room, but on film if looked large, thanks to a wide-angle lens.

Broad Arrow is an interesting place, and I suppose much like many other gold rush towns. It is a 'ghost town', 38 kilometres North of Kalgoorlie. The town was named for the markers in the shape of 'broad arrows' left by a miner to direct his friends to the discovery of gold he had made in 1893. The town boomed and at its height, it was home to 15,000 people, boasted 8 hotels, two breweries as well as a stock exchange, hospital, 3 churches, 2 banks, police station and resident magistrate: train station, and a post office. By 1920, the gold was gone, and the town was deserted apart from the Broad Arrow Tavern.

We stayed at Ceduna and my Father remarked 'how funny the soap was'. Because the water was 'brackish' you had to use special soap so that it would lather. We visited a theme park at Kalgoorlie and then crossed the Nullarbor – without a hitch, apart from Mother smelling petrol at one stage. However, there was nothing that seemed to be wrong, the smell disappeared, and we arrived safely in Adelaide.

... Mother... We decided we'd go to the Barossa Valley so off we went. The journey to the valley is through Elizabeth and Gawler then Seppeltsfield, South Australia. We saw the fermenting and the aging and the brandy distilling and the tasting. A fascinating process of winemaking was explained to us during a visit to Seppeltsfield Winery. We went to the Tanunda place. We saw the brandy and we tasted a little drop. And then we went on to Seppeltsfield which is four miles off the main road leading through the valley, and it's the largest family-owned winery in the southern hemisphere. It was absolutely, beautiful. When we got there, there was a guide, a young university student, who took us around. We saw the barrels, and the wood comes from France. Seppeltsfield Winery has just beautified the landscape. They've planted miles of palm trees and almond blossoms and cherries.

The trip continued, and we travelled inland through New South Wales to Queensland, eventually ending up back home again at Mooloolaba. It was a memorable trip for all and one that often crept into the conversations in the future.

Chapter 26
Fast and Furious

I'd had a good holiday with my parents and driven many, many miles, across 5 states of Australia. Soon after this memorable 'holiday' I returned to my normal life – that of a Drifter.

It was normal for me to continually travel and not stay too long in any one place. I'd 'blow' into a town and find a job, save some money to set me up for the next few hundred or thousand miles. I was always looking to where I was going next. I was never content, in any of the numerous places I had worked and lived to date.

It was now late 1971 and I was in my 30th year. I had been living the way of a Drifter since coming to Australia in February 1964 as a *'10 Pound Pom'*. Initially, I could say *'I was travelling around Australia',* just like many other young people – like Alex, the American who was heading to work on Daydream Island. But, after 8 years on the move, this did not ring true. I had to confront who I was, and who I had become.

Drifting had become a normal way of life, as had the highs and lows and depths of despair that go hand in hand with this life. All seemed normal. But deep down I knew it wasn't normal for me and hoped that one day soon, my life would change. It would have to, if I were to have any chance of surviving.

During the next year, I would crisscross Australia – Northern Territory, South Australia, New South Wales, Queensland, Victoria and back to the Northern Territory. Most places I would only stay and work for a very short time, before moving on. I was constantly travelling, seeking something but not knowing what, being out of work and short of money and had no real direction.

I would find myself in trouble, and in unsavoury circumstances – most, if not all, self-inflicted due to drinking too often, and too heavily. Was I trying to self-destruct? Who knows, and who cared…. I didn't seem to….

I said goodbye to my parents and headed off in my Falcon station wagon that I had driven from Perth to Queensland. I turned south, and drove towards Surfer's Paradise, with no plan of where I would end up. I saw a hitchhiker in the distance. It was good to travel with other people because they were company and often shared the driving and contributed towards petrol, making it cheaper.

I stopped and said to the hitchhiker, 'where are you going?' 'To Peko Mines –I've got a job there' was the reply. 'Which way is that?' I said. 'Tennant Creek up near Darwin, past Alice Springs' the hitchhiker replied. I responded immediately, 'if I took you there, do you think I could get a job?' 'No problems mate, I'm a miner. I'll make sure you get a job if you take me there' he said. The deal was done! Ryan the hitchhiker, got into my car.

I did a 'U-turn', and we were on our way towards Tennant Creek, Northern Territory, some 2,500 kilometres. This time I drove through Toowoomba, Roma, Morven, Longreach, Cloncurry to Mt Isa and then onwards to Tennant Creek. Unlike my last trip from Queensland to the Northern Territory, this trip was uneventful. There was no rain or floods to contend with and no problems with the car. Ryan and I shared the driving, took turns to sleep when the other drove, ate in roadhouses along the way when we stopped for petrol, and reached the open cut Peko Mine in very good time.

When we got there, Ryan thanked me profusely for the ride and got out of the car. He went into the office to sign up and talk to his boss about me and came out about a half an hour later. He said, 'She's right mate, I've fixed it with him. You can get a job, but you'd better go in and 'sign up''. I replied, 'Thanks a lot mate. I really appreciate that.' And, with that, he was gone. The transaction was completed. I went into the office and said: 'Ryan told me you've got a job for me.' 'Yeah mate, just fill in the form – you've got to join the union' was the reply. Then he said, 'the form says that with your first pay, so much is coming out for the union fees. If you don't do that, you don't get a job, so you might as well just accept it.' I told him, 'No problems, I would fill the form in. I need a job'.

I worked in the large Peko Mine workshop maintaining equipment and welded occasionally. I worked with David, a labourer like me, and George, a fitter and turner. We got on well and the three of us would travel together later. Accommodation was provided on site and I shared a large double room with another worker. We both kept to ourselves, as I noticed most others did. It was not like other mines I had worked. It was not as friendly.

But perhaps it was me who was not as friendly as I normally was? I know I was getting sick of my lifestyle and was not in a 'good place' at-this time. My behaviour when drinking indicated this. And drinking had become a very big part of my life. It was inevitable that there would be consequences of this. And there were.

There are no recordings of my time at Peko Mines. What could I say about my life that was suitable to send home? Nothing. This disinterest in recording speaks volumes of my state of mind at the time given my reliance on my reel-to-reel audio recorder for 'normality.' However, despite a lack of recordings, I vividly remember this period.

There was a bar at Peko Mines where we used to go in the evenings and have a drink. But periodically we would go into town, especially on a Friday and drink at the local Tennant Creek hotel. One Friday night I had drunk too much and refused to return to camp with my mates, and they left. At this time, I got friendly with a group of Aboriginals. I was warned to be careful and not get into a fight. I didn't, and they were a very friendly group and I got on well with them and they with me.

At the end of the session at the pub, the group of Aboriginals said, 'come back to our camp and have a few beers with us. We'll show you where we live.' I was interested in the Aboriginals, their camps and their culture and there had not been a lot of opportunity to mix and socialise previously. And they seemed to like to drink, as I did. I bought a dozen bottles of beer for us to drink 'at the party' and we left together.

The camp was about three miles up the road. We all piled into my car and I drove to the camp and we continued to drink – well into the night and early morning. I drank too much as usual, and 'crashed' at the camp. The next morning – Saturday, I got up, had a few more beers, keeping track with my drinking mates, and by this time it was round about 10 o'clock in the morning. I said, 'I've got to go, I've got to go to work tomorrow.' I thanked them as I staggered to the car and started driving.

Somehow, I got to the main street of Tennant Creek and it was there that the police stopped me. In this type of situation my rule was get out of the car when stopped by the police, before they ask you to get out. With that rule in my fuzzy head, I opened the door of my car to get out, to stand tall and look them in the eye. But, instead of this, I opened the door and fell out! I mean, I literally, fell out!

The police looked at each other and then said to me, 'Well we're going to have to lock you up, for being drunk in charge of a vehicle'. I tried to bargain with them, my words heavily slurred, 'you don't have to do that do you? I've got to go to work in the morning.' Their response was swift, 'Mate, look, you're well over the top, yes, we're going to have to lock you up and throw the key away'. 'Oh God' I thought, 'I'm really in trouble!'

Well! The next thing I knew I was in the police station, fingerprints being taken – each finger rolled across the inkpad and rolled onto the paper. They did try and get me to walk straight on a white line, but that was useless, so eventually the inevitable happened. I ended up in gaol! One policeman said to me, 'my wife will bring you something to eat shortly, although you don't look as though you could eat anything now.' He was right – I was way passed eating!

I looked around. The gaol cell reminded me of an outhouse – an outhouse with an open-air front with thick bars that did not keep the weather out. The cell was small and clean, had a concrete floor, a bed and mattress, and a stainless-steel toilet and basin in the corner.

Even intoxicated, I was aware of the predicament I was in. I recalled Rob, my mate from Benalla some years previous being booked in Sydney for drink driving and he ended up with a stint in gaol. And I remember he was never the same after he got out of gaol. What would be my fate?

When the Constable's wife brought me a meal late afternoon, I asked her, 'what is going to happen to me… do you think they'll lock me up for a long time?' She replied in a quiet motherly way, 'I don't know son – it all depends on the court. You'll have to go to court at nine o'clock on Monday and see what happens, but don't you worry love, everything will turn out all right.' 'Oh God I hope so' I said.

I was in gaol all Saturday and Sunday and ended up at court on the Monday morning. 'Please explain', said the Magistrate. I blurted out a story and emphasised how very sorry I was – and I was, it was a genuine apology. I was sorry about everything – including getting caught! But I kept this to myself.

The sentence was handed down. Thankfully, the court was generous on this Monday morning. I was fined $150, and my Northern Territory license cancelled for 12 months. But no criminal offence would be recorded. The Magistrate asked me how I was going to pay the fine? This was tricky. 'Well', I said, 'I haven't got any money on me.' 'Hmm' he said, 'well you can't leave this court until you pay the fine or we'll have to lock you up again.' Desperate, I quickly replied, 'Peko Mines might give me a 'sub'.' 'All right', the Magistrate said, 'we'll phone up Peko Mines and see if they will, but we'll have to keep you here in custody until we decide what's going to happen.' With that, they escorted me back to gaol again.

A few hours later, they returned. Peko Mines had agreed to pay my fine directly to the court and then deduct the amount owing to the mine, from my wage. So, I left gaol, and returned to Peko Mines. I had been lucky– this time. The funny thing was that the court let me drive my car back to Peko Mines and then no more, given my license had been cancelled. Not having a license in the middle of Northern Territory wasn't good. After losing my license I relied on David to drive my car.

Christmas and New Year came and went. It was now 1972. One night, in the bar at Peko Mines I again drank too much, and this time made a commotion in the bar, ending with me being thrown out of the living accommodation at the Peko Mines camp. I was not allowed to live there anymore. So, I slept in my station wagon at Tennant Creek for a week. I got up, went to work at Peko mines, showered there and ate in the dining room, and then returned to my car to sleep.

It was time to leave Peko Mines. I couldn't remain living the way I was and planned to leave. I talked David and George into leaving with me, and heading through the Red Centre, across to Whyalla, South Australia where we'd heard there were jobs, and where David's family lived. We all handed in our notice.

The night before we left, I sneaked back to the camp and we packed my car up. I was going to stay in David's cabin so that we could leave early. It was our last night at Peko mines, so we decided to go and watch an open-air film with the rest of the fellows. The night was memorable. As we settled into the chairs, the heavens opened.

There is not a lot of rain at Tennant Creek. It is constantly hot, dry, and dusty. This night, it rained – actually, poured! We were all so excited to see rain, that we all stripped to our undies, and ran around in the rain and turned the dust into mud. It was just like a rain dance! Anybody would have thought Christmas had come early! Here we all were – grown and tough miners running in the rain in our underwear! It *was* time to leave!

Early the next morning we headed off. This would be my second journey through the Red Centre. The first was memorable and enjoyable – 4 men and 3 dogs. This trip would also be memorable for the 3 of us, but for all the wrong reasons. There was nowhere to get the car checked out prior to leaving and given this car had been driven around 8000 kilometres recently [Perth to Queensland, then to Tennant Creek and South Australia] without any special care, it was inevitable that there could be problems. And there was.

David drove my car for about 20 kilometres outside of Tennant Creek. Then, I took over. My NT license had been cancelled, but I still had my Queensland license! We drove on, through Alice Springs and into South Australia, stopping only for fuel for the car and food, and to get the car out of a bog.

Further along, a tyre blew out. We changed the tyre and drove on. Not long after this, another tyre blew! This time there was no spare and we were in a very remote area. We all got out, looked around, scratched our heads and then ingenuity kicked in.

I recalled watching a TV program that showed how to pack a punctured tyre so that you could keep driving in the outback. We gathered some long dry grass from the side of the road, rolled it into tight little balls, and stuffed it hard into the tyre.

It took hours and hours to get the tyre to a stage where we thought it might work. Then, we started off, but the car thumped and thumped unevenly. We got out. The tyre was flat and the grass we had laboured so hard to pack tightly; had been squashed down as 'flat as a tack'.

We repeated this scenario several times – pack the tyre with grass tightly, test it, and then stop and go through the same process. It looked so easy on the TV, but I tell you, it was a lot harder in real life! All the time we were doing this, there was not one vehicle that drove on this road.

Eventually, it was possible to move forward – slowly. The car 'limped' into the next roadhouse, 50 kilometres away! There we took a well-earned break and bought a new inner tube. After this, we had no more problems, and drove straight to Whyalla, just stopping for fuel and food at roadhouses.

... *It's the 21st of February 1972. Here I am sitting in the room at the Hostel here at Whyalla. Looking out the window I can see the Spencer Gulf situated on the Eyre Peninsula. To the left is where the shipbuilding and smelting is carried out. More to the right is the Pellet Plant where I've been working this week – it's a very dirty and dusty place.*

... Usually David and I work in the workshops. We clean up, pull bits of machinery apart and put it together again. Just general maintenance-type stuff, that is not very hard. I don't like when we have to go up into the gantry because we look down, and there are only slats on the floor. I don't like heights. I get a bit frightened when I'm walking on these grids as you can see right down below. It's safe enough, but I always get a little bit hesitant. So, I'm always happy when we go back into our workshop and work there.

...Shift work is not too bad. The alarm is only necessary really when we're on day shift which is a terrible shift. We have to get up at 7:00 in the morning. We don't start working until 8. But when you're on the afternoon shift you hear everybody else getting up and going to work, and you just roll over and you turn up for work at 4:00 or 12:00, whichever shift you're on. So next week we're on the 12:00 shift.

... Whyalla is not a very big town really. But we go there periodically. It's situated just at the bottom of the hill. Today is the Thursday before Good Friday, so it is the 30th of March 1972. It's a very good complex I'm living in because you have a TV room where I quite often go at night and sit there and watch TV. You can't decide what channel you want to watch – you just have to watch what the majority wants. Next door there's a bigger room where they show movies. Pretty-old movies mostly, but sometimes you're shown a 'gem', like we saw last night.

...Today is Easter Sunday and we've just-been to the pictures to see 'The Spy in the Green Helmet' which is one of the James Bond movies. There are such a lot of English people here at Whyalla mostly working at BHP. They call Whyalla 'Little England'. I've never known so many English people in one place, plus Scotsmen and Welsh and all the rest of them.

... David's family live in Adelaide, so we often go there at weekends – it was very nice. His parents have quite a big house. I actually quite enjoy Adelaide, because David has a married brother, mother, and her partner Greg, and they also have a holiday house in the Adelaide Hills. I slept on the floor in the lounge and used to watch television on the little black and white TV. We have some good times.

...Greg is a funny fellow. He is obsessed with electricity and saving it. They have a huge light in the lounge, one of these big chandeliers, about 20 lights. And there is one forty-watt bulb glowing in it! Greg said, 'Got to turn off all the lights. Costs money.' I remember I was once in a boarding house in Queensland, and they used to turn my electric clock off every morning!

... David, George, and I went to Adelaide for the weekend. George was driving my car at the time and a tram hit us! It hit us! We didn't hit it! The tram put a big dent in the side of the car. It was still roadworthy, but it needed quite a lot of work done on it, and eventually I got it all fixed up. There is a chance now that I might be able to get the money back, or some of it, because the police are prosecuting the MTT. So, I still live-in hope about that.

... I must be following in Father's footsteps because I love looking around second-hand shops. I walked into one in Adelaide, and there was this beautiful alarm clock. It only cost me $1.65. It's got a marvellous ring to it. So that wakes me up in the morning now, which is a good thing when I'm on day shift.

... The car is still going very well. There is a minor defect in the exhaust that I hope to put right Thursday, and that rattle has started up again. I don't know *if another back universal has gone, but that wasn't anything to do with the accident. I got sick of waiting for any insurance money and fixed the car myself.*

... It's getting pretty cold down here now. This time of the year I suppose winter is coming isn't it.

... Next weekend when I go to Adelaide, I will go pick up a full-size roof rack that I got for $15. Dave's brother Ivan had an accident, and the roof rack is no longer any good for him because his car is being repossessed, so he's going to let me have it for $15. I think they're $30 new. So that will come in very useful. I'll put the cases on top and sleep inside. Ivan has a lot of bad luck, same age as myself, but I think we both bring it upon ourselves a lot of it.

We got sick of working in factories and left Whyalla and went to Adelaide to live in a flat. David and I got jobs in the local wool store – Elders; and George, a fitter and turner went to work at 'Iron Knob'.

David and I pressed the wool that had been reclassified and wheeled wool bales to the top floor where the wool sales were held. The auctioneers would sell the wool off to different buyers. Our main tools of trade were a bag truck and a bag hook because we used to tip the bale up, put the bag truck underneath, and use the bag hook to pull them back so we could wheel a few hundred of those around every day.

The flat was good – it had a TV, and we went to the beach. We lived as a happy family for a while and had a nice time. Then, George moved out, as there was accommodation at Iron Knob, where he was working. We visited him, and he took us around the workings there.

George and I went out one night, looking for David. I was driving, and I had been drinking. The police pulled me over and I blew into the breathalyser... there was nothing else to be said. I ended up with a fine and my Queensland license taken off me for 12 months. Now, I did not have a license at all!

I sold the car. It was a great loss, given I had spent so much money on it to fix it up and had pawned my reel to reel to keep afloat. But the car had done me a good service and had good use having been all around Western Australia, South Australia, Queensland, and the Northern Territory. Plus, it was second hand when I got it. More of a concern was the loss of my license – the second time in a few weeks – the first when I was working at Peko Mines in the Northern Territory and now here. I would not be able to get another job that required driving for 12 months.

I had seen quite a lot of Adelaide and liked it, but it was time to move on. David had a brother who lived at Redfern in Sydney and we planned to meet up with him. Before leaving I had to get my tape recorder out of the pawn – shop. This I did, and we boarded the express train from Adelaide to Sydney – a trip of over 1000 miles.

The train had a corridor down the side and cabins on the other side where you sat – like the Orient Express. David and I spent a lot of time in the buffet car – it was like a real bar. There were seats that you could sit at and you could drink beer or wine or whatever you wanted. We had beer of course and amused ourselves by drinking and eating. Occasionally we went back to our cabin.

We ended up in Redfern, Sydney and booked in at the quiet boarding house where David's brother Mark lived with his girlfriend. The room was double fronted and had two single beds. Not long after we arrived, David's brother said, 'let's go to the local pub, to meet the fellows.' It was good at the pub at Redfern especially on a Saturday night because a pianist played in the lounge and there were people singing – like karaoke. By the end of the night, we were all pretty drunk and when we stood up to sing, we all thought we were really good, and the next 'pop star' was being born there!

Money was short, so we had to get a job. Any job....

...There is a place in Sydney called 'Kings Corner'. If you get there about 6:00 in the morning, a truck comes along, and they choose the people they want to take out to the oil refineries where you spend the day cleaning out the oil refinery big tanks, they put the petrol in. Shovelling out the sludge and whatever. Not a very good job and dangerous, but it was very well paid – about $15 an hour.

When entering the gate, you had to stop and hand your cigarettes, cigarette lighters and matches to the security people on the gate. It was a criminal offence if you took any of these into the premises. The same truck picked us up in the evening and dropped us back to Kings Corner again, where we made our way home.

... That was all right on the days you worked. But the days you didn't work you got up at 5:00 or some ungodly hour; went to the market to get a drink of coffee or soup, which was our breakfast. Then we waited to be picked up. If we weren't chosen for the shift, well, you didn't earn any money that day. But we still spent it! On the way home, we passed the 6 to 6, a pub that's open from 6:00

in the morning until 6:00 at night. We would go in and stay there half a day... well sometimes longer. You think, 'I'll just have one more. I've got to go. Just one more, I'll go after this one...I'm heading home.' The next day, we would be at Kings Corner again, hoping to be told to get onto the truck.

... One good thing was the Leagues Clubs, and Parramatta Leagues Club was one of the better league's clubs in Sydney. David, Mark, and I used to go there most Sundays to see the floor show, have a few beers, and play the pokies.

... It was a rough place, Redfern. It had not improved since I last lived there some years before. Sometimes, outside our room we could see blood in the gutter where there had been fights the night before. Not a very savoury place to be, but we never got belted up or had any problems. However, I did end up with a broken nose! David and I had been drinking and we started arguing about something when we were walking up the stairs of the boarding house. He punched me sideways and hit my nose. It did not hurt that much at the time and I didn't realise it was broken! I just knew that my nose was not straight after this incident.

Within a week or so, I decided to fly back to see my parents. I stayed with them for a few days and then returned to Sydney. I went to the boarding house that I had been living with David and Mark, but it was full. There was no reason to stay.

The type of casual job I had at the oil refinery was one of the worst and most dangerous jobs I had worked. We were living and socialising in a very bleak suburb – one that I had lived before and only just escaped with my life. Plus, David used to listen to the cricket all the time on the radio in the room we shared, and I am not a fan of cricket or indeed any sport! He had also reunited with a friend he had known before and was really getting into the Sydney scene, some of which was not desirable. They were also much younger than I was.

So, I decided it was time to leave them to their own devices and move on. Without hesitating I spent my last dollars for a flight to Darwin.

Chapter 27
Raking Old Coals

I'd spent my last dollars for a flight from Sydney to Darwin, the top end of Australia. It was my second visit to Darwin, and I was determined that this time would be easier than my last. It was.

... I got a job at the Darwin Royal Air Force Base and lived at the barracks. The RAAF covers about 14 or 15 acres and is about three miles from Darwin. There aren't a lot of planes here – only a couple – as most are stationed

in Brisbane. Darwin RAAF seems to be more about intelligence, as radar and old airfields are dotted along the coast. We all hoped that if there was an invasion; reinforcements would arrive quickly!

... Well, what does a civilian do in the Air force? At-the moment I go around with a tip truck and collect boxes of stuff that people put outside the houses. There are quite a lot of ordinary houses on the base – married quarters they call them – and they are where the married staff live. During the day, I go around with the others and keep the street and gardens clean.

... I live with about 30 other air force personnel in an old pre-war hut with a partition between every two beds upstairs and downstairs. There are communal showers with about six 'shower-heads' all in a row, and the toilets have half a door for privacy. There aren't any fans downstairs, so as people leave upstairs people from downstairs move up. I was lucky, fortunate enough, to get a bed upstairs to start with because there isn't anyone downstairs at this stage, so I can go there and record hit songs from the radio.

I don't need to wear a uniform, just khaki overalls, and shoes to work in. After working hours, when you go to the beer hall, and the mess, you have to have long socks, shoes and shorts, and a shirt with a collar on. The shorts and shirts you sent me are coming in very useful, and I have worn them constantly, nearly every day, on rotation of course! I've never been dressed up so many times in all my life!

... The humidity is very, very high. I've heard people say they call February the suicide month because a lot of people just can't hack the humidity. I felt sorry today for an Englishman, who arrived at Darwin from England. He'd only been here two days, and he started work outside the sergeant's mess cutting a hedge. I don't see how he could work outside in this heat, because I remember how I felt when I worked at Oakey, and got sunstroke, as I was working without a hat. But he has been issued the right gear, and hasn't wilted that much which is good as he spent all his money coming over here.

... Queensland governs Darwin for most things including the fortnightly pay that is made up in Brisbane and then sent up here. I have to tell you about how I helped another civilian do his banking. He asked me to help him – I felt quite good to be able to help somebody, with worse problems than I have.

... There are three swimming pools here on the base – one an Olympic size pool, you can swim in whenever you want to, and it's quite refreshing at times. There are a few 'water holes' around also, and then we have the wet canteen, where a 10-ounce beer is 18c, and spirits are 20, a lot cheaper than town, because at the moment, Darwin is in the midst of another transport strike. All the buses and transport have stopped, and if the strike doesn't end by Monday, then all the prices everywhere are going to go up because the goods have to be air-freighted in. But of course, that doesn't affect us because we are not buying our own food. We let the RAAF have that added expense!

... My elbow is mending after hurting it at work. I don't know what they were talking about, wanting to operate as it is fine now – the X-rays were interesting to see.

I travelled to Alice Springs with several other civilians and air-force men from the RAAF Base in Darwin for ANZAC day. We arrived in time for the dawn service and remembered the fallen, particularly those who had died in Vietnam. After the service we had drinks and breakfast at the Returned Soldiers League [RSL], then marched down the main street of Alice Springs. After this, we came back to the RSL played two-up, had lunch and then, later on, in the afternoon, we returned to the RAAF base in Darwin. It was a memorable and sombre occasion as young men and women were still being killed and protests regarding involvement in Vietnam continued.

... I am fit, healthy, well, and happy, so all is good. It's awkward without a car. I'm going to try and buy one, I think. I'm going to save money without one though, as they seem to be such very costly items, don't they? But taxi fares cost $1.50 to go into Darwin, which I do sometimes. Saturday morning, I usually hitch hike in. The bus service is virtually non-existent. I did go by bus once. It's 20 cents by bus, which is a big difference from a taxi, but they never seem to be there when you want them.

... Anyhow we all work together and get on very well. I go into town with the fellows and drink around the pubs. One day there were whispers all around the camp: come to the golf club, 7:00 tonight, to watch a film show. So, nobody was supposed to know, but everybody came! It was porn movies – on film. Apparently the 'top brass' arranged this 'porn night', and they were there as well to see the movie. Several times we had a 'porn night' at the golf club....

You can't go in the sea at Darwin between October and May because of the blue wasps, known as the box jellyfish, that inhabit the tropical waters, along with other creatures. The jellyfish are deadly and can cause heart attacks in minutes. But I'm told that they don't keep the crocs away!

... The Darwin international airport is owned by the RAAF; and the terminal is leased out, and the control tower 'manned' by RAAF personnel. Like me, a lot of ground staff work for ANSETT and NTA in a permanent casual capacity. I have taken a casual job at the airport from 12 o'clock Friday night until 8 o'clock Saturday morning, and the same on Saturday night. I can't really go out on a Friday or Saturday night anymore.

...It doesn't take me that long really to do my casual job. It's worth about $28 a week extra, so what I can do now is bank the fortnightly pay from the RAAF and live off what I earn in my casual job.... I mainly clean out the ANSETT and Conair terminals – the latter a small company that just goes down to Katherine, and other local places. That's what we call them up here – local places, and we've got TAA and Qantas.

... When the planes arrive, we have to clean them out and load the meals up. They are building extensions to the airport. The international airport isn't much at the moment, just a bar upstairs and a lounge. There's no restaurant or any other shops, and downstairs there is a huge floor space.

... About every two weeks we get overtime on Saturday and Sunday cleaning the wet canteen and the ordinary milk bar. Unfortunately, tomorrow it's my turn, so I've got to do this night shift, and then I have to start at eight o'clock, eight to about ten o'clock, on this other one. So really, I'm going to have a bit of work, but it keeps me out of trouble, as I can never go anywhere because I'm dead tired, which keeps me away from the 'evil drop'. Well, it's Friday night, and I'm quite sober. Glad to hear that you are still on the ginger ale.

... There was a really big storm tonight. I went into town a bit earlier than normal to get to the bank that closes at five o'clock on Friday. In any case, it poured with rain, and I got drenched. I had to come back to the base to get some dry clothes on.

... I clean out all the offices, plus the main floor, which is more like a field, there is about an acre of it, I think. I had to mop and polish it and do all the rest of it. It is a perpetual headache to keep it clean over the weekend. I think tonight it's going to be pretty dirty because it's been raining, and everybody will be walking over it with dirty muddy feet. Every three weeks the floor has to be stripped right down, polish replaced and then resealed.

In this casual job, I needed to buff and polish floors – skills I had learned during my stay in a mental asylum in England before coming to Australia. Experiences and skills learned are not forgotten easily.

... It's quite fun working over at the airport, and interesting because a Jumbo jet comes in on a Friday. I look at them in awe – they are huge planes and I long to go on a trip in one, one day. You see all these interesting people coming off from the international flights. I suppose they have just come from England, or all around the world. It doesn't take me long to finish my work. I always go over there with long socks on – so when there are all these people walking around, I mingle and pretend that I'm another passenger!

... This is only a small tape, just to give you a brief outline of what we are doing. There is good food here, especially for community cooking, and Christmas, well, there were long tables in the mess hall and at the end of each table, there were dustbins filled with ice and stubby bottles and cans of beer. We had a beautiful Christmas dinner, Turkey, ham, Christmas pudding and Christmas cake. There was enough food for us all, and free drink all day! It was terrific! And it was the same at New Year, except there was a dance as well, to let the New Year in.

So, what would happen in 1973 in Australia? History books record the following:

... Every year is in some way turbulent, but not every turbulent year produces continuing aftershocks. The hike in oil prices, which followed the Arab Israeli or Yom Kippur war of October 1973, had such a profound effect, not only on the world economy, but on practically everything from international stability to individual expectations, that 1973 can be considered a pivotal year in modern world history.

The Nixon Administration continued to implode with each revelation about Watergate. Britain formally joined the EEC on 1 January, the Vietnam Ceasefire Agreement was signed on 27 January, and Papua New Guinea obtained internal self-government with the promise of full independence in 1975, and Princess Anne married Captain Mark Phillips. The Australian economy was coming out of a recession in 1973, assisted by revaluations of the Australian dollar and a decision on 18 July to institute a 25 per cent across-the-board tariff cut.

Whitlam said that the new approach was 'towards a more independent stance' in international affairs'; Australia would be 'less militarily oriented and not open to suggestions of racism' and would 'enjoy a growing standing as a distinctive, tolerant, co-operative and well-regarded nation'. The postal service first used metric weights and measures, the F-111Cs finally arrived, 18-year-olds were given the vote, university fees were abolished, and the Rolling Stones toured Australia.

I had now been in Australia for 9 years and for me, this the year of 1973 would be a year to remember.

After seeing the New Year in, I flew to Brisbane to stay a few days with my parents and then caught a train to Melbourne where I spent the night opposite the Spencer Street Station. Overnight, I decided to head back to Puckapunyal the army camp I had worked previously, to try my luck. They were very pleased to have me on board again, and I got a job in the officers' mess. But I worked there only a very short time.

I met Joe, a fellow who worked with me at Puckapunyal, who had glaucoma and his sight was getting worse. When we went to the movies at the camp, we had to sit in the first three rows because he couldn't see the pictures if we sat further back. He wanted to go to Alice Springs before his sight worsened and asked me to travel with him given I had been there before. We handed in our notice and left.

We arrived in Alice Springs and found a flat in a complex. I got a job with Parks and Gardens, maintaining the park in Alice Springs. I mowed the lawns and trimmed the edges. It wasn't a bad job, but I would only stay a very short time.

I was cooking corned beef in the communal kitchen. I really didn't know much about cooking… especially cooking great chunks of corned beef! I cooked it for an hour, and then tried to eat it. It was as tough as 'an old boot'.

Russell a bloke that lived in the same complex came into the kitchen at this time, and I said to him, 'I don't know, this meat's bloody tough and I've been cooking it for about an hour'. He said what is it? 'Corned beef', I replied. He laughed, and said, 'Corned beef? You have let it simmer on a low temperature for hours!'

Russell was originally from Kingston, Adelaide, previously a commercial fisherman, and ex-Army cook. He introduced me to his younger brother Douglas

– Doogie for short, also with a fishing and Army background; and Ron, an older man, who was also staying in the same complex.

We all got on well and started drinking together at the Spencer Hotel, quite a nice hotel, in the middle of Alice Springs. The pub at the bottom of 'Alice' was very rough and run down, and where a lot of locals drank.

Russell asked me what I was doing? I told him I was working at 'Parks and Garden'. He said, 'don't work there. You could easily get a job working for TAA – Trans Australian Airlines, a much better job. All you have to do is put your name down. Come with me.' After a few drinks, I went with him to the TAA office. Russell said, 'I've got another fellow for you. He wants casual work.'

They took me on. With this TAA job, we hung around the pub drinking, and every time a plane came in someone would come into the pub and say, 'You're wanted out at the airport.' Up we would go to the Alice Springs Airport and load up and unload the luggage. One of us got into the plane and pulled the luggage out onto the conveyor, and the others stacked it onto the truck and drove it away. That was it. So simple! No security required! When we finished, we were paid in cash, and went back to the pub! The very 'happy cycle' continued.

While we were working at the airport and waiting for the job at Papunya, Robert Morley, the well-known actor came to stay in Alice Springs. At the same time, I met a lady – about fifty-year-old in the bar and she told me that she'd love to go and see Robert Morley, but she needed a chaperone, and asked me. 'I said ok, I'll be happy to chaperone you to see Robert Morley'. She told me that, 'the day after tomorrow he's holding a barbecue in a private house with a swimming pool. Could you come with me? You'll have to be my 'brother' and I will be your 'sister'. Is that all right?' 'Yes, no worries', I replied. Seemed simple to me....

So, the next day, we went along to the barbecue to see Robert Morley. But the more beer I had, the more convinced I was that she *was* my sister! So, I kept saying, 'hey sis, look at this... hey sis, do this, do that' and she became increasingly more embarrassed! I did get to speak with Robert Morley and said, 'Oh I love all your movies'. He listened, and then asked, 'which do you like in particular?' Put on the spot, I froze! I could not for the life of me remember *one* of his movies!

I got on well with Russell and Doogie. Not long after I started the casual work at the airport, Russell and I were talking, and he said, 'I know a builder – Dowsitt Engineering. They're building a hospital out at Papunya. Are you interested? I replied, 'Oh yeah, no worries. I've been a builder. I can mix mud for the bricks and cement. I've done a lot of that.'

So, we decided that we'll hang around in Alice, go to TAA casually and when the bloke Russell knew comes into the pub and gives us the 'nod' we can go out to Papunya and get a job building the hospital. Very soon, we got the 'nod' to work for Dowsitt Engineering. At the same time, I got my Queensland license back and bought a car.

In February 1973, Russell, Doogie and I headed off to Papunya in my car. Together, we would make a quick trip back to 'Alice' for the Anzac Day ceremonies in April of this same year.

Papunya was a small, new aboriginal settlement in the Northern Territory, about 240 kilometres from Alice Springs. Before we left for Papunya, we stocked up – bought a few slabs of beer each. When we arrived, Russell, the cook, determined that cold beer was more important than keeping the meat cold, so he 'turfed' all the meat out of the fridge and put the beer in! But most of the meat was returned to the fridge.

My main job in finishing off the hospital building was working for the brickie. I had to lift the Besser blocks to the brickie, and mix the cement, called 'mud'. But the funny part about it, every 2 hours we stopped for a smoko. And, for smoko, you don't have a cup of tea out of the thermos! No way! Not in the Territory! You 'down' a beer can! So, by the end of the day we were half sloshed! Luckily, I kept the consistency of the mud up to the brickie, and as far as I know, I don't think the hospital has fallen down! I hope not.

It was a happy job. However, there was no interaction between the aborigines and the builders, at this job. After a short time, the job was completed and the whole 'gang' of builders moved to Yuendumu, another aboriginal settlement to build houses.

This decision to move with the building 'gang' to Yuendumu would alter my life's course. It would bring me face to face with my mortality, and future.

Chapter 28
The Game-Changer

It was April 1973. I was living and working in extremely remote areas of the Northern Territory. I was thirty-year-old and had been in Australia for 9 years – most of the time drifting from one place to another. Within a few months my life as a Drifter would change, finally. But it would not be an easy transition, as old challenges would be replaced with new.

Russell, Doogie, Ron and I moved from Papunya to Yuendumu with the rest of the building gang working for Dowsitt Engineering. After this, the 'gang' planned to move for work, to Groote Eylandt, in the Gulf of Carpentaria, Australia.

Yuendumu, is described by the ABC local stories program as:

'Sitting on the edge of the Tanami Desert, 350 kilometres north west of Alice Springs, the remote community of Yuendumu is one of the largest Aboriginal communities in central Australia. The drive out to Yuendumu takes you along the Tanami Road, which eventually leads to the Western Australian border. Leaving Alice Springs your last stop for petrol, food and water is the Tilmouth Roadhouse. Its watered green grass is the final vestige of everyday Australia before you hit the real desert. From here on it is spinifex, mulga, wide blue skies, and a soft peach colour in the surrounding dirt. Oh, and a seriously bumpy road.'

We started building houses and continued the normal way of life of remote building 'gangs' of the time – hard drinking, and hard playing. My one surviving audio recording of the time, talked a lot about the ways of aborigines, including some cultural aspects that I saw and heard – that is, my perceptions. In some instances, my recording may not portray a complete accurate picture due to a lack of understanding. For this I apologise. There is no intention to offend. Rather, I was just capturing a moment in time, through my eyes – someone who was fascinated with what he saw and heard.

Dear Mother & Father… Speaking to you from Yuendumu, approximately 200 miles northwest of Alice Springs.… It's July 1973. I don't think I could be in a more remote area than I am at the moment. But I have been in remote areas before and survived. This time, I think it will be easy as I am here with a lot of crew and we are building some houses at Yuendumu. Where is Yuendumu? You'll have to look on your map to find it!

…There are quite a lot of white personnel. You have the superintendent, the sub superintendent, schoolteachers, the headmaster, the mechanic, nurses, and it is going to be a town now not a settlement when the council made up of all local aborigines takes over. I suppose one of these days it will just be a town… it's quite exciting living in one of these places.

… The foreman is not much older than I am. He drives a Land Rover that has a large rack on the top that extends over the bonnet and he carries everything around on it. There is a ladder on the side that you have to climb up to get the building tools. Russell is the cook, and the rest of us are just working as labourers, building houses.

…We're eating outside, which isn't a good thing, which I'll tell you later. Our meals are prepared in a sort of makeshift hut, but the meals aren't too bad. We're all responsible for washing up. We spend the evening around the campfire, drinking, yarning, and playing roulette – Russell bought a roulette wheel from Alice Springs – told us all we would make our fortune! The only person that made anything at all was Russell!

… That siren you can hear in the background is the meat truck that has been able to get through the floods from Alice with the frozen goods, meats, milk, butter, and all the rest of it. All the people that have had stuff sent out from the store in Alice Springs are rushing to the Co-op to collect their groceries. So, we might get the rest of the crew back sometime tonight, as they have been stuck in Alice Springs for days as they could not get back to the settlement, due to the floodwaters.

… There are four tribes here altogether. Most of the people here at Yuendumu are from the Warlpiri tribe. They came originally from Western Australia – the border is only about 200 miles away from here. The smaller Pintupi tribe is the last to come in from the desert. Most of the tribes are at Papunya, which is 80 miles southwest and where I have just come from. We heard on the news a few days ago that another small settlement is going to be formed for the Pintupi – about 20 miles from here.

... Papunya is quite a lot nicer than here really, because it has a nice range of hills. And, it has more water. We seem to have a shortage of water here at Yuendumu – it goes off every so often, and so does the power....

... Some of the Aborigines are living in humpies – the same style that they've been living in for years. Others live in small basic buildings made of corrugated iron. We are building proper houses with insulation.

... It makes me wonder some nights when I'm lying warm in bed how the poor natives out in their humpies feel, but I've been told that they're quite warm if they're built properly – and they have their dogs to keep them warm. Quite often, they light the fire inside.

I got friendly with some Aborigines who were nice friendly people. We went shooting in my car. They had their guns hanging out the back windows shooting 'roos. They would shoot them and then throw them on top of their water tank for a while to cure the meat.

... I saw them make spears, boomerangs, shields and water carriers, and a lot of native goods – such as fertility beads.

... Quite a lot of Aborigines walk around selling spears, boomerangs, shields, water carriers and fertility beads. I bought two shields, one a hunting shield. It's a very thin shield. It's only about 5 inches wide. I'd hate to be defending myself with it if a spear was coming at me! They've got another show shield, which is about a foot wide. I've bought a number 7 boomerang that is supposed to be quite dear down south. I also bought some fertility beads that may be useful in the future!

... Last night was the initiation ceremony for the young men who came back in from the bush. They'd been out for six months learning the tribal customs and how to hunt and learn to be self-sufficient, to see all the tribal paintings and learn how to paint for themselves; all to prove that they are now a man, not a child. They have a ceremony which consists of them being circumcised and then accepted into the tribe at the age of about 15 or 16 as fully-fledged men.

... There is another unusual custom. We were fencing the other day. We saw a woman come tearing out of the hospital, take her top off, pick up a rock and start belting herself on the head with two stones – 'sorry stones' they are called. Apparently, her child had just died. When someone dies, they belt themselves on the head with these stones, and blood pours down their face – it's a form of expressing their grief. They cut their hair, and the immediate family cuts their hair as well, and they move completely away from where the child had been and where they'd been living. They go out to the bush. They don't speak, or if they have to, they speak in whispers so the spirit of the person who has died can't hear them. After an appropriate time of mourning has passed, they dress themselves up in paint – ochre, and they sweep the road where the child has been to sweep the spirit away. They move their humpies from the area. Then they go back to normal I suppose. Grief is shown this way towards their kin. Also, they never mention the name of anybody who has died. They never mention the person's name.

... The Kurdaitcha man is the head execution man in Aboriginal culture. Tribal law is just as strict as white man's law. They have their council, and the settlement is run by it. The town council is made up of the elders or heads of the tribes, and they're soon going to run it themselves. If somebody's done something wrong, you report it to the superintendent who hands it over to the council. They have various forms of punishment. One is they have to stand, and a spear is driven right through the top of their leg – stopping them from hunting and ultimately surviving. If you're going to be executed, they don't just kill you *outright, they do this in various ways – such as 'pointing the bone' and being outcast from the tribe.*

... Every week we put in an order for beer, and we're living quite comfortably building these houses. Every so often we have time off, and we head into Alice Springs. We've been working at Yuendumu for about a month. Then, disaster strikes.

We ran out of beer! The crew said to the Foreman, 'We're not going to do any more work until somebody goes to Alice to get some more beer. There's a party tomorrow night.' So, the Foreman said, 'which one of you are you going to select, to go to Alice Springs and get the beer'?

We all weighed up the odds. We had to give the person who was going into Alice to get the beer all the money, so he had to be pretty-trustworthy, otherwise he'd spend all the money and come back with nothing; or worse, take the money and not come back! Russell was considered, but: 'If Russell goes, he'll just stay there and drink it all!' Eventually everyone agreed that I was the one to go to Alice, to get the beer. So, the orders were put in, and there were quite a few slabs of beer to collect – about 20 slabs of beer – two-dozen cans in each slab for each worker. Off I went in my car saying – 'be back tomorrow'.

So, I took off after work about 5pm in my Falcon sedan. I was going to drive all night and return the next day – a very dangerous trip. Yuendumu is about 350 kilometres away from 'The Alice' and the road treacherous – unmade, with corrugations and 'bull dust' and unfenced.

I was travelling too fast for the road I was driving, when I saw a cow in the middle of the road! I didn't have time to come to a full stop. I slammed on the brakes but skidded straight into the side of the cow. Thud! I looked, expecting the worst, but the cow just shook its head and kept going across the road! So, I kept going as well as the car was no worse for wear. We were both lucky. I had a feed in 'Alice', refueled the car, got the beer, and started the drive back. The round trip took me around 28 hours.

When I arrived back at Yuendumu, I went straight to the party that was in Roy and Denise's very large caravan with a motorbike strapped on the back. This recently married couple were travelling and working around Australia, and had invited all their friends to the party, which was in full swing.

I opened the caravan door and was met with a hero's welcome! There was loud cheers and clapping! Thomo had arrived with the beer! I felt like a Gladiator entering Rome after a successful battle! My mates helped unload and the beer flowed! Life returned to normal. I joined in the party.

How did Di and I meet at the party? I was enjoying hero status after returning from 'Alice' with the beer in record time and talking with the men in the middle of the caravan. We were half drunk and talking about general things, which for some reason included what we'd do if our wives were unfaithful. At the time, none of us were married! I was charged up on adrenalin after my big trip, and on beer consumed since returning, and in my loud and penetrating voice said, 'I'd kill her! If my wife was unfaithful, I'd just shoot her and that would be it.' My mates laughed at my extreme response – a 'joke' at the time, and we went on talking. But then…

A tall, black haired girl came over to where my mates and I were standing. She looked me straight in the eye and said, 'You wouldn't really do that would you?' Fired up, I went on, 'Sure, I would.' The cool and calm reply from this interesting girl was: *'and what should happen to a husband who is* unfaithful?' I paused, stunned at the question, and thought to myself: 'She's nice. I quite like her – She's confident and got an opinion', and then said: 'The same'! That was that. She didn't respond, just turned, and went back to where she was sitting with her friends. The party finished and we all went our separate ways, back to our separate lives on the settlement.

Afterwards, I said to Russell, 'She was a 'bit of all right' wasn't she. I think I'm going to go around and see her.' Russell said, 'I'll come with you.' But, not having the courage, I didn't.

One day in the distance I saw her again. My mate and I were in the work 'ute', doing our daily rounds collecting the corrugated sheeting that had made its way to the roof of the humpies overnight. We were driving past the Infant Welfare Clinic and I saw her struggling with the key, trying to open the door. Just as we were driving past, she turned, and we briefly made eye contact. I smiled, waved, and said, *'how are you?'* She smiled back. She was wearing a loose, light blue uniform that I thought made her look like the shape of a triangle – a triangle with a lovely smile! I couldn't stop thinking about her. I found out her name was Dianne Ross – Di for short, that she was a Nursing Sister from Victoria and that she shared a flat in the compound on the settlement, a short distance from our camp. Soon after getting this information, I had a few beers to pluck up my courage and Russell came with me.

I knocked on the flat door and it opened. She looked surprised, and a bit uncomfortable about us being on her doorstep, but this did not deter me. She hesitated then reluctantly invited us in. She asked if we would like a cup of tea, and we readily accepted. She handed us a magazine that was lying on the table to read, as she made the tea. It was funny, the magazine had a questionnaire in it, and she said you might as well fill it in. Russell and I looked at each other – we wondered if she realised the questionnaire was about marriage?

After this first visit, Russell and I went around to her flat a few more times. Maria, her flat mate was away on leave. We just turned up 'out of the blue' when we felt like it. She was polite, but never offered us any alcohol when we visited, just a cup of tea. Once we came very late, talking loudly all the way. She met us at the door and told us in no-uncertain terms; never to come around again in the state we were in! We didn't.

Di had a friend named Jane working as a nurse at Papunya. One day, I offered to take her in my car to see her. She accepted, but brought Betty, her Charge Nurse along as well! Anyhow, we had a good day, but it took us all day to get there and back, and we had a flat tyre on the way home! I was out to impress her of my outback skills and changed the tyre in record time.

I dropped Di off at her flat late that night and we talked for a while sitting in my car. She had plans, that didn't include me, or settling down. She was twenty-one-year-old and planning to study midwifery either in Scotland, or Sydney. As she opened the car door to get out, I said quickly: 'You know, I'm going to marry you one of these days.' She responded just as quickly: 'in your dreams! I wouldn't marry you if you were the last person on this earth.' Well, I said, 'I reckon I could marry you.' And that was that she got out of the car!

I saw her again – at a dance held outside under a tree, in the red dust. She was dancing with the Superintendent of Yuendumu who was showing a lot of interest in her. Jealousy overwhelmed me, and I became very protective. Stupidly, I walked over to them and pulled her away, telling her it was best not to dance with him as he had a bad reputation. She was very, very annoyed with me and firmly told me: 'you do not own me'! I left the dance.

A tape home to my parents included the following:

*...Di is incharge of the clinic for mothers and babies. The children come with runny noses and ear infections and all the rest of it – just like any other child....
...The children have lovely brown hair. ...Di has long black hair, and she cut her hair to give to the women that make the fertility beads. They are made-out of beans – red, yellow, and orange and threaded with hair.*

Life went on, but I did not see Di. I knew it would be a while before she calmed down after what I did at the dance and before I could talk to her again. She was busy, working in the clinic, going down to the humpies at all hours of the day and night. People used to fight and use their weapons and stab themselves with spears. And if somebody died, the women would start belting themselves on the head with 'sorry stones'. Di and her crew had to fix them all up.

One evening, a builder arrived from 'Alice' to start work with us the next morning. He arrived late in the evening and lay on the top bunk in our four-bunk room. The next morning, we went to wake him, but he was stone cold dead! That was it! We didn't know why he had died or what had happened to him. He just came in very late the night before and nobody in our room had spoken to him. He lay down on the bunk and died overnight!

The Dowsitt camp was just at the back of the hospital. Di and her team were called. They came quickly and asked us to help get the body down from the top bunk. No way, we weren't going to touch him! We were terribly concerned that he may have had a disease that we would catch! There were no police stationed on the settlement to call. The Nursing Sisters confirmed death and notified the Flying Doctor Service. Some hours later, the body was collected and taken to Alice.

A few days later, another builder was due to arrive and was allocated the same bunk the fellow had died in. The Foreman told us, 'If anyone even mentions that someone died in the bunk, he'll get the sack!' The new builder arrived. We all looked at each other as he climbed into 'the' bunk. Nothing was said. Life went on.

After this episode, I started to see Di again. I felt all had been forgiven, but not forgotten. I had a long way to go to win her heart, if ever. My tape home records the following:

... I'm very lucky at the moment. I'm sitting at Di's flat, and she is cooking a Sunday meal for us.

Yuendumu had a Community Hall for recreation activities and where midday meals were served to children. The Hall had a television downstairs where occasionally cabled TV programs were shown. This day, a Walt Disney children's movie was shown. I knew the person responsible for recreation activities and he asked me if I wanted to go upstairs to see the equipment used for the TV. Interested, I jumped at the chance. He showed me a *Shibaden reel-to-reel video recorder* that had cable that connected the recorder upstairs to the television downstairs.

Whammy! A light came on in my head! My world lit up! I cannot express how deeply it sparked my interest and how pervasive this interaction was. 'How marvellous! Just put a tape on, and you've got TV! I went away thinking. 'I want one of those!' I could not stop thinking about this new 'video' and 'cable TV'!

... It's been a very wet week this week here. The road out to Alice Springs is almost blocked and only open to 4-wheel-drive traffic, and the airstrip is being closed. So, we're rather isolated. There's only about six of us left, and I've been doing the cooking the last couple of days for them as Russell was in Alice Springs. I didn't feel-like going into town this week. Anyhow, he'd gone on a 'bender', and never came back. Somebody had to cook the tea. I said I've done some cooking in my time, so I cooked the tea. It was sweet and sour, but I put a cake mix in with the meat by mistake and it came out with candy peel in it, and it was a disaster! Just when I was wondering what to do with the meal, Di and the other Sisters came around to the kitchen door and said to me, 'you don't look very well. Do you feel ill?' I said, 'I haven't felt very well for a while.' They said, you'd better come to the hospital. I told them I would after I had finished cooking and washed up. They told me 'no, you have to stop what you are doing, and come now.' I did as I was told.

... I've just come down with suspected hepatitis. It must be something like that because I'm going yellow, and my eyes are yellow. I'm in bad health really. I'm being looked after here in the hospital at Yuendumu, which is a nice hospital. It's only got eight beds in it, and I'm the only one here. I've got to know all the nurses here. They're all Nursing Sisters. The trouble is it's quite a long illness, and probably I'll be here a couple of weeks. I can stay here and watch how all the work is going. I'm not bed-ridden really, just isolated. All people who have been in contact with me have to have a needle now, which is quite a large dose of anti whatever. It's quite easy to get hepatitis because there are a lot of carriers in this part of Australia, and there was an open septic drain at the back of my camp where we used to eat our meals in the open. A couple of other Europeans have just gone down with it as well. I've just got to rest, and everything should

be back to normal I suppose. They asked me if I wanted to go into Alice Springs to the hospital. I said I didn't. The Flying Doctor said I'm all right here as long as Betty, the charge nurse can isolate me.

... All the Nursing Sisters are looking after me. I know them all personally. Today they're having a smoke over in the infant clinic. I have special cups and plates now. They have to put it in a bucket of chlorine.

There were no other patients in the hospital and no staff on night duty. I was in isolation although Russell did bring my meals from the camp and played cards with me occasionally. It was very lonely, but the isolation did give me a lot of time to think and think I did.

I thought I might have a future, if I survived. The beginnings of a vision of a future that involved Di and video were swirling around in my head. Sometimes Di came to see me in hospital in the evening after working in the Infant Clinic. We talked and talked, and I thought we were becoming closer. I had only met her about 6 weeks ago, at the party in the caravan but I *knew* she was the one, and only one, for me. But I had to convince her of this. I knew I had not done a very good job of endearing myself to her, to date. This had to change and change quickly. But here I was, at this crucial moment in my life – yellow, infectious, and feeling horribly sick! And I was not getting better. My condition was worsening.

I had to leave Yuendumu and return to Queensland, where I could have further treatment and investigation. Di wrote a letter of discharge and signed it. As a joke, rather than signing the discharge form, I placed my thumbprint on the discharge form, which was common with the locals. The discharge letter and form were then sent to Tony, my brother who is a medical doctor. When Tony received the discharge letter, he interpreted 'Di' as 'Dr', and the thumbprint as evidence that I was so unwell that I was incapable of signing my name! My family were very concerned to say the least.

For my travel, I was advised to cover up and wear my sunglasses, even on the plane from Alice to Brisbane, so that the colour of my eyes and skin could not be seen, and questions asked. My skin and eyes were brilliant yellow. I was feeling sick and looked sick.

So, was this how it was to end – me, laid up in Queensland 'as sick as a dog', and Di leaving Yuendumu in a couple of weeks to pursue her dream? I had waited so long to meet someone that I truly loved and cared for, only to be thwarted when so close to achieving my dream of marrying, settling down and having a family. Everyone seemed extremely concerned about my condition and wondered if I would survive. I knew I was ill and had literally been 'stopped in my tracks'. But my thoughts were elsewhere: Would we meet again? What could I do with the new 'video'?

I arrived in Brisbane, and caught the bus to my parents' home, still wearing my sunglasses. I stayed there for a few days and went to the local doctor. Blood tests were taken, and an appointment made to receive the results in 2 days. I returned and heard the bad news: my bilirubin level was dangerously high, and I was hastily referred to a specialist at the Royal Brisbane Hospital.

I was immediately admitted to hospital for strict bed rest and a very restricted diet. I would be in hospital some time, so was moved to a bed on the veranda. More blood tests indicated the bilirubin was still rising. There was much discussion and concern between the specialists. The general convention for my worsening condition was to be administered cortisone straight away. But the bright young liver specialist looking after me disagreed. He argued that we should wait a while longer. He expected the bilirubin would spike, remain at the level for some time, and then come down gradually. The waiting game commenced.

We waited, and waited, to see the outcome. Days passed. I had now had the debilitating condition for some weeks. The bilirubin level continued to rise. Concerns were expressed to me. I knew I was in real trouble. My body was not functioning as expected for the condition I had. The specialist resolved that there could be an additional underlying problem apart from the hepatitis that was preventing my recovery. A range of tests continued that all came back negative. A liver biopsy was arranged.

Lying in bed, I thought of Di, who I had left in Yuendumu. Before I left, she had given me her home address. I decided to write to tell her that I was ill, and what was happening to me. I also wanted to tell her that when I got better, I would come and see her in Victoria. Well, within a few days of me sending the letter, Di was at my bedside. I couldn't believe my eyes when I saw her. I was so pleased! My parents arranged to meet and take her to dinner in Brisbane. They told me 'what a nice girl she is'.

The biopsy results showed my liver was damaged. I would need to stay in hospital. My recovery would be slow. I was told I would never be able to work hard again, and my working life would be reduced. This really did not sink in at this time. Di was with me, and my days were spent thinking of her, and a future together, and of video. I was full of optimism. The longer I lay in bed, the clearer my vision of the future became. Di came to see me every day and I told her about my plans of video. She smiled and was encouraging. The next blood test showed the bilirubin level had peaked and had started to come down. She was the tonic I needed.

Eventually, I could get out of bed. On this same day, I made my way to a phone in the hospital corridor, and phoned *Shibaden*. I was forming my business. I asked about the recorder, and how much they were. I thought how Channel 7 sent tapes to outlying remote areas. I thought. 'I could do that'.

Progressively the bilirubin came down and I was able to wander further afield. At visiting times in the evening, Di would come and see me. I was able to walk a short distance now. I got as far as Outpatients one day to see Di in my red dressing gown. There were windows outside overlooking the Show Ground near my ward, and the Brisbane show – known as 'The ECHO' – was on. I asked and got permission to leave the hospital for a short time and take Di over to the Show. It was literally, our first date. Not a long date – just long enough to walk over, have a photo taken, and then walk back. I was exhausted at the end of this brief outing. It was all I could manage.

Our blossoming romance was the talk of the hospital. In the evening, the nurses would come and say quietly 'we shouldn't leave the pills on your locker, but we know you will go out of the ward to see Di tonight – just make sure you take them when you come back!' After a few weeks when it was apparent, I was getting better, I asked Di if she would have a coffee with me at the hospital canteen, when she was off duty. We arranged to meet.

I planned to ask a question that I already had a reply to a few weeks earlier. I wanted to ask but did not want to be rejected again. I looked at Di across the table, as we both sat sipping our coffee out of a disposable cup, in very ordinary and sparse surroundings. I looked her in the eye and said quietly, 'Dianne – I've loved you from the first moment I saw you… and always will… will you marry me?' I held my breath…. She did not hesitate, and to my great surprise, just simply said, 'Yes'. We embraced. It was a tender, tender moment.

My heart swelled to bursting point to think that this lovely, intelligent, and empathetic girl I had met in the most unlikely setting – way outback in the Northern Territory, had consented to be my wife. How could it be…? I was not what you would call 'a good catch' by any means! I was 'broke', unwell and had seen better days!

We walked around the gardens of the hospital discussing our new life together. Then it was time to go back to the ward.

My thoughts were racing. I needed an engagement ring, quickly! One isn't engaged until the ring is on her finger. She was not mine yet – someone else could 'snaffle' her up. While I was thinking, 'Friends of the Hospital' came around the ward and said to me: 'Hello luv, anything I can do for you'? 'Yes,' I said, 'if I give you the money, could you go and buy me an engagement ring?' They were a bit surprised and laughed saying, 'No luv, we can't do that – we're sorry – we can get you a pen and paper if you like, but we can't get an engagement ring!' After they had gone, I lay back on the bed thinking, and the day passed.

The following day, I woke up and decided: 'If no one else can get a ring for me, I'll do it myself!' With that, I put my red dressing gown on over my pyjamas. I told the nurses I was 'just going for a walk around the corridors' and they replied, 'don't be too long'. With that, I walked out of the ward, out of the main door of the hospital, and into the street. Luckily, it was a nice day.

I went to the bank and withdrew some money. Fortunately for me, 100 yards from there was a jewellery shop. I walked straight in and said, 'I would like to buy an engagement ring – a nice one'! The shop assistant proceeded to show me the engagement rings without blinking an eye! I bought one – rubies and diamonds and popped it into my dressing gown pocket and walked back into the hospital. Not one person had commented on my pyjamas and red dressing gown, or my yellow skin!

That evening, Di came to visit, and we walked to our favourite courting area – a secluded corner of the hospital, around the lift shaft. I said to Di: 'close your eyes and hold out your hands.' With that, I slipped the engagement ring on her finger saying, 'There you are dear you're mine forever.' I then said, 'I should do this properly, and ask your Father for his permission. Do you think he will agree?'

The public phone in the hospital only accepted coins. We didn't have any on us. We wanted to phone Di's Mother and Father straight away, not wait, as we were both so excited. We deliberated on whether we would wait until we had coins or make a reverse charge call. We decided on the latter and made a person to person reverse charge phone call. Would he accept the charges? Di said he would.

Di's Father answered, and wondered who I was, but did accept the charges. I blurted: 'your daughter and I have been going out for some time, and we would like to marry. Would you give us your blessing?' There was a very long silence on the end of the phone. I can only imagine what he was thinking! He asked to speak to Dianne. They spoke for a short time, then, she handed the phone to me. 'Yes', he said, 'if Dianne loves you and you love her that is good enough for me'. Relieved, I uttered 'Thank you'.

This whirl-wind romance spread through the hospital like a bushfire! Tony, Helen, Tim, and Anne drove from Lismore to visit me, and met Di in her break from duty. In the evening, they took us out to a lovely restaurant to celebrate our engagement, after I got permission to go out for a few hours.

At every opportunity I had I went to Outpatients to see Di. One day I bumped into the specialist there. 'Hello', he said, 'what are you doing down here?' I told him the news of our engagement. He congratulated me, but then said, 'If you are well enough to roam around the hospital, you are well enough to go home and get on with your life'. I agreed. I was discharged, and Di and I went to my parents' home for a short while before flying to Victoria.

We flew to Melbourne, then travelled by train to Ballarat, where Cheryl and John, Dianne's sister and brother-in-law met us and gave me a very warm welcome to the family'. Cheryl threw her arms around me and said, 'Welcome to the family', whilst her husband John beamed as he gave me a very firm handshake. I felt how genuine and warm they were, and I was right – this feeling would never change, but rather strengthen over the years. We went to have coffee and they told me about their young family. They then drove us for about an hour to Natte Yallock – to meet all the rest of the family.

I will never forget this meeting and my stay with Dianne's family. Her parents – Thelma and Keith, younger brother Dennis, and elder brother Graham and his wife Lynette, instantly made me feel at home, as did the extended family. This acceptance was extended to my family when they also met them.

I experienced the friendliness and generosity of the local community when we were provided the traditional 'kitchen tea' and dance in the local hall – something that all 'Natte' girls were given before their marriage. Dianne and I busied ourselves by fitting out the caravan we had bought to tow to Queensland with my parents' car after the wedding.

Leading up to the wedding I helped Dennis as much as I could on the farm – fencing. But the specialist was right – it would take a long time for me to recover, if ever. He had advised me on discharge, that I would never be able to do hard manual labour again. At this time, it started to sink in.

My life and how I saw myself would have to change. But I had always relied on my strong and sturdy body to do hard manual labour and earn a living. What did the future hold? I needed to rethink and plan. How was I to support a wife, and hopefully a family?

Dyslexia would always be a significant impediment. I resolved that my long-held interest in audio and perhaps the new video could provide an opportunity. But how do I go about entering this new world of video?

Dianne and I were married on December 15, 1973 at the Presbyterian Church in Avoca. Cheryl was 'Maid of Honour', and Tony Best Man. It was a perfect, perfect day in every way, and life held lots of promise.

Part 3
The Switch
1974-2017

'Life isn't about finding yourself. It's about creating yourself'.
    George Bernard Shaw

Chapter 29
My Dianne

My Dianne is my life, and my wife. We married within 9 months of meeting at Yuendumu, Northern Territory in 1973. The 1964 'Bachelors' hit song, *'Smile for me, my Diane'* could be our signatory song:

'I'm in heaven when I see you smile (see you smile) Smile for me, my Diane (my Diane)
And though everything's dark, all the while I can see you, Diane....
You have lighted the road leading home.
Oh, pray for me, when you can (when you can)
But no matter wherever I roam Smile for me, my Diane'.

But who is my Dianne?

Dianne is a quiet achiever, who shuns the 'lime-light'. In fact, she is the opposite of me! I am grateful that she has agreed to share some of her story in this Chapter. It is a story that includes something of her ancestors, her family, and her life, until we married. It is but a brief story of someone who has much to tell. Please meet *'My Dianne'*.

'...I am speaking today at Chris's request for his book and for the record. This is not something I'm particularly good at. He's much more of a storyteller than I. But I will give a little bit of background about myself, and then about when Chris and I met. My name is Dianne Lynette Thompson nee Ross, born 27/07/1951 at Stawell, Victoria, Australia. I grew up at Natte Yallock, an aboriginal word meaning 'big water-little plain'. Natte is a small farming community, between Maryborough and St Arnuad, Victoria, Australia. It's a lovely place – big red river gums beside the Avoca River that winds its way through the farming land. The Natte community are mostly descendants of those who migrated one way or another, to Australia in the 19th Century. At the time I grew up, Natte had a small primary school – Number 1347, a Methodist Church, a Post Office – a small room attached to a family home, a fire brigade hall, and a community hall, next door to the treasured sporting grounds – the centre of the community. The people were, and still are, the 'heart and backbone' of the community.

I'm fifth generation Australian of Scottish, Irish, and English descent. My first ancestor arrived in 1842, and others very soon after. Together they represent the rich and varied history of early European Australia. How they made their way to Australia was via the status of free and assisted immigrants, convict, government schemes, and by 'jumping ship'. Many had a stint on the Ballarat gold fields as miners before establishing in other areas and work. Other occupations in the early days included grocer, jockey, farming, logging and carrier, Hotel and Cobb and Co. All were pioneers and left their mark – some have been written into the history books. I will only mention a few today, but I am very proud of them all – their incredible resilience and contribution to Australia so that their descendants could have a better life.

In 1854, fifty-five-year-old Donald Ross, my great, great, grandfather, a widower and three of his sons [one Farquhar my great grandfather] and their wives travelled from Lochbroom, Ross and Cromarty, Scotland, to Australia. They were farmers and cattle dealers evicted during the Scottish 'clearances'. After serving out their 'bond' as assisted immigrants, they took the opportunity to take up land at Archdale Junction, Victoria, and subsequently prospered. The surrounding areas remain the 'seat' of this branch of the Ross clan, that includes my grandfather, John [Jack] Ross.

In 1850, sixteen-year-old, Anne Cathcart, 'Irish orphan' and my great – great, grandmother, from County Sligo, Ireland was brought with her sister to Australia via the 'Earl Grey Scheme' during the potato famine in Ireland. Her name is recorded in this historical scheme and in Hyde Park Barracks Museum, Sydney and a monument are erected in Williamstown, Victoria. We do not have a photo of her. The history of her husband – William Newman is unknown, although we do have a photo of him. His country of origin and background remains a mystery, despite much research from descendants. The 'story' is that he 'jumped ship' – a practice common at the time. Further, when he did jump ship, he believed himself a 'new man', hence the name of Newman. William and

Anne lived in Ballarat before settling in Fitzroy, Melbourne and together, had 14 children. One was my great grandfather John William Newman, who married Jane Ferris whose parents were free settlers from Wiltshire, England.

In 1842, eighteen-year-old Timothy Harrington, a jockey from County Cork, Ireland was transported to the infamous convict settlement at Port Arthur, Tasmania for 10 years, for stealing a horse. He survived this most harsh environment, gained his ticket of freedom, and became a well-known jockey in the fledgling racing industry in Tasmania. But within two years of gaining his freedom he died on the racetrack after a fall from the horse he was riding. We do not have a photo of him, but rather details contained within his records as a convict, and information regarding his death in newspapers of the time. Timothy and his wife Bridget [nee Williams] a servant and free settler from Tipperary, Ireland had one child, Mary Harrington.

In 1854, twenty-three-year-old James Beattie, a miner, and unassisted migrant from Brigham, Cumberland, England, arrived in Australia. Not long after, James was one of the thirteen men arrested at the 'Eureka Stockade' uprising in Ballarat in 1854. These men were subsequently tried for treason, but luckily for James' descendants, found not guilty! Many years after this, James, forty-six-year-old, married twenty-one-year-old Mary Harrington, had seven sons, and settled in Murchison, Victoria. After James' death in 1901, just before Federation of Australia, most of his family moved to Landsborough and then settled in Navarre, Victoria. The link between James and the 'Eureka Stockade', a significant event in the history of Australia; was not known by my family, until more than one hundred and fifty years later.

My father – Maxwell Keith Ross – known as Keith or Bill, was a very gentle man, a loving father, and an excellent farmer. He grew up on a farm at Archdale Junction, Victoria, and left school at twelve-year-old. Dad was a learned, interesting man, who enjoyed a range of conversation topics. He was sociable, well liked, and respected, and loved telling stories of days gone by and the people he knew from an early age. He was a very practical man with a knack for all things mechanical – and why his stint in the 2nd World War, saw him retained as an air-force mechanic, stationed in South Australia. He was forward thinking, embraced new technology and methods of farming until the day he died. In his own words, his only regret in life was that he never knew his mother's love [Myrtle Jane Ross nee Newman] as she died from pneumonia, when he was a very young child.

My mother – Thelma May Beattie was a loving mother, but very shy and reserved. Her farm, home, family, and the local football team, were her life. She grew up at Navarre, Victoria, and left school at twelve-year-old. Mum was academically bright and was awarded a scholarship to attend high school, but this meant either leaving home, or the family needed to move. She chose to stay with her parents and two sisters, and when they moved to St Arnuad, worked in a knitting mill and as a housekeeper. Family always took precedent and as children we benefited from her commitment. I do not believe my mother had any regrets in her life – at least none that she shared.

It was in the position of housekeeper that she met my Father, who was working as a shearer. They recalled their first meeting and laughed about it for many years. My mother had taken some time to make up a feather bed using a white bedspread, in preparation for visit from a young couple on their honeymoon. My father somehow managed to sit on the white bedspread, in his shearer's clothes! What can I say? My mother was not happy at all with my father and let him know! She obviously made an impression, as he and his brother Colin, often made the sixty-mile journey to Stawell, during the war years to court my mother and her sister Mona respectively. In time, the two couples married and eventually settled at Natte Yallock, Victoria. They lived on their own farms separated only by the Avoca River.

My mother chose not to drive at a very early stage in her marriage in fact I do not ever recall her driving a car. This meant that outings apart from family gatherings were greatly restricted – and only possible if our Father took us. I recall occasionally going to the pictures, in Avoca on a Saturday night, after football and netball, and visiting our grandparents and aunt and uncle in Stawell, which we all enjoyed. But the drive home from Stawell always followed the same pattern. My three siblings and I were tired and would constantly 'niggle' each other in the back seat of the car. Dad would 'threaten' us if we weren't quiet or 'leave each other alone', we would get the normal punishment of the time. Halfway home, he would stop the car, order everyone out, smack us on the bottom with his hand – not hard – a gesture. Then, we would all get back into the car, settle down and continue the journey home. Our other outings related to sport where we all went as a family, and Sunday school at the local Methodist Church. We either walked or rode our bikes to and from Sunday school as Mum and Dad did not attend but obviously wanted us to have the educational and spiritual experience, of which I am pleased.

I had a very happy childhood at Roslyn, our farm at Natte Yallock, Victoria. I loved my parents, brothers and sisters, aunts and uncles, cousins, and grandparents. We had a unique upbringing as two Ross brothers married two Beattie sisters and we lived next door to each other apart from the Avoca River separating us. We lived in a very small, old cottage on the farm – 2 bedrooms, a sleep out, lounge, bathroom, and kitchen, until the new, and large comfortable house was built, when I was nine-year-old. Our Grandma Beattie moved from Stawell to live next door to us on the farm when my Auntie Eileen died. Later, when Uncle Fred died, their orphaned son, my cousin Rodney, lived across the river, with Auntie Mona, Uncle Colin and their five children.

I have one sister – Cheryl, and two brothers Graham and Dennis. As children, we helped on the farm. We milked cows, fed the animals, collected eggs, turned the baled hay, moved the sheep to different paddocks, picked up sticks to clear the land and lit fires of clumps of sticks, helped in the shearing shed, and in the house. We swam in the Avoca River – only a few metres behind our house and had a paddleboat. We played with our cousins, who were our friends. It was a lovely existence.

I went to the local one-teacher primary school. On my first day, I rode my bike and propped it up against the peppercorn tree. When I walked, there was a pattern. I'd walk across the cattle pit – the entrance to Roslyn, down the gravel road winding around the river, climb through a barbed wire fence and then cut across a paddock to get to the bridge that crossed the river, and then down the dirt road to number 1347 Natte Yallock Primary School.

It was at the riverbank on the school side that I buried a dead swallow and made a cross out of twigs and placed it in the soft soil. In the puddles on the side of the road, I watched tadpoles develop into frogs. And I'm sorry to say now but in spring, I climbed trees, robbed the birds' nests of their eggs and 'blew' them so that the contents of the egg oozed out of the pin pricks in the shell I'd made, and then kept the very fragile and beautiful eggshells.

I dearly wanted long hair, but to get my mother to agree, there were sacrifices. She would tightly pull my hair back in the morning, with many hair clips and an elastic band to make it tidy, even when it was very short. Off I would go to school – walk over the cattle pit, around the bend of the road that followed the river where I would take out the hair clips and elastic band and place them in a hollow log, and happily continue to school. On the way home, I would stop at the hollow log, put the hairpins and elastic band back in my hair, and walk home. My mother was happy, and so was I.

A swarm of bees attacked me on this same road when I was ten-year-old. A young bull had gotten out of the paddock, and I was asked to go and bring him back. I found him, and started walking slowly, close behind him and next to the fence, directing him to the paddock. A very old and large tree grew next to the fence. The bull walked through the gap between the tree trunk and the fence, and when he did, his rump knocked off a nest of bees attached to the tree trunk, just as I walked through the gap. Suddenly, I was covered with very angry bees, that were ferociously stinging me all over my body. I screamed and ran, waving my hands around, and pulling off my loose top as the bees were under it and on my face and limbs and were stinging incessantly. I ran over the cattle pit, and back to home – the bees still on me, everywhere. I could hardly see. All I could think of was my Grandmother telling me about her brother who had died from a single bee sting! I took a while to recover from this incident and am still to this day, very, very wary of bees and wasps.

I developed early and did not grow any taller after twelve-year-old at which time I passed for sixteen-year-old or so, or so I was told. This was a challenge at primary school as I was very tall, and my peers were much shorter than I, with one exception – a boy, who I was always paired off with for the square dancing. I suspect he hated this, as much as I did!

I had a fantastic and inspirational teacher, Mr Brian Sword at primary school. His wife Rosemary taught us singing, and I fondly recall a very memorable song in the Maori language, which I thought was very exotic indeed! Together, they greatly influenced me in my early years. A few years ago, I realised that their daughter who was born after I had left primary school, was no other than Kirsty Sword Gusmao, the wife of the Prime Minister and former President of Timor-Leste. I was not surprised that together they had produced such a strong and committed daughter.

I had a great time at primary school until the final years when I was eleven-year-old. I was the only girl in my class, of three, and there weren't any children at all in the class below. It was a bit lonely to say the least. I loved to read, so the library became my favourite pastime. I read all the books in the school library three or four times. My mother would say, 'where's Dianne – she's probably got her head in a book somewhere' when she was trying to find me at home! She was right! Every chance I got, I read.

Because it was a one-teacher school until my final year, there were a small number of students. As such, if you wanted to play netball, the boys had to play with the girls, and if the boys wanted to play football, the girls had to play with the boys. So, I grew up with a great love of playing sport, particularly netball and tennis, at which I excelled. However, it was my aptitude for playing football at primary school that my classmates, particularly the boys, recall, years later.

We swam in the river at home, and when we were at school, we swam in a dam in the paddock next door to the school. The routine when swimming in the dam was: Swim and splash, rush out of the water onto the side of the dam, pull the leeches off our bodies, then go back into the dam water, and repeat the exercise. Our social life from an early age mainly consisted of family functions and ballroom dancing that was connected to the sporting calendar. I made my debut, as all other girls of the era did, and was escorted by Graham, my brother.

My brothers and sister and I got on extremely well. We were a happy family. There are many, many experiences I could share, but these are for another time. Some fond or significant instances I will share.

Cheryl, my sister is five years older than I, and a great lover of animals. I worshipped her as an older sister then, as I do now. I recall when I was five years old and were both in the double bed we shared at the time, Cheryl asked me to get a handkerchief for her. I was so pleased and thought, 'Oh she's asked me to do something for her and jumped out of bed to get if for her'. I was also willing for Cheryl to practice her developing skills in hair cutting and eyebrow shaping on me; and there was much practice, before she perfected the art! I learned much from Cheryl as I grew up – from caring for animals, dressmaking and the trials and tribulations of growing up being the eldest child. I was, I think, an annoying little sister, especially when she started dating.

Graham is 2 years older than I, a very gentle and placid boy, and now man. We got on well and still do. I recall Graham and I being asked by our mother to 'gut' and pull out the feathers of the rooster that she had just chopped the head off with an axe in preparation for our Christmas dinner. Each year, the old rooster would meet its fate this way, and be replaced by a younger rooster in the 'chook' pen. Anyhow, Graham and I took the beheaded rooster that was still wriggling, down to the bank of the river, and started to 'gut and pluck', although neither of us wanted to do this. Graham started dry retching, but eventually, we managed, and the unfortunate rooster was served for Christmas dinner!

Dennis is nearly 4 years younger than I, and initially, the 'baby' I could look after. We were never allowed to go near the river when we were young as our mother could not swim and was petrified that we would drown. She always told us that she went grey by thirty years old, worrying about one of us drowning. Being children, we did go near the river when we shouldn't have. One day Dennis walked out on a log that was protruding out of the river at the back of the cowshed. He suddenly slipped and fell in. He was about four-year-old at the time, and I was eight-year-old. I pulled him out and probably saved his life. We never told our mother. At the time I told Dennis, 'If you do exactly what I say, I won't tell Mum'. That threat worked for quite a while, but when he became older, he confronted me and said: 'I don't care if you do'. I knew from that time, my influence over my younger brother had ceased!

My brothers and sister have married, had children and either have grandchildren or looking forward to them. They remain in the area that we grew up. I have moved quite a bit around Australia and spent some time overseas.

My siblings and I all went to the Maryborough Technical College. We walked in all types of weather to the end of our road – about a kilometre and boarded the school bus to go to the Maryborough Technical College – 'The Tech' a trade school that took around an hour. The 'Tech' was not suited to me, but I did enjoy my time there.

One night before my completion of primary school, Mr Sword, the Headmaster, visited my parents at home to try and convince them that I would benefit from going to the Maryborough High School, which was considered more academic, and offered language studies. But my parents feared I would be 'different' to their other children if I did; and that we should all be treated equally. As such, I went to 'The Tech' as did my brothers and sister. I think that this decision held me back in some ways. I cannot speak for my siblings. What I can say is that my parents believed they did the right thing – we were all treated equally as far as the school we attended.

I secretly wanted to go to boarding school like my second cousins who lived near us did. I thought that would be very exciting and very glamorous, but none of these options were available to me. Reality was I was a girl, from a traditional farming family and therefore I could not even think what I could do or what I would do.

The 'Tech' College didn't have language studies as part of the curriculum, but did offer specific Diploma level trade qualifications, post-secondary school. I chose to study the commercial stream, which was unusual because girls like me, that is, with my background, normally continued with home economics – cookery and dressmaking. Whilst I enjoyed the early years learning about home economics, I resisted continuing, instead studying stenography, typing, and business accounting. I'm very pleased that I did. It was, one way, the only way, to express my desire to do something a little more different than what I was being groomed for.

I really enjoyed school very, very much. I won a Commonwealth scholarship in year 10 that would allow me to remain at school another 2 years to complete year 12. However, as my older siblings had left in year 9 or year 10, my parents wanted me to leave at the end of year 10. But, as I'd won a scholarship, I pleaded with my parents to let me remain at School. Eventually, I negotiated the following: I asked them to agree to let me return to complete the Leaving Certificate – year 11; and if they did, I wouldn't ask to return to finish the final year 12. Reluctantly, my parents finally agreed that I could go back to school for another year. I am not sure if my siblings felt at the time that I was shown favouritism to be able to spend more time at school. Perhaps they did. Or perhaps they were pleased they could leave school earlier.

In this final year, I was elected prefect and house captain, and won the literary award in the Wool and Wine Festival in Maryborough, with an essay titled 'The World is My Neighbour'. This essay was written by someone (me) who had never ventured any further than Melbourne – and then only once and knew only one person who was not stereotypical 'Australian' – my Italian piano teacher, Mr Bigarelli, who we all cheekily called 'Mr Biggerbelly', but not to his face! Mr Bigarelli lived in Ballarat and came to our house on a Sunday, had 'dinner', then taught Cheryl the piano accordion, Graham the banjo and me the piano.

I had an inspirational English teacher – Miss Orr – just out of university. She was just a few years older than I and talked about travelling to Europe at the end of the year. She opened my eyes to possibilities, and of deep thinking. I recall her challenging the class:

'what if we are just a figment of each other's imagination?

Prior to leaving school, I used to daydream about what I could do for a living. I used to think that 'if I was a boy… and it was always if I was a boy…I could do this, or that…. If I was a boy, I would perhaps be a doctor, or perhaps a forensic scientist.' I would always be thinking of things that I could do – *if I was a boy*. However, I kept this to myself. I repeatedly told the 'careers counsellors' on a school excursion to Ballarat in the last year of my schooling: 'what I am going to do is work on the farm'. Topic closed. I had to say this, and not allow myself to think about anything other as I needed to resolve myself to what was to be. It was too painful not to. The counsellors persisted with me, but I was resolved. How could I not be?

As a girl, the times and culture of my family dictated. My life was mapped out: stay at home on the farm, work inside and outside on the farm; marry well and preferably a local farmer. I am not sure if other girls of the district thought this, it may be just my perception. Never mind, that's how my thoughts flowed at the time.

Girls did not 'go out to work'. Girls stayed at home, until they married. This was how it was, in the family I grew up in, despite the great social revolution going on in the Western world! The 1960s, Beatles, Elvis, man on the moon, Germaine Greer, and the Female Eunuch!

Perhaps it was because of this social revolution that traditions were strongly enforced by my parents and others in the community at this revolutionary time?

Cheryl, my sister had reluctantly stayed at home before me. She wanted to complete an arts/design diploma, as she was an excellent artist, dressmaker, and cake decorator. However, she remained at home, but during this time, thrived in farming, developing knowledge and expertise relating to animals and gained wide respect in the industry she so loves to this day. At twenty-two-year-old she married John, a local farmer, and the love of her life. They are still together today, and still very happy.

At the end of 1968 on completion of year 11 at the age of seventeen-year-old I complied with my parent's wishes, and left school receiving the 'Leaving Certificate'. In 1969, I worked on the farm for nine months. I tried to fit in. I was determined that if I had to stay at home on the farm – if this was to be my life, I would try to do everything outside on the farm, learn and do it well. It didn't work. As I drove the tractor up and down raking the hay, I kept thinking about how this life was not for me, and that I really wanted to finish year 12 and find another path. But what was that path?

But then there was a stroke of luck! I enrolled in night school at 'The Tech' and studied Year 12 English and English literature. How? Our farm was some way from Maryborough [20 miles]. That doesn't sound a great distance, but in 1969, it was quite a way just to travel for 'frivolous' things such as night school; and I was not old enough to have a car license. Just to go to Maryborough at night for me to complete an English course, would not have been approved, or thought of! But luckily, Graham had started courting a young lady in Maryborough who eventually became his wife. So, on a Thursday night, he would drive to visit Lynette and I would go with him and attend night school. So, it worked very nicely for me.

I completed nine months of night school and things were going well. It wasn't long before I was to sit the final exams, but instead of doing this, I left. There was a change in my life, and I very quickly decided that I would leave home. I knew that even if I finished year 12 at night school, I would not be able to go to university, as I believed at the time that I had no way of supporting myself. So, what could I do? In hindsight, I could've completed year 12 English, pursued university studies, and worked part-time – as people do now – sounds so simple – but at the time, this thought, and direction was not clear to me. 'University' was a very foreign word, and there were no role models.

After leaving school, spending nine months at home working,' inside' and 'outside', I made the decision in early September 1969 after breaking up with my boyfriend to leave home. But where could I go? What could I do? I hadn't finished school. I could get a job – doing something… I could utilize my skills in a commerce area, but I didn't want to be a secretary. I felt that I would prefer to be in charge, of my life. This meant I had to keep learning. And, I had to support myself at the same time.

The option was nursing, teaching or hairdressing as far as girls were concerned at the time. Teaching was out – I had not finished year 12. Hairdressing needed an apprenticeship, and I had no contacts. Suddenly, I thought of nursing – I convinced myself it was the only option for me, and it would provide an income immediately.

I had made the decision. Now, how was I to go about it…?

I sat in the office at home and made a phone call to the Victorian Nurses' Board and asked which hospital I should apply for nurse training in Melbourne. I was told that if I had the grades, I should apply to the Alfred Hospital – the 'top' destination hospital for trainee nurses. I duly applied and got an interview.

My mother wanted me to go to Ballarat to train as a nurse as it was closer to home. She also wanted me to study to be a nurses' aide – an enrolled nurse as this qualification completed in a year, compared to three years for registered nursing. Her reasoning? What if I wanted to get married during the three years? In those days, trainee nurses were not allowed to marry, so in her mind it was better to study the shorter course. But I was determined, and marriage was not on my mind! I was only going to train in Melbourne, and as a registered nurse!

My Father drove me to Melbourne for the interview at the Alfred Hospital. I recall sitting in the corner of a small and sparse room in the education centre at the Alfred, looking at the 3 people in uniform who were interviewing me. It was rather daunting, but I felt I was fighting for survival! I had to really argue my point and convince them that I would stay, and not leave. They were concerned as it had not been a lifetime passion of mine to be a nurse – I had only made the decision to leave and go nursing, a few weeks ago! I thought to myself, 'I have no-where else to go – I am not leaving here until they say I can start'. They did have an intake starting on September 29th, 1969. I insisted I would be ready by this date and would not let them down.

After a long time sitting in the room being interviewed, that is, interrogated, they said they would 'give me a chance'. I was elated! So, within a week, I was in class – preliminary training school, studying nursing at the Alfred Hospital. I had only been to Melbourne once before in my life and this was when I was at primary school when we had an excursion to look over a ship docked at Port Melbourne. In this instance, Dad drove me down, along with a carload of other children. So, it was quite a big change for me – from Natte Yallock, to Melbourne. But I can say whilst the impetus for leaving was painful, the outcome of that decision was extremely positive and life changing for me. I have never regretted it.

My parents were sad to see me go and concerned. Dad knew nurse's 'reputation' [he'd been in the Air force!], and Mum was just fearful of anything that was outside of her 'world'. I recall my grandmother Beattie who I was very fond of and lived in the house next door to us on the farm saying to Mum and Dad, 'Don't worry, she'll be back'.

I was not sure at the time whether she thought that I would be back as I wouldn't like nursing or find it too hard; or, if she said it because she knew that I was determined and stubborn, and if she said I would be back then I would not be but rather stay on to complete the training! I now think the latter – stubbornness runs in the family I am told! I also have a lovely note from her written to congratulate me on my graduation. I know that she was proud of me, as my parents and siblings were on achieving the title of 'Sister', 3 years later. One of Grandma Beattie's favourite sayings and she had many, was: 'you make your bed, you lie in it'. I agree with her on this. Three years on and after many exceptional, unique and some painful experiences, I did complete my nurse training on September 30th, 1972. I was invited to stay on at the Alfred, as a Staff Nurse – a very great honour. But, along with a friend, Jane, I decided to explore further.

I was on my way overseas. I had applied to Scotland to do midwifery, and I needed to boost my finances and fill in some time before I did that. Nursing was extremely poorly paid, and I had not managed to save during my studies for books, and train travel home every 6 weeks. I was also paying off 11 acres of land I purchased in Avoca, at the insistence of Mum who managed the 'books' for it, and Cheryl leased the land for her growing herd of cattle. Just before I graduated, I saw an advertisement in a paper looking for registered nurses in Alice Springs, commencing early January 1973. I was interested and applied and approved. I thought this job would be different from what we had been doing the last 3 years – fast paced, high acuity, and enormous responsibility for our age. It would be as far away as I could possibly get from clocks and constant monitoring and observations of patients, and it seemed to be a very 'glamorous' destination.

Plus, as a remote area, it was a very well-paid position – for nursing. I would soon be on my way overseas. After graduating, I went home and worked in the local Maryborough Hospital on night duty until the end of December 1972.

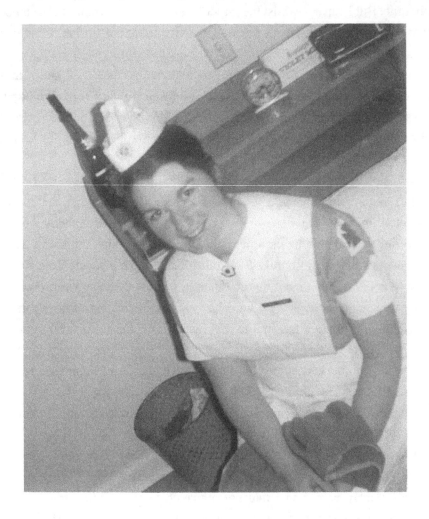

I was looking for a totally different experience and was confident that the Northern Territory would provide this. And it did.

On January 1, 1973 at 2300 I landed in Alice Springs Northern Territory, along with Jane. What was my first impression? It was like another world, and exciting. But it was nearly midnight, and it was extremely hot and humid. It was 41 degrees at 2300 when we walked off the plane into the terminal. When I got to my room at the Alice Springs Hospital, the air conditioning was not working in my room. So, it was an extremely hot and 'sticky' night.

I spent two months at the Alice Springs Hospital working at a range of environments within the hospital and as the nurse in the on-call ambulance. The ambulance often went into town when needed, attending to people after fights mostly caused by misuse of alcohol and accidents. I also went with the ambulance to attend to and collect critically ill people and bring back to hospital. Once, on the way out to a remote cattle station to attend to a man with severe chest pain the ambulance got bogged in the red soil and was dug out three times! We spent 5 hours trying to get to the sick man, and then another 5 back, after we had refuelled and had refreshments at the Station. I stayed with the patient in the back of the ambulance and administered morphine to relieve the pain, and he survived. I had some memorable and some dramatic experiences, during my time working in 'Alice'. But I'm not sharing those today.

In March 1973, I was posted to Yuendumu, an Aboriginal settlement, nearly 350 kilometres northwest of Alice Springs. I knew nothing about Yuendumu prior to this, but soon learnt that it was a settlement for Aboriginal people, on the Northern Territory and Western Australia border. There was very little induction to go to Yuendumu, so I wasn't sure how to prepare for what I would be doing.

The philosophy of community health or remote area nursing was not part of the curriculum of nursing during my training. In fact, it was not a speciality until 1975, and this was 1973. So, I was very well trained in acute care, as the Alfred Hospital was well known for receiving very sick patients from other hospitals and was a leader in many areas of contemporary care and surgery. But, at Yuendumu, I required both acute care skills for the accidents and situations that occurred infrequently, and community health skills routinely. I remember thinking 'if you arrest – cardiac or respiratory, I could save you…but how do I treat the minor ailments that may have a physical and psychological basis?' It was a very interesting experience and I had to learn quickly.

Whilst I say I had no induction to our nursing work in a remote area, what I do remember Alice Springs Hospital staff saying is: 'Stay away from the builders at Yuendumu and any other Aboriginal settlement you go to. There are a number out there building houses for the government. They're rude, rough men and it's best not to be associated with them.'

That was the only advice I was armed with when I went to Yuendumu at the age of twenty-one-year-old, with two other colleagues. Sam, short for Samantha from Lismore, New South Wales was also twenty-one-year-old, and her friend Lynn from Queensland was twenty-three-year-old. Sam and Lynn trained as a nurse together and were travelling around Australia in Sam's Kombi van and that's what we travelled in to Yuendumu.

Just as we were leaving Alice Springs Hospital, the Children's Ward staff asked us to take a passenger, a baby, named Malcolm, six months old, back to his mother at Yuendumu. How did this come about? I had nursed Malcolm in the children's ward and was rather fond of this little boy, as were other nurses. He had been in an out of hospital since birth, but this time had been in for some time with severe gastroenteritis and dehydration – a dangerous situation for a baby at any stage. He had recovered and was ready for discharge and return to his mother, at Yuendumu. I took the responsibility to return Malcolm to his mother at Yuendumu. I would have a continuing and strong connection with Malcolm and his mother during my time at Yuendumu. Sadly, soon after leaving Yuendumu, Sam wrote and told me that Malcolm had died.

Sam, Lynn, baby Malcolm and I went to Yuendumu. It was a long and dangerous drive for anyone, but there we were, 3 young nurses with a baby, in a Kombi van, travelling to remote and isolated Yuendumu! Not sure if this would happen these days, but we did it, and there was nothing said about it, and no one thought it strange.

On the way to Yuendumu, we stopped at a beautiful place to have a drink and something to eat. It was very hot. There was a riverbed and a bridge, and we opened the doors of the Kombi van to get out. I can't tell you how horrible the experience was that followed. A swarm of flies descended upon us! They were in our eyes, ears, and our mouth and all over our clothes. I quickly threw a little blanket over Malcolm to protect him and grabbed one for myself. We all had our lunch and drink of water huddled underneath a blanket! We concluded that every other person that drives to and from Yuendumu must have a 'pit stop' there as well. I will never forget it. I was used to flies but this was horrific. It reminded me of the episode of being stung by a swarm of bees in my childhood, without the pain!

We continued the journey and finally entered the arched sign stating Yuendumu. We found the hospital, and the community centre. We met Betty the Charge Nurse and Malcolm's mother came to the hospital to collect him. We were then taken to the flats where we were to live. I was to share a flat with Marie, from Colac in Victoria, but she was leaving shortly after being there some time. Sam and Lynn would share a flat together. There were two other flats with two teachers in one, and an anthropologist, a PhD student studying the language of the aboriginal people, in the other.

Our lives started as 'Sisters' at Yuendumu. Initially I worked in the Yuendumu Health Clinic and the hospital, and then later, in the Mothers and Children Clinic. I enjoyed my work and had many challenging times and experiences.

However, I came to question what I was doing in this remote area, or more precisely, the value of what I was doing for, or to, the people I was caring for. The answer I would come to would be the impetus for me to leave Yuendumu. But before leaving, I would share my reasons for leaving with an ABC crew, filming a documentary about Yuendumu.

At the time I was there, Yuendumu was considered a government model for success in aboriginal settlements. My comments, on camera, were not well received. Two instances stood out and together formed my opinion that I shared with the ABC film crew. Firstly, there was a 'mismatch' between what was required, and what was delivered. The government provided a set of white woollen clothes for newborns. As I handed out a set of this white woollen clothing to each mother for her newborn baby, that was living in a humpy in the camp, it epitomized to me the lack of understanding of the true living situation and needs of the people, in general.

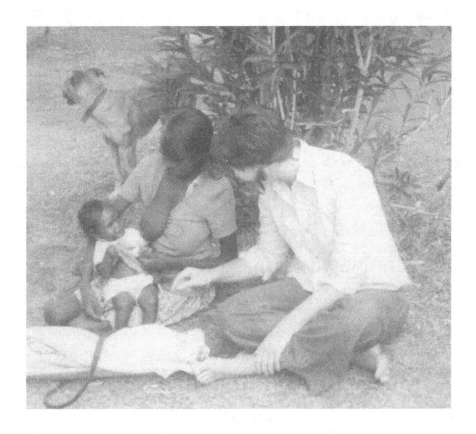

Secondly, camp life was not conducive to 'bottle feeding'. Mothers were giving up breastfeeding in favour of the bottle, despite encouragement not to do so, given the obvious problems. Hygiene regarding the feeding bottle and teat became a real issue, but the marketing image was strong and had infiltrated this remote area. Mothers truly believed they were doing the best thing for their baby by bottle feeding, but babies were consistently getting very sick, with gastroenteritis. It was a difficult and escalating problem. I became disillusioned.

The interview with the ABC crew was going well, until I was asked why I was leaving Yuendumu. I simply said, 'I didn't believe in what I was [we were] doing anymore'. The Director quickly said, 'cut'! And that was it! My response was not what they were there to record. There were no more questions, or filming, of me.

It was only a short while after starting work at Yuendumu that I met Chris. I didn't meet him in my role at the hospital or going down to the humpies to visit children or others who were unwell. I met him at a party, in a very large caravan!

I was invited to a party held by a married teacher and her husband, a builder. All off duty nurses attended. I remember sitting in a large spacious caravan and thinking it was rather strange having a party in a caravan, and not outside. Anyhow, it was all very pleasant, and it was a change, to go out socially. There was nothing else in Yuendumu to go to. Not that I wanted to, I had plans to learn, save money, and travel.

Later in the evening, the door of the caravan was flung open, and those opposite the door gave a huge round of applause, a hero's welcome because 'Thomo' had returned! Thomo had returned with the alcohol! I didn't see Thomo whoever this was, because there were so many people clustered around the doorway. So, I just kept on talking to the people in my area.

Later in the night, I heard a voice – a very distinct voice, and an accent that attracted me. I could not see the person the voice belonged to. Then, I heard this distinctive voice say loudly: 'If my wife was unfaithful, I would shoot her.' I was astounded that someone could say this. I turned and looked towards 'the voice' thinking, this can't go unchecked. The comment must be challenged!

I confronted this person, and said, 'You wouldn't do that, would you?' And the response was, 'Yes'; followed by some colourful language. 'I would.' I was stunned. I thought to myself, and then said something like 'I wonder if the same would apply if you were unfaithful to your wife?' He responded in the affirmative. With that, I moved away and started talking to others again, but at the same time puzzled at the interaction I had just had.

I did not think that this person's statement was abusive – it was the early 70's and 'abuse' was not talked about. And I knew he was joking. How could he not be? Rather, I thought: 'this is someone that believes strongly in a committed relationship'. To me, this was refreshing. I had heard – rightly or wrongly, that most people in 'The Territory' seem to be running away from someone or hiding from something. I concluded that the person I had spoken with, and his friends were in this category. We did not communicate again on this night, but I did see him again one day when I was going to work.

A few days later, there was a knock on my front door – Marie wasn't there. I opened the door, and I found the chap with the distinctive voice and his friend at my door. We had only 'met' the night of the party in the caravan due to the interaction regarding unfaithful wives. We had not even been introduced on this night – but here was this person and his friend sheepishly standing at my front door. When I looked, what did I see? I only noticed one – the one with a big smile and lots of blonde hair, and cigarette burns in the singlet top over the chest and stomach!

They introduced themselves – Chris – the one with the lovely voice and accent, and his friend Russell. I know I should have politely told them that I was busy and closed the door but didn't. But I did not know what to do with them, if I invited them in.

I hesitated, and then asked them if they would like to come in. Now they're in. What do I do with them? I was not used to entertaining in a flat. I was used to a nurses' home, where no males were allowed. I also thought we did not have a lot in common, and I was quite shy, I know. Anyhow, they're in the flat. I had broken the only rule of my induction in Alice Springs – 'steer clear of the rude, rough builders!'

I said I would make a cup of tea – I thought 'that will pass the time'. But at the same time, I was wondering what to talk about? Then I noticed the magazine on the kitchen table. It was Marie's. Suddenly I thought they can read the magazine, – that will pass a few minutes. I said, 'Why don't you do this quiz in this magazine?' I gave them a pen each to complete the quiz. I don't even know if they did it, but Russell started to read it. Later, it became a joke – how I quizzed Chris when I first met him, and the quiz was about marriage! I did not know this until a very long time after we met. Chris told me much later that he wondered at the time why I gave this quiz to him. But to me, it was just a quiz that would pass some of the time. I had never looked at the quiz and I know I was embarrassed about them calling on me.

We talked for a little while, and then they left. A few days later I was in bed and it was 1130. I was on call and in the very early hours of the morning I had to drive the 'ute' down to the humpies, to administer antibiotics to sick children and adults. I also had to be at the clinic early the next morning to give inoculations, vaccines, and antibiotics. We were short staffed, and I was working hard, long hours and doing lots of overtime.

I heard voices in the night, and they seemed to be coming towards the flat. I listened, and thought, 'I know those voices. How dare they come this late at night! My reputation will be ruined!' I could hear their loud happy voices getting closer. I was very, very annoyed, and thought, 'enough, is enough'!

I jumped out of bed, put my dressing gown on, and flung open the door before they had a chance to knock on it. Surprised, they stopped in their tracks! I said in my most firm voice: 'Number one, you do not come around here drunk.

Number two, you do not come around here and get drunk.' I opened my mouth to say, 'number three, do not come around here at all', but before I could, Chris said, 'What's number three?' And with that, the cheekiness of it, we all burst out laughing – Chris, Russell, and myself! Yes, they did come in for a short time. We talked, and they left.

I wanted to go and see Jane, the friend I went with to Alice Springs. She was working at the Papunya Aboriginal settlement about 100 kilometres away. The tribes at Papunya were a little less used to Europeans than those at Yuendumu. Chris had a car and he offered to take me to Papunya. I mentioned this to Betty, the Charge Nurse at Yuendumu and she said she would like to come as well. Betty was an interesting person with exceptional remote area nursing skills and very experienced, having worked in Papua New Guinea for many years.

So, Chris drove Betty and I to Papunya to see Jane. We had a nice day together but on the way home Chris' car had a flat tyre that he changed. Chris took me home to my flat, and we sat talking in the car for a while. I felt he was starting to care for me, but I did not want any complications as I had plans to travel and explore the world. So, attempting to 'push' him away once, and for all, I told him: 'you know nothing about me!' To reinforce this, I told him a lie. I said: 'my parents are looking after my child, in Victoria'.

It was the early 1970s and I thought he would be shocked and see me in a different light, particularly given the moral high ground he had taken about unfaithful wives the night we met in the caravan. I thought, after this comment, this will be the end of it! But I was astonished at Chris' response: 'Great – a ready-made family!' I couldn't believe that he did not get the hint… 'how blunt do I have to be?' I thought. Whilst I was thinking this, he said, 'You know I'm going to marry you and we'll laugh about what's happened here in a few years' time'. Astounded, I remember looking at him thinking, 'he's off this planet!' My response was swift, and cruel. I wanted to get my message across loud and clear and said: 'in your dreams. If you were the last man alive, I would not marry you', and with that I got out of the car!

Life went on. There was very little social life. We were many kilometres from Alice Springs and life was work, lots of it and many irregular hours. My friends and I went to an outside 'dance' at Yuendumu, near the cattle yards. Chris was also at this 'dance', but I had not gone with him. I was dancing with the Manager of Yuendumu, who I must admit had a bit of a reputation with the ladies. Chris came over to me and pulled me away and told me to be careful of the person I was dancing with. I was very embarrassed and annoyed at how he had humiliated me, and told him bluntly, 'you… do not own me!' I know he was jealous and believed he was protecting me. But I did not need 'protection'!

I did not see him for a while after that, until…he came across to the hospital early one morning and asked us to come across to his campsite as a worker who had arrived at the camp late the night before, wouldn't wake up. We went with him, and found this man was dead and he'd died overnight.

A few days after the man died, Sam and I went back to talk to Chris about what had happened. Chris was in the tiny kitchen of the 'pre-fab' hut cooking lunch. He had been allocated as the cook as Russell, the normal cook had not returned from 'Alice'. We knocked, and he opened the fly wire door. Sam and I looked at him, and then each other. Chris' skin and the whites of his eyes were yellow! Absolutely, yellow! He had a yellow shirt on, and his skin looked the same colour! He looked very unwell, and he was cooking the food! Alarm bells were raised!

We knew that hepatitis A, that's infectious hepatitis, was rampant in the Northern Territory, and particularly at this time of the year. So, we immediately told him to stop cooking and come with us to the clinic, where we took blood and so forth.

The results came back that he was positive with hepatitis A. Chris spent some time in our little community hospital. This is where we really got to know each other. I'd visit him when I wasn't on duty in the Clinic, and we talked and became a little closer. But Chris' condition was not improving. The decision was made that he should go home to Queensland, as soon as possible. His flight was arranged, and we said goodbye and he left. I never ever expected to see him again. I had decided to study midwifery in Sydney at the North Shore Hospital along with Jane. After graduating, I would head to Scotland to work as a midwife.

Life and work continued at Yuendumu.

The Flying Doctor service could only land and take off in daylight. Therefore, there was only about six or seven hours a day that the plane could land if there was an emergency. This meant we were on our own for the other seventeen to eighteen hours. As such, we had to manage a whole range of situations. And there were no police to call on – none were stationed at Yuendumu.

Yuendumu was supposed to be a dry reserve, and that meant there was no alcohol allowed there. Except, the 'whites' could have alcohol. I never liked that aspect at all – there were double standards. There was always alcohol in the community even though it was supposedly a dry reserve. There was, what we called 'Flagon Wagons' – cars or station wagons owned by aborigines who were always going to and from Alice Springs and supplied alcohol to the reserve.

A particularly significant and frightening incident happened after Chris left for Brisbane. I was leaving Yuendumu in four weeks' time. My parents were travelling by car, on their way to Yuendumu to visit and take me home. I'd moved out of the flat into a caravan waiting the time to leave so that the new nurse could live in my flat when she arrived, in two days. Betty had left Yuendumu a few weeks earlier. The scene was unfolding.

There was an incident down at the humpies. There were always 'incidents', but this was a severe one. Hitler, the leader of the tribe had been in an altercation and received a severe head injury. It was distressing, as Hitler had just started working at our clinic and was part of the group being mentored to take over the running of the settlement when the time came.

We – Sam, Lynne and I got a message from some aboriginal people to come down to the humpies to attend the injured. It was late afternoon. We took the 'ute', our ambulance that doubled as the 'meals on wheels' car and drove down to the camp to collect and take Hitler to hospital.

Straight away we could see that his injuries were severe, and the mood of the people 'strained'. We managed to lift him up and load him into the back of the 'ute', our every move watched. Sam and I got into the back of the 'ute' with Hitler while Lynne drove to hospital.

By this time, there was no way we could transfer him out or get the flying doctor in as it was far too late to call for the Flying Doctor Service plane as it would not be able to land safely. We were on our own. We cared for him as best we could, but not long after we got him back to hospital, he had a cardiac arrest, and we were unable to resuscitate him.

An extremely tense situation unfolded. The whole community was fuelled up on alcohol or /and anger. Hitler was alive when we got back to the Hospital, but in very bad condition, and he died soon after. In the eyes of the community, the nurses – Sam, Lynne and I were blamed for the death of their leader, Hitler. The reason? It was easier for some in the camp to blame the nurses for Hitler's death than confront what had happened in the camp.

The atmosphere became hostile, and we heard loud shouting and noises coming from the camp and it seemed to be getting louder. Some Aboriginals that we knew due to the clinic knocked on our doors and warned us that we were in danger. It was very dark at night when I heard this.

I decided to leave the caravan and quickly go to Sam and Lynne's flat for safety and support. Just after I got inside the flat it was surrounded by a lot of very angry people shouting. Lynne, a shooter, got out her rifle she carried with her everywhere. I asked her to put it away – I was more frightened of her with that rifle than I was with the Aboriginals that I'd been caring for, for some time.

The three of us – Sam, Lynne and I agreed that what we should do is confront them, as it would be very easy for them to get in anyway, as the glass in the windows could be broken, as well as the locked door. We decided we might as well open the door and see what happens. We opened the door and people 'swarmed' in, filling the flat and shouting angrily and waving their arms around – some with weapons. We were frightened, and 'huddled' together in the room, up against a wall.

We could not understand what they were saying – we didn't need to! It was obvious… they were expressing their anger. After about 10 minutes of this – an eternity, they abruptly stopped shouting and turned and walked out of the flat. We were amazed. We didn't sleep that night, just in case they came back.

It was a frightening experience, but I did not have time to reflect on this as my parents arrived the next day to take me home. I did not tell them what had happened. I kept this incident to myself so as not to worry them. But this incident was written up in Queensland and Northern Territory newspapers a few days after the situation. Chris, in hospital in Queensland saved the newspaper cutting his parents gave him. He was interested, but not concerned, as it did not mention my name. Little did he know!

The reason my name was not mentioned in the newspaper was simple. The journalist published the names of the nursing staff that were currently at Yuendumu when he visited. I had left with my parents and returned to Victoria, prior to him coming to Yuendumu. But I was there! I've just got my vivid memories of the incident and an inaccurate newspaper cutting of the incident titled: 'Nurse's demand protection'.

On returning to Roslyn, Natte Yallock, I started night shift at the local Maryborough hospital until I went to Sydney to study midwifery. During that time, Chris wrote me a letter. I could hardly read it – in fact I couldn't read it! I thought the scrawl was due to his poor state of health. However, after we married, I knew that this was not the case, and this was how he wrote, when he did, which was infrequently.

Chris was in hospital in Brisbane, and I could tell things weren't going well with his prognosis. I thought I should go and see him because I knew he cared about me. At this stage, I didn't admit to myself that I cared about him. In fact, it was only when an older lady said to me, 'Dianne, you've just got home from the Northern Territory, and now you're going up to Brisbane to see this man. You must really care about him', that I would admit to myself that I might, just might have felt a 'pang' of emotion!

'Darn it!' I thought. 'He's not going to derail my plans of midwifery and travel!' But he did!

However, I would finish midwifery soon after we married but in Brisbane, not Sydney. And I would travel overseas with Chris and extensively with my work at University, but not until 25 years later! There is a lot more that happened but that is another story, for another time.

Postscript:

Thank you, Dianne, for the insight into your life before I met you. Meeting you changed my life forever as you gave me hope for the future and together the final chapters that follow the success of our partnership. Thank you for bringing my stories to life. Love always, Christopher.

Chapter 30
A Roller Coaster

Dianne and I married in December 1973, and headed to Brisbane, Queensland, driving my Father's car, and towing a new Franklin caravan we had bought in Ballarat. It was a nice caravan with an annexe, and air conditioner. The caravan had a double bed at one end, and a small kitchen at the front, with a bench one side in the middle, and a table the other side. It was sufficient for the moment. However, this caravan, our first home, would become a constant 'thorn in our side', for a range of reasons.

I was still not fully recovered from contracting hepatitis A, at Yuendumu in the Northern Territory, a few months earlier. The illness had taken its toll on me physically, and financially. However, I was full of confidence, and determined to make good in the future. How could I not, with Dianne by my side?

We would spend five years living, and working in Brisbane, Queensland, before moving to Melbourne, Victoria for two years. History would record the following in Australia during 1974 – 1980:

Australian perspectives on immigration, war, sexual morality, the role of women and the environment were undergoing radical change. In 1974, the White Australia Policy was scrapped. Throughout the decade, women won the right to equal pay and maternity leave and Indigenous peoples made progress on land rights. In 1975, the nation was rocked by the dismissal of Prime Minister Gough Whitlam.

During this time of national change, our personal lives could be attuned to that of a roller coaster – never dull, and lots of ups, and downs. We would experience first-hand the worst flooding in Brisbane for over one hundred years; develop our fledgling audio-visual hiring business; Dianne would complete midwifery training and importantly, we would become parents to Sophie (1975), Benjamin (1976) and Matthew (1980). And my past would catch up to me.

We spent our first night of our honeymoon in Bendigo. The suite had a vibrating bed. I put two twenty-cent pieces in the slot in the bedhead, and the bed started to vibrate! Quite an experience! From Bendigo, we drove to Albury and spent the night in a caravan park, then headed to Yass the next day. On the way, Dianne saw a signpost for Canberra and said: 'I've never been to Canberra. Can we go now'? I said lovingly, still in the flush of the first days of marriage, 'my dear, we can go wherever you like'. So, we headed to Canberra. It turned out to be a bad decision.

Heading up a hill on a very narrow road, the car behind pulled out to overtake us, just as another car was coming down the hill in the opposite direction! There was absolutely no room for 3 cars abreast of each other, on the narrow road. I had no choice but to brake, and swerve onto the side of the road to stop a head-on collision! Immediately, our car and caravan headed towards a huge gum tree, as the two other cars remained on the road, and just drove past each other, with no problem!

I slammed on the car brakes, again, and again, to try and prevent the obvious that was about to happen, but the brakes on the caravan did not activate. The caravan pushed our car onward, and forward directly towards a large tree trunk! With a jolt, the car hit the trunk of the tree and came to a halt. The 'A' frame of the caravan made a crushing sound, as it deeply penetrated the back of the car. Dianne was winded by the seat belt she was wearing, and I ended up with a deep gash on my knee that needed suturing at the Yass Hospital.

The car and caravan were towed to the Yass panel beating shop. The news was not good. The caravan A-frame was badly bent, and needed fixing, before it could be towed. The panel beater said, 'I can mend the A-frame for you, but you'll have to fix the damage inside the caravan when you get to where you are going. And, you'll have to find some other way to move the caravan... the car is not going anywhere, it's a 'write off'.' Then, more bad news: 'I'm not sure if I can fix the caravan before Christmas....'

We had been married just three days. We were stranded in New South Wales, just before Christmas. Dianne phoned her father, Keith, for help, who immediately said, 'No worries, I'll come in my car, and tow you up to Queensland.' Keith was a very decent chap – I don't think many men would have done that. He was in the middle of harvesting but dropped everything and drove to Yass where he collected us, and then towed the caravan to Brisbane to the Amaroo Caravan Park, Holland Park, arriving Christmas Eve. We then drove to Mother and Father's in Buderim, on Christmas Eve. We had just made it!

We had a nice Christmas Day, went to a rodeo at Nambour, on Boxing Day, and visited the 'Big Pineapple'. The next day, Keith left for Natte Yallock, via Tony and Helen's, in Lismore. During these few days he spent with us, he saw where my parents lived, and where his daughter was to make her new life. We were very grateful to him, and to my father who needed to buy a new car! Luckily, he was insured.

Our newly married life commenced, with the normal settling in, and finding work. The first few weeks were challenging for Dianne, with insurance claims, for the car and caravan, complicated by living interstate to where the accident occurred. As I noted in an audio tape to Dianne's parents:

... Another fellow came to quote on fixing the caravan. We've had two now. We had a note today that the insurance company wants us to phone him up tonight. They might whisk it away in the next couple of weeks. I think if they do, Dianne will just sit in the middle of the caravan park with no caravan with a droopy annexe and just cry.

There was also copious paperwork and detail required, enabling a small settlement from Dowsitt's for me due to contracting hepatitis during working for them, in the Northern Territory. Plus, there was consistent follow up at the Royal Brisbane Hospital, for me.

Added pressure was the 'soggy' start to 1974. Continual heavy rain fell in the first three weeks of January. Then, tropical Cyclone Wanda caused torrential rain on January 23rd, leading up to the massive Brisbane flood on Sunday 27th January 1974, during the Australia Day weekend.

Dianne's 1974 diary and audiotapes to her parents, record some of the impact of the torrential rain on our caravan and annexe parked next to a stream running through the caravan park.

Tuesday 1st January 1974 – Rains – annexe flooded
Wednesday 2nd January. Air conditioner leaking and freezing up
Thursday 10th January – received the annexe floor wood. Rain ++
Friday 11th January – Annexe flooded

Friday January 25th – Rain, Cyclone Wanda. Floods. Went to Enoggera to collect pay – unable to get it – Water +++++!! Rain coming in the caravan, at the bed end!

Saturday January 26th terrible things are happening to peoples' homes. There is loss of lives with flood.

Sunday January 27th Floods +++!

Monday 28th Australia Day Holiday Lizards, spider's +++ in annexe, floods and loss of lives go on.

Dianne recorded the following:

'...We've had an invasion of spiders and little lizards. I don't mind little lizards very much because I think they're rather sweet. But I can't bear the spiders. I don't mind them so much in the annexe, but it's a bit much when they come inside the caravan, and you see them everywhere.... We've got the caravan well set up. We're almost ready to put the floor down in the annexe. It's been very wet in Brisbane, and I am afraid the annexe has been soaked quite often. Therefore, it gets very, very humid, so it's not a very good place to stay for very long. But, it will be quite nice when we get it fixed up.

...I've been to the Mater Mothers' and been interviewed and so forth, and had my uniforms fitted. I start midwifery on February 1st. The Mater is not very far from the caravan park at all via the freeway, so we're really-quite lucky. I'm quite looking forward to starting midwifery. I've got most of my books.

...I went into town today, and people can get through to the city, but there is mud, slush and a terrible smell.'

I recorded the following:

... I have managed to get a job at the army barracks here in Brisbane. I phoned up the barracks and went there for an interview, and I must have created quite a good impression because I was told to go out and see the Lieutenant at Enoggera. There was a vacancy in the officers' mess. So, I'm there as a steward. It's not quite what I'm used to, and I should hate to think that I should be doing that for the rest of my life! But it'll do for a year. It's secure and has five weeks annual leave. I get all the government 'perks'. It is shift work, so I get about 30 hours a week penalty rates, and it brings up my wage to about $90 a week, which is quite good, and keeps the 'wolf' away from the door.

... I was working Saturday and Sunday, and to top it off, Mother and Father came on the Friday to spend the night with us. They ended up staying until Wednesday. I went to work. I was on a staggered shift Saturday and Sunday. It was 6:00 to half-past 1, and then I was supposed to go back around half-past 5 to about half-past 7. On both those days I told them that I couldn't get back at night because I thought my responsibility at night, especially because it was raining, was here at home. The freeway was cut. All the bridges in Brisbane were cut, and the only way I could get to work was over the Story Bridge.

... This week I'm on early shift, and its 6:00 to 3:00, but you know the army and usually everything's done by about 2:00. So, I'm usually home about half-past 2. This job at Enoggera is shift work and it's working very well.

... I'm quite lucky now I'm driving to work. It's about eight miles away. Not at the other side of town, but it's sort of sideways, so we don't have to go through the town. We go on the new freeway and across up to Ashgrove and then to Enoggera, and eventually I arrive there. There are about 20 officers. We feed them with sandwiches and the same sort of thing as Puckapunyal. When I got there, I was introduced to the head steward and I thought that fellow looked familiar. He's German, and the same steward I worked for at Puckapunyal. He wasn't the head steward then. So, it's like old times again. He left Puckapunyal about seven and a half years ago. He recognized me, and I him, and we had a good old 'chin-wag' about old times and what's been going on.

...We've been trying to make the van into a home in-spite of the damage to the front. I've put up a shelf across the single bed, the settee. I put up a 6foot shelf above the window, and we've put the ornaments on it. We've taken the small cushion off the seat and put a small table at one end. I put a leg on the table because it sloped down a lot, and three shelves up in the bedroom, hooks, and towel rail. We've bought wood for the floor for the annexe and painted that, and we should be able to put the floor down on Monday pending the weather. The little river that runs at the back of us isn't subject to flooding thank goodness, but it has risen a few feet in the last day or two.

...Since we last spoke to you, we've become very organized and quite house-proud. We've put up those streamer things to keep the flies out at the door and laid the floor down. Dianne has been busy painting it with the sandstone colour, and it looks very nice. She's painted some of the table brown that we got from home. We have the old light that I made at school on top of the desk. Plus, we have a fluorescent strip that I put on a piece of wood with a pull cord over the desk. We've got shelves up in the annex. It looks quite homely.

... We've got some lovely pot plants too, so we're hoping they grow. I brought all the fertility beads that I got from the 'Territory', and we've strung all over the side of the annex around the table. It looks quite nice. We're hoping to get a few posters to stick up somewhere too.

... We bought pressed pine board. I painted it all with sealer, and then we're going to paint the top of the floor with sandstone varnish paint. It will look quite nice. It will match the 'lino' inside the caravan. We'll have the table and desk sent down, and we shall partition half of it off, and we shall make that into quite a nice living area. All the rest of the parked caravans have a concrete floor down in the annex except us which has rather annoyed me because I've had to spend $100 to put down a wooden floor of my own.

... At-the moment we've come down to the north coast to Mother and Father. We enjoy coming to a nice house, and it's lovely seeing them, especially as we live so close to them.

... We've settled down very well, and we're carrying on like an average happily married couple with a nice annex and reasonably nice caravan. We don't think it would be something that we'd like for the rest of our lives, but if we're both working, I think we shall probably tolerate each other in these small surroundings for the next year. Of course, we'll have children one day. Then we'll have to move....I've bought a second hand Shibaden video recorder and seven, one-hour tapes. I amuse myself recording the programs off TV and playing them back. Dianne keeps telling me that you can't do that for the rest of your life. If you like that, you'll have to get a job doing that or do something in that field. I keep saying 'Yes dear. I will do.' We'll have to see what happens.

I started looking for another job. Employment ads in the newspaper followed a set pattern. The ads commenced with professional jobs, then trade jobs, followed by labouring and menial work. I automatically looked on the labouring and menial job page.

One day, Dianne said to me: 'why do you always want to look on that page [meaning labouring and menial job], why don't you look on the other page?' I said, 'I've always had those sorts of jobs.' Dianne said: 'I think you are better than that.' So, from then on, we did look on the 'other page'. I knew there was nothing to suit me on 'the other page', but it made Dianne happy to look. If she was happy, then I was too.

My interest in electricity and electronics was obvious to all around me. The Shibaden Recorder held pride of place in the caravan, perched on a shelf I specifically made. I consistently recorded and played the tapes back. I was obsessed. Dianne, thinking she could help me, and as a surprise, enrolled me in a distance education course for technicians. The books arrived. She was right – it *was,* a complete surprise!

Confronted, my memories of school and my inadequacy with reading and writing came flooding back, and I reacted very, very badly. It was not until then, that Dianne saw my utter despair regarding books and forms. She realised that the incoherent letter I sent her when I was ill with hepatitis was not written under duress from illness, but rather, this was the way that I did write!

As a way of making up for my over-the-top reaction, and utter despair, I threw myself into developing our business. To cut down on travel, we moved to another caravan park, closer to where I worked.

In our caravan, her school Olivetti typewriter perched on the table, Dianne continued to type 'mountains' of individual contracts for our fledgling video business, in every spare moment she had. Thompson Video Recording Enterprises [TVRE] centred on renting tapes to the outback and large retail companies so they could play them to promote colour TV prior to the launch of colour television. Although colour televisions were being displayed in the shops in Queensland, there was nothing in colour as transmission was still in black and white. Coloured videotapes and recorders was the answer!

To develop my idea, I needed coloured film to be transferred to videotape. I approached all the holders of short colour film, such as travel agencies – Qantas, the Tasmanian Tourist Bureau and later to the American Embassy where I got some 16mm film of the USA, which was a magazine type film, produced each month. I was supplied the film, but now I needed to get them converted to the new format of video.

I went to Bruce, the owner of Bruce Windows Electronics [BWE] who transferred the film onto 1inch broadcast quad tape and then onto multiple Phillips videocassettes, to be played in Phillips videocassette recorders. 'Tasmania' was a great colour film. It had the seasons – summer, winter, autumn and spring in beautiful colour and the videocassette produced, was spectacular! Cassettes were hired to large retail stores such as David Jones and Myers and all other major stores in Brisbane and up and down the coast of Queensland. TVRE videocassettes became all the rage in Queensland, and subsequently the business 'took off'.

It was a very a successful marketing strategy, but not lucrative given the transfer costs of film to video. However, TVRE became extremely well known in Brisbane, and interstate, and provided an impetus for moving into other areas of video, advertising, and associated entertainment. Plus, my association with BWE led to other things. I learnt the skill and art of camera work and editing as I spent a lot of time at BWE watching and learning and consolidated this when he offered me a job in his outside broadcast van, video-taping the gallops and harness in Brisbane. Dianne also learnt the business as she worked for BWE for a few weeks after completing midwifery and during her final stages of pregnancy. The skills we learned would be useful in the future.

Video was a fledgling industry, and the time was right. We applied to lease a new U-Matic video recorder – of professional quality, with the aim of hiring it out to large advertising and event management firms. Our lease application was refused – as 'it would not be beneficial to the leasing company, or us'. Dianne's diary records this, and the defiant comment: 'who needs them'!

I was passionate about this fledgling medium, and extremely confident in my abilities in this area. Together, the business and I flourished.

It was time to move – it was not a good look for a business to have a caravan park address. We decided to sell the caravan and move to a house where we could run our business. We could not afford premises. The cost of anything related to this new medium was exorbitant. We advertised, and found a purchaser for the caravan, who offered a large deposit, but then asked if we would go guarantor for him for the rest of the money. What a ridiculous thing to ask! But I'll tell you something more ridiculous. I accepted! I accepted and became guarantor for my own caravan!

Yes, you guessed it! The 'purchaser' disappeared with the caravan! We were left having to pay for the caravan again, and we did not even have it! We employed a private detective to find the caravan. He had no luck but later he did, in a caravan park along the coast. We could not recognize it – it was derelict, a different colour and the inside modified beyond recognition! And, it was filthy with cockroaches! The chassis number was the only identifying feature left.

We had the caravan towed to the large garden at the back of the house we were then living, nearly 3 years after it had been stolen. We spent a lot of time cleaning the caravan and then rented it out, on site to a young couple. This helped to pay the caravan off again, at which point we sold it – again! It was a relief.

I became friendly with the Manager of Phillips and asked him if I could have a couple of Dutch K9 TVs which were one of the first coloured TVs out and had a 'live' chassis so you needed to be very careful when working with them. I talked fast and convinced him that I could promote his TV's at the same time as my colour videocassettes. He said to me as I left: 'you know Chris, you are an entrepreneur, but you are before your time'. He was right. I was a visionary and an early adopter of everything electronic, but as time would tell, well before my time. Timing is everything.

We planned our trip up the coast to Comalco, North Queensland to promote my colour videocassettes and to take orders for the colour TVs that I placed on a mattress in the back of our 'Ute'. Despite my enthusiasm and great interest shown from organisations in viewing colour television made possible by our videocassettes, there was absolutely no interest in purchasing the hugely expensive colour television sets! But we did have some success as my audio tape reflects:

...We sent a couple more tapes to Papunya, and we're waiting to hear from Camalco up at Weipa. I expect we'll be starting to send tapes to them soon.

Further, the trip up the coast wasn't entirely wasted for two reasons.

Firstly, we were together, and Dianne was in the mid stages of pregnancy. We chose the name of our baby soon to be born travelling along the highway, coming back from Comalco. Dianne 'felt' we would have a daughter. If we did, we would name her Sophie Louise. With such a name, she was bound to make her mark on the world – which she has.

Secondly, in recognition of my unrewarded efforts, the Manager of Phillips told me to 'keep the K9 TVs'. I immediately thought of hiring TVs and video recorders out so that advertising companies could play their advertising tapes on them, at functions that were becoming popular. However, I needed some videocassette recorders to make this work. But, video recorders were more expensive than colour televisions!

We were both still earning a very small wage – Dianne as a student midwife, and me as a steward. Every bit of spare money went into the business. But, the video equipment and everything associated with it was hugely expensive. When we moved from the caravan we moved to what we could afford – a third of a small old Queensland house, on stilts at Ashgrove. Today it would be called a 'bed sit'. Never mind, – we were so happy. And, we had an address that we could use for the business! There were a lot of things that happened during our time at Ashgrove – some happy, some not so happy, some historical, and some enlightening. And, my past did catch up with me.

Early one Sunday morning, two policemen knocked on our door. They had a warrant for my arrest for evading driving offences, in various states of Australia! I stammered and stuttered some response – I was fighting for survival! Without a license, the business would falter. I quickly made a commitment to pay the fines. The police listened – they couldn't do anything else – I did not stop speaking in case they told me what I feared – my license cancelled, or worse, jailed!

The police listened to my ramblings. After a while, they determined that 'as I was now a 'respectable married man', they would give me a warning – not to let it happen again'. Relief washed over me, and I closed the door. But then, I had to contend with Dianne who had overheard everything! Upset, she asked me: 'was there anything else in my past that was going to catch up with me in the future?' 'No', I said, truthfully. Life went on, but then....

Around two years later, the Tax Office wrote to me demanding tax information relating to jobs I had in the past. This was difficult, given my work history over the years. I had no real details – I had just worked, got paid, and then I moved on. Dianne tried to source information from everywhere. The Tax Office was not satisfied with the information or responses supplied. They kept pursuing me. Eventually, Dianne became very frustrated, and after many months of receiving demanding letters, wrote in defiance and desperation: 'Look, if he has money somewhere that has not been declared, please let me know as we could really do with it'!

We waited for a response. What would happen? The Tax Office is very powerful. Well, after that letter, we never heard from them again! It was like they knew they had pushed us to the limit, and that we genuinely could not supply any further information. Plus, it became apparent to us that they did not have anything relevant to pursue, and it was dropped!

One morning, having breakfast together at our tiny little table, we were listening to a radio program where an actor was being interviewed. I said, 'I could be an actor, if only I could read.' Just after my comment, the actor being interviewed told the announcer she had 'dyslexia', and then went on to explain what it was, and what she had experienced at school. It was like a bombshell! What she was explaining I knew only too well, but the word 'dyslexia' was foreign to both Dianne and me. The radio announcer continued and asked the actor: 'How do you learn your lines if you can't read?' She responded: 'my friend spoke the lines into a tape recorder, and the tape is then played back to me repeatedly until I memorise the lines.' This radio program, and the simple word 'dyslexia', was the beginning of an understanding of this learning disability, and in many ways a relief. There was, a reason, why I could not read or write properly; and why I had suffered, and what I had endured, all my life. I was not alone, but it was still something I hid, concluding that nothing could be done to change the situation.

I heard on the grape vine that there was a nude beach between Mooloolaba and Coloundra. Dianne and I visited. We walked to the beach down a well-worn track amongst the sand dunes. There were several people, swimming, and sunbaking, at this infamous beach. I complied with the dress code and went into the surf. Dianne was hesitant and didn't participate. After a short time, we left and did not return.

The Darwin cyclone hit and devastated Darwin on Christmas Eve. The repercussions were felt from afar. Dianne was on duty when she was told to prepare for a mass influx of pregnant women and new mothers and babies that were being flown from Darwin for care. Whole floors and wings of the midwifery hospital Dianne trained at were prepared for the influx. Those women who could be sent home were, and those that could not were transferred to other hospitals in Brisbane. They waited. And waited. Then, were told the women and babies had been directed elsewhere.

As remarkable as the introduction of colour television and the heralding of a new era was, infinitely more remarkable than this was the news that Dianne and I were to become parents for the first time! We cherished the thought of having a child, but there were some concerns.

Dianne was just over half way through her midwifery training at the Mater Mothers, Brisbane. Would she manage to finish? Then there was a self-inflicted concern. We went to the beach, and Dianne fell asleep after being on night duty. She was in her bikini and was terribly burnt with large blisters hanging off her angry and red skin. She was in terrible pain and could not bear the sheet on her skin. I helped her into a bath of cool water and she floated in this and sipped brandy. We were frightened she would miscarry.

Then, Dianne was feeling tired and in need of a 'sickie', something she was not known for. I phoned the Mater Mother's stating that Dianne was unwell and couldn't come to work. I did such a good and credible job of saying she was unwell, that the person I spoke to was very concerned as she knew Dianne was pregnant. She insisted that the on call gynaecologist should be sent out to examine her! I had to talk quickly, to ensure that this didn't happen!

With a baby on the way, I needed an additional job. I got a job behind the bar at the prestigious The Brisbane Club – the place to be for the 'Who's Who'. It turned out to be a bad choice – I was only there for one shift. It became very busy and I was the only bartender. The patrons asked for all sorts of drinks – weird and wonderful. I was managing this, until it became very, very busy. I felt that the patrons were coming at me from all directions all wanting something, quickly. I became flustered. In utter frustration I said loudly: 'Look, just line up! I'll get to you when I can!'

The 'impertinence' of telling the 'patrons' to 'line up' brought the Manager scurrying out of his office in shock at what he had just heard. He said in frustration: 'you cannot treat our Club patrons like this! Where do you think you are? You are not at the local pub! I don't think you are quite suitable for this job'! I agreed.

But it was the handling of money – adding up, giving back the change at a fast pace that brought me undone. I felt like the actor, Frank Spencer going home to Dianne saying: 'it didn't work out…' However, I did get another casual job, at the Greek Club – a nice place, where I only had to fill up the jugs whenever needed, and I didn't have to handle any money.

Colour television was due to be launched! I had been promoting this advent for so long and wanted to be one of the first to experience it. Much to Dianne's disgust, I bought a Hitachi coloured TV because I wanted to see the first colour transmission, which was 'Count Down.' We couldn't really afford it – colour televisions were extremely expensive at the time. But, Dianne condescended, and I bought one. But, she has never let me forget that it was almost the price of a deposit on a house, at the time.

Seeing colour television being transmitted for the very first time is truly a remarkable memory of mine. I vividly recall sitting in our bedsit, watching the black and white screen change to colour. In the middle of 'Count Down' on the

ABC, the colour picture slowly wiped down the screen from the top, engulfing the black and white picture. Colour was in, and a new era began! 'Count Down' was amazing in colour. The ABC pulled out all stops for this one show. The cameras were 'tube cameras' and a few tubes were 'burnt' in this event, due to the cameras being pointed directly at the bright lights for effect.

It was time to move to a larger place and we settled on a half house at Newmarket. It was tiny, with 2 very small bedrooms, with a room underneath for an office and laundry and a shared garden where I planted lots of vegetables. It was here we welcomed our first two children, Sophie Louise and 14 months later, Benjamin Marshall – whose name was chosen because it's strong – a rock, and a family name. He has lived up to this name. I chose Benjamin as Big Ben, is the most important timekeeper of the world in the houses of Parliament in England.

My passion for television and cameras intensified. Both Dianne and I attended voice classes at a local TV station, and to learn more about the industry. I knew the 'reps' from Sony in Brisbane and bought a small Sony video projector from them. In return, they lent me a huge colour studio camera for the weekend, which I took home and took videos of Sophie all weekend.

I decided to approach the television stations to see if live productions could be produced for transferring to videocassettes for renting out to those living in the outback without a television signal. Channel 7 was just up the hill from where we were living.

I made an appointment with them and proposed the following which was accepted: That TVRE will produce and organise one live variety show – 'Australian Showtime' at the Homestead Hotel, Zillmere – a very prominent venue in Brisbane. Channel 7 will record the variety show via outside broadcast [OB] and TVRE could 'do what it liked with the taped production if it organised and paid for the artists and musicians.' Channel 7 used this OB as training for staff, and TVRE was to use it as a 'pilot'. The $3 cover charge was to help pay TVRE expenses.

We retained a popular and outrageous Brisbane breakfast radio show compere – Wayne Roberts. Frankie Davidson was the star artist and supported by 9 other artists. The well-known 12-piece Sweet Inspiration Big Band provided the music. It was a very expensive exercise, but one that would pay off, eventually.

In the lead up to the variety show night, I became downright annoyed at the behaviour of some of the band who came around to our flat to discuss aspects and were constantly on our phone making bookings for elsewhere! When I queried them, the response astounded me: 'why are you worrying about the phone bill – as a business, it is tax deductible'. Tax deductible yes, but first we had to pay the bill, and then wait some time before we could claim this expense in our tax!

Advertising was crucial. I had many posters printed at The Sun newspaper – big red and white posters, the size of a newspaper. I asked: 'how do I stick them up'. The response: 'With clag mate, with clag'. 'What's that?' I said? 'I will give you some, and you just 'daub' it on, and place the poster on top', he replied. 'Great' I said.

We 'daubed' the posters very late that night, and well into the early morning. Dianne, nearly 9 months pregnant drove the 'ute' – she could hardly fit under the steering wheel! I was in the back with the clag and posters. I 'daubed' the posters on everything I could – including electricity poles, walls, and bus shelters. Sometimes I put two in the same area and stood back to admire my work! The police stopped us and asked what we were doing. We told them the truth, and they went on their way. It was a messy job, and for those who know me, I am not good with sticky, messy stuff. I ended up with clag over everything, inside and out of the Ute, and especially the steering wheel which was not a good look when I presented at a function early the next morning to set up equipment!

On the night of 21st August 1975 Australian Showtime was a great success. But no contract resulted with Channel 7. Dianne was admitted to hospital for high blood pressure and 10 days later, Sophie was born. During this time, I went to meet Terry, the ABC Program Manager, with my one-hour pilot tape in hand. I presented my vision to him, and a win-win, situation resulted.

Together, the ABC and TVRE would produce 13 episodes of a live variety program named Cabaret Time. Again, TVRE would produce the show and provide the artists and musicians. One half hour program with well-known artists would go 'live' to air on the ABC. The next half hour recorded would be adult entertainment, produced specifically for TVRE videocassettes, destined for renting to outback Australia, and Papua New Guinea. I was elated! I had hit the big time! I grew a beard, wore a cravat, commenced smoking a pipe again, and set to work to produce the programs.

I retained Pat, a singer, as compere. I went with him and a couple of other people in the entertainment industry to the Jindalee Hotel, Zillmere and asked if we could put on a show one night a week and explained the format. The Manager was keen to become a regular venue after the success our once only variety show had at the nearby Homestead Hotel recently. At the Jindalee, there would be a cover charge retained by TVRE to try and meet the expenses.

It was a busy, challenging time for both Dianne and I. Producing, and organising, one live television program per week for 13 weeks was challenging. All the major acts of the time performed in Cabaret Time. Artists were retained, and all aspects arranged – flights – first class, accommodation – 5 star, meals, transport, and legal documentation. Artists for the live to air program included singers Freddy Paris, Normie Rowe, Ray Burgess and Debbie Burns. Adult entertainment artists for the second half hour program included some well-known strippers of the time, including Janet Pleasure, who had a fire-eating act.

By the time the first program went to air, Sophie had just been born. Dianne continued with helping produce the shows, but did not attend them, but rather watched them on ABC television. I thoroughly enjoyed the atmosphere of live productions and what I had created. I was finally doing something that I felt comfortable with, and sometimes assisted the floor manager keeping an eye on things, and on occasion, assisted with the camera.

This was my 'entrepreneurial and artistic stage' where I wandered around with a beard and a pipe enjoying the attention bestowed upon me – even if it was not genuine, from artists who were looking forward to more work.

I was absolutely involved, passionate, and consumed by my work. Life was good. But, it was also a time that had temptations, and the potential to draw me back into some old ways of my previous life. This I did, on occasion, with consequences.

Driving back in the early hours of the morning after filming a TVRE adult variety show at a nightclub in Fortitude Valley, I went through a red light, and hit another car – a slight accident and no one was hurt. But, I had to retain a barrister to argue why I should not lose my licence given my previous driving offences when single. The barrister was successful – I was lucky. It was then I fully realised that if I continued my ways, I would compromise all that I held dearly.

I changed my ways.

Despite all the hard work and entrepreneurship, opportunities were lost. After 13 weeks the ABC wanted to continue the TVRE program but change the compere. I thought this was disloyal, and unfair and said as much. What a fool I was. A loyal fool! But no, not a fool, but rather, a 'bloody idiot'! The ABC did not negotiate with me – they simply lost interest in me, as they were considering me to join them in their production arm. To add insult to injury, they then developed a similar show with a similar name with the compere they wanted, and continued their live variety show, without the adult entertainment, and without me!

I had just blown one of the biggest opportunities of my life to work and progress in an industry I loved, in an environment sought after. I should have said: 'yes, just do what you like, I'll join you.' I know I could've gained a position at the ABC. Why didn't I do this? It would've been exactly what I wanted. But, the normal doubts crept in. I did not want to expose my limitations in reading and writing so, this opportunity was lost. I was invited to a great ABC Christmas party this same year and had 'an absolute ball'! After this, my association with the ABC ended. I focussed on what I was comfortable with, and where I had the support I needed.

Unfortunately, the outcome for the live variety show was not as I anticipated. The plan of renting out the Adult Entertainment videocassettes I had produced and filmed was doomed to fail. The cassettes were to be rented out for $10 per viewing, but then, the live music musicians union demanded a $30 copyright fee for every time someone viewed the tape! Disappointedly I had to discard the videocassettes after I tried unsuccessfully to negotiate with them. However, it was good fun at the time and a lot of people got a lot of entertainment out of it – including myself. It also prompted me to tape 'free to air TV' to flood the hungry market, particularly in the mining towns of Papua New Guinea.

Eventually we managed to buy a professional ¾'U-Matic video recorder. I immediately contacted all the advertising companies in Sydney and Melbourne, stating we could provide equipment and staff for the conferences and trade shows that were run in 5-star hotels in Brisbane and the Gold Coast. All they needed was to provide their U-Matic videotape cassette. The offer was taken up very quickly.

Why did it work so rapidly? Video was not 'mainstream' at this time. The average business didn't have a video recorder and domestic VHS tapes were not available. So, the only way these large companies could present and show their ads on professional standard equipment was employ a company like TVRE.

I decided to give up the full-time army job and get another where the work fitted with the hours and responsibilities I had with the business. I got a job working with a bread run with a designated route. I started at 4 am loading the bread into the van and delivered from 5am to 9 am. Early starts didn't bother me. I had a light strapped to my belt and placed the order in the bread bins. I worked fast. I needed to start my work for the business as soon as I finished. But sometimes, working fast defeated the purpose. Given I was such a good, fast worker and finished early, the Bakery asked me to do extra runs!

As soon as I finished my morning bread run, I rushed into our flat, threw my suit on and drove our loaded station wagon to various venues to set up the equipment. Dianne managed the home office and the bookings. Occasionally, when there was a clash between my bread run and the business, she would do the set up. Once, she drove to a Surfer's Paradise Hotel where a conference was booked. She had the equipment in the wagon, Sophie about 10 months in a car seat, and was also six months pregnant with Benjamin! She managed. The event was a success.

The business was expanding rapidly, and was well known, particularly by several high-profile Melbourne advertising companies. Brisbane and the Gold Coast was becoming a popular city to launch a range of national and international advertisements for products. All the major advertising companies dealt with us and our professional promotions and event hiring business expanded rapidly, but money was still tight – there was always newer equipment to be bought as advertising companies expected the best.

For presentations, our televisions were placed on strategically placed stands made of black Dexion tubing. Black cloth surrounded the frame, to cover the leads and audio-visual wires that enabled closed circuit television throughout the venue. It was a professional, sleek look. The slide presentations included three or four slide projection screens, and a tape made various beeps to change the slides. Sometimes a montage of slides was used.

Smaller functions just required me to set up at the beginning of the day and take down at the end. Larger, prestigious functions required a different approach. I went to the large advertising functions in a suit. I set the equipment up early, and had music playing when people entered. I showed the respective advertisement a few times when required. I mingled with the Company representatives, and ate the meal provided with the rest of the invited guests. It was enjoyable.

All the major advertising companies dealt with us. We did a full range of presentations including slide shows, video projectors sent up by advertising companies – for example, George Patterson and helped launch a range of new products including Four XXXX beer and Chuppa-Chupps and new ranges for example, by Rowntree Hoadley.

A large event was the TNG Insurance Company bi-centenary held at Surfer's Paradise over a full week. This production required all the equipment we owned and could rent! Plus, we had an additional challenge – the full production of a stage show that involved getting artists, hiring spotlights, and ensuring the audio was professional. I drew on my contacts that I had when working with the ABC and Channel 7 and retained a couple of good artists – Barry Crocker and Steptoe and Son. We put them in first-class hotels in Brisbane, and brought them down to Surfer's Paradise, by taxi. Dianne and I stayed at the hotel for the week, with Sophie.

Everything just had to be perfect with this stage show. The calibre of the artists was high, as were the expectations. Barry wasn't going to put up with second best. The microphone had to be the right height, the lighting and audio had to be perfect, and everything spot on. He was a real professional. I managed the spotlight on the night. Steptoe and Son were an 'eyeopener'. We had watched them on TV for years. Now we were working with them. The only time they would talk to each other was when they were on the stage. Honestly. And they had to come on the stage from opposite sides of the stage. Plus, we had to bring them down from Brisbane in two taxis. I couldn't believe it. The animosity that they showed to each other on stage was exactly as they showed to each other off stage. In the end, it was a very professional stage show. TVRE delivered.

We purchased a new Hiace Van, added the children's car seats and fitted it with windows at the side so the children could see out. It was a family 'people mover' before these came in. I parked it safely in a lane at the side of a hardware store and went inside to buy some power leads. I was at the counter paying for the power leads when I heard a *!# great crash! I rushed outside and saw my van crushed under the back of a truck! The truck had been parked on a hill, without the handbrake put on. I was lucky to be alive! But, there were pressing jobs for the business, and I needed a van. We hired one but needed to pay upfront for the month it would be out of action. Reimbursement by the insurance company would take some time. It was added financial pressure and at a time that Dianne was due to have Benjamin.

Mother came to mind Sophie when Benjamin was born – a couple of weeks early. But, work didn't stop. I took Dianne to hospital, whizzed around the corner to set up some TVs, and whizzed back to the hospital just in time for when Benjamin was born.

It was a very joyous occasion. I was like a dog with two tails. I had a beautiful little girl and a lovely baby son that I was so proud of. I was very happy. Two perfect children. It was a very happy time but tinged with sadness. Dianne's grandmother in Victoria died when Benjamin was 3 days old. And, a day after this, Mother and Father officially separated. The impetus for this separation and subsequent divorce was a very clever 'sting' that happened a few months prior.

Mother and Father had left England extremely wealthy. In their early retirement days, they owned 'Blue Horizons', apartments on the foreshore of Mooloolaba, and many other sound investments. Father then decided to 'dabble' in real estate and property development with some other 'business men'. This, we learned, well after it became obvious he had lost all his money in a 'Sting'. Father, a very private and proud man, would never talk about how he lost his fortune –in one sweep. We were never sure of the exact details but have pieced together what happened over time.

It was 1976 and Father was seventy-year-old. 'Blue Horizons' had not long been sold and money invested wisely. For some reason, he started to explore other real estate ventures in Queensland. Speculating in real estate was not uncommon – Queensland was 'booming'. However, it would be his downfall.

Initially, he had some success with the small property ventures he was involved with 'business men' he met. But, little did he know he was being groomed as a so-called 'Mark', with these 'successful' ventures. Then, he was offered a big opportunity, that couldn't fail. It required a huge investment for huge returns. Father, previously a very successful businessman, with a shrewd and careful attitude towards money, was 'sucked in' and acted in an unfamiliar manner. In good faith, he deposited his money in an account. Immediately the money, and the 'business men' disappeared. He had been swindled of his considerable fortune by a process straight out of the movie 'The Sting' starring Robert Redford that we had watched with him at the drive-in 2 years earlier. The 'business men' and Father's money were never located despite the efforts of the law. Now 'broke', crushed and humiliated, Father was understandably devastated and reacted badly.

The domino effect of this 'sting' was catastrophic for my parents. They had always been inseparable, but trouble developed after this. Their home in a retirement village their last remaining asset was sold, and a divorce settlement resolved in the courts ensued. Mother sold a piece of valuable jewellery given to her by Father many years previously and went to England to live with relatives for six months. Father bought a caravan to live in and retained his beloved boat – his solace. Eventually they both ended up living separately, and frugally in Victoria. Father died five years after the 'sting', and Mother twenty years later. It was a sad ending for a previously very loving and prosperous couple.

The Queen of England visited Australia in 1977 and opened the Brisbane Art Gallery. TVRE was retained to supply and set up the video beam projector in the middle of the foyer; and do the video camera work, to project onto this projector. A few weeks before the event, Dianne noticed a car with a man in it, continually parked on the road opposite to our home over a few days. She became concerned and pointed it out to me through the kitchen window. The man saw us, knew his cover had been 'blown' and drove off! We concluded that we had been under surveillance prior to the Queen's visit given that I would be near her and the Duke of Edinburgh during the function as I recorded the event.

It was the 11th of March 1977. The opening of the Brisbane Art Gallery was a spectacular event. The foyer was packed with flowers and a waterfall. Two cameras recorded and projected onto my large video beam projector in the foyer for the public to see, the Queen and Duke walking around the art gallery, and eventually opening it. The Queen and Duke walked within 3 feet of me. The Duke looked directly at me and said: 'I hope I don't trip over these cables.' I said 'no, no. It'll be right'. It was quite an event and went off very successfully.

Business wise, our life had been up and down over the past 4 years, but our lives were good in respect of our family. Sophie and Benjamin were happy and healthy. But, life was still challenging.

I gave up my job with the bread run to meet business commitments. We were asked to move from the half house as it was only registered for a maximum of 3 people. With Benjamin's arrival, we became a family of 4. We were happy in this relatively modern small half house and couldn't afford any more rent than we were paying.

We moved into a house with 3 bedrooms at Garden Terrace, Newmarket – just around the corner from where we were. It was a big old 'Queensland' house – on stilts, with wooden slats for windows that could be rolled up and down to capture the breeze. It was large, but very, very run down. The entrance to the house was up several very steep steps, and we were frightened the children would fall-down them. Father, an excellent carpenter put a gate up at the top of the entrance to the porch.

The mosquitoes were rife in this area, and there were no glass windows or fly screens. We all slept under mosquito nets, which wasn't that successful for young children. Again, there was no air conditioning. The back yard of the huge block was very overgrown when we moved in. Within a week, we had notification from the Council to clear it, or we would be fined! No problem we thought, we'll tidy it up even though we had not made the mess. We started, and then realised that underneath the overgrown weeds and grass was a tip – literally, a tip with broken bottles and cans, amongst other unsavoury things! It was a mammoth job to sort it out.

There was a room underneath the house that we rented out to Laurie, a chap I worked with in the army barracks who did not have anywhere to stay. I said to him 'we've got a spare room under the house and we can provide full board –

for a cost'. Laurie stayed with us for six months. Our caravan that we had gone guarantor for some months earlier was finally located and returned during that time. We cleaned it and rented it out to a young couple that stayed about 6 months until we sold it.

During our time of living at Newmarket, the demand for tapes to Papua New Guinea [PNG] exploded. Our lounge was full of equipment – recorders, TVs and U-matic tapes. We recorded the TV programs and sent them in boxes of 12 via airfreight to Companies in PNG to rent out. We recorded all day and all night – whatever was on television. We recorded current series that were on TV, plays, and sport, and gave them two options. It was a certain price if we did a straight copy of the program from start to end with the ads in. If they wanted the ads cut out, it was extra. Despite the extra cost, this latter version was the most popular. But this meant we had to watch the program all the time and cut out all the ads! Then, we duplicated the ad free master-tape to send to different clients. This was a process, and one that was carried out overnight so that the tapes could be sent off via airfreight the next day. Sometimes, we would set the alarm every hour overnight, and take it in turns to get up to put new tapes on, to meet the demand.

We were working very hard, in and out of the business, had renters in the caravan and provided full board for a renter. But, we just didn't seem to be getting ahead. We desperately wanted to not just develop the business we had but make some money. We had the capacity to make a lot of money, but we had a lot of debt. The leasing of equipment, and constant need to update equipment significantly 'ate' into any profit.

It is very hard to start and progress a business without any financial backing – absolutely nothing at all. It is also very had to develop and 'support' an electronic business that demands professional and up to date equipment. Believe me.

We also now had fierce competition in the market we pioneered. A long-established audio business with prominent premises had ventured into video. This father and son business was undercutting our prices and encroaching on our clients. To compete, we decided that TVRE needed professional premises rather than operating out of a house, in the back streets of Brisbane. But, we would need to add to what we currently offered – to spread the risk. We decided that retail – a record bar would fit with our audio-visual business. A shop became vacant at nearby Lutwyche.

I asked my very experienced Father for advice, and he gave it. 'There is a right side of the road for a shop, and a wrong side. The right side is the popular side – easy to get to, in amongst other good shops, and the side of the street where people choose to walk – you get the passing traffic'. The shop you are considering is on the wrong side. It's at the end of the shops and walk way. There is no reason for anyone to walk there. My advice is do not take the shop'.

I didn't listen. I was intent on expanding, so *Thomo's Record Bar* was created in the shop in the corner of the street that no-one walked past. Whilst I had not listened to him, my Father helped me by making the partitions to put the long-playing records in. He spent a lot of time visiting and staying with us at this time. I enjoyed his support and his company.

I tried everything to promote, including spruiking. You might think I'm an outgoing sort of person, but I couldn't bring myself to stand outside the shop spruiking and trying to sell somebody, something. So, what I did was I recorded the 'spruike', the night before. I bought some inexpensive radios to start my promotions. I started off, *'buy these radios…only $5… great for the races. Stick them in your pocket. Don't miss your favourite race'. You might win a million.'* During the day I used to play it, so everybody could hear it. I thought that was quite clever, I was spruiking, whilst selling the goods!

The one thing that did bring people into our shop without any influence was the day Elvis died – on August 16, 1977. On this very sad day, there was a run on Elvis' records and we sold out within minutes of opening!

We put a curtain across the back part of the shop and this is where Sophie played, and Benjamin walked around the playpen as Dianne managed the shop when I was out delivering and setting up equipment. Having the children at the shop was not successful, so child care a new concept was used, but abandoned within a few days.

At this stage, we employed an older gentleman with an accounting background to assist, and Dianne went back to work as a midwife, two nights per week at the Royal Women's Hospital, and minded the children during the day, at home. She enclosed the porch, laid on the mattress on the floor and the children – 6 months and 20 months played around her whilst she kept an eye on them. At their afternoon sleep, she slept.

I put a colour video projector in front of the shop for advertising, and a small speaker outside so that people would stand and look at it. Bigger fool me! We had a break-in. The robbers broke the window and for good luck, threw a can of white paint in! What goods weren't stolen, were spoiled due to the white paint.

Security called me about the break in about 2am, in the morning. I said: *'I'll be there'*. I quickly dressed and ran down the stairs to the car. It was then I realised that Dianne was on night duty, and the children were asleep upstairs! I phoned the security company and they posted a guard outside of the shop until I reached it in the morning, when Dianne returned from work.

We claimed insurance and the goods were replaced. Then, a few months later, we had another break in. We claimed but were told 'as you did not upgrade your insurance policy after the first robbery, the payout is small.' They said, 'When you have a robbery, you have to pay another premium to pay it up to the level you had it before.' I said: 'you didn't tell me I had to do this'. So, we didn't get too much back on the second robbery.

During this time, we decided to expand our retail shop and took over a book exchange nearby on a monthly, basis. As soon as we moved in, we were plagued with theft – from people shoplifting and by 'break ins'. The shop was locked and bolted at night. How did they get in? The police said, 'we know what happens here. Young kids are lifted up and get through the small side window, unlock the door and then the adults come in and whip everything out.' Shameful.

We moved the equipment and books to the Lutwyche shop. Thomo's Record Bar now included a book exchange of which 'Mills and Boon' was the most popular. We did not renew the lease on the Lutwyche shop. We decided to run the business from our home for financial and family reasons. This time, we would move to a nice house in a better suburb and operate the hiring and production business from there.

We moved to Chermside to live and combined a home and business. It was a very nice split-level brick house in a nice suburb. We bought a puppy – a Bassett hound, we named Marsha. We were a real family – mum and dad, two children and a dog. Occasionally we went to a local McDonalds' a new type of inexpensive family restaurant. We commented on how good it was to have somewhere to go with the children that was relaxed and didn't mind inevitable spillages from two small children.

We continued hiring tapes and equipment for functions. In fact, our house looked like a factory, a studio of electronic leads and equipment. The garage housed the hiring equipment; the porch, come sunroom, was a fully furnished office and our lounge was filled with recorders and TVs, churning out the tapes to send to Papua New Guinea.

One of our clients a very wealthy Chinese man who headed up a mining company in PNG was in Brisbane, and phoned, wanting to make a time to visit TVRE. Dianne was very embarrassed at the thought. Our lounge was like a 'factory', of stands, TVs, recorders, leads and tapes. There was no couch, lounge chairs or anything else that represented a home, or indeed comfort. What to do? We welcomed him enthusiastically and at the same time apologetically 'we're so sorry, but we haven't got a couch now. We're having it re-upholstered.' It was a bit of a lie, but still. He had a cup of tea, sat on a hardback kitchen chair in the lounge, and looked at the numerous TVs on stands with recorders underneath and watched the tapes he was receiving in PNG being recorded! All this, while Sophie and Benjamin played and ran around him! He continued to rent tapes from us.

Despite this 'hillbilly look', behind the scenes, we were at the top of our game when dealing with our advertising company clients in Brisbane, Sydney, and Melbourne. We often received comments on the excellent service provided, from the 'secretary' who advised the type and amount of equipment that was required for an event, to the expertise of the 'technician' who executed their order. We withstood our aggressive competitor.

I was very involved in A-V and becoming more passionate about the industry day by day. But, I was always looking for a second job to boost our income, particularly now we had two children and Dianne was working at home in our business. Plus, the income generated by our hiring and retail business was spasmodic; and leasing commitments fixed and expensive.

Dianne saw a job advertised in the paper that looked as if it would be of interest. It was at the Teacher Training College, Kedron in Brisbane. It was a temporary relief position in the A-V area as the regular employee was on leave. It was also at a time of the year that advertising companies did not normally book us for events. She had to really convince me to apply.

I could not envisage myself working in such an environment. Yes, I was at the forefront of the audio-visual area and was very confident in my abilities in this area. But how could I, who could not read or write properly and left school without finishing, work in a University? What a joke! What if I had to read and write? If it were just working with the equipment, I would be okay. Perhaps it would be?

We drove to Kedron and Dianne and the children stayed in the car. I went inside. In Dianne's words:

'The door of the car suddenly opened, and Chris jumped in, started the car and we literally took off up the road in record speed! I wondered what had happened. Something terrible must have happened. Chris was clenching the

steering wheel and driving erratically! I was confused and frightened, and said: 'what's wrong – what happened? Chris shouted in a very loud voice and with a tortured look on his face: 'they...they asked me to fill out a form!'

After a while, I stopped the car, and after much gentle persuasion from Dianne, I returned to Kedron. We had devised a strategy. I walked in, calmly picked up an Application Form and went outside to the car where Dianne helped me fill it in. I calmly returned the form and left. We waited. I got the job! And, I really enjoyed this job! I did not have to complete any forms!

One of my major roles was filming the students through a hole in the back wall, recording them teaching. One student teacher was teaching primary school students. Unfortunately, she made a mistake with the consistency of the plasticine. It was like a comedy show, from my angle, but not from hers! I was very sorry this position was just a relief position, but it was good preparation for a job in the future.

Life and business continued. We had been in Brisbane for 5 years – a tough, roller coaster 5 years. Life had not been easy. It was time to reassess. What did the future hold? There were a few personal and business factors that determined we would move to Victoria.

Dianne was getting homesick – some family had visited and stayed with us in Brisbane, and we had travelled to Victoria. But, visiting would be very rare in the future, as time and cost was a factor. If we stayed, our children would not know their grandparents or cousins, as we wanted them to. And, our children were extremely fair skinned, and we were living in a very sundrenched environment, and, Sophie reacted badly to the constant mosquito bites. Plus, my parents had divorced, and it was not known where they would end up, and my brother and his wife had decided to move from Lismore to Melbourne with their children.

Further, business wise many companies were now purchasing their own equipment for functions. Opportunities may exist in becoming a large production company, but this would mean an injection of considerable capital – something we did not have access to. Plus, it was obvious that the end of legally taping live TV programs was ending. Whilst a ruling had not been made from a landmark court case regarding copyright laws in the United States of America, all indications were that it would very soon be unlawful to record from the TV for commercial reasons.

So, we had the Melbourne paper delivered to us regularly and scanned it for suitable jobs. This time, I was looking on the 'other page'. A job was advertised at one of our major clients – Armstrong Audio-Visual in Melbourne. It sounded good, something that I would enjoy, and I applied. They were enthusiastic and said: 'Yes, we'll give you a job, just come and see us when you come down'.

I had accepted the position and then looked to sell the business. I approached my aggressive competitor, who must have thought 'why buy? He's moving. I'll just pick up his clients when he moves! We could not agree on a reasonable price. What he offered was an insult.

I determined that this business that had given me such hope during my long period of sickness, that had enabled my passion, skills, and knowledge to grow and had set me on a course for the future was *not* going to be abandoned for such a price! No matter how much Dianne wanted to move, I could not do it at this price! So, I took a gamble and said to my competitor: 'Ok, you won't buy at a reasonable price? That's ok. I'll stay, and I will advertise on every billboard to and from, Surfer's Paradise! You will not get any business!' Sensing that my determination and threat was genuine, he quickly offered a fair price for the business and I quickly accepted. My gamble paid off – luckily. It does not do to think about what Dianne would've said if I changed my mind about moving and where we would be living now if he had not purchased the business at a reasonable price.

It was November 1978. It was the end of an era for TVRE in Brisbane. It was a major effort to wind up the business and prepare to move down to Victoria, with two children and Marsha, our dog. We had arranged for our furniture to go to Dianne's parents and us to stay with them until we found accommodation in Melbourne. My Father visited us often in Brisbane during this time, sad that we were leaving. We encouraged him to move also, so that he would be close to us, but we knew he liked the hot weather in Queensland.

We chose to move to Victoria just after the Melbourne Cup, 1978 as we could send dubs of these tapes to Papua New Guinea, thus continuing making money until the last minute before we moved. The interstate removalist was booked for an early morning start but arrived the day before in the late afternoon! It was pandemonium! We were not prepared, and they would not return the next morning as booked. It was now or never!

Dirty clothes were quickly thrown in the washing machine to wash before the machine was whisked away. Other clothes were literally thrown into large garbage bags and loaded up. Sophie and Benjamin helped load our Hiace van. Benjamin was not quite two years old and was not upset by all the activity of the move, *until the fridge went.* He pointed his finger to where the fridge had been and burst out crying. With the fridge gone, the food had gone! Our beds and the little furniture we had, were loaded up and left with the removalist. We stayed in the house that night and all slept on pieces of foam.

The 'factory' our home – did not close that night. The stands, TVs, recorders, and tapes remained in our lounge and Dianne and I set the alarm for every hour to get up to change the tapes as we had some large final orders to fill, before leaving.

We left late afternoon the next day in our 'Hiace' van after packing up our TVs recorders and tapes, and went via the airport to send the last lot of tapes to PNG. It was a very ominous, stormy, humid, and sticky day… a terrible day. Then the rain started, and the windscreen wipers found it hard to keep up to the rain.

I slammed on the breaks when a car cut in front of me, and the broom on top of the load in the back came hurtling forward, between the children sitting in their car seats, then between Dianne and I, before slamming into the front windscreen! We got to the airport, unloaded the final tapes that we were sending to PNG, and finally, we were on our way.

We just got over the Story Bridge and a terrible, terrible, storm hit! I couldn't see the road or cars in front of me and pulled off to the side, as all the traffic had stopped. Then, the heavens opened and hailstones as big as cricket balls descended and pounded the van relentlessly. We couldn't hear each other speak and turned to check on the children. They were strapped in their car seats and looked petrified! Their mouths were wide open, obviously screaming, but we couldn't hear them for the noise of the hailstones. We tried to comfort them as best we could, but they could not hear us. Marsha, our dog, lay very quietly at their feet.

The storm continued for some time. We felt battered and bruised – from the packing, finalising tapes and the fierce storm that seemed to be 'punishing' us for leaving. We decided to book into a motel when we got to Wynnum, only about 25 miles from where we had left. At the motel, there was a sign 'No dogs allowed'. By this time, we'd had it! We didn't care what the sign said. We smuggled Marsha in.

During the drive across the Blue Mountains, Marsha, came on heat. We had picnics all the way down and lots of breaks to let the children run around and enjoy the trip. But, every stop we had, it seemed that every male dog in the immediate area descended on us and sniffed around. Marsha was an attraction!

We drove over the border between New South Wales and Victoria on November 10, 1978. We decided to continue driving until we reached Natte Yallock and Dianne's parents. There we were met by all the family and had a lovely meal. And, there was a surprise 2nd birthday cake for Benjamin! It was lovely – surrounded by family and all the cousins played together.

The next morning, we travelled to Melbourne to meet with Armstrong Audio-visual to discuss the position I was offered. The premises and recording studios were very impressive and staff welcoming. But there was bad news. They said: 'look, we're terribly sorry. We've just restructured, and the position we offered you has 'disappeared'. There might be something coming up later, but we haven't really got anything for you now. We thought we would have, but we haven't.' So that was that! We were in Melbourne, it was coming up to Christmas and New Year, but we did not have a job.

We chose East Keilor in Melbourne to live. It was North of the city, had easy access to the airport and was on the right side for family to visit, and us them. We found a nice brick house that seemed to meet our needs and moved the furniture from the farm. We stopped sending tapes to PNG when the ruling came from the court case between SONY and the copyright board and TV stations that it was illegal to record tapes – it was not just 'forwarding a signal'.

Dianne quickly got a part time job nursing – night duty two nights a week. It was more difficult for me, I had left a job I loved, was nearing forty-year-old, and I did lose my confidence about the future at this time. Dianne suggested that I should have my nose straightened. It had been broken when I was travelling around, and it gave me a 'thuggish' look, which may be stopping me from getting a job. I agreed and had it straightened at the Freemason's Hospital.

Just before the operation, I was offered a job as an Audio-Visual Officer at the Reservoir High School, starting in February 1979. It was a new type of position and not well paid. And, it was quite a long drive from East Keilor to Reservoir, increasing petrol expenses. In fact, I would have received more on the dole, but I had never received any assistance before, and was not going to start now.

I liked the job and did some interesting things there. Some students approached me asking if they could have a lunchtime radio station. I talked to the Principal and he said 'yes, but it would have to be recorded so it could be edited if need be; and it would be once per week.' After I set it up, 3-4 girls at a time would come in and record their half hour radio program with music. They brought in their records to be recorded, and had discussions, and the next day I would play it over the PA system at lunchtime. I got a 16 ml film licence, ordered films for the teachers, and played these to the students when requested. My confidence was increasing.

We made a little garden and grew some vegetables, and Sophie and Benjamin helped. We often walked to the little park in the centre of the shopping centre and had picnics in other parks in the areas. We had a large house warming party – a bar-b-que that all the family and extended relatives attended. We were a happy family. Unfortunately, not long after we moved, Marsha came to a sticky end. She squeezed through a hole in the fence, and we never saw her again. We were told that a truck had run over her on a busy road near our house.

My job at the school was good, but I needed to supplement our income. I did not have my business anymore, and the equipment had been sold. I was used to working all day and all night. If I stopped being busy, I went to sleep. And, I liked being busy.

I had a few jobs in addition to the AV job at Reservoir. My 16 ml film license enabled me to get some work in Melbourne at the museum sometimes showing museum-type films, on big projectors. I really wanted to get into 35 ml projection but couldn't due to lack of experience in this area, at the time. I enrolled and completed two units relating to video production at RMIT. It was a very practical course and I did well in the area. The written assignment was completed with Dianne typing what I said and rearranging it a bit. I chose the very interesting topic on the invention of television.

I had a brainwave after seeing a fascinating, new-fangled 'knitting machine'. I said to Dianne: 'I'm going to buy one of those knitting machines and make a lot of baby clothes in my spare time, to sell and make a fortune'. 'All right, dear, she said. You do that. It will keep you amused in the evening.' I bought a knitting machine – the demonstration of how to use it, looked easy. Well, I got in such a mess! There was wool and thread everywhere. It was so fiddly! And, I'm not the most patient man in the world, I admit! Within a few days, I sold the knitting machine!

I worked at the Jalna factory, making yoghurt on the pasteurizing machine. The milk is put in vats and heated up to a certain temperature to make yogurt. Quite nice stuff, but I was appalled to see how much sugar went in it. Most school holidays I worked here, which suited me fine.

I worked as a cleaner in town, cleaning offices. The supervisor would come with his white gloves and run his hand under the windowsills and elsewhere. At the weekends I used to go to Heidelberg and clean the restaurant Sunday morning after the parties on a Saturday night where a lot of singing, drinking and a lot of people 'spewed' up behind the chairs and other areas. Everything was 'sucked up' with a vacuum cleaner!

We had been in Melbourne a year, when we decided we would like another child. We had delayed long enough, due to moving and settling in Victoria. All advice received was 'Dianne, you've already had two caesareans it may be dangerous to have another'. Dianne was not daunted but I needed convincing both for health and financial reasons. Dianne persisted: 'we've got the pram and the cot; we've got everything. It's not going to cost that much.'

We left East Keilor and moved to a nice split-level brick house, in Reservoir to be closer to my work, and cut down on the travel expenses. We moved ourselves with a hire van, and it took ages to do. We had a small van; 2 small children and Dianne was 9 weeks pregnant. A few months later, we welcomed Matthew James into our family.

This time, agreeing on a name if a boy, was not easy. I did not agree with Dianne's choice of names for a boy – Samuel or James saying: 'I don't like Sam or Jim and that's what they will call him.' I remember there was an old army song years ago: 'Sam, Sam, pick up thy musket. Thy knocked it down, thy pick it up.' I thought of that every time and thought no, I don't want Sam and I don't want Jim.

Dianne was not due for a month, but started to get some terrible pains, not associated with labour, particularly when she walked up and down the outside stairs. She phoned the hospital and was told you'll have to come into hospital straight away. Her parents came down to look after Sophie and Benjamin whilst she was in hospital. Things moved fast. Dianne was quickly prepared for theatre and said, 'we have to agree on a name before I go in'. We had repeatedly talked about the name Matthew James before – one we both liked, and again a strong name.

I said okay. I waited a long time in the hospital praying for Dianne who was in theatre a long time as her uterus was badly torn and near rupturing. Then suddenly, this big nurse came out with this little baby in her arms and said to me: 'hold out your arms'. I held out my arms, and the nurse placed this beautiful little bundle in them. Matthew. She said: 'follow me'. I followed her into the nursery where she put Matthew in a humidifier crib. She said, 'you can stroke his hair if you like'. I placed my hands through the two armholes and stroked his head a little bit and thought what a beautiful baby he was. Perfect in every way, and he completed our family.

Matthew's birth was the nicest as far as I'm concerned. Things had changed in the 4-5 years since Sophie and Benjamin were born, where the first I saw of them was in their cot, in the nursery, already washed and fully clothed. No matter. Seeing your newborn for the first time is an incredibly special feeling. After seeing Matthew was safe, I then turned my attention to Dianne because she hadn't come out of theatre and it had almost been 3 hours. By that time, family were phoning me up. Is it a boy? Is it a girl? How is Dianne? I said 'I'm not telling anybody until Dianne knows. Dianne's in theatre now, and when she comes out I will tell you.'

Much later she came out, but for about 3 days was not well at all, not recalling a lot of things that happened during that time. But she does remember it was a significant time in Australia's history as the newspapers were full of how a dingo had 'taken' baby Azaria. It was discussed in hospital. Dianne always firmly believed that the parents were not involved.

As a Reservoir School employee, I was a member of the public service. A booklet was available listing all jobs in the public service. I brought it home and found that I was eligible for some of these jobs. I was in a good position to apply for one in the city at Christian Brothers, St Kilda, and one in the country at Glenormiston Agricultural College in the Western district of Victoria.

I was interviewed for both jobs, and offered both. The first time in my life I'd been offered two jobs at the same time! It was a dilemma – two good jobs, in two very different locations. Our decision would strongly influence the next few years of our life, and that of our children. I thought I am not sure about St Kilda – a lot of temptation for the children, and homes were expensive – probably we would not be able to own one.

I took the family with me for the interview at Glenormiston, near Terang. Matthew was 3 weeks old. We got up at 4.30 am and the drive was long and there were cold, windy, and bleak looking places along the way and lots of stone fences. Dianne was hesitant to say the least.

Max the deputy head interviewed me and showed me around the campus. He said we want to form an AV department, but we don't have any audio-visual stuff at all. He took me upstairs to the library and then to one big room with nothing in it. He said, 'you can have this room if you want'. I said, 'this sounds good – the room would be great for an AV department' and immediately started saying how I would set it up and develop it. He told me later that I was offered the job due to my positive attitude.

We went back home to Reservoir. We talked it over. I was not keen to go to St. Kilda. We had to think of the children, and I thought it would be a lot better for the children in a rural area where they can play with freedom. I've always tried to live and work in a rural setting, and this job suited me down to the ground. Dianne could get a job in any hospital in the area. I accepted the position at Glenormiston, and found a house to live in, near the College. Almost at the same time, we had notice to vacate the home we were renting in Reservoir. It had been sold and the new owners wanted to move in. So, overall, it was a timely decision to move.

We had a lot of plants in hanging baskets, at Reservoir. They were my pride and joy. I had them all around the patio. I decided to transport the plants myself to keep them safe. I bought wood and put shelves in the van and placed the hanging baskets on them. On the way to Glenormiston, I noticed a blue police light flashing behind me. I pulled over. They asked me to get out and open the back of the car and asked: 'what have you got in the back of your van? I said 'pot plants, hanging baskets'. They enquired: 'what are you doing with those'. 'We're moving' I replied. The police really thought I had stolen a whole lot of hanging baskets from a nursery.

The furniture van was loaded and was just about to start on its way to Glenormiston when we were phoned and told that the house we were to rent would not be vacant for another week! The removalist firm then took our furniture to Roslyn, Natte Yallock and we stayed with Dianne's parents. A week later, the furniture was reloaded and moved to Glenormiston.

It would soon be 1981. The future looked bright. Changes were coming. It seemed I had been preparing all my life for this period of my life. It would be a time where my entrepreneurial nature, my passion, and my audio-visual skills and knowledge would successfully merge – at long last.

Chapter 31
Surviving the Odds

It was October 1980 when we arrived in Glenormiston, Victoria, situated between Camperdown and Terang, and inland from Warrnambool. We would spend 6 years in this beautiful area. I worked at the Glenormiston Agricultural College, and we purchased our first home, and later, re-commenced Thompson Video. It was a time with many happy memories and provided a solid grounding for our future. But, I would also find myself facing another serious health problem.

Massive changes would occur during the period of 1980 to 1986 including that relating to technology:

1980 Saw the continued miniaturization of new technology including Domestic Camcorders and Fax Machines. The year 1981 saw technological advances: it was the first year that the Word Internet was mentioned and MS-DOS, was released by Microsoft, along with the first IBM PC. Also, in this year, Lady Diana Spencer married Charles, The Prince of Wales. 1982 saw the first CD player introduced and the use of Genetic Engineering – for example human insulin produced by bacteria is sold for the first time. 1983 was the year the world's most popular word processing programme was launched – Microsoft Word. 1984 The AIDS Virus is identified, and the PC Apple releases the Macintosh computer. 1985 As the spread of AIDS increases Governments round the world start screening blood donations for AIDS. On the technology front the first .com is registered, and the first version of Windows is released Version 1.0. Terrorists continue to perform acts of terrorism including the hijack of TWA Flight 847 and the Italian Cruise Liner 'Achille Lauro '. The Famine in Ethiopia continues. 1986 The Space Shuttle Challenger explodes shortly after take-off watched by people live on TV around the world. The Internet Mail Access

Protocol is defined which opens the way for E-Mail and the same year the Human Genome Project is launched to understand the Human Makeup, this will open the way for great advances in the treatment of many illnesses. The worst ever, Nuclear Disaster occurs as the Chernobyl Nuclear Power Station Explodes causing the release of radioactive material across much of Europe. In the UK (BSE), commonly known as mad cow disease is identified which causes many deaths over the next few years and a major reform in farming practices.

We rented a very nice house with a large garden from Athol and Carol, dairy farmers who lived in the farmhouse next door at Glenormiston. It was a very rural area – a lovely environment and my secure work was just across the paddock. Dianne would work as a midwife at the local Terang hospital when a position became available. The children could run and play and ride their bikes without any impediment, we could have an above ground pool and chooks and a dog. It was perfect, and we were very happy!

I always liked gardening and the front garden had several low growing shrubs making it hard to mow the lawn, so I decided to trim them. Athol, the owner, and himself a very keen gardener was furious. 'How dare you trim all of my shrubs – I like them like that!' So, we didn't start off on a very good footing, but as it happened, we would not be renting from him for long. We were determined to buy a house and put down 'roots' in this area.

I really enjoyed my work and the friendly staff at the College that offered diploma and degree programs to agricultural, equine and farm management students. The main historical building was situated in an idyllic setting and built by a wealthy family in a bygone era. This original home, was now the Administration building for the university [later owned by the University of Melbourne]. The College was also a working dairy farm and had a large equine centre.

I threw myself into starting up the AV department from scratch. I helped move the library from downstairs to upstairs so that the A-V department could be near the library. The top floor of this modern building was to be a 'state of the art' resource and media area including a photography darkroom. The main lecture theatres were downstairs.

I completed some major projects at Glenormiston. I wired up all the classrooms and lecture theatres with closed – circuit TV. Panels in the classroom contained plugs for TVs and remotes for the recorders so that the lecturers could operate the tapes that I had pre-cued, by remote in the control room. It was a large project to complete, but one that was very effective and proved to be an efficient system as it saved moving recorders and set up. The teachers were very pleased with the outcome.

I did a lot of telecine transferring 16mm film to tape, and placed them in the library, ready for use, until copyright became an issue. The directive came from the Principal that everything I'd copied had to be 'wiped'. Tapes I had produced for lecturers and students and edited remained.

I had a good rapport with the students and the lecturers and did some very interesting filming with them. I took a lot of black and white photographs and developed them for use in lectures. I used a micro lens, to film the bugs, grasses and soil for the agricultural students and spent a lot of time with the horse students – filming dressage and an autopsy of a horse. I was amazed at how many 'things' normally lived inside a horse!

I got on well with the librarian, and we worked together and supported each other in our respective areas. As the months progressed and the A-V department and video productions were well set up, the library expanded its opening hours and external studies were introduced. I often worked in these areas. Yes, me in a library! Dianne always thought this extension of my role was highly amusing because she knew too well that I had never liked school, didn't like books given my traumatic history, and here I was in this very learned library environment!

I used my own coloured video camera to shoot news stories relating to the College that were then shown on Channel 7 and Channel 10. This rapport I developed at this time would hold me in good stead later.

There were some very big production days that I managed for the College. One was the Melbourne Cup luncheon for ladies of the district, held on the manicured lawns that initially were used for croquet. Another was the graduation ceremony held once a year. It was a spectacular event, and a day shared with family of those working at the College.

At the beginning of the ceremony, my role was to introduce the academic staff and the students and announce: 'Please be upstanding for the students and the academic staff,' then play the pre-recorded Academic March music as the academic procession wound its way to the stage. Before I left the College, I pre-recorded my welcome, directions, and the Academic March music on cassette.

Years later Darryl an employee of Thompson Video went to the College to record the graduation as a news story. He came back amazed saying: 'Suddenly, just as I was getting ready to film, your voice came over the speakers! I'm immortal, at least on graduation day at Glenormiston Agricultural College!

Dianne's land in Avoca was on the market and sold quickly. We had a deposit to buy a house! We looked at a house to purchase right in the town of Terang – very sensible 1950s house that we could move straight into, without any renovations. Then, we drove past a little cottage on 2 acres for sale in Noorat a small village between Terang and Glenormiston and immediately knew it was for us.

The cottage was built in 1850 by a 'horse breaker' at the base of Mt Noorat a large dormant volcano. Alan Marshall, the famous author of '*I can Jump Puddles*' was born in Noorat in 1902.

Noorat village had a post office, small grocery shop, a milk bar, a fire brigade station, an excellent primary school, a bulk cheese factory outlet, a Presbyterian Church, and a pub popular with the students from Glenormiston Agricultural College.

The cottage did not have any immediate neighbours. The house and garden were positioned next to the Show Grounds with a row of very large, old pine trees along the fence line. The acre of land on the other side of the house gently sloped down to the next building. Two very tall and impressive date trees – one either side of the footpath leading to the front door added enormously to the appeal.

Two elderly sisters – spinsters lived in the house, and had done so, all their lives. The house and garden were extremely run down. Time had stood still. Large plants had grown and still had the tins they were originally potted in, embedded in their trunks. At some stage, the roots of the 'pot plants' had burst through the base of the rusted tins, allowing a forest to grow. But, the house looked so 'cute'.

We had 'stars' in our eyes! We both fell in love with the house and the setting and promptly bought it. We could make it into a home. But, it would be a lot of work and money, but we were not frightened of work, and we would stagger the renovations. The date to move in was set and we started packing. But a disaster was about to occur – one that would have huge implications for the immediate future and subsequently the rest of my life.

Within 3 months of moving to Glenormiston, and just before moving into our first home at Noorat, I was diagnosed with testicular cancer. One testicle became red, swollen, and bigger and bigger – the size of a tennis ball! Dianne said one of the ducts might just be blocked. So, I went to the doctor in Terang and it became obvious that something was wrong. I was immediately booked into have tests and a biopsy at the local hospital, then wait for results and then action if necessary. I phoned Tony and he advised differently. He said, come straight away to the Austin hospital, Melbourne where the tests can be performed quickly, and if necessary, immediate action taken, on the same day.

We travelled to Melbourne and I was admitted to hospital, and Dianne and the children stayed at Tony and Helen's. On March 12, 1981, I signed to have a biopsy and further surgery if the biopsy revealed cancer. It did. The testicle was removed.

Dianne has her own memories of the day Tony told her that I was out of surgery, and the diagnosis was cancer and I would need radiation therapy, in Melbourne. She was holding Matthew – 6 months old, on her lap in the lounge at Tony and Helen's. She could hear Sophie 5 and Benjamin 4 playing happily outside. But, she felt 'numb'. She vividly recalls holding Matthew close and gently putting her face on his warm head and sadly thought: 'he will grow up not knowing his Father'.

Meanwhile, I was in a hospital bed and had been awake from the effects of anaesthetic a short while. A nurse came and said, 'You can go home now' and started to get me out of bed. I spluttered: 'But, I've just had a serious operation'. Then, another nurse rushed up and said to the nurse attending me:

'No, no, no', explaining that it wasn't a blocked duct, but rather, I'd had further surgery. They decided to wheel me to the lounge, but as there was no spare wheelchair, they used a commode to push me there! Dianne and the children visited, and it was lovely to see them.

I recall Dianne's strong but kind words and heeded them. She said: 'I don't want any psychological problems from you having one testicle! It doesn't bother me so don't let it bother you. We have too much living to do, and children to bring up to let something like this dominate our life'. With that, I have never let it bother me. But, it has brought some problems, particularly in later life. One cannot have a bout of mumps orchitis that affected one testicle badly and the other removed and subsequent radiation, without having some problems later in life. All I can say is 'thank goodness Matthew was conceived when he was!'

It was a stressful time for all and would be for some time to come. I had just started a new job 3 ½ hour drive from Melbourne, we were due to move into a dilapidated house, the children were very young and needed to be cared for. Tony was very upset about the whole thing and took control. He said to me, the next thing you need to do, is go to 'Peter Mac' Hospital and have radium treatment and 'all the tests under the sun'. It was arranged. I went, and the staff said: 'the scar hasn't healed yet. We don't usually get people as early as this'. I said my brother is a doctor. They understood and did a lot of tests to see if it the cancer had spread into the lymph glands and subsequently everywhere else. It was good news. It seemed that the cancer had been contained and removed. However, to be sure, radium treatment was ordered and undertaken. A very, very unpleasant experience, but 'Peter Mac' did a great job.

I hadn't been working at Glenormiston very long and I was concerned about how we would live during the time I needed to have nearly three months away. I asked Dianne to meet with the Principal of the College to express my concerns. He was supportive and understanding and the College paid me throughout the time I was recovering, during the radiation therapy time and when check-ups continued over the months thereafter.

The time of radiation therapy tested me mentally and physically. Initially, I stayed with Tony and Helen, and Helen took me to Peter Mac every day during the week to have radium therapy and cared for me. I was, and still am extremely grateful to them. On occasion, I stayed with Mother in her flat at Hughesdale. But, every Friday I drove home to Noorat to Dianne and the children. It was a very long and extremely uncomfortable drive – I pulled over often to be sick beside the road – but it was a trip I knew I needed to do. My family were what sustained me during this time. On Monday morning I would get up early and drive back to Melbourne and the process started again.

To me, radium treatment in 1981 was 'like putting your head into a gas oven every day. You knew what was going to happen. You were going to be 'sick as a dog' afterwards, and you just walked in to get sick!'

Not long after my treatment commenced, we moved into our home at Noorat. Dianne's father and brothers came with their truck and moved the furniture from our rented home at Glenormiston to our first home at Noorat. It was a big day and I can only imagine the mixed emotions of that day, as I could not share it as I was in Melbourne having treatment. But emotions and stressors were to continue.

Between the move into our dilapidated home, my illness, and treatment in Melbourne, and living a long way from family support, it was obviously going to be very, very stressful for Dianne. While we tried to shield the children, they did sense the disruption and trauma that had unfolded. Sophie at five years old was at school during the day and she seemed to cope well. Matthew at six months old was too young to be aware of the upsets. It was four-year-old, Benjamin that became very upset when I left to return to Melbourne for treatment and displayed signs of anxiousness. He would not let Dianne out of his sight during the week, constantly calling out and wanting to know where she was. Understandable.

Our house was in dire need of renovation, but prior to this, a large amount of demolition – such as the old double fireplace in the kitchen prior to extending, converting a room into a bathroom, and putting in a new soak away system as the septic tank was blocked. I was still having radiation therapy and we needed assistance.

We called on Sam [Samantha] and Jeff, a married couple and our friends who lived at Coleraine. Sam was one of the nurses that Dianne went to Yuendumu with, and Jeff was the farm manager there. Sam and Jeff married after we left Yuendumu and someday after this, they returned to Jeff's farm at Paschendale, Victoria. They answered our call for help and came down with their two children to stay and work for a couple of weekends to help us out. It was both a relief and a reunion. We talked, worked and the children played. Sam and Jeff were a really great help to us and exceptionally good people, and good friends.

I never realized there were so many bricks in a fireplace! Especially a double sided one – built to last in the 1850s. Incredible! It was getting near winter, and we lit a fire in the fireplace to heat the house a few times before we took it down to start renovations.

We hired Jared, a dairy farmer and carpenter to complete the renovations. He came when he could – after milking in the morning to late afternoon when he returned to milk his cows. At this pace the extensions continued for a very long time, but it gave us a chance to accumulate some money to pay for both building materials and wages.

Overall it was a tense time intensified by the state of our home that we had moved into. It was barely liveable. What we had seen as cute and lovely just a few weeks ago, became a constant source of dismay when we lived in it and realised the true extent of what needed to be done, to make it comfortable. Plus, Dianne and the children were on their own during the week – I was not there to support or protect them.

Dianne held everything together but worked extremely hard during this time and for many, many months to come. At this time, we joined and attended the local Church and the children went to Sunday school. Matthew was christened at Noorat, amongst family. It was truly a happy occasion at this very torrid time in our life.

There were challenges enough without having to contend with possums that lived in the pine trees next to the house and in the roof space of our house! Prior to renovating, possums over ran the house. They pounded the corrugated roof at night and slept in the space between the ceiling and roof around the chimneys where it was warm during the day.

We set a legitimate mesh type cage, obtained from the council to try, and catch and remove them before the new ceiling was sealed. We placed an apple attached to a spike and a spring in the cage so when the possum touched the apple, the cage door snapped closed. We were successful in catching possums, night after night, and in the morning, I would release them a long way from home in an area they would survive. I swear to this day, they came back to us again, along with their friends! The cycle was repeated, again, and again, with no obvious decline in numbers!

The day came when the ceiling plaster was to be finalised. All other areas of the roof had been secured and possums would not be able to squeeze into the roof after tomorrow. It was a day we were looking forward to, but we knew there was one possum still in the roof space. If we didn't get it out it tonight, it would die, and there would be a decaying smell for months – something we were familiar with when a cat crawled under our rented house at Glenormiston and died. Eventually, the smell was so bad under the floor of our bedroom, that I crawled under the house, located the remains, and placed them in a bag and brought them out. I did not want this to happen in the roof of our house.

But I was exhausted from the continuing radium treatment. Dianne on the other hand had a plan. She pitted herself against this old possum, with greying fur. She knew his pattern at night as she had watched him through the gap in the doorway. Early in the morning, he would climb down from the roof, into our new family room extension and walk around before going back up into the roof. She had tried unsuccessfully to get him out and thought he seemed to sense her spying on him. She said 'he looked in my direction, with pride and defiance, his piercing look telling me plainly: 'this is my house – I have lived here a very long time. You are the intruder. I am not going anywhere.'

It was a battle to be fought between them. He was not going to leave, without a fight. She respected him, but this was her house! She was sick of living with possums – possums running over the crockery in the laundry that doubled as a kitchen and bathroom when the extensions were being done. Possums crawled into incredibly small spaces making noises that kept us awake at night and left their stain on clothing that was impossible to wash out!

Tonight, the night before the plastering was to be completed, she would implement the plan again. This time she must succeed as she had with all other possums that had lived in her house. Firstly, she placed some tempting apples near the wide-open back door and positioned herself on a chair behind the adjacent passage door that led to the bedrooms. This passage door was left slightly ajar, so she could see through the slit where the hinges attached to the doorframe. It was very quiet, dark, and cold, but she waited and waited. She planned to slam the passage door and frighten the possum just as he was nearing the food at the wide-open back door. If this old possum jumped in fright back into the house, and not out, that would be it. The possum would be sealed in the roof space forever.

In early morning, the old possum repeated its normal pattern. He climbed down into the family room and walked very slowly over to the food, its nose twitching. Just as the possum got to the apples Dianne slammed the passage door. Which way would the possum jump? Frightened by the noise the old possum jumped to the nearest exit – out into the dark night. Dianne rushed to close the back door petrified that he would turn and scamper back into his 'home'. The plan worked perfectly! She hadn't slept at all, but she had *her* house back! Dianne believes in live and let live. But she has never recovered from this time of living with possums and the grief and angst it caused at an already hugely stressful time. She does not like possums…and nothing will change this!

Renovations continued, and the house became liveable, and a good family home. We concreted the large back veranda and carport with the help of a few friends. We made a lovely garden, with lots of vegetables and flowers and, I built a large play area for the children. We had a dog, chooks and chickens and a couple of goats in our paddock next door to keep the grass down, until they started to get through the fence.

We had a lovely uninterrupted view from the large windows in our family room. The view overlooked our garden and fishpond and extended to a lush green paddock with cattle grazing and onwards to the enormous and elegantly shaped Mount Noorat. Dianne painted the outside of the house, a fresh pale green. It was a very big job, but the house was then 'reborn'.

The children were happy and helped us with everything. Benjamin was my little helper and Sophie, Dianne's. Matthew, still young, helped us both as much as he could. Dianne started working as In Charge midwife and nurse at Terang and District Hospital on Friday and Sunday evening from 4pm – 12midnight when Matthew was 10 months old. This is when I bonded with Matthew properly as it had been a hard few months before this and I was preoccupied.

I was still not fully recovered, and my stamina was low. However, I was riding a bike to and from work so that Dianne had the car for the children and work. Until I could better manage, Dianne who left for work at 3.30pm arranged for Floss, a local lady to come in to look after the children, prepare dinner and bathe them by the time I returned home from work.

As time went on and the children got older, Floss stayed until I got home, but I cooked and did the bedtime routine. The children loved the pancakes and vegetable patties I cooked. And they loved Friday nights – movie and lolly night! Some favourite movies included *Willy Wonker and the Chocolate Factory* and Sophie's all-time favourite 'Grease'. At 7.30 we would routinely phone the hospital so that the children could say goodnight to Dianne.

One night, I returned from work extremely tired. The children's bedtime couldn't come quickly enough. I had a 'brain wave'. I would trick the children into thinking it was later than it was. I wound the clock forward by an hour and told them it was bedtime. But they didn't 'buy' it! Although they could see the clock and understand the time, their 'body clocks' just didn't believe the time! I didn't try this again as it literally took me twice as long to get them to bed than other nights where the clock was left at the right time!

The children went to the Noorat School a short walk from the house. They rode their bikes down the large, grassed strip between the main road and service road. They studied music and played sport and had great friends – many whose parents worked at the same College I did.

Dianne joined a local playgroup consisting of six families and attended weekly with Matthew. Each mother hosted the playgroup in their home and provided a 'speciality' for the children. Dianne's was play dough – all colours that she made herself. Activities provided by other mother's included pony rides, painting, and planting. The children enjoyed the playtime, but the mother's enjoyment seemed greater, and strong friendships developed and yearly grown-up dinners at 'posh' restaurants in Warrnambool ensued.

Dianne read to the children at night – a popular story was the 'Cat in the Hat' series. I recorded her reading children's books so that I could play the cassette at night to the children when she was working. When they could read themselves, I no longer needed to play the cassettes and they read to me.

The showground next door to our house was used regularly for events, particularly football during winter and Dianne and her local friends ran laps during the week. Once a year the Agriculture show was run over a weekend. It was an exciting time for all. Before the show, people, caravans, and trucks arrived and set up their homes in the paddock at the back of our house. The show ground next to our house was transformed with rides, music, and events. Weird and wonderful species of fowl were placed in pens alongside our fence, waiting to be judged.

Sophie loved music and musicals, especially 'Grease' and wore the videocassette out by repeated playing of the cassette! She explored the world at an early age when she climbed out of her bedroom window with her packed case to run away. She told us when she returned that she got as far as the school, and then turned around and entered the house the same way she left! We did not even know she had left until much later when she told us! Probably the most significant thing that Sophie learned at this time was about loss of life when a friend in her grade at school died from an acute asthma attack in the car that her parents were driving from their farm, into the local hospital. She was five-year-old. The grief in the small community was palpable.

Sophie displayed entrepreneurship and business skills at an early age. We had an account at the local milk bar where we sold our eggs and bought milk, bread, and Friday night lollies. At seven-year-old, Sophie used our account to buy lollies – not for herself, but for those who were in the school yard waiting for their parents who lived out of the village, on farms to collect them. Sophie was able to go out of the schoolyard as she lived in the village and was able to walk or ride home from school. We were not aware of her activity after school until the owner of the milk bar mentioned it to us. We were horrified, but when questioned it was obvious that Sophie was just doing what she had seen us do. That is, go into the milk bar and 'book up' what we wanted, on account. It was simple.

Benjamin found 'fishing' at an early age after 'going fishing' with his friend Ben, and Ben's father. His love of fishing remains. But he was prone to climbing trees. One day, he climbed a large fir tree beside our home. He climbed onto the fowl pens and then up the main trunk and then out onto a limb. He got to a stage that he couldn't get back as the limb would not support him. He was 'waving' around precariously on the small end of the limb, yelling *'Dad, Dad, help me. I can't hold on anymore'*. I rushed and got into our high ace van with a stand on the top of the roof and drove quickly around to the showground. I stretched my arms out as far as I could and said, 'Ben jump into my arms.' He did, and I managed to get him down.

Another day at Terang Racing Club, Benjamin decided he could fly. He put his arms out and jumped off the grandstand, and ended up flat, bang onto the floor just missing the seats of the stand. He just lay there. I gathered him up quickly and rushed into the hospital where Dianne was working but there was no real damage. Benjamin climbed and fell from a wet and slippery tree at the Hamilton Races and broke his arm. Sophie and Matthew brought him back to us, his forearm mis-shapen. He spent the day in hospital in Hamilton and had his arm set in plaster. When we picked him up in the evening, he said 'Hello Mum and Dad. They've been giving me ice cream. I've had a lovely day.'

Matthew was inseparable from his siblings and joined in with everything. They in turn, were very protective of him. At two years old Matthew gave us a really, big fright. When Dianne and I worked in the garden or on renovating our house, the children had their jobs, and played around us and were usually very tired by the end of the day.

We had all worked hard in the garden on the Saturday and were entertaining friends at lunchtime on the following day. Dianne went to check on the children. Sophie and Benjamin were present, but there was no sign of Matthew. This was unusual, as the three of them were always close together. We all called out 'Matthew', and quickly looked in and around the house and play area. There was no answer. Panic set in as we lived on a very busy road, a dangerous road, on the top of a crest and there was always milk trucks travelling along the road. We had more than one dog killed on the road. But Matthew was always compliant, and never ventured near it. But where was he?

Our friends who had older children tried to calm the situation. They told us that once, one of their children had gone missing at their home and was found hiding in a closet and didn't answer when called. Perhaps Matthew was in a closet hiding? We looked, but there was no Matthew. Then, again Dianne went through the bathroom, through the laundry and past the toilet to the back door. The door to the toilet was half opened. She pulled the half open door right back. Relief! There was Matthew, sound asleep, sitting on the 'potty', mouth open, with his head supported by the wall. It had been a very tiring weekend for a little two-year-old!

We held our children's birthday parties at our home, and we learnt the hard way that it was not advisable to have too many six – seven-year-old children at a party. Our children used to climb the old peppercorn tree and then jump off onto a wood play area I'd made for them. It was very safe to do so, and they enjoyed the experience. But one very inexperienced and over-protected child at the party joined in and climbed out to the very end of a branch on the tree and then promptly shouted: 'I can't hold on anymore'. We shouted 'hold on' as we ran towards him, but he just let loose and fell like a limp rag – he did not try and protect himself at all! Plunk! He hit the ground with a thud! He was unconscious. But was he? He was not breathing, and Dianne couldn't feel a pulse. She resuscitated him while I called the ambulance. He survived. The doctor Dianne worked with at the hospital said: 'We heard what happened, I hope your insurance policy is up to date.' It was, but we did not need it thank goodness.

Our dear nephew was accidently killed not long after we moved to Noorat. It was devastating. Dianne received the call and immediately said *'I must go home'*. We packed and left in a few minutes of receiving the call, commencing the long drive. When we arrived, Dianne realised that she was supposed to be on duty at the Terang hospital in 2 hours. She asked me to phone and tell them she would not be at work for the next few days. I called directory assistance and got the number of the Terang Hospital and phoned them. I was astounded at the response as they told me that they didn't have a staff member named Dianne Thompson, and what's more, never had! Frustrated and confused, I responded: Well, where the 'bloody hell' has she been going two evenings a week, for the past few months? After a lot of discussion, we got to the stage of realising that the number I had phoned was the Kerang hospital, and not the Terang hospital! I had been given the wrong number.

It was the 16th February 1983. Ash Wednesday. A memorable day, 'burnt' into our memories. I saw a wisp of greyish smoke in the far distance on my way back to College from the University at Warrnambool. Once back, I collected my bike and started to ride home to Noorat. I could see a dark plume of smoke rising in the distance and smelt smoke in the air. I thought, 'this looks serious.' Arriving home, I saw my neighbours and others congregating on the verge and the word was: 'all males go to the fire station immediately to be on standby.' The fires were 'lapping' at the Terang racetrack and if the wind changed, it would be a straight path to Noorat.

Dianne was at work and the children at Floss' who lived across the road from our home. If the wind changed, I feared for our safety and that of our home given the large and combustible Showground pine trees were right next to our home. Dianne was battling the situation in a different way at the Terang Hospital. It was high drama. She tells the story:

'It was a horrible day, hot, windy, wild and threatening. The unusual day was noticed first when I tried to close the back door of our house to go to work at around 3.45pm. I needed two hands to pull the door shut due to the strength of the wind, and only then I could just manage. I was late, so I jumped into the car and drove the few kilometres to work. I was in charge of the hospital when I worked, and it was a diverse and busy hospital – midwifery, general, children and aged care residents, downstairs. We also had an emergency centre, one ICU bed and a surgical theatre.

I walked into the staff room and saw a colleague who lived at Garvoc, between Warrnambool and Terang sitting in the chair with her baby. I knew she wasn't working on that day and asked is everything all right? She said she had been phoned by her local fire brigade to get out of their house and go somewhere safe as there was a fire heading her way – but she didn't know where exactly, and further, she didn't know where her husband was.

We received handover – me, a registered nurse and midwife, 1 registered nurse and 2 enrolled nurses. Just after this the police phoned and said the fire was nearing and that all cars had to be removed from the car park of the hospital as it was directly in line with the fire's path. The oxygen and other gasses were near the car park and the concern was that they would explode; then the cars combust, and the car fuel would worsen the situation. We scrambled, taking it in turns to move our cars down the street and then return. After this one communication, there was no more from either the police, or fire brigade. It was not known what was happening. The wards were full including a postoperative patient, a newborn and mother to care for and someone in the final stages of dying. It was a busy time.

Then, around 30 minutes later I smelt smoke coming in the hospital rooms and assumed it was from outside. With all telephone lines down, and a full hospital, I suppressed my concern and fear and calmly went into all the rooms and handed blankets to the patients just saying it's best to leave these on your bed. There was no mention of fires so as not to alarm anyone, but the blankets were in case we needed to evacuate quickly. But where would we evacuate if necessary? The car park was our evacuation point and this was not safe. Remain calm Dianne.

Then, a policeman, and a fireman, arrived telling me the hospital was to be evacuated as it was directly in line with the path of the fire. We were directed to 'get everything you need for some time', I asked, how do we get to where we are to evacuate to – a facility at the opposite end of the town? They were arranging a bus to take all patients and staff to a facility at the opposite end of town, was the response.

Get everything you need for 24 hours for elderly residents and patients sick, dying, unwell patients on all types of medicines, IV fluids etc., plus having to get everyone into the bus – most not able to walk? Think about this, and 4 staff members…

In amongst all of this, one staff member panicked, concerned for her young family, and abruptly left. I did not see her leave; I just knew she wasn't around. Luckily, about the same time as this, other off duty staff members who lived in town heard that the hospital was to be evacuated and turned up to help. It was a godsend. It took numerous bus trips to get the evacuated patients and equipment required down to the other facility and set them up. If the fire had stayed true to its course, we would not have made it. It didn't stay true, and the hospital was saved.

But, by leaving, we had jumped from the 'fat to the fire'. Not long after we had finished moving everyone, the word came that the wind had changed and the facility we had moved to was now in the direct line of the fire! I recall the feeling. Nowhere to go – we are here. Squashed into the facility, waiting…waiting. What would be our fate?

I was extremely worried about Chris and the children and there was no way to know if they were safe. There was no communication at all –phone lines were down and mobile phones not available or common. I was torn, but I was on duty, in charge of my patients and my duty of care was evident. I believed that Floss would look after the children to the best of her ability until Chris came home.

But then, Chris appeared at the door, with the fire fighters! I was relieved to see him, but at the same time so angry. 'Why aren't you with the children? Where are they? Are they safe? What if the pine trees go up in fire – Floss' house will explode?' He had come to see if I was all right, and if he could help. He knew the children were safe, but I didn't, and I was under much pressure and responded out of character. I felt if I couldn't be with the children, he should be, to protect them. He could see my frame of mind and the pressure I was under, so he left saying he would go home to the children. I continued my work until the danger ceased – some hours, at which time everyone was taken back to the hospital.

The devastation of the fires was horrifying and long lasting. Houses can be rebuilt, but not lives. There were many problems that arose after the fires that I saw first-hand at work. Lives were lost, and others destroyed. It was hard for many to pick up the pieces. The baby, born the day of the Ash Wednesday fires, lost its Father in the fire. There were many, many other sad stories. Evidence of the pressure people were under, continued for months and indeed years after the fires. Many walked through the doors of the hospital seeking help as a last resort.'

I was enjoying my job, my life, and my family, but knew there was something else for me. We went to the local races at Terang one day as a family. I am not interested in horse racing, but I am interested in filming – anything. I took my new small amateur video camera and tripod to see how it worked. This day was significant as by the end of the day a 'seed' – an opportunity was formulating in my mind. I could film the races, as I did in Brisbane for Bruce Windows Electronics. Dianne encouraged me to approach the President of the

Terang Racing Club to follow up on my vision. I did and on the same day he invited me to present my proposal at the next club meeting at the Garvoc pub.

I arrived at the pub and set up my presentation equipment including a TV, video recorder and the video tape of the footage of the Terang races. It was like old times, but on a much simpler scale.

I presented my proposal to the committee. I spoke passionately and with authority. I knew what I was talking about and convinced them that country gallops should not be the 'poor cousin' of the metropolitan gallops. I convinced them that country races should be video recorded for stewards' patrol, owner and punter enjoyment, and posterity, just as was done in the metropolitan area. And I convinced them that, all of this, I could do!

Despite the amateurish video footage, I showed, they were enthralled. I had used what I had available to film – my own small camera with an inadequate lens. The result was far from professional. The horses looked like 'flyspecks' in the distance until they came onto the straight and the footage was jerky due to the cheap tripod. Luckily, the committee members were visionary and saw the potential. I pointed out the flaws but at the same time, told them 'I'll get a bigger camera with a better lens and friction tripod'. They didn't seem to care, but I did. My footage was to the best it possibly could be.

My proposal was accepted, and history was made! No one had recorded country gallops before! The Club paid me to film the races on a trial basis, and I was in my element! I had the security of Glenormiston during the week, but the excitement of a new project on a Saturday.

I brushed off the dust of our 4 Dutch K9 TVs we had from Brisbane, loaded them into the station wagon with the rest of the equipment and headed to the racetrack. I positioned the TVs in the bar and other places around the racetrack, and linked them with coax, creating closed circuit TV enabling the races to be shown.

It was an amateurish start. I stood on the Terang grandstand, in amongst the spectators. The best position to stand and film just happened to be in an area where there was a gaping hole in the floorboards. I straddled my legs either side of the hole and started to film. It was successful – the punters, owners and trainers loved it and said: 'can we buy a copy of the races? How much?' I replied '$30 per dub'. The response: 'that's all right. No worries. This was a very good price, but it needed to be, given the expensive equipment and commitment we would have with AGC at a whopping 15% interest. At this time, I designed a form! Yes,

I designed a form to take and record the orders! And the Terang Club decided to build me a tower to stand on, at the side of the grandstand.

Thompson Video was back!

Word spread like wildfire in the industry. The Stawell Racing Club phoned: 'we hear you're doing the races at Terang. Do you think you could come do the races at Stawell for us? How much? 'I went to Stawell. Then Horsham Racing Club phoned: 'we hear you're doing the races at Stawell....' So, I went to Horsham...then Warracknabeal... then Edenhope...then Nhill and then Penshurst.

Within 3 months of the filming the initial meeting at Terang, I was video recording the races at all the Western District and North Western District Gallops and supplying dubs of the race meeting to owners and punters alike. Some collected the dubs on the day of the races and others placed orders by phone to Dianne during the week. I did the dubs in the evening after work, and we sent them via the post.

I was making a name for myself in the wider community. I went back to AGC and leased a professional JVC camera – a red one with a 12:1 lens and a new tripod with a friction head so that I could 'pan' smoothly. This new equipment made a huge difference to the footage – the picture was greatly improved.

My equipment was valuable and cherished and needed protection in travelling in the station wagon, and later vans. I asked David, a friend and carpenter at Glenormiston to make some solid, lined boxes to transport the TVs safely, and used hose reels to wind up the coax.

As things progressed, we bought a proper van that I fitted out with equipment on specially built benches, with wiring like a control panel, to meet the expanding demand. Some clubs wanted numerous TVs dotted around their racetrack. At these times, we hired extra televisions. Dianne would travel to Warrnambool with the children on a Friday afternoon to collect them, and we would return them on Sunday.

In these early days, the races were a family affair – we left very early in the morning to travel long distances to the towns where the race meeting was held. I would set up a recorder and small TV in the van so that the children could watch it while we travelled. Some clubs were 5 hours away, and on these days, we went from 5am – 12 midnight. On arrival, we set up the equipment and had music playing by the time the public came. I filmed the races and Dianne operated the recorders and did the dubs for punters. The children played around us, and Matthew just two-year-old when we started filming the races had an afternoon sleep on a small foam mattress beside the van. We always stopped on the way home somewhere to have dinner – it was a real treat. As time progressed, and the children got older, they would all help, in different ways. But it took its toll. It was a very tiring day – up early, home late.

At one stage, Benjamin about six-year-old, collected cans at the racetracks to save and buy a BMX bike. When he was about seven-year-old he would come to the races with me to help, at times. I would ask him to 'start the recorder off in the van' as I ran up the ladder to the tower, to start camera and film the races. He did a really good job.

Once I got lost on the way home from the races – between Natimuk and Horsham. It was dark, and petrol was low. Benjamin got concerned – he thought we would run out of petrol and starve. I said, 'don't be silly, we have enough lollies in the car to keep us going a month!' His teacher told us at a parent-teacher interview that she couldn't wait to go to school on a Monday morning to hear 'show and tell' sessions about the adventures Benjamin had over the weekend!

The children stopped coming to the races all the time when they started team sport on a Saturday. The children had enough. They said they never wanted to go to another race meeting in their life! At this stage, I employed Jarrod, a local 'lad' still at school, and the headmaster's son. He was a clever chap, determined to be the Prime Minister of Australia. He helped put up the TVs, wind out the coax and then start the recorders.

Both my Mother and Father visited us at Noorat – separately of course, but sometimes it was like a 'revolving door'. Mother would stay for 2 weeks and return to Melbourne, and then Father would come for 2 weeks. Father had an operation at the Terang Hospital and stayed with us to recuperate and Mother celebrated her 80th birthday at Noorat.

Unfortunately, my Father died in Robinvale, Victoria just before I started Thompson Video again. He was due to visit us for Sophie's 6th birthday but died a few days prior to this. When we travelled to Mildura to finalise things and to pack up, there was a jewellery box on the table, with a card for Sophie. We had tried unsuccessfully to get him to move to Terang with his caravan to be near us, but the cold weather deterred him.

I would've liked for him to see me on the cusp of success with Thompson Video, but it was not to be. He on the other hand, would've liked me to take the time to talk to him when he stayed with us, but this was not to be. I still found it difficult to talk to him, as the past was still raw, despite the time that had elapsed and some tolerant times we had in Queensland all those years ago. But I think with the added pressure of my parents divorcing and me trying to be fair to both made me the 'meat in the sandwich'. Dianne told me that he said to her as he left our home at Noorat for the final time before his death: '…I don't really want to go…. I would like to have a chat with Christopher – perhaps next time.' Then, he looked around and said: 'this is a lovely spot to live, and I can see you are very happy here. But you know you will want something more in the future – some more culture for you and your children and your children's education.'

Dianne recalls this conversation vividly for two reasons. The first because she could not say: 'you don't have to go, please stay longer.' She could not say this as Mother was arriving the next day to stay, and he did not know this! Secondly, she could not comprehend why he would say we would want any more than what we had at this very moment. We had everything we could ever want. We had just exhausted ourselves with renovations and getting our home looking perfect. We had three happy and healthy children. We were content in our jobs and had security for the first time in our married life. Moving was not remotely in our thoughts. However, just as his advice on the shop at Lutwyche was sound, his vision of our future would also prove to be correct.

There was a time when it was right for us to move. It was 1986 – 6 years after my diagnosis for cancer, which had not returned. I wanted to explore the full potential of my business, and this meant tendering for weekday race meetings, something I couldn't do and stay in my present position. Plus, the College was restructuring and working towards merging with a College in Gippsland, where the A-V department was to be relocated. Neither of us wanted to move to Gippsland. The children were getting older, and we wanted to send them to a private school for their secondary education and Dianne wanted to pursue further studies and gain work at a University. This was all at a time when we had bought our first computer – a BBC and had some educational programs to use. It seemed a bold and exciting new era was unfolding.

We considered living in Geelong, Hamilton and Ballarat and weighed up the pros and cons. These were all cities that would meet our needs and Thompson Video could still meet its racing – gallops obligations. Ballarat won out as it is a beautiful and historical city, we would be closer to Melbourne and Dianne's family; and the health and education facilities were second to none. It was a decision we never regretted.

Dianne scoured the Ballarat paper for houses and jobs. She found a place in Lydiard Street, Ballarat to view. It was a big, renovated house in a good position in historical Lydiard Street. It had originally been built for a family of 10 during the depression and recently been a 'halfway house'. There were five big bedrooms, a combined formal lounge and dining room, kitchen with an old-fashioned fireplace, family room, bathroom, and an attached laundry. It had a tall fence and a nice big tree in the front garden, with a thick hedge running the full length of the block at the side, and a bus stop out the front. And there was space to build a large garage, to accommodate our vans and planned edit suite. We decided that we'd buy it and put Noorat up for sale.

Before we moved, Dianne obtained a part time clinical teaching role at the University of Ballarat [then Ballarat University College], the first year that nursing was offered in the university system. She travelled early in the morning two days a week to Ballarat and returned to work at Terang Hospital for the afternoon. We planned to move at the end of the school year but were advised to move earlier as the vacant house had been broken into and there was the potential for squatters. Matthew, five-year-old drew a picture at school of our new house in Ballarat and described it to his teacher as 'a house with stripes'. This was correct – the house had the look of an English Tudor house – a house with 'stripes'. Our house at Noorat sold just after we moved to Ballarat.

Sophie and Benjamin entered Ballarat Grammar School, as Matthew did a few years later after finishing primary school at Ballarat North, a block from our house. We used the small amount of money I inherited from Father to purchase the initial uniforms and pay the first term school fees. We agreed this was appropriate and was comforting as he always said he wanted his grandchildren to have the best education we could afford. They did, and in a small way, he contributed to this.

At this time, I commenced working part time – 3 days per week at Glenormiston Agricultural College. I stayed at the hotel at Camperdown during this time. There was a small fridge in the kitchen that contained bacon and egg, and bread and milk. You could help yourself, to the food, and make your own breakfast before you went to work. The same system operated in Tasmania when I was there years ago. But it got lonely in the evenings. You just had the option to drink in the bar, which I didn't do; or sit in your room. After six months I felt I did not fit any more, that is, I was no longer a part of Glenormiston or Noorat. We had to decide what to do. And we did.

I took the 'plunge' and resigned. It was now or never. Thompson Video not only had to survive but thrive!

Chapter 32
A Major Player

By August 1986 we were living in Ballarat, an impressive city rich in both history and culture and with excellent education and health care facilities. It would be our home from 1986-2006. We were an hour's drive from Dianne's family, and my Mother came to live in a hostel on the banks of the beautiful Lake Wendouree, Ballarat. We put down strong roots in this environment and the family and the business thrived.

Our children grew and matured and took every opportunity to follow their interests and passions. We joined the YMCA where the children swam and learnt defensive judo, but learning music was abandoned, as were the Japanese language lessons attended briefly on a Saturday morning.

Sophie's interests were broad at school. She excelled at mathematics and was fully involved in sport and social activities and loved listening to music and watching TV. She was an excellent swimmer, played in the first basketball team, and won the head of the lake in the firsts rowing team. She attended *Sovereign Hill* as a volunteer in costume of a young lady of the era demonstrating handiwork and worked part time at a local grocery store.

Benjamin was house captain and prefect, excelled in physical education studies and pottery, for which he was awarded a scholarship. He was a passionate and formidable sportsman – especially rowing and a member of the firsts team for 4 years. At sixteen-year-old, he won the under eighteen Victorian Yarra Banks Sprint Erg championship, in Melbourne. In his final year at Ballarat Grammar, he was awarded the prestigious Sportsman Medal of Honour – only awarded every 6 years for sports achievement at a high level in football, soccer, basketball, swimming, rowing, and athletics [cross country running, shot put, discus and javelin]. Interests outside of school included shooting, archery, and martial arts; and he worked part time at Mars Confectionery.

Matthew was prefect and school captain, excelled in acting and languages, and was in the first rowing team at Grammar. At fourteen-year-old he won the under 16 Victorian awards for Latin, and at 15-year-old, travelled to Avignon, France for a twelve-month student exchange. It was here that he was a member of the team who won the French National head of the lake for the school he was attending. He worked part time at McDonalds and at Sovereign Hill in Ballarat, the latter in costume as a 'redcoat' soldier and performed on the popular television program of the time: *'Hey Hey its Saturday'* in the segment *'Red Faces'*, with the singing act of *'Big Bad John'*.

Muffy our dog – a Scottish terrier bought from the RSPCA pound was loved by all the family despite her 'reflux' problem. Muffy was obsessed with balls and consistently climbed up the hedge beside our house to retrieve a ball. Matthew made a wooden box lined with foam, for her to sleep at the back door of the house. The box had a cut out area for her to rest her chin in comfort while she 'guarded' the house. The children spent hours playing with Muffy, but unfortunately, she died when she was five-year-old, after visiting the vet. The children were distraught and furious and insisted that the vet give Muffy a post-mortem as 'the vet killed their dog!' The vet obliged and found that Muffy had numerous problems – all of which made her life painful and could've killed her at any moment. She was lucky she lived as long as she did.

Dianne followed her dream and passion and completed degree and higher degree studies, while working full time in academia, and contributing to the business. She would finally travel overseas for the first time, with me in 1996. After this, over the next 10 years, she would travel overseas extensively and frequently in her role at the University of Ballarat – now Federation University.

I would relish working with the equipment and industry that I loved. I was a businessman and joined Rotary. After 30 years in Australia, I became an Australian Citizen – something I had resisted, for the sole reason that 'we are all British.' However, with the children asking why I wasn't 'Australian' *when I could be;* and the change in policy of the government of the day that a visa is required to get back into Australia if you left on a British passport; the time seemed to be right. In 1993 I took the plunge and attended the Australian Citizenship ceremony in Ballarat with Dianne and the children, repeated the oath and received a small native shrub and planted it at Lydiard Street.

Together, Dianne and I contributed to, and embraced, all aspects of the social life connected with the children's school. We attended and filmed the school musical and theatre productions and became involved in supporting rowing. It was Dianne who went with the children to their sporting events. Every weekend and public holiday, I was at the races, working. But I was still involved in their sport when I could be. I enjoyed their rowing years in the way that I knew – behind the video camera lens. Every so often the rowing coach would ask me to go out in a motorboat to film the training sessions so that the technique of the rowers could be examined in detail. But I always saw them row in the Head of the Lake in Ballarat and joined in the festivities afterwards.

Our holidays consisted of one week at our timeshare – Kyneton, or through exchange for units in Queensland or New South Wales when the children were older. At Kyneton the children roamed, rode their bicycles, swam, yabbied, and played tennis. I joined Dianne and the children when I could, given the commitments I had with the business. Sometimes I drove to Kyneton, stayed overnight, and returned home the next day. The holiday season was 'jam packed' with race meetings and I needed to keep my 'eye on the ball'.

There were many stories from the children's school days and growing up. Some stand out.

Matthew was twelve-year-old and attending orientation for senior school. One of the older boys – a known bully, targeted him for no reason, apart from seeing him as a 'threat' to his power. He walked up to Matthew who was sitting on a bench seat with other boys, grabbed him by the lapels of his jacket and started belting his head against a wall. The deputy principal, phoned me and said,

'Matthew's been in an altercation with an older boy... you don't have to come...he's all right.' I immediately said: 'I'm already there' and slammed the phone down.

The deputy principal tried to stop me at the front gate. I pushed passed him saying: 'just show me where he is!' I would have gone through steel. Benjamin, sixteen-year-old had heard about the incident and had taken it a bit further by the time I got there. He'd cornered a boy and was getting ready to give him a hard time, but then he then learnt just in time, it was the wrong boy!

The deputy principal a very calm and capable man told me afterwards: 'it was the worst day of my life. I had you coming like a mad bull through the front gate at one end of the school, and I had Ben coming at the other end'. Benjamin and I were both going to protect Matthew whatever happened. It all calmed down in the end. The boy who had caused the problem on this day had a long history at the School. He had caused many problems and had numerous warnings since arriving at the School. This, his most serious incident, was the final straw. The School expelled the boy – I commend them for this.

Life was busy and commitments many. The children normally rode their bikes or got the bus to and from school. One night, it was getting dark and quite late, and I suddenly thought Benjamin should be home by now. Concerned, I phoned up his friends asking if he was at their home. He wasn't. I was getting very worried and eventually phoned up Dianne who was working late that night. She said 'you were supposed to collect him from school today. Maybe you should go see if he's still there.' I thought if he *is* at School why hasn't he come home? I drove to the School and there he was! He was sitting on a box at the front school gate! He quietly said: 'I thought you'd pick me up eventually.' He has never let me forget that I abandoned him! I must admit it was not the first time I had forgotten to collect him.

Sophie was passionate about TV. She loved it and watched it intently. I understood this. We used to think if she could be *'in'* the TV, she would be perfectly happy. Programs such as *'A Country Practice'*, a series about a doctor in the country, were excellent and provided an opportunity to talk about the diverse range of topics that are often hard to broach with teenagers. We watched this hour program each week as a family and talked about anything that came up. But, when Sophie watched TV too often, I implemented my method of 'parental control'. I simply cut the electricity plug off the TV lead! You can imagine the outbursts and frustrations! This crude method was effective, but as the situation occurred repeatedly, the lead to the TV got shorter and shorter. Each time I cut the plug off, I would have to rewire it as everyone, including myself loved watching films on television! When a proper adaptor became available to screw over the plug, I used this, and the lead didn't get any smaller!

Our Friday night movies at home continued, but our long-time child treats of lollies were replaced by grown up chocolate. One Friday night, the fire was burning brightly and the family ready to watch the movie. The children started to argue incessantly about how many squares of chocolate they should have in the shared chocolate bar. Frustrated with the 'bickering' with no resolution, I stood up, grabbed the chocolate bar, opened the door of the heater, and threw the whole family block of chocolate in the fire and closed the door! The children were quiet as they watched the chocolate ooze out of the unopened packet! This image is imprinted in their brains and they recall it to this day. In this instance, actions spoke louder than words!

Satellite TVs were all the rage in the 1990s. The thought of accessing unimpeded vision beamed down from the heavens from all around the world captured my interest. As an early adopter of all things electronic, I just had to have one. I took Benjamin with me to Melbourne, to buy a satellite kit to erect on the back lawn of our home. The kit consisted of a small satellite dish about 2 metres wide on a stand with a LNC suspended on top of the dish that picked up the signal from the satellite. A cable ran from the LNC to the decoder that was hooked to the TV.

Lo and behold after alignment we saw a picture and we were all ecstatic! The 'raw footage' without ads was coming from Channel 7 Sydney to Channel 7 Melbourne. The first program we saw coming off the dish was 'Happy Days.' It was terrific – just a second of black where ads would be inserted later and then the program resumed. This new technology also provided an insight into the behind the news scenes – a bit like the forerunner to 'reality TV'! The newsreaders waiting for the recording of the news behaved 'naturally' – not at all like the edited version on TV that night. They scratched their heads and said things that they wouldn't say on air. One person who appeared very pleasant on TV when reading the nightly news was obnoxious on the raw feed! It was most interesting, and we all watched the raw feed for quite some time, day after day.

I thought there is a market for satellites and so did my neighbour, a telecom technician. We banded together and purchased a large and expensive dish about $5000 – 8 metres wide, with a tracker that could pick up countries like Spain,

Russia, and America. We dug a 1-meter by 1-meter hole in my garage floor and cemented an upright pole that penetrated the roof of the garage, extending high into the sky. We mounted the satellite on this secure pole and welded it in place. We ran coax down the pole and into my TV and desk and split the signal enabling the coax to go around the back of the garage to my neighbour's house.

The satellite looked impressive. I was so proud of this satellite dish that I shone a spotlight on it at night! Together, my neighbour and I picked up a huge range of signals and had a lot of fun. Technology was expanding rapidly, and it was a tremendously exciting time. Later, when we put our home at Lydiard Street on the market, the buyer would only buy, if the satellite dish remained. Reluctantly, I had to agree to his demand, and mourned the loss.

They were good family years and exciting times electronically. At the same time as our family life unfolded, the business developed and expanded.

When we arrived at Lydiard Street Ballarat, we registered Thompson Video Pty Ltd. We built a deep retaining wall given the slope of the block, and a large garage to accommodate 2 vans, an office, edit suite and storeroom. Up until this point and in the future when there were multiple race meetings, Dianne and the children went with me to race meetings at the weekends. I enjoyed the family time despite the pressure. And there are some good memories.

I was never interested in horse races as such, just the production side. But occasionally, I would have a 'flutter' on the races – when Benjamin came with me, just to make the day more interesting. Benjamin was too young to bet but read the racing guide and chose the horses for a win/place. Together we would go to the TAB and I would place the bet. Once, I forgot the horses' name and turned to Benjamin and said: 'what was the name of the horse we wanted? The person in the TAB picked-up on this and said: 'you know he's not supposed to bet at his age'. I said: 'he's not betting. I'm betting'. But it was obvious that I didn't know what I was doing, and Benjamin did!

Once at the races a well-known punter had won 'big time'. But, when he went to collect his winnings, he couldn't find his ticket. A murmur went around the racetrack. Matthew, about 7 at the time, quietly looked around in amongst a lot of discarded tickets, and low and behold he found the punters winning ticket. He showed me the ticket, and I said he had to give it back to the owner who was a punter that purchased tapes from us. To this day I wished I'd advised him otherwise!

The Racing Industry is an unforgiving one, with a challenging lifestyle. Race meetings are held all through the week, weekends, and every public holiday. Often there were two meetings held per day, sometimes 3-4 per day, particularly when there were long weekends and in the holiday period. The preparation both before and after the meetings was considerable. The children were all proficient at their responsibilities, but when they commenced team sports such as rowing, and increasing school commitments, there was a need to put the business on a professional footing and find some others to assist.

We set about finding someone to go with me to the race meetings at the weekends. But who other than me would like this work style? It was not an easy job – a bit like a member of the travelling circus – long hours spent travelling to a race club early in the morning – sometimes through fog, rain and sleet, and long hours travelling back from a race club, late at night on country roads. Arriving early with the 'crunch' of the frost still underfoot, or the rain still 'bucketing' down to methodically set everything up for the days meeting. This included running out numerous power leads and coax cable, lifting heavy televisions onto very high stands and positioning cameras in the right position. Sometimes this meant running up and down 'rickety' steps, or very high ladders, all with the contract needing everything running smoothly by 'show time' – 1230, when the first race was run.

It was a job with a lot of pressure, that increased rapidly as extra specialised equipment and responsibilities was added over the years, by the relevant Clubs and Boards. Basically, you arrived at a clear landscape and within hours you had to weave the magic so that the stewards, race callers, Sky Channel, the totaliser, punters, and every patron had access to your vision and sound.

I contacted St Patrick's College, Ballarat as they had a developing media department. They recommended Darryl, a sixteen-year-old – the youngest of 6 sons of a 'good Catholic family'. He looked the most unlikely person to employ when I met him. He was small, skinny, and very, very, shy, and nervous. But he was obviously very interested in audio-visual and knew about the equipment including cameras and computers and importantly, loved horse racing. I said: 'I'll give you a go –the races this weekend is at the Terang Racetrack'.

Darryl turned out to be a perfect choice – he enjoyed the whole atmosphere of the work at race meetings and travel did not bother him. He developed his skills and knowledge over time, and when he left school at 18, he worked for me full time. He ended up being a great asset eventually taking charge of the production side of the races and editing. He became my right-hand man for many years and my children even referred to him as 'my third son'.

I employed many other staff over the years to service the growing business – at peak, six full time staff and fifteen part-time. For the races, I tended to employ those who needed a chance, and showed promise in some way. They came from all sorts of backgrounds – cooking chickens, factory workers, and unemployed. In a way, they were all like me, in my youth. Waiting for someone to see their potential, and to give them a go.

I found the effort of training most of my staff, was well worth the energy and time. They had integrity and commitment. But there were some that were not so honest. Like the person who supplied a forged driver's licence and worked for me for 6 months before 'chatter' of the employees led me to approach the police about his licence. They said, 'we can't tell you if the licence is authentic or not, but what we can tell you is that the photo on the licence doesn't match with the name listed on the licence.' And, like the person working for me part time who 'skimmed' cash by not writing receipts for some dubs done on the day of the races. This I only found out when other employees refused to be rostered with him, and under some pressure, told me why. Their claims were backed up when a punter requested a re-dub of a tape that he had paid cash for at the race meeting. When asked the receipt number, he said he wasn't given one.

My first question on interview to potential employees was: Do you like going to the races? If they said 'yes', I knew they had the beginnings of what may be a good employee for this type of work. I resolved I could train them in the audio-visual side no problem, but if they weren't interested in the races – they wouldn't stay with me no matter how much they enjoyed working with audio –visual equipment. I never employed anyone from a television station for the races, despite their specialised skill. I needed people with diverse skills, a combination of audio, camera work, editing and good people skills, and able to stand very hard work and at a time when many others were socialising, combined with lots of travel and pressure on the day to perform. It was a tall 'ask' to find people with the combination of skills and attitude required. Training from scratch became the preferred method for those who liked the races!

Employees learned the required skills and craft on the job with my supervision. I was a firm employer and demanded commitment and a quality product. Staff learnt, sometimes the hard way, that a six o'clock start, meant six o'clock in the van ready to go. Occasionally, when staff hadn't arrived by 5 minutes to 6, I would pull Benjamin out of bed, and take him with me, still leaving at 6am. He never complained, and he worked well despite his young age.

The late staff member would knock on the back door of the house at 5 past 6 or later, and Dianne would say, 'I'm sorry, they've gone – they left at 6am'. 'But the 6 o'clock news is still on' they would splutter in disbelief. Dianne would repeat: 'I'm sorry, he left at 6 o'clock'. They soon got the message that sticking to the time required was crucial.

This strict approach was justified. There were so many things that could go wrong on the day without leaving late and putting extra pressure on all involved. Problems faced could be van breakdowns and accidents on the way to the meeting. And in the early days there was no communication – there were no mobile phones – we could be stranded without communication. When 'brick cell phones' came in we abandoned the CB radio and communication was possible. Our strategy for breakdowns or accidents was simple. We had a contract with a local towing firm to attend the breakdown as a priority wherever it was and place the van on the tow-truck and take it along with all the equipment inside, to the racetrack. While an expensive strategy, the alternative was worse. At least this way, we could meet our racing contract obligations without penalty.

Then, there were the unexpected things that could occur at the racetrack. The real possibility of equipment malfunctioning; was handled by always taking extra crucial equipment and improvising. It was imperative that we got to the racetrack early and finished setting up well before the first race. Then, and only then, we could relax while eating the lunch provided and watching and listening to our setup in action – the pre-programmed TVs or tote, the music playing, and the crowds 'pour' into the racetrack to enjoy the audio-visual environment provided by Thompson Video.

My famous quote that guided staff was: 'it does not matter if you finish one hour earlier than the first race is due to start. If you do this, you can relax and enjoy yourself. But you can never get time back!' But there were often unplanned changes that we had no control over and made things difficult. Sometimes at a whim, particularly at Cup Meetings and picnic meetings the Secretary and I would have a conversation that would go something like this as we walked around the track:

Secretary: 'We'd like to put a tent here.' [This tent was probably 100 yards away from anywhere else that had power, coax etc.]. 'We're going to put a tent here… and a bar over there, and we'd like you to put TVs in all of them if you could. Is that all right?

Me: 'No worries. We can do that for you', all the time thinking, more coax, more power leads to plug into already overloaded power plugs where sometimes you competed with the ladies boiling kettles for cups or tea; more splitters to retain the signal; and more time to set up – time we didn't have at this late stage of the day.

We managed, but it's a wonder we didn't all electrocute ourselves particularly when it poured with rain and water was sloshing around. We just used to plug the TVs in and hope for the best. Luckily there were no incidents in these 'pioneering' days.

The work ethics and skills of my staff were well recognised in the industry. Often, the local television stations would 'poach' them. This was a compliment to my training and their ambition, but it left me with a constant throughput of staff and constant training of new staff.

Despite this, it is with pride that when Thompson Video ceased, my full-time employees took up substantial positions in other media firms and running their own business. Darryl became head cameraman with WIN TV. David, who came from the 'Red Rooster' restaurant to work for me, became a Steward at the harness racing, and then, head of a multi-screen production company. Paul, who came from a muffler factory to work for me, now has his own successful video business. They all flourished in their own ways, and I am proud of them all.

But one, Simon, has excelled. He came to work for me as an unemployed eighteen-year-old, and after experiencing a significant family loss. When he started, he was exceptionally well groomed, very particular about everything he did, but almost non-communicative. I could not roster him to a position that required customer interaction, such as at the races. Plus, he was not interested in the races. But he demonstrated exceptional graphic and edit suite skills, so this developing area became his position at Thompson Video.

Many years later and under different circumstances I met Simon on a train. We were pleased to see each other. He said: 'come and sit with me'. He had matured and was confident and obviously successful, from his mannerisms and dress. He quietly told me his story. He was still working in computer graphics and had developed a significant reputation in the industry having worked on many well-known big productions. He had his laptop with him and showed me what he was currently working on. He asked about my family and we chatted.

As I departed, he thanked me for the opportunity I provided that helped him on his way. Without it, he was not sure where he would've ended up. I was humbled by his generosity of thanks and proud to know he had done so well after such a bumpy start.

I often told Dianne that if I had a lot of money, I would purchase some land and build a home on it for young men who needed some guidance and support. It is only now I can see that in a round about way this is what I did do with Thompson Video, without the house and land. That is, provide an opportunity for young men who needed someone to believe in them and had an interest in what I knew. But only if they were willing to work hard and learn new skills. After all, if someone like me can succeed despite all the odds stacked against me, then so can they.

So, what was that success that I achieved beyond all expectations? This falls into two areas. Starting and developing a successful business in a competitive environment that offered opportunities for all involved – I see as a success. But my greatest achievement by far is bringing up my family and watching them grow and mature to become all they possibly can be. This is my greatest success.

Having premises at the back of our garage was financially prudent and convenient when the children were young as when the races weren't on, I was at home when they were.

But, with our clientele increasing and many coming to our edit suite for post-production, we were told in 1993 by Channel 10 'if you want to keep doing production and editing work for us, you need to move to business premises.' It was not a good image for their clients, especially as Muffy was starting to give clients a gentle 'nip' to their heels when they were leaving, just to remind them who the boss was! Plus, there were other factors to consider.

The children were getting older and were sometimes home by themselves. But because it was a business, they often opened the door to strangers who knocked on the door, wanting to collect or order videotapes, or to book in work. This practice was potentially inviting trouble. And there were criminals prowling at night. One of our vans was broken into and equipment stolen when it was parked, as was Dianne's handbag stolen from our car when it was parked in our driveway. The police told us something like: 'there are criminals that have an area to 'prowl' at night. It is their routine 'job'. They do the rounds, and some nights, there will be mistakes made by owners. On this night the robbers are successful.'

Our home business premises were accessible 24 hours and professional punters, and owners knew this. There was no down time. Many times, they would ask to collect tapes at odd hours. Once, Dianne opened the door at 6 am to a man who had arranged to pick up a tape early in the morning as he was travelling through Ballarat to a race meeting that day. She knew who he was instantly and told me later who had collected the tape. He was no other than the well-known Australian rules footballer, who in later life was admitted to the 'Hall of Fame', received an OAM, and had a prominent new bridge in Melbourne named after him – the E.J. Whitten Bridge.

It was then I recalled an interaction with a 'Ted Whitten' at the Terang races. It was at the end of the day when several people were staying back to collect tapes they wanted 'there and then'. The conversation with him went something like this:

Ted: 'I need you to dub me a tape of race x now as I've got to go.'

Me: 'You'll have to wait your turn – it'll be about half an hour – there are a number of people ahead of you.'

Ted [frustrated]: 'Don't you know who I am?'

Me: 'I haven't got a clue.' [I went on with doing what I was doing]

Ted: 'I'm Ted Whitten!

Me: 'Nice to meet you Ted, but you are still going to wait in the cue!'

I did not know who Ted Whitten was, but I could see that he believed I should know, and that he should get special treatment! He never got it from me. Nor did anyone else. The racing industry is a tough industry in which to operate. My approach – that is one of no compromising ever, no colluding ever, would soon be recognised at the highest level, and rewarded. But for now, we needed to take stock of our situation and find suitable premises.

After I returned from my first trip back to England in 1993, we moved the business from our home to double fronted brick business premises at Norman Street, Wendouree. Originally a video shop that hired videos it had an open plan space with one full width partition at the rear sectioning the shop from the double garage that opened into a secluded yard to park the extra vans, trailer and satellite dish used for picnic meetings when required.

We moved the partition forward to enable room to park our long line vans inside ensuring security given they held expensive equipment, ready for the races. At the front of the partition we built a secure storeroom, dubbing room, edit suite, office, and conference room. Later we added an audio recording studio and purpose-built wall for filming. Large business signs were placed out the front of the building and a state or the art security system installed. We successfully operated from these premises.

Despite the security, we did have a break in. Dianne and Lauren, our niece who started work for us on the day after I flew out on a trip to England, were confronted with the evidence and managing the aftermath. All our dubbing recorders were stolen. Dianne immediately contacted a friend – a JVC agent who we had bought a lot of equipment from and asked for assistance. He brought the new equipment replaced by insurance and set up the dubbing suite – a big job – so that it could be operated. We never missed a beat.

I always suspected somebody knew about me going away and took the opportunity. But who knows…? What I do know was that there was some animosity towards us – the 'tall poppy syndrome'. We were 'outsiders' who blew into town, 'seen to be doing well', and could be 'taken down a peg'. However, perhaps it was the simple fact that recorders were easy to 'dispose of', and we had plenty.

There are always financial pressures in business. Some you can plan for, some you can't such as extremely high interest rates up to 22% at one stage for business and 16% interest for our housing loan. We were keeping our head above water but there was no surplus cash at this time. Then suddenly, without warning, our bank – the Westpac called in their small business loans! Official records refer to this: 'in late 1989 – 1992 Westpac suffered a $1.6b loss, a record for any Australian corporation at the time. Staff were let go 'en masse', and the bank called in a number of loans.' We were required to pay Westpac $10,000 in two weeks. Well, Dianne and I were absolutely astounded that the bank could do this and at such short notice. Dianne always quotes her wise Father: 'Banks will give you an umbrella when you don't need it but take it away when you really need it.' It's true.

To capture a different market, Action Channel with the logo 'you name it, we'll tape it' was launched. Under this name, commercials, filming of stage plays, and musicals, weddings, parties, and funerals were filmed with professional recording and editing equipment; and conversions for distribution overseas was undertaken.

And we became a 'Stringer' supplying news vision to local and Melbourne TV stations. There are many stories relating to this era, some stand out.

We shot news stories around Ballarat and District and further afield for local and Melbourne television stations. I got to learn that news stories are only valued news if they are a little more than 'news'. That is, 'we only want vision of a fatal accident, and preferably multiple pile up or fatalities, not just an accident.' Once when there was an exceptional 'newsworthy story', the television station sent a helicopter to pick up the tape we had recorded the news on. But mostly, the news story was sent via the 'Trig Point', outside the main post office in Ballarat. We were provided a key to open the Trig Point and send the video feed straight to the relevant Channel. When more than one television channel wanted the same footage, diplomacy was paramount.

Channel 10 phoned: 'We want a story about the terrible snowstorm in Ballarat – have the footage sent down by 5pm at the latest so it can go on the evening news.' 'OK' I said and put down the phone just as it rang again. This time it was Channel 7 asking for the same footage and timeframe. No time to muck around. I called Neil, a semi-retired cameraman who used to work at WIN TV who sometimes did news stories for me, particularly when all staff were at the races. Neil filmed one side of the street as I filmed the other. We sent both down the line, one after the other, to the respective Channels. We managed to shoot two completely different news stories in the space of a few metres and a few minutes later it was on both news channels!

I had a good relationship with the television stations. Channel 10 asked me to shoot some footage in Nhill with my equipment for them to make a television advertisement. They said I could take the family – all expenses paid by them. So, we all went and stayed the night in a motel – two rooms and meals provided. Room service? Ok. We were not used to this lifestyle, and it was a real treat. Ben, even at a young age, loved oysters and ordered a dozen for starters, and we all enjoyed ourselves. We also went to the *Little Desert* and went on a tour. Channel 10 were shocked with the bill, but they paid it. This Channel was very generous – they gave me a bottle of whiskey every year for being a 'Stringer'.

I developed a wide circle of professional employees at this time – including Tim and Martin both working at television stations and looking to produce, direct and edit a range of productions outside of their normal work. Tim, a creative editor, made a promotional tape for Action Channel. He was what you might call a stereotypical 'artiste' – creative, with a volatile temper and intolerant of the 'mundane'. Together, Tim, and Martin a Director, produced some exceptional work. I enjoyed working with them, despite Tim jokingly referring to the Thompson family as *'The Simpsons'*, a program that was hugely popular at the time, and which I guess, we fitted perfectly in a few aspects that I am not sharing!

A pilot program *Action Channel* produced for the ABC was *'Horsing Around'*. It was a five-minute segment about aspects of the racing/horse industry and designed for scheduling just before the news. The ABC considered the pilot but did not take it up. What they did do was produce a similar program!

We moved on to other things including producing a promotional tape to send to overseas relatives – an idea of Martin's. I said 'I've got family overseas – my cousins – Rosemary, Judy and Andrew that I haven't seen for a long time and we've drifted apart. We'll make it for them.' The 'shoot' was both hilarious and frustrating!

It was the middle of winter, in Ballarat. But I thought it's Australia – we'll have to have a barbecue! I went to the local butcher and said: 'I want some really thick steaks. I'm sending a promotional video to family in the UK, and I want to give a good impression.' His steaks did not disappoint.

I persuaded Dianne and the children to play their part. We were all outside in the very late afternoon and shooting was about to commence after many hold ups. I said to the children: 'You've got to smile; you've got to look happy'. It was very cold, and we just had short-sleeved shirts on, to make out it was a warm, balmy evening, and we were really enjoying life. By the time we got to cook the barbecue, it was about 9:00 at night and we had to have lights on! But the videotape did have the effect I wanted. After viewing it, my extended family started communicating and this has continued. It was great.

Twenty-nine years had passed since I'd left England as a twenty-one-year-old in 1964. It was time to return. Dianne was supportive, and thought I was returning to say 'goodbye'. I don't know what I thought, but I knew I wanted to see the countryside again and visit where I had lived as a child. As it turned out it was not goodbye, it was 'hello' as this would be my first of many trips back to England. But on the next trip in 1996, Dianne and I would go together – a memorable trip for several reasons. We would not only visit England, Scotland, and Ireland – where Dianne's ancestors lived before immigrating or being transported, we would also visit Matthew in France as an exchange student, when travelling in Europe.

On my first visit back to England I was very fortunate to be shown around CNN and Sky Channel Sky studios and editing rooms in London. Seeing how these organisations operated were highlights of my trip. Sky Channel staff told me their process: Sky Channel in England sent the European raw footage to America where the credits were put on and then it was beamed up to satellite for broadcasting. Nothing was sent directly from England up to the satellites for broadcasting. Sky Channel 'had a lot of Australians working here – they seem to be better at productions.' 'If only I thought'…. It was so interesting. I didn't know it then, but I would soon be intricately involved with Sky Channel, in Australia.

On return I wanted to get further involved with satellite TV and followed the technology closely. I attended the Commonwealth building in Melbourne where the bidding for the wave bands for satellite pay TV was held. History was being made and I was there in the room when the first paid satellite TV license was handed out to the major players – Austar and Foxtel.

My recognition in the industry enabled me to tender for service contracts with Club Keno, Sky Channel and Austar. These contracts required extra staff and 7 day a week service commitment. Club Keno was simple – just replacing equipment that malfunctioned. Sky Channel and Austar was much more complicated. But none of the contracts were well paid.

I was already dealing with Sky Channel for the races – providing a clean feed to them and 'barrier cam'. Sky Channel approved our mobile satellite dish to be taken to small country race meetings, like Avoca and Great Western to beam footage to Sky Channel for distribution. When satellite dishes became more widely used, I tendered for the contract to install and realign satellite dishes, mainly for pubs that provided sports footage to patrons. I attended Sydney for orientation and training, and on return I taught my staff the intricacies of satellite dishes.

Thompson Video staff attended Sky Channel service calls at the weekend. But on this one particular Sunday all available staff were working at the three big race meetings leaving Dianne and I to attend to any service calls.

A phone call from Sky Channel came in: 'A unit has failed at Golden Point Club Hotel and there is as huge boxing event scheduled in about 30 minutes.' We jumped in the car and drove quickly to the Club and walked in. There was a room full of keen betters all stirred up, drinking beer and ready to 'kill' the Sky Channel representatives as there was a blank screen on the super large televisions in the Club! I set to work feverishly. I replaced the decoder, phoned Sydney, gave them the number on the back of the decoder and waited for them to activate the signal that would take 5-10 minutes. Timing was crucial – it was 5 minutes before the fight started! I phoned Sky Channel back and said, 'look. Get this thing on quick! I've got about a thousand people here getting ready to punch me up if we don't get this match going shortly!' With just a few minutes to spare vision appeared on the huge screens. There was an explosion of cheers and shouting from the punters. We were relieved and safe! It was a memorable moment. To this day I am not sure what the outcome would've been if the vision had not come on in time to see the opening round!

The Austar – Pay TV sub-contract we had, focused on installing small dishes mainly for domestic situations in Ballarat and the very wide surrounding rural area. The contract enabled us free access to Austar but otherwise just covered costs with installers using our van, equipment, and phones in return for a flat rate for installation and minimal supervision.

In 1996, Dianne and I went overseas on holidays – it was Dianne's first trip overseas. We were travelling down a tiny little road at Whitchurch, England, when we received a phone call from the main contractor at Bendigo on our 'super-duper' roaming mobile phone of the time. The phone call was not good news. In the time we had been away travelling there were reported delays in hooking up and positioning of dishes culminating in several complaints about our Pay TV team. The main contractor did not 'mince' his words. Our contract would be cancelled unless service improved. We immediately phoned Darryl, ordered a Polaroid camera, and asked staff to take a photo of the final installation for proof the job was done properly. This worked well, and the contract was saved. But the $2000 cost of the 'roaming' phone whilst overseas crippled us financially. It was in the days that you had to pay for two exchanges – each country charged for the one call! Never again would I go 'roaming'.

We retained a business manager to get our business on a good footing. We developed policies and procedures and our staff had a smart uniform – one with our logo and their first name for easy recognition for our clients. Our variety of productions increased, and corporate clients grew in profile and included McCains, Mars Confectionary, City Council and Her Majesty's Theatre. These domestic, corporate, and commercial obligations were being managed at the same time there was a surge in technology requirements and contract obligations for race meetings. It was a very specialised and unforgiving environment and the risks many and rewards – well, not so many. But I am very proud of the part I played and the outcomes of the business in this extremely professional and stressful environment.

There were formidable high-profile competitors in the racing industry. I was fully involved in the regular meetings but needed to win the contract for the more lucrative TAB meetings in my district, for the business to grow. But for me to be successful meant that a current provider of TAB meetings would need to lose out.

I continued planning to tender for the TAB meetings. But, before I could submit my tender, the Gallops Racing Board sent a letter to all of my regular clubs saying that they would not agree to Thompson Video doing the oncourse video at the lucrative TAB meetings as they did not have the appropriate equipment – the 'Bods' – equipment that channelled all of the prices at TAB meetings. A secretary from one of my regular clubs phoned me and read the letter to me over the phone. He told me that my regular clubs wanted Thompson Video to do the TAB meetings. I was thankful to them for letting me know and incensed that the Gallops Racing Board had 'assumed' that I could not do the TAB meetings!

I responded decisively. I immediately phoned, and then sent a letter to the Gallops Racing Board, writing something like: 'how can you say that I can't do a TAB meeting? Nobody has even asked me for the 'Bods'! Of course, I can do it! I can do anything that any club wants!' I sent a letter out to all of my clubs, telling them I could do the TAB meetings – I had the 'Bods'. All agreed that if I had the 'Bods' I could do the meetings.

At this point, I didn't have the 'Bods' but set about locating this very specific, and unique equipment. A competitor had made his own 'Bods' based on the original inventor – a Sydney company. I contacted the owner of the Company in Sydney who was still livid with my competitor who he said, had 'stolen his idea' – his patent. He immediately wanted to help me beat my competitor. This was a good situation to be in. Normally, in the industry I was in I had my back up against the wall, but here was someone willing to help me. He said: 'No worries mate. I'll give them to you at a good price. You can have the 'Bods' for $2,000 each. They're usually dearer, but you can have them for that price'. I bought three 'Bods' and gained the TAB meetings.

However, the most stressful and challenging meetings were those relating to the TAB, as there were large amounts of money at stake. If the 'Tote' link/feed was disrupted for any reason, betting ceased by the professional punters on track. If it were determined to be Thompson Video's fault that the tote 'went down', heavy fines would result. Fortunately, this never happened, but there was one very tense time at Camperdown where neither the tote nor Sky Channel feed would work. Whose fault, was it? The Tote? Thompson Video? Sky Channel? We all worked under a very heavy 'black cloud' that day. After the day was over, it was determined that it was not Thompson Video's fault. The relief to Dianne and I was immense.

We had some good times at Thompson Video. We had a Christmas party at the Golden Point Club Hotel one year, and other years I bought take-away and beer for the party held at the premises. Once a fortnight we had a staff meeting in the conference room and had pizzas afterwards.

One day a couple of staff members said to me quietly after a staff meeting: 'we won't work with 'X'. We don't want to go to the races with him.' I said, 'why not?' 'We just don't want to go with him' was the reply. But when pressured they told me. One person was skimming cash derived from dubs on the day. Easily done – no receipt was provided to the punter or owner and the cash tally at the end of the day matched the receipts given. This staff member had been going to the different race meetings long enough to know what the approximate number of dubs were for the day, and the associated cash received. He only skimmed what he thought would not be queried. The fellows just wouldn't work with him because they were honest. Without any real evidence, I approached 'X' and simply said: I cannot employ you anymore – for some reason, none of the staff will work with you'.

I had another person who worked for me – nice, pleasant chap, but 'light fingered' in relation to equipment. After he left Thompson Video and went to a competitor in Melbourne, I was contacted for a reference for him. I said: 'pleasant, good worker, good skills, but everything around him should be screwed down'. He got the job, but my competitor knew what I meant, and how to handle the situation.

Another, with a full security clearance entered and left the premises at odd times, as reflected in the official security log. Sometimes he would be in the premises up to 2 hours or more. Why? I knew that private dubs of the race meetings were being done for racing mates. This I tolerated as the benefits this person brought to the business far outweighed his misdemeanour.

But there was one instance in which I strongly reacted. It was a lovely summer day and I had brought our barbeque from home to have a BBQ after the normal staff meeting, for a treat. We were halfway through the staff meeting and could smell the steak and sausages cooking on out the back ready for when the meeting finished. Then, a part time staff member said: 'By the way, we've got a union rep coming after this meeting. You're not allowed to attend because you're the boss. It's just for the workers.'

I was incensed. I left the meeting, picked up the hot BBQ with the meat still on it and put it in the back of the van ready to drive to the lake to sit for a while.

Just then, the staff member who told me about the union visit came out of the meeting and said: 'mmm...something smells nice.' I said, 'you're joking mate... if you're going to pull those stunts on me and pull the unions in, you're definitely not going to have any treats.' The union meeting was held – apparently, and nothing more was said. The staff member left soon after. My family ate cold sausages that night.

I always had tea, coffee, and biscuits on hand for staff every day. I even filled the biscuit tin up with chocolate biscuits. Mostly people treated me right, and I them. It was about trust. But the culture of the organisation was changing, as is normal when expanding.

In the very serious environment of the horse racing industry, there were some 'blips' and light-hearted moments. But it was only after the long day was over that you could share the relief and have a bit of a laugh. One instance is memorable and went like this: The horses had crossed the finish post at Warracknabeal. The winner could not be announced until after the jockey was 'weighed in' and any interference ruled out by the Stewards. Dianne gave me the recorded 'Stewards' tape, and I walked to the Stewards Room and handed it to the Head Steward. 'Job done', I thought.

Not long after, I was summoned to the Stewards Room. I thought: 'Oh god'... I wonder what the problem is.' I went inside and saw the jockey who was under scrutiny for his ride in the last race sitting on the seat opposite the Stewards. He had a big smile on his face, and I thought – strange...I don't think I'd be smiling in his position. In contrast the faces of the 'bank' of Stewards were very serious indeed.

The Head Steward looked at me intently and said sternly: 'Mr Thompson. How can we conduct a serious investigation when *this* is shown at the end of the race?' With that statement, he pressed the play button on the cued recorder. Vision appeared on the screen. To my immense surprise, and horror, what did I see? I saw a naked woman with her legs in stirrups, in the final graphic stages of childbirth!!! And so did the Stewards, and the smiling jockey!

Acutely embarrassed, I spluttered a profuse apology and confirmed with them that this would never happen again and quickly retreated. But how had it happened?

Tony, my brother, and a doctor had given me some 30-minute tapes that he no longer wanted. I had not asked if there was anything on them or indeed if there was anything at all. I just thought that the tapes are a perfect length for each race and could be used as stewards' tapes – that is, tapes that can be recorded repeatedly! After the day was over, I could see the funny side and Dianne, a midwife, took all the tapes to her work. I never wanted to see them again!

Punters bet in thousands of dollars and were well looked after by the racing clubs. They were encouraged to attend the racetracks by special incentives including the use of a private room, provision of free food and beer and wagered their bets at a designated tote window. The tools of their trade to choose winners included copies of our video footage of every race at every meeting we filmed. There were six professional punters we dealt with and we priority dubbed and couriered the tapes to them the day after each race meeting. The dubbing room was extremely busy.

The racing industry is tough, and one that seems to be able to make or break people. The word around the track was that a well-known professional punter was 'cleaned out' during a weekend of race meetings. He had bet big and subsequently lost – not at the racetrack, but in a card game in a local hotel where he and others were staying during the Cup Meeting.

Another time, a discrepancy occurred between a punter and Thompson Video. The professional punter a long-standing client of ours always paid his account on time. Then, his bill mounted and mounted. It got to a certain point that we needed to ask for payment on the amount owing from previous months. We advised that we could not send any future tapes to him until the invoice was paid. These tapes were his 'lifeblood', without them he could not punt successfully. After receiving the final demand, he contacted me claiming that the $2,500 outstanding had been paid, in cash at the Thompson Video van, a few weeks earlier. We had no record of such a payment, and he could not remember which race meeting he had paid the cash, nor the staff member it was paid to. All my racing staff stated that none of them had received this substantial amount.

A few phone calls between us followed trying to sort out the discrepancy. If he was correct, I needed to write off his amount owing. But there was no way of proving what had happened. Then, a phone conversation with me, and then Sophie who worked part time in the business, whilst studying at University made me act quickly and decisively. The Punter said something like: I'm having family problems, and this is sending me over the edge'. 'I paid the money to Thompson Video; I've got nothing to lose. If you don't credit me and send me tapes, I will come and get you… I know where you live.' This latter statement was chilling. Sophie was physically upset when she told me. I immediately phoned the Punter and said the amount would be written off if he supplied a statutory declaration. He did, and we wrote off the debt and continued to supply him tapes, on a month-to-month payment plan.

After this, we advised Punters we would not be accepting cash from them at the races. They needed to pay on invoice, directly to the business. We also changed the way we receipted and stored cash at the premises. It went from initially placing the takings in an envelope with the receipt book and reconciliation form and left in the dubbing room in the early days, to placing the cash with the receipt book, reconciliation and evaluation form in the strong box that was bolted to the desk in the dubbing room.

Sometimes, things just 'fall into your lap'. Sometimes. Not very often. But the harness racing contract did fall into our lap. But we had to fight to retain it.

It was 1993 and four o'clock on a Friday afternoon. I was dubbing gallops meetings for regular punters in my edit suite in Lydiard Street. Dianne was at work and the children were at after school sport. Muffy was keeping 'guard' outside. The phone rang, and I answered. It was the Harness Racing Board [HRB]. The conversation went something like this: 'we have just had a disagreement with our on-course video contractor. We want you to do four race meetings in your district until the contract expires. New tenders will be requested after this time. Can you do that?' I immediately replied, 'Yes'. Then, 'Could you start next week?' I replied, 'Yes, I could'. Then, 'we'll do a contract – let us know your prices.' It really was that quick!

Without any effort we had secured a lucrative contract for the next few months! This contract would have widespread commitments and financial ramifications. Our meetings would increase by 25% and as some harness meetings conflicted with gallops meetings, particularly in the spring racing season we would need to buy a further van and fit it out with the edit module and extra equipment. We could then manage 3 race meetings on one day. On the days that there were 4 race meetings scheduled, I hired an extra van and TVs, placed the spare edit module and equipment in it, and wired it up. Any picnic meeting that clashed with the 4 meetings on one day I used our car with a trailer that was fitted out the same way. I could now offer my best men full time work and retain them. Each would have responsibility for a race or harness meeting.

I had jumped at the chance, but we needed to seek accounting and business advice to ensure the fees charged were realistic. There were several factors to consider. Given the contract was for less than a year at this stage, and we had to gear up considerably to meet the requirements [vans, cameras, recorders, and staff], we were advised on a fee to charge which to us seemed way over the top. But the HRB did not hesitate – they agreed to the price!

Dianne and I were over the moon and we celebrated! How? We went out to lunch a few times per week, when the children were at school. We had never done this before, but we both remember this small window period as 'the good times'.

We provided the on-course video as required and were invited to submit a tender for the next 3 years. Once we had it, we did not want to let it go. We knew the HRB 'normal contractor' would be gearing up to get it back after losing the contract to us for the past few months.

We submitted a tender for the next 3 years for our 4 local harness racing clubs and waited. The fee we charged was not as lucrative this time around – there was competition, and we already had the equipment. We waited, holding our breath. Luckily, we were successful, and the years of the contract went quickly. During this time there was pressure from the bank to reduce our overdraft. We determined to sell our house to access the considerable equity and move further out to where we would one day retire. Eventually, we found just the house, in Black Hill, with a beautiful view. We set about putting our touch on it and made it a very comfortable house.

Towards the end of this HRB contract we were invited to submit a tender for the next 3 years. We had done well in the previous years and felt confident that we would gain the contract again, in our area. But when we read the Tender, we had considerable doubts. The requirements for the tender were different from the previous one. This time there were only two discrete tender opportunities. One for Melbourne, which had the most frequent harness race meetings, and one for the rest of Victoria. The tender demanded that the on-course video provider tender for the whole state of Victoria, except for Melbourne. There was no opportunity to tender for segments of Victoria, as was the case previously. It was obvious that the HRB wanted to work with 2 on course video providers and not 4 as they had previously. This meant that two contractors would be unsuccessful. Who would they be? We determined it would not, could not be Thompson Video who was unsuccessful.

Dianne and I drove to Melbourne and I attended a meeting at the HRB to discuss the tender. I had heard that the HRB were requesting the provision of a free tape and dub to the winners of each race. My understanding was that my competitors had already complained to the HRB about this aspect of a free dub, given that it was not specifically in the Tender, and the fact that the 'cream' was in the dubbing revenue. My competitors had apparently bound together and told the HRB: No way, we are not going to give free dubs.

My competitors had not approached me – I'm glad of that. I was viewed as a 'clean skin'. To me, it was obvious. If you did not submit to this one request from the Head of the HRB, you were not going to be successful in the tender. It was worth the trip to Melbourne to confirm with them that I agreed with their request. However, giving an owner a free copy of a race meeting means that you're giving it to about 20 other people because the owner, naturally, will copy it for all the other people in the syndicate of the horse. So, the on-course video contractor is going to lose out on dubs – big time. But I knew that without resolving this point in favour of what the HRB wanted the day would not be successful.

The meeting went something like this:

HRB: 'First thing we've got to talk about is… I want a free copy of each race to go to the winner. Are you prepared to do that?

Me: Yes… I can't see any problems in that. We'll give them a free copy of the race meeting – any stipulation of what and how and when?

HRB: No, no. We don't care – as long as they have a free VHS tape of the race.

Me: Okay. We'll give them a free tape from the start of the race to the finish of the race. All right? Right.

HRB: You know you're up against big odds. There's Pro Video, Sports Cover and you've got Purcell – he's throwing his hat in the ring as well. You might not be lucky. So, you just have to wait and see.

Me: That's fine. I'll submit quotations in three.

We went back to our accountant who knew our situation and worked with us on tenders before. He was very familiar with large tenders. Brainstorming commenced, and we worked feverishly. We needed to win the tender – it was our life-blood – we couldn't lose it. We had normal family commitments and leases to pay off.

The tender was very tight with not much 'fat' in it. Each aspect was examined in detail. It had to be. The only time the contract would vary would be in the case of increase in wages – based on official employment pay rates. Rise in petrol costs would need to be absorbed by the on-course video provider. We knew we had to be competitive. But we also knew in all honesty that we could not be due to the equipment they were requesting – specific high-grade professional equipment, and the amount we would need to purchase to provide a service to all of Victoria [apart from Melbourne]. But the free ten-minute tape in a no frills brown envelope for each winner of a harness race was not a problem. It was factored into the cost of the HRB meeting.

The Tender was prepared. We reviewed it and were not happy with the amount the HRB would need to be charged. We felt it was too high and would automatically exclude us from being successful. And yet, what good is it submitting a tender that would see us go out of business? We needed to rethink, as the cost of equipment and the amount we would be required to purchase to meet the obligations right across Victoria was such that we knew we would not get a loan from the bank to purchase it. The cost came to thousands and thousands of dollars. We determined that even if we were successful, we knew we would not get a loan for the hundreds of thousands of dollars required to gear up. We also didn't know if we wanted to be in so much debt.

Dianne and I looked at each other and agreed: 'we have no option than to try'. But we needed a new strategy. I was convinced that there was a cheaper way that would deliver the same professional outcome. The HRB just had to be convinced. But I also knew you should not vary from what is listed in the tender.

I decided to put in two tenders: One that met all of the HRB criteria that contained extremely expensive equipment and resulted in a huge cost to the HRB; and the other that met all of the HRB criteria, but replaced the extremely expensive equipment with a new format that gave the same outcome based on audio-visual industry approval and backed up by research. I hand delivered the 2 different Tender responses to the HRB and waited. It was a very tense time.

We were successful! The tender based on the less expensive equipment was successful! I was elated that the strategy had worked, but our competitors were livid to say the least! My main competitor strongly appealed the decision, as the quote did not meet the required elements of the Tender! It was a tense time. First, I was told I was successful then I was summoned to the HRB to fight for the business!

The HRB Committee, my competitor and myself sat around the conference table and argued our cases. I had to defend the equipment I had listed in the second tender and my ability to offer the service to all the State. I exuded confidence, knew the equipment intimately and could quote industry research, had a demonstrated excellent trackrecord and a professional and loyal team to deliver the service. I drove back to Ballarat on tender hooks and waited.

The re-awarding of the contract to Thompson Video Pty Ltd was confirmed! But now the real fight began. I did not have access to the funds required to meet the equipment contract obligations. And I wasn't sure if our bank would come to the party and provide the funds in these times.

When your back is against the wall it is time to come out fighting! We had a substantial and secure contract from the HRB and detailed analysis of income and outgoings surrounding this contract. But it was not easy to get the loan required to service the contract we had just secured! I had to do a lot of fast-talking to gain a loan to purchase the 'not so expensive equipment' that was, still incredibly expensive.

We visited our business bank manager, who unfortunately had a 'nervous twitch' at any time. I said: 'Come on, I'll take you out to lunch and we can talk about it… there's no risk at all – the monies in the bank – a secure contract from the HRB. Plus, we haven't factored in the amount we'll get from dubs that we're going to get which might be $500 or $600 each race meeting. After considerable effort, the bank manager recommended our application to head office for approval. It was a tense few days. Finally, the loan was approved.

We successfully managed commitments to the gallops, harness, and other contracts. The business thrived, and life was good for some time – until changes in the industries we serviced impacted.

The Gallops industry was changing. Instead of individual clubs retaining on course video providers, Head Office was to be in control. And they were to follow the same structure and processes that the HRB had implemented. This meant less security for Thompson Video.

The HRB also was implementing wide sweeping changes. The tender process was delayed, the contract expired, and we were retained on-a monthly basis, for a slightly increased fee. This situation went on for several months, and we knew that changes were coming.

We *really* needed one more contract to enable us to finish the leases we had and make some money to sustain us over the next few years. We continued our obligations as we had no other option, but as time went on, we were not confident that we would be awarded the contract next time around. We projected that the end may be in sight for a significant component of our business and started to plan for this. But we did not for-see what the impetus to the end of Thompson Video in its current form would be.

It was August 1997 – just before spring and when the race meetings started in earnest. I was busy at the racetrack setting up for a very large race meeting. I was setting up power and coax to the televisions for patrons to view the races from their special advantage point – in tents in the *middle* of the racetrack. Rushing across the 'straight' of the track, my foot sunk into a hole covered by grass – I presume that of a hoof print. I felt an incredible pain in my knee at the time but continued with the priority – setting up. I 'soldiered on', hobbling around the racetrack, until the meeting finished. But my knee was very sore and got worse and worse over the day. By the time I drove home, I could not put any weight on my leg, and needed to hang onto furniture to move around. I thought I had just twisted my knee, and all would be well. But it wasn't.

The point is with a job, you have to be able to do everything that you ask your employees to do. That's very important because once staff see there's a weak link and you can't do it, they don't respect you anymore. At least that is my opinion and that is how I worked and built the business. And I guess when they see a weakness at the top they fear for their future.

'Managing people and situations is very hard unless you can sort of wield the pick at the same time they can'. Once I asked an employee to dig a trench to put a cable in because we were running coax for a satellite dish. He had the pick and tried, then told me: 'it won't work. It keeps bouncing off the soil'. Frustrated I said: 'give me the pick!' I swung the pick with gusto and managed to dig the trench. I said: 'that's how you do it!' Another time an employee was rolling up the coax onto the reels at the end of the racing day. He was going so, so slowly. I thought if he doesn't go any quicker, we won't finish until midnight and then we have to drive four hours! I said: 'give it here. This is how you do it'! I rolled the coax up in record time. I even got blisters on my fingers doing it! But I never let him know ... I'd made my point!

I couldn't sleep with the pain and worry about the situation that was becoming more obvious to me every day. I sat on the edge of the bed and thought. I knew that everything was ending. I had been going to the race meetings hobbling and using a walking stick. I thought my knee would not get better before the next big race meeting. It didn't, and with that one life changing incident and the changes coming to both the gallops and harness industry, spelt the end of Thompson Video Pty Ltd.

I could not guarantee all staff the employment they were used to. With sad recognition I turned to Dianne and said: 'I just can't keep going, dear'. I have to tell the HRB'. Dianne was not surprised at my comment. She fully knew the situation and what was to be done. She just typed the letter to the HRB explaining the situation. And that was it.

We always knew that the business was 'for now'. It would not continue in its present form. Therefore, we never wanted the children to become part of the business or encouraged them to do so. A life on short-term contracts, in a very hard and dynamic industry, utilising expensive and sensitive equipment is difficult, and would always be so. However, we had hoped for one more contract to build for our future. But the best laid plans....

We were in shock and grieved for our loss of livelihood and the impact of the injury on my ability to work as I had always done. What did the future hold?

I had a substantial injury to be resolved. We had two children at university and one due to start the final year of secondary school. We had another three years to go on our lease of the premises and one year left on our lease for the equipment.

Life as we knew it, quickly unravelled.

Chapter 33
Clawing Back

In 1997, at the age of fifty-five I was disabled, heavily in debt, and facing a very uncertain future. Dianne and I started the long process of clawing back, what we could salvage, to survive.

Over the next few years, we would face many challenges with the business and our personal lives. Our parents would pass away – Mother – 26/9/2003 and Dianne's parents Keith – 21/1/2007 and Thelma 7/10/2011. All are buried at Natte Yallock, along with Father who died on 6/9/1982. But there were moments of great joy and sense of achievement also. Our children graduated from University and set off to explore their chosen paths, and later marry Sophie and John (2005) Benjamin and Jayne (2008) and Matthew and Zara (2014). Grandchildren followed. But all of this was in the future – well into the unknown future. For now, survival was paramount.

I needed to find work, but what sort? I approached a Melbourne production company that did on course video. I had thought about applying to them almost 17 years earlier, when we lived in Melbourne. The owner was very supportive when I met him, but when I tried to walk up the stairs at his premises, it became evident to both of us, that the thought was ludicrous. The injury to my knee prevented working in any job that required even the slightest physical effort. And dyslexia prevented me from pursuing any other sort of job in the industry I had made mine.

My livelihood had gone – disappeared in an instant. I was redundant and mourned the loss. We sought legal assistance – could I 'pursue' the club for an unsafe working environment? No was the answer – the government of the day had removed this option. Years later, the option was returned by a different government, but I was prohibited, as the retrospectivity ended two years after I had injured my knee. We were on our own, but after 2 years, I did receive some worker's compensation in the form of a small weekly wage.

At the time, we responded to our situation hastily, and on reflection, not wisely. But hindsight is a wonderful thing. At the time, the imperative was to survive – day by day. We sold our house in a relatively exclusive and secluded part of Ballarat and bought a small two-bedroom cottage near the business premises enabling me to continue at home, some aspects of the business such as copying videos and format conversions. The imperative was to meet our financial obligations that were substantial. There was never any question of choosing the bankruptcy route. This, we believed was not right, and certainly not a fair option to our creditors. We fought on, and the bank supported us, 'providing an umbrella, when it was pouring with rain'.

We approached the owner of the business premises requesting a release from the 3 years left on the existing lease. He refused, stating: *'business is business.'* He kept this hard-line approach despite the obvious state I was in, and the number of approaches I made requesting release. When the lease finally expired, he sent a thank you card to me, stating I was: 'an honourable gentleman, and one he respected.' I cannot say that I appreciated these words at the time, or even later, as the trauma had been too great.

During the 3 years of the remaining lease, we sub-let one side of the premises, and sold the professional equipment we could. We stored the excess business documents and tapes at the properties of my brother in laws, who helped us during this time. It was seven years later that we finally went through and sorted the tapes, and documents. I felt like I was foraging through a loved one's belongings, long after their death.

I offered the large library of professional video footage of commercial business, government organisations and the races to the respective parties. There was absolutely no interest in this historical or copyrighted footage. Many years later, the Harness Racing Board contacted me wanting the harness footage, but by then, the tapes had been recycled, and sold. My professional tapes were copyrighted and could not be sold. They ended up in a big hole on a farm, alongside dead cattle, and then covered with earth. It was torture.

We met our obligations. But it was at a very great personal, and financial cost. Envelopes with a clear window at the front, arriving in the post, indicating a bill to pay, sent me into an uncontrollable sweat. Each month, I ticked of the amount I paid to our creditors. The list of names, and the amount owing, gradually reduced. I still cannot bear this type of envelope arriving in the mail.

For two years after the accident, I struggled to walk, and needed a walking stick. Finally, I consulted with a well-known, and respected orthopaedic surgeon who told me bluntly that I had severe arthritis all over my body and needed a full knee replacement. He explained in graphic detail 'I'll chop it off and throw the old knee away and put a new alloy one in!' I was shocked: 'no way' I said, I'm not going to have that'. I reacted strongly as his method was so drastic and I could visualise exactly what he explained. I had previously filmed a knee replacement at St John of God Hospital and the memory of what I saw, and heard on that day, came flashing back. I decided to get a second opinion.

This time the response of the surgeon was palatable: 'yes, you are too young to have a knee replacement. If you do, you will probably need at least another two in your lifetime. But by then, there will not be enough bone left, to do a replacement. So, I suggest you have a 'clean out of the area', and some injections – a new method to help the cartilage grow back. You can only have three of these injections, after which time it becomes dangerous – you may have a reaction.'

I had the three painful injections and waited. The knee became worse. The surgeon said: 'Hmm, the treatment hasn't worked. I can do a partial knee replacement – just replace the side of the bone that is the worst – not the full top of the bone.' I had this painful operation – the top of the bone on the worst effected side was sawn off and replaced. Constant rehabilitation followed. I was advised that if I looked after my knee – not stress or strain it, the replacement would last several years.

But, despite looking after the knee – no jumping, no carrying heavy weights, within eighteen months, I was in trouble again. The arthritis in the other side of the knee bone had worsened. As I was placing a lot of pressure on the 'relatively good knee', to protect the other, it was also showing signs of extreme stress.

I was in a real 'pickle'. 'Eating humble pie', I returned to the orthopaedic surgeon I visited initially, who greeted me saying: 'I knew you would be back – as I said, you need a full knee replacement. Without it, your other knee will need to be replaced shortly.'

I had a second painful knee replacement, but immediately got a blood clot in the leg operated on and it could not be manipulated in case the blood clot moved. As such, the crucial period for moving the knee enabling the best outcome was lost. I ended up not able to bend my knee very well. The physio said: 'the muscles have set and you're never really going to get proper movement in it unless you go back into hospital again and under anaesthetic, the knee worked to 'break' all the scar tissue and then the physio will work.' I was told I would not be able to kneel ever again, but I went to the hydrotherapy pool every day, and 'sank' down to the bottom, and rested on my bent knee. I put in the 'hard yards', and happily, I've got 95% movement in my knee. But this was not the end of the saga.

Some years later, the metal shaft threatened to protrude through the bone and pierce the skin. The knee was replaced for the third time, with a very large and long shaft. Then a warning – it could not be replaced again. Before this operation, both shoulders were repaired, and a hip replaced.

I enjoyed the very hard physical work that I did in my young life and when working around Australia. But it was at a time that the words: work, place, and safety, were not joined together! Workplace safety was not spoken about – work was work, and no precautions taken. This, coupled with severe arthritis, has significantly impacted on my wellbeing in later life. It is not evident that I am being held together with cement, metal screws and metal shafts, except when I go through security to board a plane. I beep with gusto!

After the demise of Thompson Video and my accident, I still wanted to work. My dilemma was that physically I could not manage labouring work and I did not have the skills required to work in an environment that required good written communication. What could I do? My thoughts returned to what I knew I could do, and do well: that is, converse with people from all 'walks' of life and cultures.

I applied to be a 'doorman' at a large Hotel in Melbourne; but did not hear back from them. As Christmas was approaching, I decided to have the first knee operation that I had been putting off. This way, most of the rehabilitation could be completed over the long holiday period, and I would not have an obvious limp and could discard the walking stick.

There are some funny moments in my life that stand out. One relates to taking a phone call I received immediately after returning to my hospital bed from the operating theatre after having the knee replacement. I was very uncomfortable and a bit fuzzy from the anaesthetic, and heavily under the influence of the *lovely* Morphine! Dianne was giving me ice to suck and answered my mobile phone when it rang. It was the Manager of a Hotel in Melbourne, and he 'wanted to speak with Christopher Thompson'. Calmly she said: 'One moment please....' She frantically put another pillow under my head to raise me a little and handed me the phone. I mustered up an act that I am proud of to this day: 'Yes, I am still interested in the position of doorman, and yes, I am able to come for an interview. But I am taking a planned holiday… I could see you in say, 2 weeks-time, is that ok?' It was – I was to contact them again 'when I returned'.

I went for an interview and got the job. Then, the hard part began. I had to demonstrate my ability to do the job. Another new employee, a young girl, discretely helped me fill in the form, and then I joined a 'team working' activity – but really, it was a test of your physical status in the pretence of teamwork bending, lifting and the like. Luckily, I had dosed myself up on painkillers before I went in, but it was still a very painful experience. I waited, then, the phone call came…I was successful! I had met the physical! Now, the next hurdle – I had the job, but where was I to live?

Dianne and I arrived at 6am in Melbourne on the following Saturday morning and parked around Albert Park Lake. We scanned *The Age* newspaper we'd bought on the way, for suitable rental properties. We targeted a 'bedsit' near King Street and a tram ride away from the hotel. We drove into the CBD early, spoke with the agent and put in a completed application, then viewed the bedsit along with a few other people. We waited. On the same day, I was contacted. The dark and dingy bedsit was mine! I would share it with numerous resident cockroaches.

I crossed my fingers that my knee would hold up to all the standing required for the job and signed a short-term lease. If I liked the job, we would move to Melbourne. So, a mere six weeks after my operation, I started full time work at the Swanston Street Hotel – 2 x 4 hour shifts per day early in the morning and then late afternoon into the evening, during the week.

I was happy there – I liked the people I worked with and the environment, and one month, I was nominated by clients as the most outstanding employee. I was also commended on my demeanour and common sense when the Hotel received a bomb threat, and clients needed to be evacuated. I remained at the entrance, calmly advising people they could not come into the Hotel at this stage – it was closed for the time being. But one woman persisted: 'why can't I go in… I'm paying good money for my room'! I could see that my restrained approach was not working so I bent forward, lowered my voice and quietly and firmly said to her: 'Madam, a bomb is due to go off in 3 minutes!' She did not retaliate this time, but rather, took off up the street as fast as her legs could take her!

But the constant standing seriously affected my knee and leg. After each shift ended, I would return to my bedsit and put ice packs on my knee to reduce the swelling and pain. At weekends I returned to Ballarat, my leg enormously swollen and painful – the healed but red and angry suture line almost ready to burst. The weekends went so fast. A lot of the time was spent buying what might be more comfortable shoes to assist with standing, and a better pressure bandage than I had used the previous week to stop the swelling! But one weekend was different.

Our modest home was slowly being renovated. There was a wall that needed removing, and we had been advised that it was not a 'load-bearing wall'. One weekend, after a steak and a bottle of red wine, I knew I could do anything! Without a moment's thought, I grabbed the sledgehammer and swung like fury. The wall came down – horsehair plaster and all, and the room was opened. It's surprising what a glass of red wine will do!

During the week that followed, I received a phone call from Dianne who said the inside roof where the wall had been removed looked to be 'dipping' and was concerned. I told her to phone the builder, who came immediately, and put an emergency beam in the roof. It was then it was realized that a very large hot water tank was positioned in the roof and was being supported by the so-called 'non-load-bearing wall'!

Each Sunday night I boarded the train with my trolley of groceries and returned to my bedsit thinking: 'this week will be better…It has to be.' It never was. Reluctantly I accepted reality and resigned. But the Hotel wouldn't accept my resignation and offered me more money to stay – the first time ever I had been offered more money to stay, anywhere! I really wanted to stay, and under different circumstances I would have.

I could not tell the Hotel I was leaving due to my knee. Instead, I told them that I needed to return to Ballarat to care for a family member who was unwell. This was true. My Mother was becoming very frail, and I am grateful for the time I could spend with her.

I returned to Ballarat. I volunteered at Sovereign Hill as a concierge. I became involved in Community TV as a program manager. I supplied Peter, who leased a channel from Neighbourhood Cable with some programs that Thompson Video and Action Channel had recorded, plus obtained films to transfer onto computer, from the film archives in Melbourne. And I produced and filmed the show *'Out and About'* – sometimes with the assistance of Benjamin and Matthew when they were around.

Colin and Lyn were friends of ours and they had given us enormous support during the demise of Thompson Video. Years later, Colin and I decided to film a cooking show at their house for community TV. Colin emigrated from England many years previously after resigning from the army. He developed a hardware business before retiring in Creswick and marrying Lyn. He was witty and had a good persona on camera. I recorded Colin cooking the meal – a glass of wine in hand, lots of idle 'banter' and then we would all enjoy eating the meal afterwards. It was a fun show and enjoyable to film and aired frequently on community television.

At this time, I joined the local library. Yes, me, entering the doors of a regular library! I had discovered audio books and became an avid listener. They are part of my day, and night. I always have an audio book on the go – it transports me to different places and times and assists me with debilitating tinnitus. My taste of books extends to many genres, but I have developed a liking for the writing style of authors Bryce Courtney and Geoffrey Archer. I prefer English and Irish accents, and stories that are well read, and go into detail, enabling my imagination to flow, and visualise the stories being told.

In the early days, I transferred the basic audio books from the library onto portable CDs to listen. With smart phones, I download directly from audible, increasing the selection of books I could 'read'. Audio has always been a constant in my life, and would continue to be, influencing me in years to come, in telling my own story. But this is well into the future. For now, I was restless and started thinking about what to do next.

Dianne and I discussed what we saw as our future. Our children were now fully supporting themselves. We thought there was a 'small window period' in our lives to do as we pleased, before the next stage of our lives unfolded. This stage would probably include– children marrying, the arrival of grandchildren, and the need to be close to ageing parents.

I am nearly 10 years older than Dianne, who had a very good and interesting position at University that she enjoyed. She often travelled overseas with her work, and I sometimes joined her in Hong Kong. I also visited our children in England, Canada, and China when they were working there. But I could not continue to do this routinely. What then, was *my* future? I felt I had not finished my working life, but there was not a lot of opportunities for me in my current environment. It was a dilemma.

It was a comment from Dianne that persuaded me what I could do. She simply said: 'if I were in your position, I would pursue every avenue, and take every opportunity available. Why not? Life is short. We are at different stages in our life, and I am happy doing what I am doing – you should have that choice too.' She encouraged me to seek what I was looking for. I did, and over the next few years had a few interesting jobs and experiences.

I prepared myself by going to BRACE – an adult education centre for short courses. It was not easy. Entering the building was a really, really, hard decision. If I did not want to change my life so badly, I would not have entered. But, once I was inside, I found things had changed over the years, and there was much assistance, and ways to prove you knew things. I didn't tell my teacher my situation; she found out anyway. When I told Dianne that I had to write an exam in class, she phoned BRACE unbeknown to me and spoke to my teacher who said: 'His verbal responses to questions in class are excellent – it is obvious 'he knows his stuff', but I must admit, I could not understand the writing he submitted.' Anyhow, I ended up with being assessed verbally and became competent in food preparation and tending a bar.

I determined I would look to England for work. I searched the Internet and found my way to the website of Moggerhanger Christian Conference Centre, eight miles outside Bedford, England. They were advertising for volunteers – that is, no pay, but accommodation was provided. We sent them an email. They replied – they were happy for me to stay with them and contribute. Perfect I thought.

I arrived in England during winter. Moggerhanger Christian Conference Centre [now Moggerhanger Park] was a grade 1 listed Georgian Historical house building set in beautiful surroundings and was being renovated as a conference centre with accommodation. The house was set in 33 acres of lawns, and a walled garden, underground ice chest and woodland at the rear of the house building with lots of bluebells growing. There was a functioning kitchen and tearooms and a souvenir shop.

I worked in the kitchen with Jim the head chef, making baguettes, bread and butter pudding, and prepared the cakes for afternoon tea. Jim told me that I was too generous when slicing the cakes into portions, and in the fillings of the sandwiches. But the customers loved them! Jim was a nice fellow and said to me, 'you can't keep working for nothing. I don't think it's right. I'm going to tell them they have to pay you something.' So eventually they did pay me a small amount.

I lived in a Gatehouse, a shared house at the entrance to Moggerhanger. Alex, who lived in Birmingham, was another volunteer who came periodically and shared the house with me. He had obvious problems that apparently commenced after he had been stabbed and had not fully recovered, mentally. We each did our own shopping and cooking, but I did not shop much as I had plenty to eat in the kitchen during the day. But often I would return to the Gatehouse in the evening after completing my shift in the restaurant and find strangers there – volunteers who had come to stay for a couple of days. On these days, it was incumbent on me to provide them with food – my food.

My thoughts went back to my roaming days and I automatically fitted in with where I was, and what was expected in the environment I found myself in. I attended the regular prayer sessions and other activities at the Centre. Praying was constant, and the answer to both small and large challenges. Once, Jim was not sure what to cook for Sunday lunch. Should he cook pork or roast beef? We all held hands and prayed for guidance. It was a serious occasion. In any case the answer must have come through because Sunday lunch was roast beef! After a long six months I returned to Ballarat and continued with community television.

In early 2006, Dianne and I returned to Moggerhanger. Dianne took long service leave to attend Bournemouth University, to gain registration as a nurse in England. Our intention was to stay there for around 8 months, and on return, we would make our home in Melbourne, and Dianne would travel to Ballarat to continue her position at University. I worked in the kitchen, and as a security guard – opening and closing the entrance gates, as security had increased since I last visited. We lived in the Gatehouse, under the same system as my previous visit. That is, people would come and go, and you were never sure who was living there, and who wasn't.

Soon after we arrived at Moggerhanger, Prince Charles visited, with his entourage to encourage and view the progress of restoration of the building. I was the designated official photographer for the occasion and was told that I was not to talk to him unless he spoke to me, which he never did. Moggerhanger extensively distributed the photos I took of the day.

Dianne loved England, but was extremely uncomfortable with the living arrangements, and some other aspects at Moggerhanger. But, as she travelled to Bournemouth once a week, and stayed overnight, it was manageable, for a time. We fitted into the rural surroundings – we rode the bus and trains, shopped in the local market town, Bedford, went on the underground trains in London, and made some memories.

I started looking for paid work in hospitality. I boarded the train to Edinburgh early one morning, and attended an interview at a well-known Castle, next to where the Royal Edinburgh Tattoo is held. It was beautiful, and I could see us living in Edinburgh for a time. Dianne and I would be together, and she would nurse in Scotland as she dreamed about, many years previously. The interview went well, and proceeded to the 'showing around', of the restaurant. It was then, that reality set in. I had to negotiate the numerous stairs in the winding staircases. Everything needed to be carried up and down. It was obviously not a position I could manage. Disappointed, I got on the train, and returned to Moggerhanger.

When Dianne finished her course and applied to register as a nurse in the UK, we took a holiday of 2 weeks. We drove around Northern England tracing family histories and enjoyed the time together. On our way back to Moggerhanger, Dianne received a phone call saying her Father was very unwell, and in hospital in Ballarat. In this moment, Dianne decided to return to Australia, and left that night. I was responsible for security at Moggerhanger and could not leave without notice. I stayed for 3 days, then packed my case, and flew home to join Dianne, in Melbourne. We made our home in South Melbourne, and it was there we celebrated the birth of our first grandchild, born in 2006.

I returned to England later and boarded with Jean, an elderly churchgoing lady I had met at Moggerhanger previously. Jean lived in Biggleswade, a small village near Moggerhanger. At this time, I also travelled and visited relatives in England, and Scotland. I have not returned since this time, but 'hanker' to do so.

Benjamin, my son, was working around the Cairns area and knew I was looking for something to do and said to me: 'I'll pay all the expenses and you can sell heat packs at the Cairns market – we'll make a fortune!' Heat packs are plastic bags that have a mixture of compounds so that when you press the button inside, the liquid heats up. The packs are used for arthritic pain and this is a topic I know a lot about and experience it first-hand. I jumped at the chance, and Benjamin organised the lease and goods.

The next thing, I was in Cairns, working at 'Sun Pod' at the night market, selling heat packs. The demo heat packs were well used. Once the button inside the pack was pressed, the liquid became hot, and after a time, solidified. To set them again you had to boil them in hot water that liquefied the content and when cooled down, they were ready to be reset again. But the demo heat packs became more sensitive each time they were 'set off'. Eventually, it seemed that just looking at them would set off the process! It was very frustrating. I was there for about three months and really enjoyed it. *Sun pod* closed when Benjamin was transferred. I returned home, thinking of the next thing I could do.

I found an agent for acting as an extra. I had always been interested in films and movies and liked being in this environment and had acted in 'Around the Twist' when I lived in Ballarat. This time, I appeared in the series, 'Underbelly', 'City Homicide', 'Home and Away', and 'Knowing', a movie filmed in Melbourne starring Nicholas Cage. I also was an extra in some comedy shows for 'Mad Dog Productions'. I completed a Santa course, and liked doing this for the short time available. I was an excellent Santa!

So, what now? Working as an extra was interesting, and I loved the buzz and the interesting people I met and the equipment and environment. But it was spasmodic work and very time consuming for little rewards. Often you needed to bring to the set, several changes of clothes for the different scenes in the day 'shoot'. And some sets were a long way from where we lived, and transport was a problem.

But I like working.

Dianne suggested being a security officer after seeing an advertisement for a six-week course. I hesitated: 'I don't know. I'm not good at writing and spelling, and all that.' Dianne said: 'it doesn't matter these days. You just speak with your teacher like you did previously, and tell them you're having problems, and they'll help you. There's no stigma these days. Just go and give it a go… I will help you'.

I did the six-week course and passed, with much assistance and an oral exam, and received my Victorian Security Licence. Then, I got one of my favourite jobs ever – the security of the 'Spirit of Tasmania' – a car and people ferry, that docked at and departed from, the historical Station Pier, Melbourne, every day.

Many migrants had arrived at this pier in days gone by, and now I was working here. The work was mainly outside near the sea, and diverse in activities. Cars, caravans, trucks, and luggage were searched, looking for fruit, vegetables, contraband, guns, and stowaways. People and luggage were scanned, and sometimes the police called. It was a good job, and I was happy there.

I worked at Station Pier until I was 70, then Dianne and I went on a cruise. After this, we moved from South Melbourne to Ballarat to reduce the driving to University for Dianne. There we had more contact with Dianne's family and caught up with family, friends, and previous Thompson Video employees.

This move was short-lived – only one year, at which time we moved back to Melbourne for Dianne to take up a new position at Lawson College Australia. I also work one day per month at this same organisation when the Occupational English Test, is delivered. It is my social outlet, as well as work. It is a very multicultural environment on this day, and one where mostly young highly qualified people, who are desperate to achieve their potential and contribute to their adopted country, gather to sit the very important exam. Their enthusiasm and commitment amaze me.

***

My days of 'sir' have long gone. I am now in that period that comes to older people whether they like it or not. That is, being referred to on occasion as: 'luv' or 'darl' and 'grumpy gramps'. The latter reference I don't mind, it is from my grandchildren, and a form of endearment, and furthermore it is correct! The former – 'luv' and 'darl', I detest. It is demeaning, but I know that it is meant in misguided kindness.

I do reflect on times gone by, and the active life I led for so many years and the experiences I had in 'my time'.

I have noticed things about this time in my life. There are some benefits of ageing, like the time to reflect. But reflection also causes some consternation. I can see things clearly now about my past life – particularly in the early stages. If only….

But 'if only' thoughts are futile – they keep you tied to the distant past, and continually experiencing the past. The dreams I have are not happy ones. I am always stuck somewhere, in trouble, without money, looking for a job, or missing filming the start of a race. In my dreams, and in real life, I am, very critical of myself – in my character as a young man, and lost opportunities in my youth, teenage years, and early adult life.

I constantly think of where I can travel to where it is warm, and on a stringent budget. Why? Maybe I am trying to capture the freedom and adventure of my drifter years in Australia. But, after much thought, I concluded that I have both seen, and experienced, a lot of it in the space of my years. And, for this, I am grateful. Others have not been, nor will ever be, that lucky.

I am not social in my older years. I do not 'fit in' with the 'normal' older person, and their interests. In my waking hours I think of where I can get a job. Why? I am seventy-five-year-old. Prospects are gone. I hanker for what work gives you –purpose and contact with interesting people. But I would only want it, on my terms. I have done volunteer work in the past, but arthritis in my hands and shoulders prevented me from continuing.

I would like to live in a peaceful, quiet rural setting again, in a little cottage, with my Friesian cows grazing in the field. But then, I would not have the other environment I like: cinemas, lots of interesting shops, restaurants, trams, and trains at my doorstop!

I do live in comfort, amid my family. I live in a vibrant community with strong links to its media past, including television productions like 'Countdown'. I can be part of this environment and feel 'at home', but I do not have to be 'with' people unless I want to be. In fact, I have everything that I could ever want. I am lucky.

If a man is judged on his family, I have excelled. Our family is our pride, and joy. We are very lucky. We have a strong, and supportive, family unit. We have three caring children, [Sophie, Benjamin, and Matthew], a great son-in-law [John], two terrific daughters-in law, [Jayne and Zara], and seven beautiful grandchildren [Jack, Emily, Lucy, Maxwell, Oscar, Eleanor and Samuel].

Until now, my family have not known about this full and diverse account of my life. They had only heard some 'snippets' of my stories. I hope they continue to be generous in their understanding of my life, as written.

I hope my children's journey, my grandchildren, and their children's children, is a life that they choose, and excel in. I hope they have unswerving confidence in themselves, and abilities, and pursue their dreams without fear – no matter what, and no matter where, their dreams lead them. And I sincerely hope they remain positive, and resilient, no matter what life throws at them, during 'their time'.

Finally, I wish you green lights and blue skies, all the way.

Epilogue

'We don't stop playing because we grow old; we grow old because we stop playing.'

George Bernard Shaw

Instead of succumbing to what is expected and becoming 'invisible' as you do with age, I decided I would grasp life, and make something new with what I have.

But what do I have now?

I have always liked telling my stories, and those who heard them in the past, seemed to enjoy them, and have a laugh with me. Perhaps they were being polite – I don't know. But these stories are what I have, that is unique. So, in 2006, I seriously went back to the past – more than fifty years ago.

I listened to the young man talking on my reel-to-reel audiotapes recorded in England, and in Australia. I listened to him – but did not know him. He did not know who he was, or where he was going, from one day, to the next. Mostly, I did not like what I heard. If I could've talked to that young man, I heard speaking on the tapes after so long, I would've said harshly: 'get a life, be your own man, follow your dreams'! I felt I was listening to a stranger – someone else, not me. Perhaps we would all feel like this, if we had the opportunity to listen to our young self?

But I have mellowed since then. If I went back today and spoke with that insecure and lost youth in England, I would encourage him and say: 'Shake of the shackles, look to the horizon, and not the alternative'. But I am not sure he would listen to me. The quote of George Bernard Shaw rings true: 'Youth is wasted on the young'.

I went back to my past, to share my life stories – 'warts' and all in the time of now. I shared my stories with you, in new and exciting mediums – a blog, then Amazon and Audible. They are mediums to which I feel infinitely attuned.

Listening to my young self and recalling my past has not been easy. But there have been unexpected rewards in this journey.

Over 1.5 million people arrived in Australia during 1945 – 1975 as a *'10 Pound Pom.'* I was one of them.

There were many success stories and famous *10 Pound Poms*, who made contributions at the highest level to their adopted country, for example, Julia Gillard, ex-Prime Minister of Australia, music groups such as the Bee Gees, singer, Kylie Minogue, musician, Red Symons, and actor Noni Hazelhurst.

Along with many thousands of others, I have not achieved any such type of recognition in this country I call home. But in a very small way, recognition has come to me. And, when it did, it was a humbling and genuine surprise.

In September 2016, some years after working on my 'book', Dianne saw on the internet that the *Immigration Museum* in Victoria were looking for *10-pound Poms* to share their stories: *'Calling all Ten Pound Poms, Nest Eggs and British Migrants'*. There had been a surge of interest in the era of the *'10 Pound Pom'*, and the Museum was putting together an exhibition that would run for 2 years and visit every state of Australia.

I visited the Museum with the first few chapters of my book and some photos that had been posted on the blog. Staff at the Immigration Museum were polite, took the printout of the first few chapters, and recorded the 'Onemoretale.com' website details. I was told: 'They would be in contact if they were interested in my stories, after determining the focus of the Exhibition'. In July 2017, the call came from Sophie, the Curator. I was selected to be part of the British Migrant Exhibition, as 'Adventurer'.

I am honoured and filled with pride that in some small way, my memoirs represent part of the political and social era between 1964-1973 of Australia and the United Kingdom.

Dianne and I and our children attended the opening of the British Migrant Exhibition on November 25, 2017, at the Immigration Museum in Victoria. It was amazing to see one's life spread out in animation, audio, and photos. But at the same time, it was confronting, and emotional.

I am eternally grateful for what Australia has given me, and proud to be an Australian citizen.

Postscript

This memoir is not a literary work of art, nor is it meant to be. It is a true account of my life and evidenced by photos and audiotape quotes. The terminology in the quotes may not reflect what is used today but was not altered to ensure the integrity of my stories and the era they represent. It has been a hard slog over many years to write this book, and some painful and stressful memories have surfaced.

Vivid memories of my early childhood and potent school days were recorded onto a CD and transcribed. Original audiotape narratives from my days as a Drifter in the 1960s and 1970s, were transcribed and specific quotes embedded in the stories. Together, these stories provided the impetus for the book, co-authored by Dianne and me. I hope you have enjoyed reading 'my story'.

Christopher Guy Thompson, December 2017.

CHRISTOPHER THOMPSON

Chris, who suffered from undiagnosed dyslexia, was looking for a new start in Australia far away from his father and a childhood of institutional abuse. Chris worked his way around Australia as a manual labourer for nearly ten years—until an Australian nurse made him wonder if it wasn't time to settle down.

Chris Thompson leaning against his Falcon, Darwin, 1970.
Source: Museums Victoria.
Copyright: Christopher Guy Thompson.

Name	Christopher Thompson, aged 21
Motivation	New opportunities and a fresh start
Left UK	1964
Where from	Coton, Staffordshire, England
Occupation in UK	Farmer
Where to	All over Australia
Occupation in Australia	Jackaroo, farm labourer, landscape gardener, factory worker, farmer, builders labourer, nightcart driver, rubbish collector, pie seller, miner, drover

"

My brother was a doctor and he sponsored me to come out to Australia. He was sending slides home, from Nambour and of course mum looked at slides and said 'Look at that Chris, isn't that terrific. Tony just went for just 10 pounds. You could go there. There might be something for you there. You only have to stay there for two years.'

I got a job at the Hereford Stud farm out at Oakey in Queensland. It was so vast you know. We could see for miles. So that was a cultural shock. Everything looked different, felt different, and was different.

I think in school you were told that you were not good enough and that was drummed into me that I wasn't good enough for anything you know. And then of course when I came to Australia the whole thing opened up. I have been successful and I thank Australia for that.

Christopher Thompson

Chris Thompson holding a Koala at Lone Pine Sanctuary, Brisbane, 5 April 1964.
Source: Thompson Family.
Copyright: Christopher G.S. Thompson.

ACKNOWLEDGEMENTS

British Migrants: Instant Australians? was developed in 2017 by Museums Victoria with support from the Australian Government Visions Touring Fund.

Many talented Museums Victoria staff as well as our valued contractors and community contributors contributed to realising this project. The core Museums Victoria project team were: Project Lead, Emily Kocaj; Lead Curator, Dr Moya McFadzean; Project Curator, Dr Sophie Couchman; Editors, Kate Chmiel and Richard Gillespie; Lead Experience Developer, Hamish Palmer; Lighting, Phil Spinks; Digital Media, Hayley Townsend; Lead Conservator, Karen Fisher; Lead Exhibition Collection Manager, Sarah Parker; Creative Lead, Dan Koerner (Sandpit); Lead Exhibition Fabricator, Scott Jones. The core external team were: Creative Lead and Experience Design, Sandpit; Exhibition Design, Anna Tregloan; Communication Design, Nick Lewis; Animation and Illustration, Vera Babida (Love and Money Agency); Sound Design, David Heinrich; User Experience, Rey Takeshima.

We thank in particular the following individuals for the generous contributions of their stories, objects, photographs, perspectives and their time: Jen and Bill Barlow, Susan Blunden, Eric Bogle, Carolyn Briggs (Boonwurrung Foundation), Tony Burgoyne, Tasneem Chopra, Jan Coolen, Nigel and Tony Crowther, Dr B. Hass Dellal AO (Australian Multicultural Foundation), Trish Flew, Jay Gordon, Tammy Gordon, Dr Jim Hammerton (La Trobe University), Merle Hathaway, Dermot Henry, Sheila Howell, Paul Jennings, Peter and Rachel Legge, Isobel Morphy-Walsh, John Patten, Cliff Pester, Jo Pritchard, Professor Kee Pookong (University of Melbourne), Lesley Silvester, Magda Szubanski, Christopher Thompson, Professor Alistair Thomson (Monash University), Dr Ben Wellings (Monash University) and Dr Sara Wills (University of Melbourne).

CPSIA information can be obtained
at www.ICGtesting.com
Printed in the USA
LVHW041503290322
714698LV00010B/352